THE NAVAL CHRONICLE

VOLUME V

THE NAVAL CHRONICLE

The Contemporary Record of the Royal Navy at War

Volume V 1811 - 1815

Consolidated Edition
containing a

GENERAL AND BIOGRAPHICAL HISTORY

of

THE ROYAL NAVY

of the

UNITED KINGDOM

During the War with the French Empire and American Republic

*War Reports, Commanding Officers' Gazette Letters of Naval Actions, Narratives
taken from Foreign Sources, Intelligence Reports on the Fleets of Europe and of the
American Republic, Letters from Serving Officers on Naval Strategy, Tactics, Gunnery,
Ship Design, and Professional Concerns, and With a Variety of Original Papers on
Nautical Subjects.*

*

*Under the Guidance of Several Literary and Professional Men,
and Prepared for General Use by:*

NICHOLAS TRACY

CHATHAM PUBLISHING

LONDON

Copyright © Nicholas Tracy 1999

First published in Great Britain in 1999 by
Chatham Publishing,
61 Frith Street,
London W1V 5TA

Chatham Publishing is an imprint of Gerald Duckworth & Co Ltd

British Library Cataloguing in Publication Data
A catalogue record for this book is available from the British Library

ISBN 1 86176 095 7

Typeset by Linda Jones
Printed and bound in Great Britain by Bookcraft (Bath) Limited

Contents

Introduction to Volume V

The last five years of the war against the French Empire were not marked by any great naval battle, and the fiasco on the Scheldt in 1809 discouraged attempts at large-scale amphibious operations. The naval war became one of minor operations, largely in support of British and allied armies fighting near the coast, and of cruiser work in defence of trade. The coast-wise operations in the Mediterranean continued to the end of the war, and those in northern Spain eventually carried the British army across the French frontier, and into Bordeaux. At the same time, the shores of the North Sea and Baltic were gradually freed from French control. Trade protection and control was essential to the ability of Britain to pay the subsidies needed by her continental allies if they were to keep in the field the armies which were ultimately to defeat Napoleon. Unfortunately, it also had disastrous consequences for Anglo-American relations, and was to lead to war in 1812. It was a war not wanted by American trading interests, but the provocations at sea were used by those who had ambitions to incorporate Canada into the American Union. The defence of Canada was to involve naval operations on the Great Lakes, and along the American seaboard where the American capital was burnt, and finally to an ill-conducted assault on New Orleans. The American war was also to be marked by frigate actions in which the American super-frigates proved highly successful, shockingly so to the readers of *The Naval Chronicle*.

Napoleon's 'Continental System' by which he planned to destroy the British economy was soon shown to be incapable of that instrumental goal, and was transformed during the last years of the war. In 1810 Napoleon ordered the destruction of British goods throughout French-controlled Europe, and there were bonfires lit in every city presided over by French officialdom, but the flames were fuelled by the least valuable but most bulky of the British manufactures and produce. Clearly, the demands of the marketplace were stronger than the fear of French power. Tacitly acknowledging his inability to strangle Britain by his trade controls, Napoleon altered his system in order to cash in on the high fees that smugglers could charge. The Trianon Tariff dropped the ban on colonial products. British manufactured goods were still in theory to be burnt, but a licensing system was introduced. The licensee was permitted to import British manufactures provided Britain took French items in return. This change of strategy transformed the Continental System into something more nearly resembling Britain's effort to monopolise trade, but, given the relative weakness of the French economy, it had no chance of success. In 1810 the British Government issued 18,000 licenses, totally transforming Britain's pro-forma trade blockade into a system of protected trade. Enemy shipping interests were encouraged to trade to British ports, and even provided with convoy.

The licenses for trade to Britain became an important source of revenue, and Napoleon began to regard his conquests in Europe less as a means of denying markets to Britain than as a means of ensuring them for France. This change of economic objective, however, made the controls all the more irksome for the French vassal states. The stubborn conflict in Spain and Portugal had been one consequence for France of the attempt to enforce the Continental System, and the final break with Russia in 1812 was to be the knell of Napoleon's ambitions.

1811 – Naval News

THE EARLY PART OF 1811 was relatively quiet, dampened by the continuing constitutional crisis, and the after-shocks of the failed Scheldt expedition, but the smouldering crisis in British–American relations was gradually moving towards the open warfare of 1812. The deliberate attack by an American super-frigate, the USS *President* under the command of Commodore Rodgers, on the deminutive *Little Belt* was a sign of the growing tendency in the United States to resist British exercise of maritime commercial control, even if that put the republic in the balance on the side of the Buonapartist Empire. The most positive development, from the British point of view, was the defeat of the French before Cadiz, and their expulsion from Portugal.

Apart from the *Little Belt* incident, the only significant naval actions of the period were squadron engagements in the Mediterranean. Early in March a small British force of four frigates commanded by Captain Hoste encountered off the island of Lissa, the modern Vis on the Dalmatian coast, a French squadron of five frigates, and nine smaller vessels. Its commander, Captain Dubordieu, immediately attacked, forming his force into two columns with the intent to employ Nelson's tactics to break the British line. However, during two hours of action, Hoste forced three frigates to surrender, Dubordieu's own ship ran aground and eventually blew up, and his objective of landing a garrison on the island was defeated. On 30 April Captain Barrie with two frigates and a sloop attacked three French frigates lying in Sagone Bay in Corsica where they were loading ship-timbers under the guns of coastal fortifications. All three were set on fire, and the Toulon dockyard lost a much needed supply. Smaller forces were equally successful on the Calabrian and Neapolitan coasts, and in the Adriatic Captain Gordon captured or destroyed an entire convoy. In the Atlantic, Captain Bourshier, commanding HMS *Hawke*, succeeded after a desperate engagement in forcing two enemy brigs, two luggers, and a convoy of fifteen ships onto the Normandy coast. In August Captain Ferris of HMS *Diana*, and Captain Richardson of HMS *Semiramis* passed into the Gironde under the guns of the coastal fortifications, using French colours, captured a convoy, and destroyed a force of gunboats.

1

Other news during this period included the plans of the American Government to establish a colony on the banks of the Columbia River where a trans-pacific trade could be conducted; a court martial which exhonerated Lieutenent Kent in connection with the mutiny at Botany Bay which displaced Captain William Bligh as governor; and the text of Sweden's reluctant and formal declaration of war against Britain. The capacity of merchant ships to defend themselves from privateers was a centre of interest, as was the High Court of Admiralty's decision that a captured British-owned ship fitted for the now illegal slave trade, but not carrying any slaves at the time of capture, and naturalised under the Portuguese flag, was a legal prize.

From 'Naval Anecdotes.' XXV *19-28*

American Expeditions to the Columbia River

The government of the United States has recently sent out an expedition by sea, and another by land. The former sailed to the southward, for the purpose of doubling Cape Horn, of traversing the Pacific, and reaching Columbia. The latter was to proceed westward, to follow the Missouri, to cross the great ridge of mountains, and to arrive at the same river by this long, though, in point of actual distance, much shorter route. The expedition of Captain Merewether Lewis (noticed in former Volumes of the *Naval Chronicle*) was only preparatory to the present, which is to settle a new colony either in the bay of the Columbia, or more probably at its mouth or on its shores - a colony which will perhaps hereafter conduct a vast trade with different parts of the East. The naval expedition conveyed stores and necessaries for the settlement of the new colony. A principal object in view is to open a communication between the Missouri and the Columbia; or, in other words, between the Atlantic and Pacific, with as short, or as commodious a carrying place over the mountain tract as can possibly be found. The great obstacle, indeed, to an extensive intercourse between the eastern and western sides of the North American continent - an obstacle which time only can surmount, and after all imperfectly sur[veyed], is the intervening ridge of mountains, which is broad, and supposed to be free from snow only about three or four months in the year. These months will therefore be hereafter busy months for the transport of commodities. The want of roads, of culture, and of population, time and industry will remedy; and that the Anglo-Americans will hereafter carry on across the Pacific a vast and lucrative commerce with China and Japan, in spite of the present timid and jealous character of their governments, can scarcely be doubted.

Settlement of Accounts

The master of an American merchant vessel at Cadiz having requested the captain of a British man-of-war to take out of her a refractory English seaman (who, by the way, had one of those certificates of his being an American subject, so easily obtained in America), the officer applied for the man's wages, which *Jonathan* discharged by the account, of which the following is a literal copy from the original:

John Levey, to the Ship *Fabius*,   Dr.
August,
1810

3.	To a month's advance	$28.00
13.	To my travelling expenses to go to Philadelphia after you, when you ran away with the ship's boat	$3.00
14.	To the Squire's fee of office	$0.50
	To cash advanced you at the Squire's office to pay a debt that you were sued for	$0.25
	To cash paid two constables to commit to prison until an opportunity offered to send you on board	$0.50
15.	To coach-hire to Newcastle for you, the constable, and myself, at $1.50 – 1.00 each	$4.50
	To your travelling expenses	$0.50
	To the constable's dinner and Squire, etc	$1.00
	To coach-hire for the constable back to Philadelphia	$0.25
	To goal fees paid for you	$1.00
	To the constable to go with you to Newcastle	$3.00
	To three gallons of rum at Newcastle	$3.00

$52.52

(E.E.) John Daly

Gallant Action

A more gallant action than that recorded in the following letter, has not been fought by a merchant ship against the enemy's privateers this war, nor in any preceding one. The Lords of the Admiralty have, in consequence, been pleased to express to the committee for managing the affairs at Lloyd's, their lordships' satisfaction at the gallantry exhibited on this occasion, and their intention to grant to each of the crew of the *Cumberland*, as a mark of their lordships' favour, a protection from the impress for the term of *three years*.

Deal, January 15
Sunday night the ship *Cumberland*, Barrett, master, arrived in the Downs from Quebec, under a jury foremast and bowsprit, having pitched her bowsprit and foremast away in a heavy gale of wind off the banks of Newfoundland. From seven till eight o'clock on Sunday morning, she was attacked by four French lugger privateers, between Dover and Folkestone, the first of which hailed to know if he wanted a pilot; Captain B. having suspicion of her, replied in the negative: immediately after another privateer ordered him to lay back his main-yard, and the whole then commenced a fire of musketry, and two of them ran alongside and boarded the *Cumberland*, previous to which the captain had ordered all the ship's crew into the cabin; they being armed with their boarding pikes. As soon as about twenty men came on board, the captain ordered the ship to be

sheered off from the privateers, leaving the Frenchmen no good retreat; and on the ship being boarded, the privateers ceased firing: in the mean time the ship's company rushed forward and cleared the deck; the greatest part of the boarders being killed, and the remainder jumped overboard. Immediately after, another came alongside, and told the captain they would give no quarter; on hearing this, the ship's company cheered them, and they were boarded and cleared in like manner. This was repeated three times afterwards, with the like success on the part of the ship's crew, and their taking three prisoners, two of whom were wounded, and one has since died of his wounds. Immediately after this, Captain Barrett discharged three of his carronades loaded with round and canister shot; the first was seen to carry away the mainmast of one of the privateers, and the second carried away the bowsprit of another, and it was supposed destroyed many of the men, as they were heard to cry out, and the shots were heard to strike the vessel. They then made off, and the *Cumberland* proceeded for the Downs. We are sorry to say Mr. Coward, chief mate, is wounded in the shoulder, and that one man on board the *Cumberland* has died of his wounds. The loss on the part of the enemy is supposed to be nearly 60. Captain B. killed three himself, one of which he was obliged to put his foot on to extricate his pike.

This is supposed to be the most gallant defence made by any merchant ship during the war; as her crew consisted only of twenty-six men, and those of the privateers, according to the prisoners' statement, up to 270 men.

Extraordinary Sentence of a Court Martial

During the course of the last summer (1810) a young gentleman, a midshipman of H.M.S. *Edgar*, Captain Paints, then cruising in the Belt for the protection of our convoy, having been disrated for some offence, was sent to row guard during the night; and, wishing by every means in his power to recover the favour of his captain, he unfortunately landed on the island of Sayer. To this he was induced by the honourable hopes of distinguishing himself, and recovering his former situation. According to his expectation, he fell in with a party of Danish soldiers, whom with the utmost gallantry he attacked and defeated, but unfortunately had one man killed; not finding any vessels which he could carry off, he reembarked, carrying with him some fowls, and two sheep. On his return on board, he was immediately put under arrest, both legs put into irons; and after remaining in that condition 14 days, was tried by a court martial, of which Rear-admiral Dixon was president, and the following very severe and extraordinary sentence passed upon him, which was executed with the utmost rigour, viz. "And the Court do hereby sentence you to be stripped of your uniform publicly on the quarter-deck - mulcted of all your pay - rendered incapable of ever serving his Majesty as an officer - and, finally, on the arrival of your ship in England, you are to be drummed ashore." Although the conduct of the midshipman was certainly exceedingly improper, and wholly inconsistent with the standing orders of the service, yet surely, in consideration of his youth, his eminent gallantry on several occasions, particularly in the capture of the gun-boats by the boats of the fleet under the orders of Captain Martin, in the Gulf of Finland, the Court might have passed a more lenient sentence than one which has essentially blighted his promotion in the most honourable of services, that of his King and Country.

The Best Method of Defence Against Privateers
From 'Correspondence.' XXV 44-45

"H.Y." to the Editor, Deal, December 16
I am of opinion, that the most effectual method of preventing their successes, would be
for the masters of merchant vessels, and coasters in particular, to adhere strictly to
those instructions, which desire them, on the appearance of a suspicious vessel in the
night, to fire guns, burn false fires, or throw up rockets, with which they should always
be provided, and this would immediately apprize the cruisers of the proximity of an
enemy; and I am persuaded the alarm it would excite in a privateer would frequently
deter him from attacking a vessel who had recourse to those measures. If, however,
capture becomes inevitable, not a moment should be lost in cutting the haulyards, sheets,
braces, &c. In short, nothing should be left undone that could, by retarding the enemy,
in carrying the vessel to a French port, afford our cruisers a chance of recapture. This
attention, so highly desirable on the part of the masters of merchant vessels, would at
once obviate the necessity of the construction of launches, and of the increase of the
naval establishment, and it would facilitate the protection of the trade, and operate
more against the successes of the enemy than any expedient I can think it possible to
devise.

From the 'Naval History of the Present Year,' 1810-1811
December-January. XXV 68-70; 82

Regency Bill Passes Lords

The Bill for appointing his Royal Highness the Prince of Wales Regent of the United
Kingdom, for a limited period, in consequence of the illness of his Majesty, was agreed
to in the House of Lords, and returned to the Commons, with several amendments, on
the 29th of January. It is expected that it will have passed through all its stages by the 2d
of February, when the Prince will be fully invested with his powers, as Regent, and
proceed in state to the House of Peers.

Capital Sentences to be Referred

The Board of Admiralty have come to the resolution of submitting all sentences of
capital conviction in his Majesty's navy, for the approbation of the Attorney and Solicitor-
General, before such sentences are ordered to be carried into execution.

Opportunity for Sailors to Buy Out of the Service

The Admiralty have settled a plan for receiving a certain sum for the discharge of seamen,
according to their different ratings.

8th Report Published Recommends Piece Work in Yards

The long-expected 8th report of the Commissioners for revising the civil concerns of
his Majesty's navy, has at last made its appearance, and commenced operations in
Plymouth dock-yard on the 1st of January. It comprises a new system of pay for all the
artificers and other workmen belonging to his Majesty's several dock and rope-yards, in

reference to a very extended scheme of task and job-work, for each respective description which accompanied the same, together with sundry regulations for the internal government of the yards: and, it is presumed, will be found not only highly beneficial to the state, but satisfactory to every class of workmen, to whose skill and exertions we are so much indebted for our maritime ascendency and national defence.

Brig Feared Lost

The *Conflict* gun-brig, Lieutenant Batt, it is feared, has foundered off the north coast of Spain. On the 9th of November, while cruising in company with the *Arethusa*, they were caught in a violent gale, and the former was seen towards night in great distress, since which time no accounts have been received of her.

Spanish Coastal Operations

We learn from the Spanish papers, that the *Volontaire*, Captain Bullen; and the *Cambrian* (frigates), Captain Fane, have been employed on the coast of Catalonia, from Tarragona, nearly to Rosas, in destroying the batteries which the enemy had obtained possession of, and levying contributions upon the partizans of the French. Colonel O'Roman commanded the Spanish troops that embarked in the frigates; and he omitted no opportunity of harassing the enemy. In proceeding to destroy the Castle of Medas, the *Cambrian* lost her rudder. From Cadeguez they obtained 19 ships, six of them laden with grain and wine, which they manned and sent to Tarragona. Captain Bullen was wounded during these services; but we trust not dangerously. Both ships had returned to Tarragona.

Reward for Live Saving

The crew of his Majesty's sloop *Childers*, has presented an elegant sword, with a suitable inscription, to Mr. George Wilson, master of that ship, as a mark of their esteem for his jumping overboard at sea, and saving, at the risk of his own life, one of their shipmates from a watery grave, who had fallen from the fore-yard-arm, and was in the act of sinking.

Foreign Levies for French Fleet;
Norwegians Rebellious Against Denmark

The Emperor of Russia is reported to have acceded to Buonaparté's request, in placing a certain number of Russian seamen at his disposal. - In Norway, however, the seamen lately raised for the service of the French fleet, have refused to embark; declaring, at the same time, their perfect willingness to engage in the service of their own country. Nearly the whole of Norway is reported to be a state of open insurrection, and has offered to throw off the Danish yoke, provided she could obtain the protection of Britain.

An extensive maritime conscription has been ordered in France, of which farther notice will be taken in a subsequent part of this volume.

Hanse Towns Annexed to France

Hamburg, and all the Hanse Towns, have been formerly annexed to the French empire.

US News

Mr. Madison, the American president, in his message to congress, on the 5th of December, anticipates the existence of doubts and difficulties as to the operation of the Non-intercourse act, in the event of our Government rescinding only the retaliatory Orders in Council, and continuing our other orders of blockade in force. The Danish government, it appears, has not made any reparation for the depredations committed by its cruizers upon the American commerce. The message explains the extent to which the president had interposed in the affairs of West Florida. He ordered possession to be taken of a district, alleged to be included in the territory of Orleans, which had been ceded by Spain to France, and by the latter to the United States . . .

January - February. *XXV 153-154*

Isle de France Captured

The account of the capture of the Isle of France, and of the other proceedings in the Indian Seas, recorded in our *Letters on Service*, will be read with much interest and satisfaction. [See Volume IV, pp352-361.]

Banda Captured

Of unofficial intelligence, the most important which we have to announce, is that of the capture of Banda, the chief of the Dutch Spice Islands. It was carried by a *coup de main*, early in August; the assailing force, under Captain Cole, of H.M.S. *Caroline*, not amounting to more than 180 men while that of the garrison numbered 1000. The property, to the captors, is estimated at £600,000; and, what renders the news eminently pleasing, is, that the rich prize has fallen into our possession without the loss of a single life.

Baltic

Some arrangements, inimical to the interests of Buonaparté, are thought to be forming amongst the Northern Powers.

The World's Insanity - *Editorial*

In North America, they, who ought daily to offer up thanksgivings for being at a safe distance from the din of arms, seem madly ambitious of war, with the certain annihilation of their present enviable advantages! In South America, the Spaniards are cutting throats to establish the authority of Ferdinand VII; who, as a power, does not exist! At what period between his extremes of *delirium* and *insanity* does Doctor W— place such *derangement?* But let us not laugh as if we were mere lookers-on. With respect to any one of those, it may be said with the grave-digger in Hamlet, "In England they are all as mad as he." Have we not in face with an enemy at the gate, and another (of paper) within, been profoundly debating away whole weeks and months, whether the Regent or the Queen should have the *Buck-hounds?* To say nothing of tying the hands of him who is to defend us, by a solemn act of those who represent us, and pretend to be our "brains!" Of this species seems to have been the mania which prevailed at Constantinople when the Greek and Latin churches were disputing whether the sacramental bread should be *leavened or unleavened*, while Sultan Mohammed II was laying siege to the city![1] So at Jerusalem,[2] while mighty ruin was impending, the Jews were deeply considering the heresy of the Sadducees! As none of these can be reckoned amongst the acts of reasonable men, we are compelled to account for such conduct by referring it to the old adage, which saith, "Heaven first makes fools of those whom it wills to destroy,"[3] or to adopt Voltaire's fearful apprehension, that "our little terraqueous globe is neither more nor less than the mad-house of the universe."[4] In these retrospective remarks, the reader will be pleased to observe, that we have spoken merely of folly - generously avoiding all mention of knavery.

Captain Bligh's Charge Against Lieutenant Kent
Naval Courts Martial. XXV 79-80

[Captain William Bligh, who placed the charges against his lieutenant, was the same who had survived the mutiny of his crew on the *Bounty* in 1789 by making an unprecedented boat voyage 3618 miles across the Pacific to Timor. He had made another voyage to the Pacific in 1791, in which he was assisted by Matthew Flinders who was then 17 years old. For his efforts Bligh received the Society of Arts medal. He was a Member of the Royal Society, and commanded the *Glatton* at the first battle of Copenhagen in 1801, and had then been appointed in 1805 as Governor of New South Wales. While there, however, he again suffered mutiny in 1808 and was kept in confinement until his return to England in 1810.]

On the 8th of January, an interesting Court-martial commenced on board his Majesty's ship *Gladiator*, at Portsmouth, Vice-admiral Hargood, president; for the trial of Lieutenant William George Carlisle Kent, late acting commander of his Majesty's ship the *Porpoise*, in New South Wales, (and on whom the command of his Majesty's ships devolved, on the suspension of Captain William Bligh, the late governor of that territory) in consequence of his having exercised his own judgment, in proceeding to relieve the dependent settlements, when all communication was cut off between him and the said Captain Bligh.

The charges preferred against the prisoner by Captain Bligh were,

1st. His having sailed from Port Jackson, without his orders.

2d. Having hauled down the prosecutor's broad pendant, which he was ordered to keep flying on board his Majesty's ship *Porpoise*, then under his command, and again proceeding to sea, without his orders, or any person duly authorized to give the same.

3d. For having permitted Lieutenant James Symons to quit his Majesty's service, and carry home despatches from the persons who had usurped the government, and not apprehending him and bringing him to punishment.

In support of these charges, which caused Lieutenant Kent one year and eleven months' confinement, the prosecutor, out of above a dozen witnesses whom he summoned, only called one, being Mr. Griffin, his secretary; and then closed the prosecution, by delivering in, about noon, the following written paper to the Court:

---

1 The consequence was, it fell into the hands of the Turks, and the last of the Constantines lost his empire and his life. See Gibbon, Decline and Fall of the Roman Empire, VI 481 4to.
2 Josephus, Wars of the Jews.
3 "Quos Iupiter vult perdere prius dementat."
4 "J'ai bien peur que notre petit globe terraqué ne soit precisément les petites maisons de l'univers."

Port Jackson, New South Wales.

View of Port Jackson, New South Wales. Engraved by Baily, from a drawing by W. Westall.

Port Jackson, situated about five miles to the north of Botany Bay, is one of the finest harbours in the world. The annexed view, by Mr. Westall, was taken from Garden Island. - The ships appear off the entrance of Sidney Cove, the chief settlement. Plate 297

Mr. President, and Gentlemen

Taking it for granted, that the court will not think it right to inquire into the propriety or impropriety of the dispossessing me of the civil government of the territory of New South Wales, as that is to be made the subject of investigation before another tribunal; and the Lords Commissioners of the Admiralty directed me, in framing the charges upon the present occasion, to confine myself to those points which were in breach of the naval articles of war, I have no further evidence to trouble the Court with. Should, however, the prisoner put his defence upon that ground, and the Court think it right to enter into the inquiry, they will, I trust, hereafter permit me to call witnesses to answer to any charges which may be attempted to be established against me in justification of that measure. Until I hear what they are, it is impossible I can answer them; and to enter, by anticipation, into a general history of my government, would, I apprehend, be an unnecessary waste of time to the court.

WM. BLIGH

After an investigation of three days, the prisoner was *acquitted of the whole of the charges* alleged against him, agreeably to the following sentence:

"The court proceeded to try the said Lieutenant W.G.C. Kent, on the charges preferred against him by Captain William Bligh, and having heard the evidence adduced in support of the charges, and by the said Lieutenant Kent in his defence, and what he had to allege in support thereof, the Court is of opinion that it appears that the said Lieutenant Kent, did sail with the said ship, from Port Jackson in the two instances stated in the above-mentioned charges, without the order of the said Captain William Bligh; that he did not so sail under the persons asserted therein, to have illegally, and by force, dispossessed the said William Bligh of the government of New South Wales, and did not improperly strike the broad pendant of the said William Bligh. That it appears that the said W.C.Kent, under the extreme and extraordinary difficulties he was placed under, shewed every disposition to obey any orders which the said William Bligh might have thought fit to have given to him; that he was actuated by a sincere wish to perform his duty for the good of his Majesty's service, and that he was justified in the conduct he pursued on such an occasion; and the court is further of opinion, that the said third charge has not been proved against the said Lieutenant Kent, and doth on the whole adjudge him to be honourably acquitted of the whole of the above charges."

Captain Shortland's Dog

From 'Naval Anecdotes.' XXV 197-198

The late Captain [John] Shortland, a memoir of whose life and services was given in the preceding volume, had a favourite dog, which constantly attended him during those acute sufferings which preceded his death, licked his hands, and displayed every mark of the most affectionate attachment. Captain Shortland's servant brought this faithful creature to England, after the decease of his lamented master, but, unfortunately, the animal was almost immediately lost. Many of our readers, we doubt not, will be much gratified to learn, that he has recently been recovered, under the following remarkable circumstances:

"The dog, it appears, was stolen, at the Elephant and Castle, Newington, taken on board a ship, and carried back to Halifax, Nova Scotia, where one of the crew of Captain Shortland's ship, who had been very severely wounded in the action between the *Junon* and the French frigates, met the dog, and, instantly recognising him, demanded him of the man in whose possession he was. The fellow refused to give him up (although the dog remembered his old friend, and immediately answered to his name, *Pandore*); in consequence of which the sailor very properly applied to Admiral Sir J.B. Warren, the commander-in-chief on the Halifax station, stating the particulars of the case. On the dog's exhibiting, at the sailor's command, all the tricks which he had been used to, the admiral insisted on his being delivered up to the tar's care, who brought him safe to England, and, on Sunday the 3d of March, took him to Mrs. Shortland's, in London. The dog, a middling-sized terrier, is now old, but very handsome. Mrs. Shortland's

An eye sketch of Hunter's River, Port Jackson, discovered by the late Captain John Shortland, R.N. Engraved by Simpkin, from Captain Shortland's sketch.

H.M.S. Reliance, Sydney Cove, Port Jackson, September 10, 1798
My Dear Father, About a twelvemonth since I went on an expedition in the Governor's whale boat, as far as Port Stephens, which lies 100 miles to the northward of this place: in my passage down I discovered a very fine coal river, which I named after Governor Hunter; the enclosed I send you, being an eye sketch which I took the little time I was there. Vessels from 60 to 250 [tons] may lead there with great ease, and completely land-locked. I dare say in a little time this river will be a great acquisition to this settlement. The short time I remained at this river we had rain, which prevented my doing so much as I otherwise should.
(Signed) J. SHORTLAND Plate 322

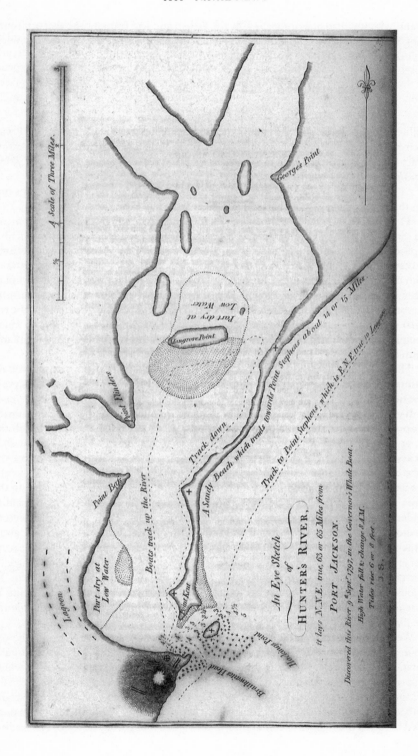

A Scale of Three Miles.

George's Point

Part dry at Low Water

Mangrove Point

Point Finders

Track down

A Sandy Beach which trends towards Point Stephens about 14 or 15 Miles.

Track to Point Stephens which is E.N.E true to Leeward

Point Bars

Boats track up the River

Logoon

Part dry at Low Water

Point Kent

Brathbourne Island

Hexham's Point

An Eye Sketch of HUNTER's RIVER, it lays N.N.E. true, 63 or 65 Miles from PORT JACKSON.

Discovered this River 9ᵗʰ Septᵣ 1797, in the Governor's Whale Boat.
High Water falls change 8 A.M.
Tides rise 6 or 8 feet.
J. S.

servant, who was also one of the crew of the *Junon*, and had brought the dog up from a puppy, was recognized by the animal the moment that the door opened; and the happiness its return has occasioned in the family, is hardly to be conceived."

Atrocious Conduct of the French Captain, Hamelin

From 'Naval Anecdotes.' XXV *197-198*

To illustrate the character of Hamelin, the commander of the French frigate, *la Venus*, which captured the *Africaine*, Captain Corbett, in the Indian Seas, we insert the following extract from the account which the *Quarterly Review* gives of Peron's *Voyage aux Terres Australes*:

"The favourable reception which the officers and naturalists of the two ships met from the government of Port Jackson, far exceeded their expectations.

The English received Captain Hamelin, (of the *Naturaliste*) from the first moment, with that great and polite generosity which the perfection of European civilization only can produce. The most distinguished houses in the colony were open to our companions; and during their whole stay there, they experienced that delicate and kind hospitality, which confers equal honour on him who practises it, and on him who is the object of it. All the resources of the colony were placed at the disposal of the French captain. - "In one word," says M. Péron, "the conduct of the English government with regard to us was so marked by magnificence and generosity, that we should be wanting in every principle of honour and justice, were we not to record in this work the expression of our gratitude."

The same kind attention appears to have been paid to them by the inhabitants; all, continues M. Péron, seemed to feel the important truth, "la cause des sciences est la cause des peuples."

It gives us pain to observe, after reading these and similar passages, that the gratitude of Captain Hamelin scarcely survived the period of its record by M. Péron. This officer is at present commodore of a squadron of frigates in the East Indies. Last year they attacked and completely destroyed the small and defenceless settlement of Tappanooly on the coast of Sumatra. Forgetful of that delicate and kind hospitality with which he was received at Port Jackson, Captain Hamelin not only permitted, but assisted in the pillage of private property: he even stood by and saw the wardrobes of the ladies plundered, and was base and malicious enough to order his people to tear in pieces, in presence of the owners, several articles of dress which were not worth carrying away. He then compelled the whole of the civilians to embark for the Isle of France, leaving orders that every house in the settlement should be set on fire. When on ship-board, he called the English ladies upon deck, and with savage exultation pointed out to them the glorious blaze which their houses exhibited. This is that very Captain Hamelin, at whose disposition, even in the midst of war, "all the resources of the English colony" were placed!

We have been induced to notice this infamous conduct in an officer of the old school, as it tends to prove, among a thousand other instances now before us, how totally the national character of France is altered and depraved by the military despotism which has sprung out of the Revolution. - Her age of chivalry is, indeed, gone - we fear for ever; and its place is supplied by a systematic ferociousness, a rancorous mode of warfare, wholly destitute of that urbanity of manners, that generosity of sentiment, which once served to soften the rigours of contention, and stripped it of half its terrors. The leading

Portrait of Captain Matthew
Flinders, R.N. Engraved by
Blood, from a Miniature in the
possession of Mrs. Flinders.
Plate 422

principle in the modern school of military France, is to renounce humanity altogether; to mortify, to insult, and trample in the dust a vanquished foe, not so much for the gratification of personal hatred, as for the unworthy purpose of ministering to the dark and stormy passions of the most malignant and revengeful of tyrants."

From the 'Biographical Memoir of Captain
Matthew Flinders, R.N.' XXXII 177-191

[At the Glorious First of June], when Lord Howe broke the French line on that decisive day, the second ship from the *Queen Charlotte* was the *Bellerophon*; her guns would bear on three of the enemy's ships, and some of those on the quarter-deck having been left leaded and primed by her men while called off to trimming sails, &c. Mr. Flinders, having at that time no other but the general order to fire away as fast as possible, seized a lighted match, and at the instant his ship was passing under the stern of a French three-decker, fired in succession as many of the deserted guns as would hear, right into her. Commodore Pasley having observed his actions, shook the young hero violently by the collar, and sternly said, "How dare you do this, youngster, without my orders?" Mr. Flinders innocently replied, "he did not know, but he thought it a fine chance to have a good shot at 'em."

[Flinders, however, is better known for his service under Captain Bligh in 1791-3, and for the voyage of exploration in HMS *Investigator* which sailed from England in July 1801 and circumnavigated Australia.]

In the beginning of 1811, Captain Flinders received the commands of his superiors to undertake the publication of his voyage, in order to form the sequal to those of Cook and Vancouver. And it was during this period of literary seclusion, that the *Naval Chronicle* being presented to his notice, obtained no small share of his regard. Besides answering the established biographical enquiries with the utmost candour, Captain Flinders was always accessible to reference touching any nautical or scientific points upon which the Hydrographer (without personal acquaintance) took the liberty of consulting him, and liberal to the greatest degree in imparting his knowledge.

From the 'Naval History of the Present Year,' 1811
February - March. XXV 248-249

Assault on Cadiz Repulsed

The most important event, within our knowledge, which has occurred during the month
of March, is the combined naval and military attack, which was made upon the French
besieging army at Cadiz. "General Graham's division," as is concisely stated in the
Earl of Liverpool's communication of the news to the Lord Mayor, on the night of
March 24, "marched from Tarifa on the 25th ult. (Feb.); on the 5th inst. after a night's
march of 16 hours, they arrived at the ridge of Barrosa, about four miles to the southward
of the St. Peter River, and commenced a well conducted attack on the rear of the enemy's
line near St. Peter, by the vanguard of the Spanish army, under General Ladrizabel,
and opened a communication with the Isle de Leon. Lieutenant-general Graham having
received the directions of the Spanish commander-in-chief to move down from the
position of Barrosa to that of Torre de Berringa, received notice on the march that the
enemy had appeared in force on the plain, and was advanced towards the heights of
Barrosa: in this position a most desperate action took place, in which the enemy was
completely repulsed, with the loss of an eagle and six pieces of cannon. The General of
division Rufin, and the General of brigade, Rousseau, were wounded and taken. The
chief of the staff, General Bellegarde, an aide-de-camp of General Victor, one colonel,
nine captains, and about 480 rank and file were made prisoners. - The field was covered
with the dead bodies of the enemy, and it was supposed that their loss amounted
to about 3,000 in killed and wounded. The loss on the part of the British troops amounts
to 2 captains, 5 ensigns, and about 190 rank and file killed; 5 lieutenant-colonels, 1
major, 14 captains, 26 lieutenants, 8 ensigns, and about 940 rank and file wounded. It
appears that the enemy had about 8,000 men engaged, and that the British, with the
Spaniards attached to them, amounted to 5,000. Lieutenant-general Graham, with the
troops under his command, had crossed the St. Peter River, and re-entered the Isle of
Leon."

By Sir Richard Keats's despatches, (vide letters on service) we learn, that, from the
tempestuous state of the weather, the naval attack, which was intended to operate as a
diversion in favour of the land forces, did not take place until the day after the battle of
Barrosa. An attack was then made on the enemy's sea-defences, from Rota to St. Mary's.
Several redoubts were taken, and dismantled, and their guns spiked. - We deeply regret
to add, that the Spanish army of reserve consisting of 11,000 men, under the commander-
in-chief, General La Pena, did not fire a shot, or advance a step, in support of the
victorious but suffering Britons fighting in their cause; and that, merely because they
were not led on by their superior officer! It is the general belief, that had the Spaniards
done their duty, the enemy must have lost every man, and the siege of Cadiz have been
raised. On the representation of the British minister, Mr. H. Wellesley, General La
Pena has been superseded, and put under arrest. - A second effort to raise the siege was
to be made; in which the chief command of the Spaniards was to be assumed by General
Blake. According to a private letter, that officer had crossed the bridge over the Santi
Petri, on the 11th, and was engaged with the enemy. A flotilla of gun-boats had sailed,
to co-operate in attacks on the French positions, along the coast of the bay.

General Massena commenced his retreat from Santarem on the 6th of March, in
consequence it is supposed, of the expected arrival of Lord Wellington's reinforcements,

in Sir J.S. Yorke's squadron. Lord Wellington as soon as he was apprized of the event, went in pursuit of the enemy.

Empress Gives Birth

Buonaparte's young wife presented him with a son, on the morning of the 20th of March.

Sidney Smith to Command Secret Expedition

It is said that Sir S. Smith is appointed to the command of a squadron, which is immediately to sail on a secret expedition, the destination of which is not publicly known. It is also stated, that Sir Sidney himself was the planner of the enterprise he is about to execute.

March–April. XXV 335-337

Portugal Liberated

At length we have the satisfaction of knowing, that, instead of the French having driven the English into the sea, as the *Moniteur* vauntingly threatened should be the issue of the contest, the English have completely driven the French out of Portugal! Excepting spies and prisoners, not a Frenchman now remains in that country.

Massena's retreat from Santarem, and Lord Wellington's consequent pursuit, were announced at page 249 [*vide supra*]. Most warmly was the enemy chased; severely was he harassed in his retreat; and whenever he endeavoured to make a stand, he was defeated with great loss. The last action, which took place on the 3d of April, near Subugal, is mentioned by Lord Wellington, as one of the most glorious in which British troops were ever engaged. . . .

Massena, in his retreat, or rather flight, inflicted every where the most wanton and horrid barbarities; burning the towns and villages through which he passed, as if the pursuing army could diet on their walls and beams. Such was the conduct of that general, whose master complained through the usual organ of his slanders, the *Moniteur*, that Lord Wellington, in his retreat, [to the lines of Torres Vedras in the autumn of 1810] drove the cattle, and burned the granaries. . . .

Parliament has voted the sum of £100,000 to be applied for the relief of the suffering Portuguese; and large subscriptions are raising in the metropolis, for the same laudable and benevolent purpose. . . .

Report of Revolt in The Netherlands

It is reported, that the oppressive measures of Buonaparte have at last produced a serious revolt in Holland and Flanders. When the accounts left the Dutch coast, all communication between Holland and Walcheren was said to have been cut off for three days; and it was inferred by the people at the latter place, that the inhabitants had overpowered the military. The Amsterdam post had been stopped in consequence of an insurrection in that city and at Dort. - It is also stated, that the populace had risen upon the garrison of Rotterdam, and had taken possession of the batteries and ports, and that the French troops had been disarmed there and at other places. It is said that these insurrectionary movements have been the cause of the recall of the French guards and other troops from Spain.

French Draw Cordon Along Baltic Shore

French troops are assembling on the shores of the Baltic, for the purpose of forming a cordon, to resist any debarkation that may be attempted from a British fleet. . . .

4-Decker Proposed

The draughtsmen of Plymouth-yard are said to be, in consequence of orders to that effect, engaged in preparing drawings for the inspection of the navy-board, of a first rate ship of four decks, with a circular stern, round which guns will be planted. The vessel will, of course, carry an immense number of guns, and will be the largest ever built.

The British Navy

There are at present in commission, 159 ships of the line, 20 from 50 to 44 guns, 108 frigates, 158 sloops of war, 5 fire-ships, 174 armed brigs, 37 cutters, 76 schooners and luggers, making altogether 792 ships of war; besides which there are building, repairing, and in ordinary, as many as make the grand total of 1,005, of which 256 are of the line.

Buonaparte's Lucky Escape
From 'Naval Anecdotes.' XXV 387-388

Last summer, a story was generally circulated throughout the North Sea fleet, that Buonaparte, with several of his general officers, and the commander of the fleet at Antwerp, had nearly been captured, when on an aquatic excursion near Flushing, with the Empress, by H.M.S. *Nymphen*, Captain Maxwell. The *Nymphen*, it is stated, fired several shot at the yacht in which Buonaparte had embarked.

Danish King Equally Fortunate

The King of Denmark had also a narrow escape from us. The sloop in which he was taking a passage to Keil, in Holstein, where her Majesty the Queen resides, was boarded by an English man of war, in the Belt; but esteeming her of no value, she was allowed to pass. His Majesty concealed himself below, where, unfortunately the lieutenant did not go. This story is related on the credit of a Correspondent.

Swedish Proclamation of War
Naval State Papers. XXV 406-409

We, Charles, by the Grace of God King of Sweden, of the Goths and Vandals, &c. &c. Heir of Norway, Duke of Schleswig, Holstein, &c. &c. make known. Whereas, in order completely to do away the doubts which have been expressed concerning the situation of our kingdom with respect to England, and in order, in a more effectual manner, to confirm the ties of amity and confidence that exist between us and his Majesty the Emperor of the French and King of Italy; as also, in order, on our part, to contribute to the common object of the powers of the Continent, namely, the conclusion of a general and speedy peace; we have been inducted hereby to declare war against the United Kingdom of Great Britain and Ireland. . . .

Slave Traders Condemned
Admiralty Court. $^{XXV\ 419\text{-}420}$

A cause relating to the slave trade lately came on to be tried in the High Court of Admiralty, the result of which will give general satisfaction. It appeared that the ship *William and Mary* proceeded from America to Madeira, to obtain Portuguese papers, and to sail under a Portuguese flag, as the slave trade is prohibited by law in the United States of America. When the ship reached Madeira, her name was changed to the *Fortuna*, and a Portuguese master was named as Master. Matters being thus arranged, the ship was to proceed to Angola for the purpose of taking in a cargo of slaves for the *Havannah* or Cuba. The vessel was captured by the *Melampus*, Captain Hawkins, and sent into Plymouth, where, after unlading, the platform, for making a stage for slaves, was discovered, and in the hold were the iron bars, chains, and diverse other abominable instruments, for confining the unfortunate beings destined for slavery. There were also found papers, concealed, proving the ship to be the adventure of an American. On the discovery being made, it was represented that one of the parties concerned had laid violent hands on himself. - The learned Judge condemned the ship and cargo as subject to confiscation.

The bill brought in by Mr. Brougham renders the carrying on the slave trade, after the 1st of May next, felony, rendering the parties liable to be transported, for a term not exceeding 14 years; or imprisoned, and kept to hard labour, for a term not exceeding five years, nor less than three.

From the 'Naval History of the Present Year,' 1811
April-May. $^{XXV\ 423}$

Squadron Victory in Adriatic

The most important naval event which has for some time occurred, is the victory obtained by Captain Hoste, over a French squadron in the Adriatic. For its extent, the engagement was unquestionably one of the most severe, and, for us, one of the most brilliant, that has taken place during the war. Captain Hoste's force consisted of H.M.S. *Amphion*, *Cerberus*, *Active* and *Volage*; mounting, in the whole, 124 guns, and carrying 879 men: to this was opposed a French squadron, of five frigates, and various smaller vessels; numbering, in guns, 272, and in men, including 500 troops, 2,665! The result of the action, which lasted six hours, was, that two of the enemy's frigates were captured, and one destroyed; the remainder owing their escape to the crippled state of the masts and rigging of his Majesty's ships. Our loss, unfortunately, amounted to 50 killed, and 150 wounded; but, considering the great numerical superiority of the enemy, in ships, guns, and men, the wonder is, that it should not have been heavier. - It has been fairly remarked, that the very name of Captain Hoste inculcates the old axiom - *Fas est at ab Hoste doceri.*

He certainly will long be remembered by the enemy, who may have gained experience by their discomfiture.

Gold medals, descriptive of the action, are preparing, and will be presented to the Captains Hoste, Hornby, Gordon, and Whitby, to be worn by them in the usual manner.

We understand that Captain Hoste was first taken to sea by his Norfolk countryman, Lord Nelson, under whom, and other commanders, he served in thirty-six actions, without a wound, until the last. He was in that of Trafalgar, and was honoured by the dying request of his immortal patron, that he might succeed to the *Amphion* frigate, (in which he so recently distinguished himself) which Lord Collingwood instantly obeyed.

[Captain William Hoste's account of the action was published in Vol. xxv, pp430-436.]

French Prisoners of War
From 'Naval Anecdotes.' XXV 460

The following letter (circular) has been transmitted to the acting magistrates of the country of Middlesex:

"Sir, It having been discovered that French prisoners of war are in the habit of absconding from their places of abode, with a view of effecting their escape; and for their protection in passing through the country, make use of the usual parole certificates, with which they are furnished by the Commissioners of the Transport Service, having first extracted, by a chemical process, the names and descriptions of places and persons originally inserted in writing in the blanks of such certificates, and afterwards filled up the said blanks in their own hand-writing, so as to suit their particular purposes; I am directed by his Grace the Duke of Portland, Lord Lieutenant and Custos Rotulorum of the country of Middlesex, to notify you, that all passports filled up in a French hand, whether they bear the seal of the Transport Office or not, are to be considered as forgeries, under which the parties making use of them can claim no protection.

I have the honour to be, Sir, Your most obedient humble servant,

HENRY COLLINGWOOD SELBY
Clerk of the Peace for the County of Middlesex"

A Correspondent Protests the Dangerous Practice of 'Manning the Yards'
From 'Correspondence.' XXV 465-466

London, June 15th, 1811

Mr. Editor, I beg leave, through the medium of your publication, to offer a few remarks upon a practice which, though far less general than formerly, is unfortunately still too prevalent in the navy, to the utter reproach of all such as have power to command, or influence to procure its total abolition.

The custom to which I allude, is that of "manning the yards," either in honour of some illustrious visitor, upon hoisting the flag of some admiral, or in commemoration of some splendid victory, or of some regal nativity.

That this exhibition has proved fatal to many of our brave seamen, I believe the memory of almost every officer will amply inform him: that from its very nature it must always be attended with risk, perhaps none are sufficiently prejudiced to deny.

That the means to which recourse must be had to recruit the loss thus needlessly sustained, are harsh and distressing, and such as every officer of feeling would willingly avoid; that they are such as can be justified only by imperious necessity, and are even such as, after every exertion has been used, are found incompetent to supply the defection, are truths too apparent to be questioned. Why, then, whilst we acknowledge the existence of the evil, shall we delay the application of the remedy? Why shall we barbarously and wantonly continue to sacrifice that of which we have long and proudly felt the value, that of which daily experience teaches us the scarcity?

Of our admirals, it is well known that they are too sensible to enjoy, and too firmly convinced of the attachment of their tars, to require such a testimony of their zeal or affection; nay, there are many who, to their eternal honour, have forbidden such a compliment any more to be paid them. That this show affords great gratification to such persons of distinction or parties of pleasure, as occasionally honour his Majesty's ships with their presence, is perhaps a position more easily advanced than maintained; for, by many intelligent naval officers I have been assured, that of their visitors there were few that could look upon it without an emotion of terror rather than delight, or that did not feel more concern for the safety of the seamen than fascination at the splendour of the spectacle! But, allowing it were otherwise, if the sight were capable of exciting the most pleasurable sensations, what could warrant such exposure of life to calamity? What compensation could lull the agony of fractured limbs? - Surely humanity herself pleads powerfully against it. Justice condemns; reason reproves; compassion weeps. . . .

ORION

From the 'Naval History of the Present Year,' 1811
May-June. XXV 502-504

US Attack on HMS Little Belt

The disputes between Great Britain and America have not yet been settled; but, on the contrary, an incident has occurred, which seems likely to operate as a fresh obstacle to the adjustment of differences. In the month of May, the *National Intelligence*, which is usually considered as the organ of the American Government, contained the following remarks:

"Within the course of a few days past, several cases have occurred of impressment by British vessels on our coast from coasting vessels. These impressments have taken place under aggravated circumstances, and have excited, as they ought, a very general indignant feeling. The Unites States frigate *President*, put to sea from Annapolis, under such circumstances as justify the impression, that the object of her sailing was to obtain the release of these men, and rumours of an engagement off our Capes have reached us, which we present to our readers, barely observing, that it is well understood that the commanders of public vessels are generally instructed to submit to no question from any foreign vessel, which shall wear the semblance of a threat, in manner or in words."

Respecting the engagement alluded to above, the *Norfolk Gazette*, of May 24, presented the subjoined report:

"The following account, after being drawn up, was shewn to one of the Gentlemen who came up from the *President* yesterday, and may be relied upon as an accurate statement:

'The United States frigate, *President*, Commodore Rogers, arrived off the Hook yesterday forenoon from a cruize, and her captain of marines, Captain Caldwell, and Lieutenant Perry, came up to town in the afternoon, in a pilot boat. It appears that about nine o'clock in the evening of the 16th instant, the frigate *President* fell in with a sloop of war, about forty miles N.E. of Cape Henry; that when they had come up within fifty yards of her, Commodore Rogers hailed to know who she was and where from. - The Commander of the sloop of war answered by asking who and what the frigate was. Commodore Rogers, conceiving himself entitled to the first answer, hailed a second time, and instantly after received a shot which struck his main-mast: he returned it; upon which the sloop of war poured a broadside into him. He ranged up alongside, and an action commenced, each being ignorant at that time of the other's force. The sloop of war, after two broadsides, ceased firing for a few moments, and Commodore Rogers supposing she had struck to him, gave orders immediately for the frigate to cease firing. But a few moments elapsed before the sloop of war, taking the *President* for a French frigate, commenced her fire again, and the battle was renewed, which lasted about ten minutes, when the sloop of war struck her colours. Commodore Rogers, judging from his superior force, that he must have injured her very much, determined to lie by her during the night, and early the next morning sent his boat with a Lieutenant on board, and finding that he had (to use a cant phrase) completely riddled her, crippled all three of her masts, and killed and wounded thirty of her men, offered his assistance to get her into port, which the commander of the sloop of war politely declined, saying, 'He believed he should be able to reach Halifax without any assistance.' On being asked how he came to fire into the *President*, he answered, 'That he thought she was a Frenchman.' - The *President* has received little or no damage, and had only one boy slightly wounded in the arm.'

The British vessel was the *Little Belt*, of 18 guns, Captain Bingham. We have seen several private letters, all of which flatly contradict the assertion, that Captain Bingham fired first; and add, that the *President* fired the first single shot, and also the first broadside. The official particulars of this unfortunate affair have not yet arrived."

French Capture British Sloop

A naval action has taken place, off Corsica, between an English sloop of war and a French frigate; in which strangely as it may sound in this country - and in France too, we conceive - the latter gained the victory!

[After a short engagement off Corsica the *Alacrity* of 18 guns surrendered to the *Abeille* of 20.]

1811 – Army Co-operation in Spain and Portugal

THE EARLY MONTHS OF 1811 saw very active campaigning in Portugal and Andalusia by British, Portuguese and Spanish forces. These were largely land operations, but the navy was involved in operations to clear the walls of Cadiz of the French army which had been weakened by units drawn off to fight in the interior. Four thousand British and 8000 Spanish soldiers were embarked, and taken to Algeziras because the weather would not allow them to be landed closer. The soldiers returned along the terrible roads, with the navy moving their guns in boats along the coast. At Barrosa General Graham fought a desperate uphill action which routed the French, and in an hour and a half killed 4000 men. The lack of co-ordination of the allied effort, however, prevented the garrison of Cadiz profiting from the victory.

Supplement to the 'London Gazette Extraordinary'
Admiralty Office, March 25 1811. [XXV 338-341]

Captain Carrol arrived at this Office last night with despatches from Sir Richard Goodwin Keats, K.B., Rear-admiral of the Red, addressed to John Wilson Croker, Esq. of which the following are copies.

Milford, Cadiz-Bay, March 7, 1811
Sir, I have the honour to enclose, for the information of the Lords Commissioners of the Admiralty, copies of my despatches to Admiral Sir Charles Cotton, Bart. of the 20th and 28th of February, and 7th of March.
 I have the honour to be, &c,

R.G. KEATS

Milford, Bay of Cadiz, February 20
Sir, An expedition having been determined upon by the Spanish Government to which Lieutenant General Graham has consented to give his personal assistance, together with that of a considerable portion of the troops under his command, I have felt it my duty, after fully stating in council the uncertainty and risk to which at this season of the year all measures connected with naval operations on the coast are subject, to lend the

expedition all the aid and assistance in my power, and a body of troops, exceeding 2,000, including cavalry, various military stores and provisions, are at present embarked, either in his Majesty's ships named in the margin,[1] in such transports as I could avail myself of, or in Spanish men of war and small transports of our ally: and the whole, together with a numerous fleet of Spanish transports, in which a body of 7,000 troops of that nation are embarked, are waiting in this Bay a favourable opportunity to proceed into the Straits, with a view to force a landing between Cape Trafalgar and Cape de Plata at Tariffa, or at Algesiras in failure of the two former places. General La Pena is the commander-in-chief of this expedition, and as the object is to unite the Spanish forces at St. Roche with the troops sent from hence, with a view to make a combined attack on the rear of the enemy's line before Cadiz; at the same time some demonstrations, and an attempt to open a communication with our troops, are to be made from this quarter, which is thought to require my particular attention; I have therefore placed the execution of the British naval part of the expedition under the able command of Captain Brace of the *St. Albans*.

Milford, Bay of Cadiz, February 28
Sir, I have the honour, in further reference to my letter No. 20, of the 20th instant, to inform you that it being determined to let the troops of the expedition proceed by the earliest opportunity, and it being conceived, from the appearance of the weather, that the Spanish part would be able to get out on the afternoon and night of the 21st, the British naval part, under Captain Brace, put to sea accordingly, and with the exception of one transport, got into the Straits; but it being impracticable to make a landing either in the vicinity of Cape Trafalgar or Tariffa, Captain Brace proceeded to Algesiras, where General Graham and the troops were landed and marched to Tariffa, to which place (the roads being impracticable for carriages), the artillery, provisions, stores, &c. owing, as the General is pleased to express, to the extraordinary exertions of the navy, were conveyed in boats, notwithstanding the unfavourable state of winds and weather. The Spanish part of the expedition, though it twice attempted to get out, was driven back to this bay; and it was the 27th before it was enabled to reach Tariffa.

Milford, Bay of Cadiz, March 7
Sir, I have the honour to inform you, that the combined English and Spanish army, under their respective commanders, General La Pena and Lieutenant-General Graham, moved from Tariffa on the 28th ult. towards Barbate, attended by such naval means as circumstances of weather would permit. Preparations were made by me and our ally, and acted upon, to menace the Trocadero and other points, in order as the army advanced to favour its operations; and arrangements were made for a landing, and real or feigned attacks as circumstances might determine; and to this end the regiment of Toledo was embarked on board his Majesty's ships in the Bay. On the 1st instant General Zayas pushed across the Santi Petri, near the coast, a strong body of Spanish troops, threw a bridge across the river, and formed a tete-du-pont. This post was attacked on the nights of the 3d and 4th with vigour by the enemy, and though he was eventually repulsed, the loss was very considerable on the part of our ally on the 3d. As the weather, from the earliest preparation for the expedition, had been such as to prevent the possibility of landing on the coast or bay, even without great risk, and with no prospect of being able to re-embark, should such a measure become necessary; the apprehension of having

1 *Saint Albans, Druid, Comus, Sabine, Tuscan, Ephira, Steady* and *Rebuff.*

a force, which, with such prospects, I could scarcely expect actively to employ, when its services might be positively useful elsewhere, in defending the tete-du-pont, or in opening a communication with the army from the Isla de Leon, induced me to state my sentiments on the subject, and the regiment of Toledo was in consequence disembarked. The sea on the coast having considerably impeded our communications, we were still uncertain whether the advance of the army would be by Medina or Conil, and of its precise situation, until the 5th, when at eleven A.M. I was informed by telegraph from the Isla de Leon, that it was seen advancing from the southward near the coast. But though the *Implacable* and *Standard* weighed, the pilots refused to take them to their appointed stations, and in the opinion of the best informed, the weather was of too threatening a cast to venture a landing, and which as the army was engaged by noon, according to the telegraph, would not have favoured its operations. Under such circumstances our measures were necessarily confined to feints, whilst the British troops, led by their gallant and able commander, forgetting on the sight of the enemy their own fatigue and privation, and regardless of advantage in the numbers and situation of the enemy, gained by its determined valour (though not without considerable loss) a victory uneclipsed by any of the brave achievements of the British army.

Milford, Bay of Cadiz, March 7
Sir, I have the honour to inform you, that the wind having come off the land, and the sea much abated, two landings were effected, by way of diversion, yesterday morning, between Rota and Catalina, and between that and Santa Maria's, with the Royal Marines, commanded by Captain English of the *Implacable*. 200 seamen of the squadron, and 80 of the Spanish marine, one division of which was under the direction of Captain Spranger of the *Warrior*, the other under Captain Kittoe of this ship; at the same time Catalina was bombarded by the *Hound* and *Thunder* bombs, and that fort and the batteries on the east sides of the bay were kept in check with much spirit by the gun and mortar boats, under the respective commands of Captains Hall and Fellowes. One redoubt of four guns, near Santa Maria's was stormed by the marines of this ship, led by Captain Fottrell; a second, to the south of the Guadalete, was taken by Captain Fellowes's division of the flotilla; and the guns of all the sea defences, together with the small fort of Puntilla, from Rota (which the enemy evacuated) to Santa Maria's, with the exception of Catalina, were spiked, and the works dismantled. Preparations were also made to attack the tete-du-pont, and other defences of the bridge of Santa Maria's, but a strong corps of the enemy, consisting of 2,000 cavalry and infantry, rapidly advancing on the road from Port Real, aware that our troops had crossed the Santi Petri into the Isla de Leon, and that the purposes of a diversion had been answered, I ordered the seamen and marines to re-embark, and the boats (which got on board with difficulty) had not put off many minutes before the enemy arrived on the spot. The enemy had one officer and several soldiers killed and wounded, and an officer and 30 prisoners were taken in the redoubt that was stormed, the rest making their escape. Lieutenant W.F. Carrol, whose conduct on all occasions has been conspicuous, having had his gun-boat sunk before Catalina, thereby sustained a considerable loss. I have given him six weeks leave of absence, and with it duplicates of my despatches. I enclose a list of killed and wounded, and I have the honour to be, &c.

Admiralty-Office, March 30, 1811. ^{XXV 341}

Copy of a letter from the Honourable George Cranfield Berkeley, Admiral of the Blue, &c. to John Wilson Croker, Esq. dated at Lisbon, the 8th of March, 1811

Sir, I have great pleasure in informing their lordships of the evacuation of the strong post which the enemy possessed at Santarem, and that our army are now advancing in pursuit. Lieutenant Claxton, of the *Barfleur*, who commands the gun-boats, in co-operation with the division of the army under Marshal Sir William Beresford, on the south side of Tagus, yesterday, informed me, that on the evening of the 5th instant, in reconnoitring under Santarem, he perceived the enemy departing; and immediately crossed, with the officer of the British piquet, and gave the intelligence to Lord Wellington. He then went to Santarem, where he found the enemy had left three rough built boats or pontoons, two rafts, and twelve or fourteen of their heavy cannon, the carriages of which had been burnt. The army is now moving on, and the boats are ordered to follow them up the Tagus, the navigation of which is now cleared up to Abrantes.

1811 – The Gallant Defence of Anholt ^{XXV 302-305}

THE NAVAL CHRONICLE'S reporting of naval operations in the Baltic, apart from the major expeditions of 1800, 1801, and 1807, tended to be patchy. This reflected the nature of the issues at dispute, which were those of maritime commercial jurisdiction. Extensive coverage was given to diplomatic settlements which determined how naval officers were to approach their task of protecting and controlling trade, but the trade operations themselves were seldom such as would attract much attention in the journal, and less so in this Consolidated Edition. Occasionally, however, an event such as the defence of Anholt occurred which became a major story.

Anholt, which has been some time in the occupation of the English, as a *dépôt*, and point of communication between this country and the Continent, is an island of Denmark, situated in the Cattegat, and surrounded by sand-banks. A light-house was erected on the island, in consequence of the dangerous nature of its coast. - It lies in longitude 11°55' east of Greenwich; latitude, 56°38' north.

The official details of the late defence of Anholt will be found amongst our *Letters on Service*; but the affair was altogether of too brilliant a nature to be passed over, without the record of farther particulars. Captain Maurice, R.N., the governor of the island, was already well known to his country, by his distinguished defence of the Diamond Rock, at Martinique, in the year 1805; and the present achievement has greatly added to his military fame.

It is proper to mention, that the assailing force consisted of a Danish flotilla, of 33 sail, amongst which, according to our Gazette account, were 18 heavy gun-boats, carrying nearly 3,000 men. Our little garrison, including officers, seamen, marines, &c, amounted to only 350 men; yet, with the loss of only two killed and 30 wounded, we killed the Danish commander, three other officers, and 50 men; and took prisoners, besides the wounded, five captains, nine lieutenants, and 504 rank and file! Three pieces of artillery, 500 muskets, and 16,000 rounds of cartridge, also fell into our possession; and two gun-boats, and 250 more prisoners, were taken by his Majesty's ships *Sheldrake* and *Tartar*, in their retreat!

25

Captain Maurice's Dispatches

Letters on Service, from the 'Supplement to the London Gazette'
Admiralty-Office, April 9, 1811. ^XXV 343-349^

Captain J.W. Maurice to Vice-admiral Sir James Saumarez
Fort Yorke, Island of Anholt, 27th March, 1811

Sir, I reported to you in my letter of the 10th ultimo, my having received information of an intended attack on this island by the Danes. On the 8th instant, I received corroboration of this intelligence, but as every exertion had been made to complete the works as well as our materials would allow, and as picquets were nightly stationed from one extreme of the island to the other, in order to prevent surprise, I awaited with confidence the mediated attack.

Yesterday H.M.S. *Tartar* anchored on the north side of the island. The enemy's flotilla and army, consisting in all of nearly four thousand men, have this day, after a close combat of four hours and a half, received a most complete and decisive defeat, and are fled back to their ports, with the loss of three pieces of cannon, and upwards of five hundred prisoners: a number greater by one hundred and fifty men than the garrison I command.

I am now to detail the proceedings of the day. In the morning, just before dawn, the out-picquets on the south side of the island made the signal for the enemy's being in sight. The garrison was immediately put under arms, and I lost not a moment in proceeding with the brigade of howitzers, and two hundred infantry, accompanied by Captain Torrens (who had hitherto acted as major-commandant to the battalion), in order to oppose their landing. On ascending an elevation, for the purpose of reconnoitring, I discovered the landing had already been effected, under the cover of darkness and a fog, and that the enemy were advancing rapidly, and in great numbers.

On both wings the enemy now far outflanked us, and I saw that if we continued to advance, they would get between us and our works; I instantly ordered a retreat, which was effected in good order, and without loss, although the enemy were within pistol-shot of our rear, and seemed determined to enter our batteries by storm: but Fort Yorke and Massareene batteries opened such a well-directed fire of grape and musketry, that the assailants were obliged to fall back and shelter themselves under the sand-hills. As the day lightened, we perceived that the enemy's flotilla, consisting of eighteen gun-boats, had taken up a position on the south side of the island at point-blank shot. I ordered the signal to be made to the *Tartar* and *Sheldrake*, that the enemy had landed, upon which these vessels immediately weighed, and under a heavy press of sail, used every endeavour to beat up the south side, but the extent of shoals threw them out so many miles, that it was some hours before their intention could be accomplished. The gun-boats now opened a very heavy fire on our works, while a column of about six hundred men crossed the island to the westward and took up a position on the northern shore, covered by hillocks of sand, by breaks and inequality of ground. Another column made many attempts to carry the Massareene battery by storm, but were as often repulsed, and compelled to cover themselves under hillocks of sand, which on this island are thrown up by every gale.

The column on the south side had now succeeded in bringing up a field piece against us, and Captain Holtoway, who had commanded at the advanced post, joined us by water. I had been under great apprehensions that this officer had fallen into the hands of the enemy; but finding after several gallant attempts, that he was cut off from reaching head-quarters by land, he with the coolest judgment, launched a boat, and landed his party under Fort Yorke amidst the acclamations of the garrison. Immediately afterwards Lieutenant H.L. Baker, who, with Lieutenant Turnbull of the royal marines, and some brave volunteers, had, in the *Anholt* schooner, gone on the daring enterprise of destroying the enemy's flotilla in his ports, bore down along the north side of the island. Things were in this position when the column on the northern shore, which, divided by the sand hills, had approached within fifty paces of our lines, made another desperate effort to carry the Massareene battery by storm; the column to the south-east also pushed on, and the reserve appeared on the hills ready to support them; but while the commanding officer was leading on his men with great gallantry, a musket-ball put a period to his life. Panic-struck by the loss of their chief, the enemy again fell back, and sheltered themselves behind the sand-hills. At this critical moment Lieutenant Baker, with great skill and gallantry, anchored his vessel on their flank, and opened a well-directed fire. The sand-hills being no longer a protection, and finding it impossible either to advance or retreat, the assailants hung out a flag of truce, and offered to surrender upon terms; but I would listen to nothing but an unconditional surrender, which after some deliberation was complied with.

In the mean time the gun-boats on the south side, which had been much galled by the fire of Fort Yorke and Massareene battery, got under weigh, and stood to the westward, and the column of the enemy, which had advanced on the south side, finding their retreat no longer covered by the flotilla, also hung out a flag of truce, and I sent out an officer to meet it. I was asked to surrender; the reply that I returned it is unnecessary to mention. The enemy finding my determination, sought permission to embark without molestation; but I would listen to nothing but an unconditional submission, and I have the pleasure to inform you, that this corps also laid down their arms, and surrendered themselves prisoners of war.

The prisoners, which were now more numerous than my small garrison, were no sooner secured, than operations were commenced against the reserve, which had been seen retreating to the westward of the island.

I took the field with Major Torrens (who, though wounded, insisted on accompanying me), and Lieutenant and Adjutant Steele; but, as our prisoners were so numerous, and as we had no place of security in which to place them, I could only employ, on this occasion, the brigade of howitzers under Lieutenants R.C. Steele and Bezant, of the royal marine artillery, and part of the light company commanded by Lieutenant Turnbull. When we arrived at the west end of the island, we found that the enemy had formed on the beach, and were protected by fourteen gun-boats, towed close to the shore; to attack such a force, with four howitzers and forty men, seemed a useless sacrifice of brave men's lives; I therefore with the advice of Major Torrens, halted on the hills, while I reluctantly saw the reserve embarked, under cover of the gun-boats, and the flotilla take a final leave of the island.

I am happy to say our loss has not been so considerable as might have been expected, from so desperate an attack, we having only two killed and thirty wounded. The enemy have suffered severely; we have buried between thirty and forty of their dead, and have received in the hospital twenty-three of their wounded, most of them have undergone amputations, three since dead of their wounds, besides a great number which they carried off the field to their boats. I have the honour to be, &c.

J.W. MAURICE, Commandant

To Vice-admiral Sir James Saumarez, Bart. and K.B., &c.

1811 – USS President and HMS Little Belt

THE UNPROVOKED ATTACK by the USS *President* on the sloop *Little Belt* was misrepresented in the United States at the court of enquiry. It appears that Commodore Rodgers had set out to act aggressively, and did so. The episode was indicative of the frustration felt in the United States at the means being employed by the British Government to defeat Napoleon's attempt to destroy by economic protectionism the only independent state in Europe which was beyond his military reach. Perversely, that frustration drove the American republic to favour the French empire.

Letters on Service
Admiralty Office, July 16 1811. XXVI 81-84

His Majesty's Sloop Little Belt, May 21, 1811, Latitude 36°53'N Longitude 71"49'W. Cape Charles bearing West 48 miles
Sir, I beg leave to acquaint you, that in pursuance of your orders to join H.M.S. *Guerriere*, and being on my return from northward, not having fallen in with her, that at about eleven A.M. May 16th, saw a strange sail, to which I immediately gave chase; at one P.M. discovered her to be a man of war, apparently a frigate, standing to the eastward, who, when he made us out, edged away for us, and set his royals; made the signal 275, and finding it now answered, concluded she was an American frigate, as he had a commodore's blue pendant flying at the main; hoisted the colours, and made all sail south, the course I intended, steering round Cape Hatteras, the stranger edging away, but not making any more sail. At half-past three he made sail in chase, when I made the private signal, which was not answered. At half-past six, finding he gained so considerably on us as not to be able to elude him during the night, being within gun-shot, and clearly discerning the stars in his broad pendant, I imagined the more prudent method was to bring to, and hoist the colours, that no mistake might arise, and that he might see what we were; the ship was, therefore, brought to, colours hoisted, guns double-shotted, and every preparation made in case of a surprise. By his manner of steering down, he evidently wished to lay his ship in a position for raking, which I frustrated by wearing three times. About a quarter past eight he came within hail. I hailed, and asked what ship it was? He repeated my question. I again hailed, and asked what ship it was? He again repeated my words, and fired a broadside, which I immediately returned.

28

The action then became general, and continued so for three-quarters of an hour, when he ceased firing, and appeared to be on fire about the main hatchway. He then filled. I was obliged to desist from firing, as the ship falling off, no gun would bear, and had no aftersail to keep her to. All the rigging and sails cut to pieces, not a brace or bowline left, he hailed, and asked what ship this was; I told him; he then asked me if I had struck my colours; my answer was, no, and asked what ship it was? As plainly as I could understand, (he having shot some distance at this time) he answered, the United States frigate. He fired no more guns, but stood from us, giving no reason for his most extraordinary conduct. At day-light in the morning, saw a ship to windward, which, having made out well what we were bore up and passed within hail, fully prepared for action. About eight o'clock he hailed, and said, if I pleased he would send a boat on board; I replied in the affirmative, and a boat, accordingly, came with an officer, and a message from Commodore Rodgers, of the *President*, United States frigate, to say that he lamented much the unfortunate affair (as he termed it) that had happened, and that had he known our force was so inferior, he should not have fired at me. I asked his motive for having fired at all; his reply was, that we fired the first gun at him, which was positively not the case. I cautioned both the officers and men to be particularly careful, and not suffer any more than one man to be at the gun. Nor is it probable that a sloop of war within pistol-shot of a large forty-four gun frigate should commence hostilities. He offered me every assistance I stood in need of, and submitted to me that I had better put into one of the ports of the United States, which I, immediately, declined. By the manner in which he apologised, it appeared to me evident, that had he fallen in with a British frigate he would certainly have brought her to action; and what further confirms me in that opinion is, that his guns were not only loaded with round and grape shot, but with every scrap of iron that could possibly be collected.

I have to lament the loss of thirty-two men killed and wounded, among whom is the master. H.M. sloop is much damaged in her masts, sails, rigging, and hull, and, as there are many shot through between wind and water, and many shots still remaining in her side, and upper works all shot away, starboard pump also, I have judged it proper to proceed to Halifax, which will, I hope, meet with your approbation. . . .

I have the honour to be, &c.

A.B. Bingham, Captain

To Herbert Sawyer, Esq. Rear-admiral of the Red, commander-in-chief [of His Majesty's Ships and Vessels on the Coast of North America]

[The editor's comment was: 'Had it been the object of the commander of the *President* to claim the restoration of some American seamen who had been forcibly impressed, which the American papers pretend gave rise to the rencontre, he would naturally have made the demand in an amicable manner, at least in the first instance; and the only motive which we can assign for his conduct, was a determination to proceed to acts of hostility where the inferiority of force opposed to him gave him a fair chance of success. It remains to be seen whether his conduct will receive the approbation of his own government.']

Several American Opinions
From 'Naval Anecdotes.' *XXVI 32-41; 197-199; 205-206*

[The *New York Evening Post*, of 25 May 1811, was reported to have observed:] "A belligerent .. by the law of nations, has an unquestionable right to conceal her condition, and even to have recourse to artifices to deceive. She may wear false colours, she may give false answers, or refuse to give any answer at all; in short, she is at liberty to have recourse both to simulation and dissimulation, to mislead her enemy. - Very different, they continued, is the case of a neutral. She is supposed to be on terms of friendship with all the rest of the world; she has no right to hoist a false flag; she has no right to give false answer, nor to attempt to deceive or conceal her situation. On the contrary, she is bound to observe civility and courtesy to every one she meets with in her course, provided she receives no provocation to act otherwise."

[*The Boston Repertory* of 8 June was equally sceptical of Rodgers's account, and critical of his justification, while the *Quebec Mercury* of 17 June expressed its contempt in sarcasm.]

Proceedings of the American Court of Inquiry
From 'the Columbian.' XXVI 423-426

The Court of inquiry on the conduct of Commodore Rodgers, in the action between the *President* and the *Little Belt*, has now closed the testimony in the case.

> This Court consists of-
> Commodore Stephen Decatur, President,
> Captain Charles Stewart,
> Captain Isaac Chauncey - and
> William Paulding, jun. Esq. Judge Advocate.

Of the evidence furnished to this Court, on the oaths of the several witnesses examined, we present a brief outline, in the order it was adduced; and leave the public, in a case where doubt is impossible, and conviction irresistible, to make its own comments. Whenever the proper leave is obtained, the proceedings, in their official shape and extent, shall be given to our readers.

[The evidence almost universally supported the contention that the *Little Belt* fired first, improbable as that may appear.]

The Present State of the American Navy XXVI 41

The following is a List of the Navy of the United States:
FRIGATES - *President, Constitution*, and *United States*, 44 guns each; *Chesapeake, New York, Constellation*, and *Congress*, 36 guns each; *Boston, Essex*, 32 guns each, and *John Adams*, 26 guns. Sloop of war, *Wasp*, 16 guns.
BRIGS. - *Syren, Argus, Oneider* [sic], and *Hornet*, 16 guns each; *Vixen*, and *Nautilus*, 12 guns each.
SCHOONERS. - *Enterprise, Ferret*, and *Revenge*, 12 guns each.
170 gun-boats, and the *Vengeance, Spitfire, Aetna*, and *Vesuvius* bombs.
The subsequent only are in commission, the remainder being laid up in ordinary:
FRIGATES - *President*, Commodore Rodgers; *Constitution*, Captain Hall; *United States*, Captain Decatur; *Essex*, Captain Smith.
CORVETTE - *John Adams*, Captain Evans.
SLOOP OF WAR - *Wasp*, Captain Jones.
BRIGS - *Syren*, Captain Tarbett; *Argus*, Captain Lawrence; *Hornet*, Captain Hunt; *Vixen*, Lieutenant Bambridge [Bainbridge]; *Nautilus*, Captain Sinclair.

SCHOONERS - *Enterprize,* Lieutenant Read; *Revenge,* Captain Perry; *Ferret,* Captain
Gunsden.

Impressment of American Seamen
From 'Naval Anecdotes.' XXVI 195-196

The subjoined copy of a letter from Admiral Sawyer, in answer to one from Colonel
Barclay, relative to the case of Gideon Caprian, who, a short time ago, was impressed on
board H.M.S. *Guerriere,* will be regarded as a proof of the conciliatory spirit of the
British government; and, as placing in a fair light, before the American public, the
manner in which such impressments are regarded by the proper authority:

Rear-Admiral H. Sawyer to T. Barclay, Esq.
Halifax, 25th June, 1811
Sir, I had the honour to receive your letter, dated the 20th ult. relative to the persons
named in the margin [John Digio, Gideon Caprian, Josh Leeds], on my arrival at Halifax,
the 19th instant, which had been previously opened by Captain Pechell, of H.M.S.
Guerriere, the senior officer, who immediately discharged John Digio, in compliance
with your request.[1] He would have given up Gideon Caprian also, had he not *entered
into his Majesty's service,* and wished to remain; from which circumstance, he conceived
it to be his duty to detain him for my decision respecting him. But having received your
letter, expressing his father's request to have him sent home, I have now sent him to
New York, by the *Prince Ernest* packet; and will order the discharge of Josh. Leeds, on
the arrival of H.M.S. *Eurydice,* if he is (as I suppose) on board her.

I assure you, Sir, I shall be happy to receive any representations you may be pleased
to make to me, with all the deference to which they will be entitled; as I perfectly
coincide with you, that when American citizens are impressed by mistake or otherwise,
they should be immediately released.

Statement by the Officers of His Majesty's Sloop Little Belt
Of the Action between that Sloop and the United States Frigate President

Marine Law. XVII 57-64

[The statements of the subordinate officers of the *Little Belt* corroborated the service
letter of their captain, Bingham. More interesting is the following account by William
Burket or Burkit, who served on board the USS *President.*]

Province of Nova Scotia, Halifax
The examination and information of William Burket, mariner, taken before John Howe
and Thomas Boggs, Esquires, two of his Majesty's justices of the peace for the country
of Halifax, this 22d day of June, in the year of our Lord, 1811; who being duly sworn,
deposeth and saith, that he was born at Deptford, in England; that he is about 23 years
of age; that he has reason to think he has a mother still living at Deptford; that he left
home about three years ago, and went to Montego Bay, Jamaica; that he left that place
afterwards, and proceeded to New York, in a brig called the *Pizarro*; that some time in
August, 1809, being in a state of intoxication, he was forcibly carried on board the

---

1 "I must here, in justice to Captain Pechell, of H.M.S. *Guerriere,* assure you, that he never was, by
leagues, so near the American coast as has been represented." (Editor *Post* American Newspaper.)

United States armed schooner *Revenge*, in which he continued until she was cast away in Long Island Sound; that he was afterwards transferred to the United States ship, the *President*; that he entered on board the *Revenge*, and afterwards on board the *President*, by the name of Elijah Shepardson; that he was on board the *President*, the first week in May last, when that ship was lying at Annapolis, in Maryland; that Commodore Rodgers suddenly came on board from Havre-de-Grace, where he had been with his family; that instantly after the arrival of the Commodore, all was bustle in the ship; that the sails, some of which were unbent, were immediately bent, and the ship got ready with all possible expedition to proceed to sea; that she got under weigh next day, and proceeded down the river; that they spoke a brig, which said they had been boarded the day before by a British cruiser, and that she had taken a man from her, who had been sent back again; that, as they were going down the river, they got up a much larger quantity of shot and wads than had ever been customary on many other occasion, while he was on board the ship; and that he knows this to have been the case, from having held the station of quarter-gunner; that after proceeding to sea, they cruised on the different parts of the coast, without any thing materially happening until the 16th day of May: that at twelve o'clock on that day, being below at dinner, word was brought that a frigate, supposed to be British, was in sight; that orders were then given for clearing away the bulk-heads, and preparing for action; that, soon after, all hands were beat to quarters; that every thing was then immediately got ready for action; that at this time it was about two o'clock; that all sails were then set, and they went eagerly in chase of the supposed frigate; that orders were soon after given for pricking and firing the guns; before dark, while they were approaching nearer the chase, orders were given to take the aprons off the guns; and at that time this deponent looked at the ship they were in chase of, through the bridle port, and he saw her colours flying; that he saw red in them, but could not correctly ascertain what colours they were; that at the distance they were, he is satisfied that with glasses they could easily be distinguished; that he heard Lieutenant Belling, who had a glass, and who commanded in his division, say, that her colours were British; that when this deponent looked at her, he could see her hull, and was satisfied that she was a small ship; that they continued after this period to approach her until between eight and nine o'clock, when they were within pistol-shot; that Commodore Rodgers then gave orders to stand by their guns, and not to fire till orders were given; that the commodore then hailed; and when he was hailing a second time, a gun in the division to which this deponent belongs, being the second division, went off, he thinks, by accident; and that there were four or five men leaning on the gun at the time; that he instantly turned to acquaint the Lieutenant that the gun had gone off by accident, the Lieutenant then standing only three guns from him; that before he could do this, the whole broadside of the *President* was discharged; and that immediately after a general order was given, "fire away as quick as possible;" that before the firing of the gun of his division, which he thinks went off by accident, and the broadside which immediately followed, this deponent is satisfied, as he was looking out of the port, and distinctly saw the *Little Belt*, that not a gun had been fired from her; that the *President*, he thinks, continued firing about half an hour without cessation; that an order was then given to cease firing; that the *President* then filled her main-top-sail, and stood from the *Little Belt* with her head to the southward, and continued all night on that tack without heaving-to; that the Commodore, before he steered from the *Little Belt*, hailed her to know if she had struck; the only part of the answer given that he could distinctly hear or understand was, that she was a British ship.

This deponent further saith, that the *President* was wounded in her fore-mast and main-mast, a 32-pound shot having entered each of them; that the rest of the night after the engagement, they were employed in repairing the damage sustained in the rigging. This deponent farther saith, that the crew of the *President* consists of about 500 men, upwards of 300 of which he knows to be British seamen, from having conversed with them, and having heard them declare they were so, and from many of them having designated the places they came from; that the engagement with the *Little Belt* had excited great disgust in the British seamen on board the *President*, who had manifested their reluctance to fight against their country; that one man in particular had so plainly expressed this feeling, as to have drawn on him the resentment of Commodore Rodgers, who had put him in irons; in which situation he remained when this deponent left the ship, for the aforesaid offence, and for having said that the first gun was fired from the *President*.

This deponent farther saith, that, after the *President* came into New York, and was lying in the North River, that by the assistance of his hammock lashings, he got in the night from the fore-chains into the river, and swam to a place of safety, and has since procured a passage to Halifax.

WILLIAM BURKIT, his X mark

Sworn at Halifax, the day and year aforesaid, before us,
    John Howe, Thomas Boggs, Justices of the Peace.

After the insertion of the preceding important documents, we feel ourselves called upon, for the first time, to offer some remarks upon this case; remarks which will be found the more interesting, in consequence of the American President's Message, at the opening of Congress, as given in the preceding sheet. [See above p7.]

The readers of the *Naval Chronicle* have already perused the letters of Commodore Rodgers and Captain Bingham to their respective governments, (as referred to below) each charging the other with being the aggressor. They have also seen the minutes of the American Court-martial, proving that the *Little Belt* fired first; in addition to which, we now bring forward what they were before strangers to - the minutes of a Court of Inquiry holden at Halifax, *proving*, in like manner, that the *President* fired first. So far, therefore, Great Britain and America are equal; they carry their defence to the same length, and support it by the same testimony. But we go much farther than this; for we have now also inserted the depositions of two seamen - the one an American, we believe [not reproduced here], the other an Englishman, - who were on board the *President* at the time of the action, and who swear that the first shot was discharged from their ship: to this testimony we solicit proper regard. Nor does England's excess of evidence over that of America rest even here; for we have long ago seen Captain Bingham's instructions, charging him to treat the citizens of the United States with the utmost respect; while the American has hitherto studiously concealed the instructions under which Commodore Rodgers sailed.

According to the deposition of one of these seamen, the first shot was fired by accident; than which nothing is more likely among inexperienced persons: and how strongly does this confirm the opinion of the agitation which must have prevailed on board a vessel, manned by mariners who had never before been in action!

But to recur to another topic, no less essential to the dispute than firing the first shot. A gun may, as we have seen, go off and do mischief by accident: but a threatening position cannot be assumed but by intention. Who, then, *intentionally first* put himself

Outside view of St. John's Harbour, Newfoundland. Engraved by Baily, from a
Drawing by Pocock. ^{Plate 342}

in a posture of offence? Commodore Rodgers, clearly, by his own acknowledgment,
and [by] Captain Bingham's assertion, supported by the evidence of his officers at
Halifax. These are the words of the two captains, speaking at the same moment of time:
– "By his manner of steering down, he evidently wished to lay his ship in a position for
raking, which I frustrated by wearing three times." (*Vide Captain Bingham's Letter, and
the evidence of all his officers to the same effect.*)

What says Commodore Rodgers to this? – "At fifteen minutes past eight, I directed
Captain Ludlow to take a position *to windward of her, and on the same tack,* within short
speaking distance: this, however, the master of the chase *appeared, from his manouevres,
anxious* to prevent; as he wore, and hauled by the wind on different tacks, four times
successively, between this period and the time of our arriving at the position which I
had ordered to be taken." – (*Commodore Rodgers's Letter*). – Why did Commodore Rodgers
assume this position? To speak to us. But, why did he wish to speak to us, to windward
upon the same tack, or, in other words, in the most formidable position for raking us;
and that, too, after he saw that we had three or four times avoided suffering him to do it?
Let him, or any one else for him, answer that.

We again request attention to the depositions of the two seamen, particularly that
taken at Halifax. It is evidence of much more than the mere commencement of the
action. The fitting out of the *President* – the arrival of Commodore Rodgers on board –
the taking in of shot and wads – all these points, we fear, argue "a foregone
determination;" but still, if America be content to disavow the act, perhaps it would be
more politic in us to believe, or seem to believe, her assurance.

1811 – The Fall of Tarragona

NAPOLEON BUONAPARTE'S STRATEGY FOR 1811 was systematically to occupy all the Spanish principal towns. Towards the end of April General Suchet, with forty thousand infantry, six to eight thousand horse, and a hundred guns, arrived to lay siege to Tarragona. A vigorous resistance was conducted by the garrison, which expected to be relieved by a Spanish army under General Campo Verde, and on 26 May a British force from Gibraltar, under the naval command of Captain Codrington, arrived off the coast of Catalonia. However, by then the French had so effectively breached Tarragona's defences that Colonel Skerritt did not consider it proper to land his small embarked army. The French assault found the garrison demoralised, and the British watched as they were hunted down in the streets, and flung themselves from the walls.

Letters on Service
Admiralty Office, August 16 1811. *XXVI 169-174*

Copy of Letter from Admiral Sir Charles Cotton, Bart. late Commander-in-chief of H.M. Ships and Vessels in the Mediterranean, to John Wilson Croker, Esq. Secretary to the Admiralty, dated San Josef, off Toulon, 5th July, 1811
Sir, The Lords Commissioners of the Admiralty will be informed by my despatch, No. 108, of the 4th ultimo, of the state of affairs in Catalonia, up to the 24th May. I have now the honour to transmit accounts of the further events in that quarter, to the 1st instant, contained in the accompanying extracts of communications from Captains Codrington and Adam, and Lieutenant-colonel Green, . . . by which their lordships will regret to see that the last accounts, brought me this day, by the *Volontaire*, state the town of Tarragona to have been stormed, taken, and set fire to, by the French force under Suchet, on the 28th June.

I have the honour to be, &c.

CHARLES COTTON

No. VII

Captain Edward Codrington to Admiral Sir Charles Cotton
Blake, off Tarragona, 29 June, 1811
Sir, Yesterday morning, at dawn of day, the French opened their fire upon the town;

about half-past five in the afternoon a breach was made in the works, and the place
carried by assault immediately afterwards. From the rapidity with which they entered,
I fear they met but with little opposition; and upon the Barcelona side a general panic
took place. Those already without the walls stripped and endeavoured to swim off to
the shipping, while those within were seen sliding down the face of the batteries; each
party thus equally endangering their lives more than they would have done by a firm
resistance to the enemy.

A large mass of people, some with muskets and some without, then pressed forward
along the road, suffering themselves to be fired upon by about twenty French, who
continued running beside them at only a few yards distance. At length they were stopped
entirely by a volley of fire from one small party of the enemy, who had entrenched
themselves at a turn of the road, supported by a second a little higher up, who opened a
masked battery of two field pieces. A horrible butchery then ensued; and shortly
afterwards the remainder of these poor wretches, amounting to above three thousand,
tamely submitted to be led away prisoners by less than as many hundred French.

The launches and gun-boats went from the ships the instant the enemy were
observed by the *Invincible* (which lay to the westward) to be collecting in their trenches;
and yet, so rapid was their success, that the whole was over before we could open our
fire with effect.

All the boats of the squadron and transports were sent to assist those who were
swimming or concealed under the rocks; and, notwithstanding a heavy fire of musketry
and field-pieces, which was warmly and successfully returned by the launches and gun-
boats, from five to six hundred were then brought off to the shipping, many of them
badly wounded.

I cannot conclude my history of our operations at Tarragona, without assuring
you, that the zeal and exertion of those under my command, in every branch of the
various services which have fallen to their lot, has been carried far beyond the mere
dictates of duty. . . .

I have the honour to be, &c,

EDWARD CODRINGTON

Captain Codrington further states, that he had gained intelligence that General Contreras
was wounded and made prisoner, and that the general personally distinguished himself;
that the governor (Gonzalez) with a handful of men, defended himself to the last, and
was bayoneted to death in the square, near his house; that man, woman, and child were
put to the sword upon the French first entering the town, and afterwards, all those
found in uniform or with arms in their houses; and that many of the women, and young
girls of ten years old, were treated in the most inhuman way; and that after the soldiers
had satisfied their lust, many of them, it was reported, were thrown into the flames,
together with the badly wounded Spaniards; one thousand men and been left to destroy
the works; the whole city was burnt to ashes, or would be so, as the houses were all set
fire to; the only chance in their favour was the calm weather, and the sudden march of
the French, by which some houses might escape.

General Memorandum

Whereas from the present distressed situation of Tarragona, many families may be
obliged to embark without the necessary means of existence; until they can be conveyed

to other places on the coast, where the customary generosity of the people will ensure them a share of what they may have for their own subsistence:

It is my direction, that the ships of the English squadron furnish them with such provisions, for the time of their embarkation and transport, as the humanity and liberality of our country will dictate.

A separate account of the provision so expended is hereafter to be given to me, regularly signed by the proper officers, for the information of the victualling board, instead of the people being borne for victuals as passengers usually are.

EDWARD CODRINGTON

Blake, in Tarragona Roads, 25th June 1811

[Letters accounting operations around Valencia were published in Vol. XXVI, pp492-500.]

1811 – Continued

IN 1811, ALTHOUGH THE AMERICAN theatre was very active, subsequent to the *Little Belt* incident it did not yet represent a scene of war. In September there was a report that an accommodation appeared possible with the Americans. However, President Madison's declaration to Congress in early November set the American Government on the road to war with Britain the following year.

From the East Indies there was news of the defeat of a squadron which had sailed with reinforcements for the Isle de France before its capture was known in Europe. It sought shelter at Madagascar, and there it was hunted down and destroyed. There was also news of the sailing of an expedition intended to capture Batavia from the Dutch and French.

Marine Law
Middlesex Sessions ^{XVI 59-60}

Rescuing Impressed Men

G.M. Bluckhart, landlord of the Queen's Head public-house, Gravel Lane, and Janson, a foreigner, were indicted for rescuing a man from the press-gang, on the 14th of September last. It appeared that, on the evening above-mentioned, Lieutenant Donadieu and a party of men under his command, being on shore in the impress service, passed by the defendant's house (the Queen's Head), and hearing a fiddle and dancing, he ordered a midshipman and two seamen to go into the house, and endeavour to pick up a man: they, accordingly, went in whilst the lieutenant stopped at the door. There were several seamen in the room, who, on the midshipman's asking them who they were, said they were man-of-war's men on shore with leave of absence. The officer desired to see their certificates, when two of them not being able to produce any, he was proceeding to take them away; a scuffle ensued, and some blows passed; the officer and his men, however, succeeded in taking the two men out of the house; but, on their coming out of the door, the defendant Bluckhart followed, and calling to the mob, who stood round the door 'go it boys, rescue them,' the mob attacked the press-gang, and, in the scuffle, one of the impressed men escaped.

Mr. Alley, on the part of the defendant, Bluckhart, contended that he was justified in what he had done, Lieutenant Donadieu, to whom the impress warrant was directed, not having entered the room with the midshipman, that officer could have no legal authority to act, and, therefore, the resistance made to him in the house was legal, and

38

the resistance without side of the door was merely a continuation of that which commenced within the house. Neither had any proof been produced that the man who escaped was a person proper to have been impressed, he, therefore, contended that the defendant, Bluckhart, must be acquitted.

The Court, however, over-ruled both the points taken by the Learned Counsel, and the jury found the defendant guilty. - Sentenced to be imprisoned six months. Janson, against whom there was no evidence, was acquitted.

From 'Naval Anecdotes.' XXVI 137

French Naval Force in the Mediterranean, in April, 1811

Majestueux, 120 guns, Admiral Gantheaume, chief admiral d'Etat, Major Duranteau, permier adj., Captain Violet; *Austerlitz*, 120, Vice-admiral Allemand, Captain Guier; *Commerce de Paris*, 120, Rear-admiral Cosmez, Captain Brouard; *Donaumert*, 80, Captain Infernet; *Ulm*, 74, Captain Durlos; *Danube*, 74, Captain Henry; *Breslaw*, 74, Captain Allemand; *Suffren*, 74, Captain Laville; *Genovis*, 74 Captain Montalvert; *Magnanime*, 74, Captain Jugan; *Ajax*, 74, Captain Petit; *la Boree*, 74, Captain Sency; *Hannibal* (E.) 74, Captain Maitre.

FRIGATES - *Penelope*, 40, Captain Dubourdieu, C.V.; *Pomone*, 40, Captain Losamel; *Pauline*, 40, Captain Montfort; *Amerie*, 40, Captain Maynard; *Proserpine* (E.) 36, Captain Gantheaume; *Incorruptible*, 40, Captain Martin, C.F.; *Themise*, 36, Captain Villen; *Adrien*, (new) 40, (unknown); *le Victorieuse*, 22 carronades, Capt. -.

BUILDING - *Monarque*, 120 guns; *Sceptre*, 74, at Toulon, launched. - A line-of-battle ship and a frigate, at Genoa.

STORE SHIPS - *La Maviere*, 800 tons, 30 guns; *la Baleine*, 800 tons, 30 guns; *Durance*, 500 tons, 26 guns.

AT CORFU - *La Danar*, 40 guns, Captain Decauche; *la Flore*, 40, Captain Lambert.

AT LIOBAT - *La Girafe*, armed store-ship, 800 tons, 30 guns, burnt by H.M.S. *Pomone, Unite* and *Scout*, on the 1st of May, 1811. *La Caravau*, armed store-ship, 830 tons, 30 guns.

AT LEGHORN, PORT ESSINE, AND GENOA - *L'Abeille*, 18 carronades, 36-pounders, commanded by Murat, L.V.; *le Courier, l'Endymion, Janus, la Ligurie*, 16 carronades each.

AT PORT VENDRE - *La Fatigue*, 20 carronades, 36-pounders; *la Fleche*, 10 carronades, 16-pounders, (a schooner).

N.B. They have more store-ships, but at present their names are unknown.

By a letter from off Toulon, dated May 13, 1811, the ships building in April, were found ready for sea, which made the French ships 15 sail, and four sail are still building.

NAPLES, MAY 13 - One ship of the line building.

From the 'Naval History of the Present Year,' 1811
July-August. XXVI 165-166

American Negotiations

Nothing decisive is yet known in this country, respecting the progress of Mr. Foster's negotiation with the American government.

Russia

Russia is, at this time, understood to be very favourably disposed towards this country: so much so, indeed, that a free commercial intercourse with her is expected. A belief continues to be prevalent, on some parts of the continent, that hostilities will shortly commence between France and Russia. The war has been renewed between the Russians and Turks.

New Spanish Ambassador

The Duke del Infantado has arrived in England, to succeed Admiral Apodaca, as ambassador from Spain.

August-September. XXVI 253-255

Buonaparte At Boulogne

Buonaparte having arrived at Boulogne, a grand marine *fête* took place for his amusement, and under his immediate direction, on the 20th and 21st of September. On the former day, after much bustle and pomp of preparation, the great Emperor, in his barge, visited several vessels of his flotilla. Seven praams, of 12 24-pounders each, then stood out to attack H.M.'s frigate *Naiad*, Captain Carteret, which awaited their approach with springs on her cable. After a distant cannonade of three quarters of an hour, the praams were joined by ten brigs, of four guns each, and a sloop of two. The engagement continued for two hours longer; when the *Naiad* weighed anchor and stood off, partly to repair some slight damages which she had received, but chiefly, by getting to windward, to get within shore, if possible, of a part of the French flotilla. The enemy, however, retreated under the batteries.

On the following morning, "covered with glory," the seven praams, and fifteen smaller vessels, renewed the attack. The *Naiad* had, in the mean time, been joined by the *Rinaldo, Redpole,* and *Castilian* brigs, and the *Viper* cutter. The enemy were drawn within pistol-shot; and then, by the judicious and incessant firing, from both sides of H.M.'s cruisers, they were thrown into inextricable confusion. The French admiral himself very narrowly escaped being taken; and one of the praams, bearing a commodore's pendant, which came up to his assistance, was secured and triumphantly borne off! - In this action, Lieutenant Cobb, of the *Castilian*, and two seamen, were killed, and about 16 wounded. The loss of the enemy is supposed to have been considerable. On the former day, not a man of ours was hurt. . . .

[Captain Philip Carteret's accounts of this action, dated HMS *Naiad*, off Boulogne, 21 September 1811, were published in Vol. XXVI, pp340-343. A description of the praam, with an illustration, has been inserted in Appendix 2 on Ship Design, Volume I, p360.]

French Ports Embargoed

Buonaparte is said to have laid an embargo on all the French ports; probably with a view of favouring the putting to sea of the Scheldt fleet, which is said to consist of 25 sail of the line. The general belief is, that it will attempt to go north about; consequently, an extra number of men of war have been ordered on the Loughswilly station. - Buonaparte is expected to visit Rotterdam, in the course of his tour.

Yellow Fever

The yellow fever has broken out, with considerable violence, at Carthagena.

US Language More Conciliatory

The last American papers are milder in their language, than we have, for some time past, been accustomed to witness. It is certain, however, that the negotiations between the two governments have been suspended, till Mr. Foster shall receive farther instructions, in answer to despatches which he some time ago transmitted to England.

Orders in Council

The expected Order in Council, retaliatory on the Non-importation Act of the American Congress, has not yet appeared; but the Gazette of September 7, contains an Order, grounded on an Act passed, by the late administration, in the 46th of his Majesty, and entitled, "An Act for authorising his Majesty in Council to allow, during the present war, and six weeks after the ratification of a definite treaty of peace, the importation and exportation of certain goods and commodities in neutral ships, into and from his Majesty's territories in the West Indies, and Continent of South America." By this order duties are imposed upon a variety of articles, the produce of the United States of America, which will naturally affect the lucrative commerce which the Americans have so long maintained with our colonies, to the no small discouragement of our North American settlements and possessions. . . .

Royal Marines

In filling up the late vacant naval colonelcies of the Royal Marines, two of the three nominations seem to have given dissatisfaction, both in and out of the service; as those captains who have particularly and individually distinguished themselves, were not thought of, such as a Moore, Foote, Blackwood, Brisbane, Berry, E.Hamilton, Rowley, Seymour, Hoste, &c. The only justification and policy for these sinecure colonelcies and generalships to continue independent of the serving corps, can be but to reward extraordinary merit in the naval service.

September-October. XXVI 335-339

Two French Frigates Captured

We have the gratification of recording the capture of two more French frigates- the *Astrea* and *Renommée*; of which the following are some particulars: - On the 21st of June, 60 leagues to the southwest of the Isle de France, the *Fox* spoke H.M.S. *Harpy*, Captain Bain, who informed her, that an action had taken place off Tamatavé, in the Isle of Madagascar, between the *Astrea*, *Phoebe*, and *Galatea* British frigates, and the *Clorinde, Astrea,* and *Renommée* French frigates, and that after a severe action, the two last mentioned French frigates were taken, but the *Clorinde* made her escape. One of the prizes had arrived at the Isle of France before the *Harpy* left it; the other was in Tamatavé, rigging jury-masts. They had each 200 troops on board, for the relief of the Isle of France. They had communicated with the island, but on hearing that we were in possession of it, they made two attempts to land and re-take the Isle of Bourbon, but were repulsed. The action was fought at night. According to private accounts, the *Galatea* lost between 50 and 60 men.

The *Clorinde* arrived at Brest on the 24th of September; on which day she had a very narrow escape from the *Tonnant*, which chased her through the Saints, and would have run her down, had not a violent squall carried away her fore-top-gallant-mast, by which means the enemy got off. The *Tonnant* had fired three broadsides into her.

On her passage from Madras, the *Clorinde* captured the *Swallow* Jamaica packet, when within a week's sail of Barbadoes. Captain de St. Cricq, after taking what he thought proper out, chiefly eatables and drinkables, of which he was in great want, some sails and cordage, gave up the packet to the captain, (and she arrived at Falmouth on the 28th of September, having some poultry, plenty of wine, porter, and spirits, and salt provisions, remaining) not suffering the sailors to plunder the packet's crew. He behaved very handsomely. The *Clorinde* bore evident marks of having been severely handled. There was a box of plate, value £440 on board the *Swallow*, for General Morrison, of Jamaica, which narrowly escaped the Frenchmen. - Captain de St. Cricq's report of the proceedings of the *Clorinde*, will appear in a subsequent part of this volume.

Expedition Against Batavia Sailed

By the *Fox* frigate, which brought the news of the capture of the *Astrea* and *Renommée*, we learn, that the last division of our expedition against Batavia, sailed from Madras on the 29th of April. Commodore Broughton had assumed the chief command of the squadron in the Indian Seas, and had appointed R. Festing, Esq. to be captain of the *Illustrious*. The governor-general had embarked on board the *Modeste* frigate.

HMS Dover Wrecked

The *Dover* frigate, Captain Tucker, has been lost in Madras Roads. The *City of London*, which came under convoy of the *Fox*, fell in with the *Indian* soon after leaving the Sand-heads; and from that ship she learned, that, on passing Madras Roads, the *Indian* saw the *Dover* and some merchant vessels on shore; but with respect to the fate of their crews she knew nothing.

The *Dover* had not long returned from her successful expedition against the Spice Islands; for which the officers and crew (if preserved) will have to share very considerable prize-money.

[Captain Edward Tucker's letters accounting the capture of Ternate, 31 August 1810, are published in Vol. XXVI, pp70-78.]

Order in Council

The *Gazette* of October 5, contains an Order in Council, revoking a previous order of 12th April, 1809, by which the subjects of countries in amity with Great Britain, were permitted to trade in their own vessels with the Cape of Good Hope and its dependencies, and declaring, that from and after the 12th of April, 1812, the trade with that country shall be carried on in British vessels only. It is, however, provided, that ships belonging to states in amity with Great Britain, may enter the ports of that settlement for repairs and refreshment, and, under such circumstances, a part of the cargoes may be disposed of to defray expenses: such vessels also being laden with provisions and furnished with licenses, which the governor is permitted to grant, are also allowed to enter the said ports.

Buonaparte Ends Tour

Buonaparte reached Amsterdam, in the progress of his coasting tour, on the 9th October; and is believed, by this time, to have returned to Paris.

Scheldt Blockade Suspended

Admiral Young, the commander-in-chief of the North Sea Fleet, with Rear-admiral Sir Richard Strachan, and Vice-admiral Ferrier, arrived in the Downs on the 18th of October, with 13 sail of the line, from off Flushing. The blockade of the Scheldt, except by a small squadron, for the purpose of observation, being for the present suspended. It is generally understood, that the French fleet which was assembled at Flushing, is gone up the Scheldt towards Antwerp, not being sufficiently manned and equipped for the sort of service they might have encountered if they ventured out to sea.

Texel Blocked with Sand

A letter from Deal states, that, by the sudden shifting of the sand, a bar has risen at the entrance of the Texel, which renders it impossible for the squadron in that harbour to come out. . . .

Boulogne Flotilla

The following particulars relative to the Boulogne flotilla have been received: - the flotilla consists of 16 ships (praams) with 12 24-pounders, and 112 men each; 28 brigs, with false keels, from six to eight 24-pounders, and 112 men each; 28 brigs, with false keels, from six to eight 24-pounders, and from 70 to 80 men; eight schooners, of 13 guns and 40 men each, and 300 gun-boats, with two 24 pounders, and 26 men each; the sailors chiefly Flemish and Dutch. Five hundred impressed men lately arrived from Holland. Several gun-boats out of repair. The crews are mustered on shore every Sunday, and taught infantry movements.

Maritime Conscription in Hanse Towns

Buonaparte has issued a decree, for a maritime conscription, in the Hanse Towns. A Hamburg article, dated September 30, also says - "By a decision of the commission of government, dated the 27th instant, all proprietors of ships, of whatever description, are ordered to furnish, within a specified time, to government, a declaration of such ships, their description, tonnage, the port to which they belong, and the place where they are at present. The ships, the proprietors of which have not complied with these formalities, shall be placed under sequestration, until their condemnation be pronounced." . . .

Popham Improves Signal System

Sir Home Popham has just completed a new code of signals, which extends and amplifies his former code. The Admiralty have adopted it, and it is printing for their exclusive promulgation.

The signal-posts established on the coast, for observing the enemy's cruisers, are undergoing a complete revision by Admiral Browne. . . .

Greenwich Fire

Fire at Greenwich Hospital - About one o'clock, on the morning of the 1st of October, an alarm of fire was given by the sentinels on duty in Greenwich Hospital. It was observed to proceed from the top of the north-west angle of the infirmary. The most prompt and vigorous assistance was given by the seamen of the hospital, and the inhabitants of Greenwich; but without being able to stop the fury of the flames for several hours. The difficulty of procuring water was the reason of so much damage being done, as very little was procured until the arrival of the London firemen, who dug up the pavement, and cut the pipes in several places.

November-December. XXVI 491-492

US President's Statement to Congress

The message of the President of the United States to Congress, at the opening of their Session on the 5th of November, will be given at length, amongst our State Papers, in the succeeding volume. The conduct of the British Government is still the theme of complaint. The message also bears a hostile expression towards France, though not on the ground of the Berlin and other decrees of Buonaparte, inimical to neutral commerce, which the American Government consider repealed, but on account of internal regulations, by which American property has been unjustly seized in France. These, it is recommended, should be met by restrictions on French imports into the United States.

American papers, of a more recent date, inform us, that the affair of the *Chesapeake* has at last been adjusted between the British and American governments, by the agreement of the latter, to accept of reparation, on the principle formerly proposed by Mr. Erskine, but not ratified by the English ministry!

State Papers XXVII 28-32

Message of the President of the United States, James Madison, to Congress, 5 November 1811

Fellow Citizens of the Senate, and the House of Representatives
In calling you together sooner than a separation from your homes would otherwise have been required, I yielded to considerations drawn from the posture of our foreign affairs; and in fixing the present, for the time of your meeting, regard was had to the probability of further developments of the policy of the belligerent powers towards this country, which might the more unite the national councils in the measures to be pursued.

At the close of the last Session of Congress, it was hoped that the successive confirmations of the extinction of the French Decrees, so far as they violated our neutral commerce, would have induced the government of Great Britain to repeal its Orders in

Council; and thereby authorise a removal of the existing obstructions to her commerce with the United States.

Instead of this reasonable step towards satisfaction and friendship between the two nations, the orders were, at a moment when least to have been expected, put into more rigorous execution; and it was communicated through the British envoy just arrived, that whilst the revocation of the edicts of France, as officially made known to the British government, was denied to have taken place, it was an indispensable condition of the repeal of the British Orders, that commerce should be restored to a footing that would admit the productions and manufactures of Great Britain, when owned by neutrals, into markets shut against them by her enemy; the United States being given to understand, that in the mean time a continuance of their non-importation act would lead to measures of retaliation.

At a later date it has indeed appeared that a communication to the British government, of fresh evidence of the repeal of the French decrees against our neutral trade, was followed by an intimation that it had been transmitted to the British Plenipotentiary here, in order that it might receive full consideration in the depending discussions. This communication appears not to have been received. But the transmission of it hither, instead of founding on it an actual repeal of the orders, or assurances that the repeal would ensure, will not permit us to rely on any effective change in the British cabinet. To be ready to meet with cordiality satisfactory proofs of such a change, and to proceed, in the mean time, in adapting our measures to the views which have been disclosed through that minister, will best consult our whole duty.

In the unfriendly spirit of those disclosures, indemnity and redress for other wrongs have continued to be withheld; and our coasts and the mouths of our harbours have again witnessed scenes, not less derogatory to the dearest of our national rights, than vexatious to the regular course of our trade.

Among the occurrences produced by British ships of war hovering on our coasts, was an encounter between one of them and the American frigate commanded by Captain Rodgers, rendered unavoidable on the part of the latter by a fire, commenced without cause, by the former, whose commander is therefore alone chargeable with the blood unfortunately shed in maintaining the honour of the American flag. The proceedings of a Court of Inquiry, requested by Captain Rodgers, are communicated, together with the correspondence relating to the occurrence between the secretary of state and his Britannic Majesty's envoy. To these are added the several correspondences which have passed on the subject of the British Orders in Council; and to both the correspondence relating to the Floridas, in which Congress will be made acquainted with the interposition which the government of Great Britain has thought proper to make against the proceedings of the United States.

The justice and fairness which have been evinced on the part of the United States to France, both before and since the revocation of her decrees, authorised an expectation that her government would have followed up that measure by all such others as were due to our reasonable claims, as well as indicated by its amicable professions. No proof, however, is yet given of an intention to repair the other wrongs done to the United States; and particularly to restore the great amount of American property seized and condemned under edicts which, though not affecting our neutral relations, and therefore not entering into questions between the United States and other belligerents, were nevertheless founded in such unjust principles, that the reparation ought to have been prompt and ample.

In addition to this, and other demands of strict right on that nation, the United States have much reason to be dissatisfied with the rigorous and unexpected restrictions, to which their trade with the French dominions has been subjected; and which, if not discontinued, will require at least corresponding restrictions on importations from France into the United States.

On all those subjects our Minister Plenipotentiary, lately sent to Paris, has carried with him the necessary instructions; the result of which will be communicated to you; and, by ascertaining the ulterior policy of the French Government towards the United States, will enable you to adapt it to that of the United States towards France.

Our other foreign relations remain without unfavourable changes. With Russia, they are on the best footing of friendship. The ports of Sweden have afforded proofs of friendly dispositions towards our commerce, in the councils of that nation also. And the information from our Special Minister of Denmark shews, that the mission had been attended with valuable effects to our citizens, whose property had been so extensively violated and endangered by cruisers under the Danish flag.

Under the ominous indications which commanded attention, it became a duty to exert the means committed to the Executive Department, in providing for the general security. The works of defence on our maritime frontier have accordingly been prosecuted with an activity, leaving little to be added for the completion of the most important ones; and as particularly suited for co-operation in emergencies, a portion of the gunboats have, in particular harbours, been ordered into use. The ships of war before in commission, with the addition of a frigate, have been chiefly employed, as a cruising guard to the rights of our coast. And such a disposition has been made of our land forces, as was thought to promise the services most appropriate and important. In this disposition is included a force, consisting of regulars and militia, embodied in the Indiana territory, and marched towards our north-western frontier. This measure was made requisite by several murders and depredations committed by Indians; but more especially by the menacing preparations and aspect of a combination of them on the Wabash, under the influence and direction of a fanatic of the Shawanese tribe. With these exceptions, the Indian tribes retain their peaceable dispositions towards us, and their usual pursuits.

I must not add, that the period is arrived, which claims from the Legislative Guardians of the National Rights a system of more ample provisions for maintaining them. Notwithstanding the scrupulous justice, the protracted moderation, and the multiplied efforts, on the part of the United States, to substitute, for the accumulating dangers to the peace of the two countries, all the mutual advantages of re-established friendship and confidence; we have seen that the British Cabinet perseveres, not only in withholding a remedy for other wrongs so long and so loudly calling for it; but in the execution, brought home to the threshold of our territory, of measures which, under existing circumstances, have the character, as well as the effect, of war on our lawful commerce.

With this evidence of hostile inflexibility, in trampling on rights which no independent nation can relinquish; Congress will feel the duty of putting the United States into an armour and an attitude demanded by the crisis, and corresponding with the national spirit and expectation. . . .

(Signed) JAMES MADISON

Washington, November 5, 1811

From *'Correspondence.'* XXVI 397-398

Social Inequality a Service Issue

Tom Starboard to the Editor, dated Cable-street, 12th November, 1811
Mr. Editor, The court martial held in the Tagus a few months since, for the trial of
Lord William Fitzroy, captain of the *Macedonia*, for putting in irons the master of that
ship, sentenced his lordship, after two days' investigation, "*to be dismissed from the command
of his ship, and struck off the list of the Royal Navy.*" The master was afterwards tried for
"Contempt" to Lord William Fitzroy, sentenced "*to be dismissed his Majesty's service,*
AND RENDERED INCAPABLE OF SERVICE AGAIN AS AN OFFICER." The sentences appear rather
extraordinary, from being so widely at variance in their effects on these officers; one
having an opportunity of being restored, while to the other that event can never be
attained. It is very far from my wish to offer any disrespect to the members of the
court, individually, or collectively, as, without doubt, they fully exercised their abilities
to the utmost extent human knowledge can ever be supposed capable of attaining; and
in the construction of the two sentences they acted, in their opinion, for the benefit of
his Majesty's service. It appears very evident, from the public papers, that Lord William
Fitzroy has availed himself of the opportunity in the construction of his sentence,
and is actually restored to his rank of post captain; and I have been informed the master
has, encouraged by his lordship's success, applied for his restoration, and met with a
negative. This can, I suppose, only have happened from the sentence being so decidedly
against him.

The papers insinuate, that the restoration of Lord William Fitzroy was effected by
the Prince Regent (which is certainly the fact), but keep out of view, from ignorance, or
other motives, that it was on the *recommendation* of the Admiralty Board. Perhaps
many of your friends, Mr. Editor, are unacquainted with the method by which an officer
regains his rank in the navy, and I will therefore state it. An officer dismissed the
service by the sentence of a court martial, sends in a memorial to the council (which is
merely left in an envelope at the Council Office, Whitehall), stating his services, character,
&c. and praying restoration to his former rank. After it has been read to the Council
Board, it is referred to the Admiralty, to consider and report their *opinion* as to the
propriety of the prayer being complied with. Should they, in their WISDOM, think
the officer's request may be allowed, he is restored by an order in council; but should
their opinion be the contrary, all his hopes are vanished, "and leave not a wreck behind."
This is certainly a case of some hardship on the unfortunate master, who is doomed to
everlasting disgrace, and his wife, if he has one, deprived of a pension from that fund to
which her husband has perhaps for years been contributing, which she would be entitled
to, provided she outlives him.[1]

The following anecdote I heard some years ago, and it may not be undeserving of
being placed in the *Naval Chronicle*, although it is not very modern. A cook belonging
to a man of war at Portsmouth, had been guilty of some improper conduct, particularly
drunkenness, and of course disobedience of orders: for these crimes he was to be tried
by a court martial. On the morning of his trial he was extremely low spirited, which a
messmate perceived, and inquired the reason of: the cook, it is said, replied, "Why I

---

1 The pension allowed to a master's widow, from the Charity appointed for the relief of commissioned and
warrant officers, is £40 *per annum*, and they are enabled by a late regulation to receive it quarterly.

should not so much mind it, were the court to be composed of cooks; but as that can't be the case, I am damnably afraid I shall go to leeward, and it will be all over with me."

[Lord William Fitzroy's career was quite unaffected by his disgrace, being eventually promoted to Admiral of the White in 1855. Other letters and papers relating to the problem of discipline have been located in Volume III, Appendix 6, pp338-357.]

1811 – Action at Madagascar

SOON AFTER THE CAPTURE of the Isle de France it was learnt that three French frigates under the command of Captain Roquebert with an embarked army intended for reinforcement of that colony had arrived in the Indian Ocean. These proceeded to Madagascar for water, and there they were hunted down by Captain Charles Marsh Schomberg, commanding HMS *Astraea*, *Phoebe*, *Galatea*, and the brig *Race-Horse*. After a ten-hour chase they were brought to action in the dark, and only the *Clorinda* managed to escape. On her return to France, her captain, St Cricq, was subjected to a court martial, dismissed the French service, and condemned to penal servitude.

French Report of the Proceedings of the Clorinde Frigate
From 'Naval Anecdotes.' XXVI 388-394

The *Moniteur* of October 5, presented the following extract from the Report of Captain St. Cricq, commander of the *Clorinde* frigate; which, as stated at page 336, effected her escape into Brest on the 24th of September:

"The frigate, the *Renommée*, commanded by Captain Roquebert, who was also commodore of the squadron, the *Nereide*, Captain Le Maresquier, and the *Clorinde*, under my orders, sailed from Brest Roads, at forty minutes past four, in the afternoon of the 2d of February, 1811. The first night of our putting to sea was so frightful, it caused so much damage to the squadron, that we had only to console ourselves for such an unprosperous outset, by the consideration that we had at least succeeded in keeping together; a surprising circumstance so near the coast, and exposed to one of the most violent hurricanes that any of us had ever experienced in our lives.

Our ships sustained considerable damage in their sails and rigging; and the *Clorinde*, from the breaking in of the sea, lost some gunpowder and a great deal of biscuit in this tempest, as sudden as extraordinary. During eighteen successive days, we struggled with contrary winds, without being able to get out more than 200 leagues from the point of our departure.

On the 12th of February, I received orders to sink the English brig *Summer*, laden with grain, from Liverpool to Lisbon.

On the 22d the commodore ordered a schooner to be sunk which was on its voyage from Spain.

49

On the 24th the *Renommée* brought-to a Portuguese three-masted vessel, armed with 22 guns. This ship was poorly laden, and had a great many people on board. The commodore released it.

On the 21st of March, we captured and released a Portuguese slave-ship. Our meeting with it was a misfortune; for each frigate took some negroes on board, and they communicated the small-pox to us. Many of our crew on board the three frigates caught the disease.

Here ended our captures during a voyage of 93 days, from Brest to the Isle of France; during which time we had seen only two English flags; and circumstances did not permit us to chase the ships which carried them.

We were constantly under a press of sail; for Captain Roquebert was unwilling to lose a moment, particularly, as, from the Lisbon gazettes, we had reason to suspect that the Isle of France was at that moment attacked, if it had not been so some months previously. The object was, to save that colony; all our anxiety had that direction. We had not to complain of calms; it was contrary winds which constantly retarded us. In struggling with them we lost masts, sails, and provisions. We crossed the line on the 13th of March; we doubled the Cape of Good Hope on the 18th of April, in latitude 38; and we arrived within a league and half of the southeast port of the Isle of France, on the 6th of May, at eleven at night.

In consequence of orders from the commodore of the squadron, I immediately sent on board the *Renommée* the best boat's crew which I had. It consisted of eight excellent seamen, all armed with muskets, commanded by M.K. Karadec, enseign de vaisseau, and by M. Dauvais, sub-lieutenant.

At half an hour past midnight, the yawls of the *Renommée* and *Clorinde* set out together and made for the land. It was nearly a calm all night, and we did not hear a single musket-shot. This circumstance was encouraging; but our alarm naturally commenced at day-break, when we saw the French flag floating on the Isle de Passe, without any of the signals agreed upon with our officers being made.

At sun-rise, we perceived successively five sail, which we took to be a schooner, a brig, and three frigates; the whole more or less to leeward of us, from one to four leagues distance. The coast made signals of three ships of the French empire to windward, according to the old signals of the island. The enemy, therefore, had got possession of the signals after the surrender of the Isle of France. Our fears increased more and more. The fort of the islet had hauled down the French flag, when its commander saw that he no longer deceived us. At last the boat of the *Renommée* returned about mid-day, having had the good fortune to escape. It informed us, that the Isle of France had been near five months in the possession of the enemy; and two Creole negroes, whom the officer who commanded the yawl brought off with him, gave the Commodore all the information in detail.

My yawl, M. Karadec, M. Dauvais, and eight brave men, were therefore made prisoners! It was no longer possible to doubt it, on seeing no appearance of them by sunset.

Two of the five vessels seen in the morning disappeared during the day: first the schooner, which was probably only a coaster; and then one of the three masts, which I believe was one of the frigates we afterwards fought at Madagascar, but which probably had not then her complement on board. There then remained but two frigates and a brig. The wind favoured them, and they gained considerably upon us. We continued our course to the east all the night. On the following day (May 8), the Commodore made a signal that he would attack, and in our turn we chased the enemy. It was almost calm; nevertheless we gained upon them, though slowly, and at night Mr. Roquebert gave orders for discontinuing the chase, because the English ships were carried by the current between isle Ronde and Serpent's isle, where it would have been very dangerous to engage them. We did not see them again for some time.

Mr. Roquebert summoned the captains on board his ship; we repaired thither at seven o'clock. He ordered us to reduce our crews to two-thirds allowance; and resolved to go to reconnoitre some point to windward of the Isle Buonaparté [Bourbon]. On the 11th of May, after beating about for three days, we passed twenty leagues to windward of the Isle of France, and bore up for that of Buonaparté; we made the land on the same night. The boats which we sent to land could not disembark their men on account of the heavy surf. Our officers saw about forty armed men, whom he could have easily beaten, had it been possible to land. In this state of things, Captain Roquebert resolved on going to Madagascar for provisions.

On the 19th of May we neared the land of Madagascar, and ran along the coast to the Isle of Prunes, the entrance of *Tamatavé*. There were two small vessels at anchor. Our Commodore sent two boats to land; the return of the boat of the *Renommée*, next morning, with an English soldier on board, sufficiently informed me that our boats had made some prisoners.

We spent the night in beating about. On the 20th of May, at daybreak, we were to leeward of the Isle of Prunes. We perceived four ships in the N.N.E. which were soon discovered to be three frigates and a brig; the same which we had seen at the Isle of France, with the addition of a third frigate. Our Commodore gave the signal for a decisive action, and we made preparations to engage.

At noon, being two leagues to windward of the enemy, the signal was made to form in line of battle. At fifty minutes after three the commodore gave orders to commence the engagement; nothing more was wanting, as we were within cannon-shot. The brig was in close line with the frigates; the *Clorinde* was a-head of our line, the *Renommée* in the centre, and the *Nereide* in the rear.

I did not wish to attack first, on account of the distance; but the *Renommée* attacked the frigate which led, which soon found herself near the *Nereide*; then I engaged successively, and always at the same distance, the second and third frigates. The most perfect calm succeeded the first discharges. I attempted several times to bear up, but could not succeed; the movements were too slow, and the *Renommée*, who also could not bear up, annoyed me continually. She made many signals, which the weather prevented me from clearly distinguishing; those who supposed they saw them, thought they ordered the *Clorinde* to take in her sails.

But, first, we could no longer guide the ship; secondly, I was so close to the *Renommée*, that, if she had pulled out a little, she would have masked my fire for a long time; I therefore did not think this was the signal. Mr. Roquebert then sent a midshipman, in a boat, to tell me to put down a boat, and get myself towed. This was more reasonable, and I had already done it; a yawl had been towing me for some minutes. The enemy, equally with us becalmed, committed the fault of not making use of their boats, which proved to their disadvantage, as the frigate nearest mine presented her stern to us for more than a quarter of an hour, during which time I kept firing into her. A second frigate was in the same situation with respect to the *Renommée*, and it was with difficulty that these two vessels were again able to present their broadsides to us. If we had fortunately been nearer, they were inevitably lost, for never was fire more dreadful. – They were severely handled, that is beyond a doubt.

In regard to the *Nereide*, profiting by the remains of the breeze at the commencement of the action, she had come up with and closely engaged the frigate which led, and apparently with advantage, but there was not much damage done on either side.

At six in the evening a trifling breeze sprung up; the calm had sent us to a distance from Captain Maresquier. I received a verbal message to take post behind the Commodore, who fought from both sides, which I obeyed. The fire thus continued till eight at night, when the enemy's ceased; and, assisted by a light breeze, he got to a distance from us. We followed; when the fire commenced, and lasted till half-past ten at night, at which time we tacked, to place ourselves in a line with the *Nereide*, which appeared damaged. The *Renommée* put out her lights, and hailed us to conceal ours. We approached Captain Maresquier, to whom I communicated similar orders. - I thought I perceived his main-top-mast, sails, &c. were damaged. We tacked twice to support the *Nereide*, which no longer had the wind. The enemy, on his part, seemed to rally. A light wind now blew from all points, and we found ourselves engaged by the enemy, who all at once opened his fire, nearer than we expected. Taking advantage of a momentary change in the wind, I sailed towards our frigate, for the purpose of disengaging and supporting her. I did not again see the *Nereide*. I believe her also be amid the fire, and perhaps she was there.

We arrived at twenty minutes after eleven in the midst of the contending vessels, from which we were not more than two musket-shots distance, at the commencement of the action. Then, although very near each other, within half pistol shot at the most, the fire ceased on both sides, in the fear of the frightful mistakes which might occur in a dark night.

At this moment a ship in the group shewed three Bengal lights in those parts of the vessel from which the signals were to be made, agreed upon between the *Renommée* and the squadron, for night engagements. I instantly replied by shewing my number, and manoeuvred to approach that frigate. The *Nereide* did not answer.

Without doubt, the remains of the smoke, the variety of the winds, joined to the obscurity of the night, were the cause of my new uncertainty. I found myself in the middle of four ships, within pistol-shot of two of them; and the *Renommée* was still hidden from us. I again made the night-signal with Bengal lights.

I perceived, in return, only such English lights as enabled me to comprehend that I was not with my friends. The frigate nearest me fired two cannons, which I did not answer. I sought the *Renommée* and *Nereide*, but could neither by signals nor otherwise discover their situation. I have already said that a frigate made signals I did not understand; the three other vessels which surrounded me answered them. Our frigates, then, were no longer near us, for they shewed no lights. How, without wind, could they get to a distance? They must have had a breeze which I did not experience! and this breeze must have driven them, in spite of themselves, far from me; for both these captains would willingly have sacrificed their lives for the power of saving me.

I was nearly enclosed, and without sails; which gave the enemy an opportunity of molesting me with their bow chasers. In the hope of discovering our frigates' situation, I stood in towards the land, which we were close upon.

It now was impossible for me to do otherwise without running into the enemy's division, which would have directed all its force against the *Clorinde*. The enemy would then have cut me off. I was ignorant of the position of our frigates. - Where were they? What winds had they experienced?

I was constrained to proceed along the coast, which required the adoption of the measures I successfully took; and, in proportion as I got my sails hoisted, I found myself the less harassed by the enemy. Two of their frigates, whose bowsprits nearly touched the *Clorinde*'s stern, cannonaded me. The two remaining ships dropped so far astern, that I could not any longer distinguish their lights. The two which pursued me did not cease making signals. At a quarter past four o'clock, I perceived the enemy for the last time. In the battle, one man was killed, one drowned, and six badly wounded.

At sun-rise we perceived nothing; and I had time to reflect upon my situation, and that of the frigates from which I was separated. Mine was sufficiently melancholy; in addition to the damage sustained in the combat, I had twenty-five men sick, from the small-pox, and the scurvy, and fever. My stock of provisions was much reduced, and two of my masts gave me constant uneasiness.

The Seychelles isles seemed the least dangerous spot I could repair to, where I hoped that the other French frigates might likewise rendezvous. But in the light of the 21st, four ships were seen to windward of us, one of them visibly smaller than the others. This was doubtless the English squadron; at three o'clock they were no longer visible. From this I concluded that the *Nereide* had had time to repair the little damage which she had sustained; and that our two frigates, no longer seeing the enemy or myself, had either got off without opposition, or had entered Tamatavé, a course which I could not follow, because the English squadron was on my route to that place.

I therefore steered for the Seychelles, and anchored under the little isle St. Anne. A fishing boat informed me, that there was only one Englishman on the isle; he was a lieutenant of marines. I made him prisoner, in order to be exchanged for M. Karadec, taken at the Isle of France.

On the 7th of June, I left the Seychelles, on my return to France. On the 26th, I reached the isle of Diego Garcia, the bay of which is in lat. 7° 18' and long. $70^\circ13'$. There I found, to my surprise, that some of the inhabitants of the Isle of France had formed an establishment, where cocoa-oil and tortoise-shell were the only kind of speculation in which they could engage. Certainly their gain can be only a slight recompense for the frightful misery to which these unfortunate people are condemned by the very nature of the soil which they inhabit. It is so dry, that there is hardly the depth of an inch of vegetable soil to be found on the whole surface of the Island. Reduced to cocoas, some fowls, and tortoises, the unfortunates who inhabit Diego Garcia, must renounce the habits of other living beings.

I purchased about thirty turtle, which afforded some relief to my crew, and particularly to the sick. We also laid in a great number of cocoas, a little wood, and some excellent water. I sailed on the 28th of June; and, on the 1st of August, I doubled the Cape of Good Hope. The wind forced me to near the western coast of the African continent. On the 23d of August, in four degrees of south latitude, I captured a Portuguese brig, from which I took eleven days' provisions, and let her go. On the 4th of September, I took an English packet; I found in her about 20 sacks of biscuit, and some salt provisions. Her mail was thrown into the sea when she first saw us. The want of water prevented me from destroying this vessel, which had about 30 men on board, who would thereby have suffered a great deal, and added too much to our consumption. I gave her a cartel of exchange, of which I have brought a copy; and released her, after making her throw overboard her twelve cannon. Several American ships, which I met on the 29th of August, the 5th, 8th, and 16th of September, made some slight addition to our provisions.

On the 18th I fell in with the English sloop *Narry*, bound to the Newfoundland fishery. This ship was in ballast. I contented myself with giving a cartel of exchange, and sent her to Madeira.

On the 24th of September, at six in the morning, being only ten leagues from the Saintes, I fell in with an English ship of war, which had the advantage over me of having seen the land the evening before, and which manoeuvred to cut me off from the passage Du Raz. I was not disconcerted, but struck right into the Raz, amidst the copious rain, and a very thick fog.

The enemy struck into the passage at the same time with me, keeping within musket-shot. It blew very fresh; the ship of war was in full sail; though he gained upon me, I was prudent enough to take in mine a little and I had soon the pleasure of seeing his main-top and mizen-masts dismasted, at the moment when he cannonaded me severely, and was at least within pistol-shot. The enemy, obliged to haul off, molested me no longer, and at five o'clock I came to anchor in Brest Roads.

                                          J. SAINT CRICQ, Capitaine de Frigate
Dated Brest Roads, on board
the Clorinde, September 24, 1811"

Schomberg's Dispatches

Letters on Service
Admiralty Office, November 16, 1811. ^{XXVI 431-434}

Copies of two Letters, and their Enclosures, from Captain Schomberg, of his Majesty's Ship the Astraea, addressed to Captain Beaver, of the Nisus, Senior Officer at the Isle de France, and transmitted, by the latter, to John Wilson Croker, Esq.

His Majesty's ship Astraea, off Foul Point, Madagascar, May 21, 1811
Sir, I had the honour of communicating to you, from Round Island, my determination to quit that station, in order to follow the three enemy's frigates with troops on board, which had appeared off Mauritius on the 7th instant, and also my reasons for supposing they would push for a near point, perhaps Tamatavé.

I have now the satisfaction to report to you, that the enemy were discovered on the morning of the 20th instant, far to windward, and well in with the land, near foul Point, Madagascar. The signal to chase was promptly obeyed by his Majesty's ships *Phoebe*, *Galatea*, and *Racehorse* sloop. The weather was most vexatiously variable during the whole of the day, which combined with the efforts of the enemy to keep to windward, rendered it impossible to close them until nearly four o'clock, when the *Astraea* being about a mile a-head and to windward, they wore together, kept away, and evinced a disposition to bring us to action. The enemy then commenced firing; I regret to say, at a long range, which soon so effectually produced a calm to leeward, as to render our squadron unmanageable for three hours. No exertion was omitted to bring his Majesty's ships into close action, during this very critical and trying period; but all was ineffectual. The enemy's rear frigate neared the *Astraea* a little, who lay on the water, almost immovable; only occasionally bringing guns to bear, while his van and centre ships, preserving a light air, succeeded in rounding the quarter of the *Phoebe* and *Galatea*, raking them, with considerable effect, for a long time.

At this, his favourite distance, the enemy remained until nearly dark, when a light air enabled the *Phoebe* to close the near frigate, in a good position to bring her to a decisive action. In half an hour she was beaten. Her night signals drew the other two frigates to her assistance; the *Phoebe* was, in consequence, obliged to follow the *Galatea*, which ship brought up the breeze to me. At this time I was hailed by Captain Losack, who informed me, that the *Galatea* had suffered very considerably, and, as she was passing under my lee, I had the mortification to see her mizen, and, soon after, her foretop-mast fall. Having shot a-head, she made the night signal of distress, and being in want of immediate assistance, I closed to ascertain the cause, when I was again hailed by Captain Losack, and informed, that the *Galatea* was so totally disabled as to prevent her head being put towards the enemy to renew the action, as I before had directed.

My determination was immediately communicated to Captain Hillyar to recommence action, when the *Phoebe* was in a state to support me. She was promptly reported ready, although much disabled. The *Astraea* then wore, and led towards the enemy, followed by the *Racehorse* and *Phoebe*; the conduct of which ship, as a British man of war, did honour to all on board. The enemy was soon discovered a little a-head, and his leading ship, the Commodore, was brought to close action by the *Astraea*. In twenty-five minutes she struck, and made the signal to that effect, having previously attempted to lay us athwart hawse, under a heavy fire of grape and musquetry from all parts of the ship. Another frigate, on closing, struck, and made the signal also: but, on a shot being fired at her, from her late Commodore, she was observed trying to escape. Chase was instantly given, and continued till two o'clock in the morning, with all the sail both ships were enabled, from their disabled state, to carry; when I judged it advisable, as she gained on us, to wear for the purpose of covering the captured ship, and forming a junction (if possible) with the *Galatea*. At this moment, the *Phoebe*'s foretop-mast fell: sight of the *Galatea* or captured ship was not regained until day-light, when, to the credit of Lieutenants Rogers (second of the *Astraea*) and Drury (R.M.), who, with five men, were all that could be put on board the latter in a sinking boat, she was observed making an effort to join us, a perfect wreck.

The captured frigate proves to be *la Renommée*, of the first class (as are the other two), of forty-four guns, and four hundred and seventy men (two hundred of whom were picked troops), commanded by Capitaine de Vaisseau (with Commodore's rank) Roquebert, Officier de la Legion d'Honneur, who fell when gallantly fighting his ship. The senior officer of the troops, Colonel Barrois, Membre de la Legion d'Honneur, is dangerously wounded. The ship that struck and escaped, was *la Clorinde*; the one disabled by the *Phoebe*, *la Nereide*, having each two hundred troops on board, besides their crews. . . .

May 28, 1811
Sir, In my letter of the 20th instant, detailing the action between his Majesty's ships under my orders and those of the enemy, I had the honour to inform you, that it was my intention to reconnoitre this port, as I had received information that the enemy had landed and surprised the garrison on his first arrival on the coast.

The state of his Majesty's ships *Astraea* and *Phoebe* did not admit of their beating up quickly against the currents and very variable winds; the *Racehorse* sloop was, therefore, despatched in advance, to summon the garrison of Tamatavé to immediately surrender.

On the evening of the 24th instant, Captain De Rippe rejoined me, reporting his having seen a large frigate anchored in that port: a strong gale prevented his Majesty's ships from getting in sight of her until the afternoon of the 25th instant, when every thing being ready to force the anchorage, I stood in, and observed an enemy's frigate, placed in a most judicious position within the reefs of the port, for the purpose of enfilading the narrow passage between them, supported by a strong fort in her van, within half musket-shot, full of troops; there were also new works in forwardness, to flank the anchorage.

Not having any body of local knowledge in either of his Majesty's ships, and it being almost impracticable to sound the passage between the reefs, which was intricate, and completely exposed to the whole concentrated fire of the enemy within grape distance, I judged it expedient, under existing circumstances (both ships being full of prisoners, and having a proportion of men absent in *la Renommée*, besides sick and wounded), to defer, until necessary, risking his Majesty's ships.

I, therefore, summoned the garrison and frigate to immediately surrender; when, after the usual intercourse of flag of truce, I have the honour to inform you, that the fort of Tamatavé, its dependencies, the frigate and vessels in the port, together with the late garrison (a detachment of the 22d regiment), were surrendered to, and taken possession of, by his Majesty's ships under my orders.

I was induced to grant the terms (a copy of which, together with the summons, and answer thereto, I have the honour to inclose), in order to prevent the destruction of the fort of Tamatavé, the frigate, and vessels - a measure they intended to adopt.

The enemy's frigate proves to be *la Nereide* (one of the finest, only two years old), of forty-four guns, and four hundred and seventy men (two hundred of whom are choice troops), commanded by Capitaine le Maresquier, Membre de la Legion d'Honneur, who fell in the action of the 20th instant, in which she suffered very considerably, having had one hundred and thirty men killed and wounded. She was much engaged by the *Phoebe*.

The crew of *la Nereide*, together with the French garrison of Tamatavé, I intend sending to the Mauritius as soon as possible, fifty excepted, who are too severely wounded to survive removal.

The whole detachment of his Majesty's 22d regiment retaken, being ill, of the endemic fever of this country, I mean to embark on board the *Nereide*, so soon as she is in a state to receive them; when, after having dismantled the fort, and embarked the guns, &c, I shall proceed with her, under convoy, to the Mauritius, in company with the *Phoebe*.

I have the honour to be, &c.

C.M. SCHOMBERG, Captain

Captain Beaver, his Majesty's Ship Nisus,
Senior Officer at the Isle of France

[The articles of capitulation provided for the repatriation of the prisoners to France, without their being considered prisoners of war.]

Report of the French Minister of the Marine, to His Majesty the Emperor, Relative to the Proceedings of La Renommée, La Nereide, and La Clorinde

Marine Law. XXVIII 151-157

Sir, I am about to fulfil the painful task of laying before your Majesty, an account of the occurrences which have taken place with respect to the division of frigates under the orders of Captain Roquebert, on the 20th of last month, as they have been represented by the several reports which have been received.

The division, consisting of *la Renommée*, commanded by Captain Roquebert, *la Nereide*, Captain Le Maresquier, and *la Clorinde*, Captain St. Cricq, being on the 19th of May in the latitude of Tamatavé, in the island of Madagascar, Captain Roquebert sent two armed boats into the bay of that place, to take some vessels which had anchored there.

The expedition, which took place in the night, did not experience any obstacles, and the person who commanded the boats exceeding his orders, surprised the fort, and took 100 prisoners.

On the 20th, at day-break, the boats had not yet reached their ships, when a division came in sight of three of the enemy's frigates, and a large sloop of war, several leagues to windward.

Captain Roquebert determined to attack this division, but instead of acting on such a determination, he remained the greater part of the day lying-to, while the enemy was endeavouring to come up, with a press of sail; in the mean time, one of the boats, which had been taking possession of Tamatavé, came on board.

At three quarters of an hour after three o'clock, the two divisions were within cannon-shot, on opposite tacks, and the firing commenced. They soon, by a manoeuvre of the enemy, came on the same tack, but were at so great a distance, that the carronades did no execution. . . . etc.

[The account of the action adds little to our understanding, but the summation is interesting.]

Captain Roquebert was at perfect liberty either to give battle or to decline it. He is not to be blamed for the determination he formed to fight, and even to engage in a decisive action, for which, according to the report of Captain St. Cricq, he made the signal. But when this resolution was taken, how had it happened that, in place of bearing down upon the enemy together, and in order, he spent eight or nine hours in tacking, so that the action did not commence till four o'clock in the afternoon, whereby he exposed himself to all the variations of the wind, which, at the time, was in his favour, and to all the chances of a nocturnal engagement, for which he had no advantage to gain?

How came it that he did not profit by this delay of nine hours, to concert with the captains upon his plan of attack, and the manoeuvres which it would be necessary to make? When resolved upon a decisive action, why had he not [sic] engaged the enemy at such a distance, as would not only render his musketry useless, but be without the range of his carronades?

Why had he not, when at the commencement of the battle he saw the *Nereide* more to leeward than himself, bring the *Clorinde* and *Renommée* up, in order to close equally with the enemy? and, above all, why had he not hurried this movement of closing with the enemy, when he saw the *Nereide* obeying his signal to the very letter, and every moment nearing still more, with a view to engage yard-arm and yard-arm the compact line of the enemy? Why, when the enemy had recourse to his sweeps to rally three ships against the *Nereide*, had not Captain Roquebert practised the same manoeuvre to cover her, in place of remaining with the *Clorinde*, to engage at a great distance a single enemy's frigate?

When towards evening the *Renommée* and *Clorinde* had disengaged the *Nereide*, which they perceived in a condition rendering her incapable of manoeuvring, why had

View of Porto Praya, in the Island of St. Jago. Engraved by Hall, from a Drawing by
G.T.

Porto Praya is a town and harbour of St. Jago, the most fruitful and best inhabited
of all the Cape de Verd Islands. Captain Cook, who anchored at Porto Praya, on his
second voyage, thus describes the harbour:

"Port Praya is a small bay, situated about the middle of the south side of the island
of St. Jago. The water is tolerable, but scarce, and bad getting off, on account of a
great surf on the beach. The refreshments to be got here are bullocks, hogs, goats,
sheep, poultry, and fruits. The goats are of the Antelope kind, so extraordinarily
lean, that hardly any thing can equal them; and the bullocks, hogs, and sheep, are not
much better. Bullocks must be purchased with money; and price at that time was 12
Spanish dollars a-head, weighing between 250 and 300 pounds. Other articles may
be got from the natives in exchange for old clothes, &c. The sale of bullocks is
confined to a company of merchants, to whom this privilege is granted, and who
keep an agent residing on the spot."

Porto Praya has long been a place where the outward-bound Guinea and Indiamen
(whether English, French, or Dutch) have been accustomed to touch at for water
and refreshments; but few of them call on their return to Europe. The town consists
of about a hundred small huts, one storey high, built of wood, thinly scattered. It
has a fort, or battery, upon the summit of a hill, which entirely commands the
harbour; and, were it properly mounted and garrisoned, it would be a place of great
strength. It is, however, almost in ruins. The gaol is the best building, and next to
that the church. The Governor resides in a small wooden barrack, at the extremity
of the plain, commanding a view of the bay and shipping. Earl Macartney, on his
embassy, was received by him with due honour and respect; but as he had shared in
the general wretchedness, occasioned by the long drought and arid winds, which at
the time prevailed, he had neither wine nor any other refreshments to offer.

Porto Praya is situated in longitude 23° 51' W. of Greenwich; latitude, 14° 53' 30"
N. Plate 333

not orders been given to the *Clorinde* to take her in tow, the sure means of preserving her, and which would have prevented the fatal separation that took place a few hours afterwards?

In short, why had not the *Renommée*, when she could no longer perceive the *Clorinde* in her wake, manoeuvre with a view to rejoin that vessel, and why had she exposed herself singly to the fire of the whole English squadron, without foreseeing what must be the result of these partial actions, in which, whilst each vessel contended separately, they must all be captured one after another?

There hangs over this last resolution, by which Captain Roquebert threw himself singly into the midst of the enemy's division, a veil which cannot be removed until the arrival of the officer who succeeded him in the command of the *Renommée*, for this officer concludes in these words the report which he has addressed to me: "It is impossible for me to explain to you how Captain Roquebert came singly into the midst of the enemy before the ships of his division were rallied. It is a misfortune of which I can give only a verbal account." . . .

To the copy of the above Report, published in the *Moniteur*, was affixed the following order, from Buonaparte:

The Minister of Marine shall put the laws of the Empire in force. The Commandant of the *Clorinde* shall be brought before a Council of War, for having taken so small a share in the action – for having abandoned his Commodore – for having preferred his life to his honour – and for not having fulfilled his mission and executed the orders he received, to proceed to Batavia, and carry thither his cargo and the troops he had on board.

(signed) NAPOLEON
The Minister Secretary of State,
(Signed) Count DARU

Palace of St. Cloud, November 23, 1811

[Jacques St Cricq was cashiered, condemned to three years' penal servitude, degraded from the Legion of Honour, and required to pay the cost of the trial.]

1812 - Naval News

THE WINTER GALES OF 1811-1812 proved most destructive to the Royal Navy. On the night of 4 December the *Saldanha* 32-gun frigate, commanded by the Honourable Captain William Pakenham, was lost with all hands off Lough Swilly on the coast of Ireland, and on the 23rd the *Hero*, 74, Captain James Newman, escorting 120 sail in the North Sea, was driven with twenty of her convoy on the Texel, and all hands were drowned. The next day, and a little farther north, the *St George*, 98 guns, with Admiral Robert Carthew Reynolds on board, and the *Defence*, 74 guns, under the command of Captain David Atkins, were both stranded on the coast of Jutland. Of their two crews only seventeen men survived.

Apart from the perils of the sea, the most interesting item of naval news was that of the final reduction of Batavia, in which the East Indies squadron provided transport for units of the army. Other items of interest were the arrival in Britain of a ship commanded by an American black, son of a liberated slave; the ordering of a new naval uniform; and the court martial of Captain Robert Preston, of HMS *Ganymede*, for the severity of his punishments. He was found not guilty, but was cautioned about his methods. The change of attitude in the fleet to service discipline was becoming evident. Finally, a correspondent warned that the inventor of a new incendiary round, not receiving encouragement from the Admiralty, had taken his invention to the United States.

The great campaign of 1812, which led the British army under Wellington's command to the capture of the fortresses of Badajoz and Salamanca, the defeat of Marshal Marmot, the liberation of Madrid, and eventually to the precipitant retreat from Burgos back to the Portuguese border, were naval operations only to the extent that the communications between Britain and Spain were kept open. The principal threat was from privateers, but there was always the chance that a French battle-squadron would escape from its blockade and disrupt the flow of shipping. Wellington's campaign did at least succeed in persuading Marshal Soult to raise the siege of Cadiz so that French forces could concentrate.

During the first months of 1812 the final efforts were made to resolve the dispute with the United States over maritime rights. Before the year was over, the navy was to find itself fighting United States warships, and it was to take some time before it learnt how to manage the threat mounted by an American navy, the strength of which consisted of a few exceptionally powerful frigates. Had American politics reached the stage of seeking war five years earlier, when the Continental System was at its most effective, it could have ensured the triumph of the French empire throughout Europe. As it was, the impact on British mercantile trade was to be severe.

Napoleon Buonaparte's diplomatic manoeuvres succeeded in making the British appear to be the only party unwilling to meet American demands. His virtual abandonment of the restrictions on British trade, and its replacement with a tariff, apparently in response to American complaints, were also most useful at a time when he was planning a campaign to invade Russia and needed funds for the purpose. The Americans failed to see through his game.

Traumatic as the American war was to be, especially for those in Canada who did not relish being 'liberated', Napoleon's resolution, to put an end by force of arms to Tsar Alexander's rebellious failure to comply with French economic strategy, was to be a matter of much greater importance. Before the final break between the United States and Britain became known, Napoleon left Paris to join the army invading Russia.

In domestic news, Viscount Robert Melville, son of the First Lord who had been driven into resignation by the impeachment proceedings of 1805, succeeded his father, and more immediately, Charles Yorke, in that office.

Loss of the St George
From 'Correspondence.' XXVII 119-121

Tim Weatherside to the Editor
Mr. Editor, The losses attending the Baltic fleet at the close of the last year are truly deplorable; and though, like every thing else in this country, they have only occasioned a nine days wonder and regret, I had hoped to have seen so important a subject more fully discussed in your *Chronicle*.

It certainly, Mr. Editor, does appear most extraordinary, that the *St. George* should have been allowed to leave Wingo Sound, at such a season, under jury masts, and with only a temporary rudder: for as to having two ships to attend her, it is clear, that when a ship gets on a lee shore in a gale of wind, or even when at sea when boats cannot live, no other ship can be of service to her. The fate of that unfortunate ship has been truly disastrous. It was fixed that she should leave Hano Bay the last of October, 1811, with convoy; by some fatality, her sailing was delayed to the 9th of November, when the wind came foul, and they could not move for some days. During their passage down the Baltic, they were obliged to anchor with the convoy near Laland: a gale of wind came on, and a large ship of the convoy drove in the night athwart hawse the *St. George*, and broke her adrift. Her other anchors were immediately let go, but she would not bring up; the gale having increased to a hurricane.

The admiral, although the ship was driving towards the shore, resisted for a long time the advice of the captain and officers, to cut away her masts; but at length he gave orders so to do. The ships however struck, and beat hard, and in the course of the night knocked her rudder off – the wreck of her masts also gave them a great deal of trouble. Twelve of the convoy were seen next morning wrecked on the enemy's coast, and several foundering at their anchors; some put back, but 30 were totally unaccounted for. When it became moderate, the *St. George* was got off by the assistance of the King's ships that were in company; and having rigged jury-masts, and made a temporary rudder, she proceeded through the Belt towed by the *Cressy*, and reached Wingo Sound. While lying there, a Pakenham's rudder was made; the *Cressy* and *Defence* were selected to attend her to England, and the *Hero* was appointed to take home the convoy that had sailed from Hano under the *St. George*.

Thus had every thing been arranged, when on the 17th of December, 1811, the *St. George*, *Cressy*, and *Defence*, sailed from Wingo Sound, in company with the *Victory*, *Vigo*, *Dreadnought*, and *Orion*; which ships soon parted from them. The *Hero* and her convoy sailed at the same time. Three of this convoy were lost on the Scaw Point, several near the Holman, and some were wrecked with the *Hero*, on the coast of Holland. At the time of their sailing, the days were not six hours long, the weather proved very unfavourable, and the *St. George* became unmanageable, from being under jury-masts: this ship, with the *Cressy* and *Defence*, had not been long out, before, in consequence of thick weather and strong currents, the whole three were nearly lost on the coast of Sweden. Having, however, escaped this danger, they proceeded down the Sleeve; when on the 22d of December it came on to blow strong from the N.N.W. (which is right on the Jutland shore) until it gradually increased to a gale of wind. At night on the 23d, the captain of the *Cressy*, thinking they were getting near the shore, and that they were on the wrong tack, called his officers together, and laid the situation of their ship before them. They were all of one opinion – *To wear the ship*. In wearing they ran to leeward of the *St. George*, and remained very close to her for some time: when, finding that the latter took no notice of the *Cressy*, she set her main-top-sail and fore sail, and lay up west. The *St. George* was at that time under her stay-sails, the *Defence* was without any sail set, staying by her; and, by continuing so to do, shared her fate. These things I have thought it right to send you, Mr. Editor, that the public, and the profession in general, may have a more correct statement of facts, than what can be found in the papers. The list of the British navy does not contain better officers, or more excellent characters, than Admiral Reynolds, Captain Guion, and Captain Atkins. I wish you would publish a biographical memoir of the public services of poor Newman; he was a friendly, good-hearted man, as brave and as generous as a Lion.

I hope you will not let the attempt pass unnoticed, that has been made, to raise the merit of Lord Minto, at the expense of poor Admiral Drury. I have only time left to throw out this hint for some abler correspondent.

A.F.Y. to the Editor

My Editor, As it is some time since I have seen the *Naval Chronicle*, I know not whether you have published the narrative of John Anderson, one of the survivors of the unfortunate crew of the *St. George*. This was sent to Admiral Reynolds' family; and, if you have not received it, it is much at your service.

A.F.Y.

"On the 22d of December, 1811, lying off Salls, the wind at W.S.W. made signal for a pilot, who came on board. The wind chopped round to the N. by E. stood off to sea, and shaped a course for England.

Sunday 23d, the wind N. by W. we continued our course. Monday evening the wind came round to the W.N.W. blowing a strong gale, with a heavy sea; at nine lost sight of the *Defence*; at nine 30 the *Cressy* passed us to leeward, and stood to the southward. About 11 the wind changed to N.N.W.; at 12 the Admiral made the signal to wear and stand to the westward; in vain we tried to hoist the jib, but it was blown away before half up; after it was gone, hands were sent up to loose the fore-top-sail; it was no sooner gone from our arms, before it was blown away. All our head sails being gone, we got the hammock cloths in the fore-rigging, which, however, had no effect. Then got a nine-inch hawser, and bent it to the spare anchor, the stock and one fluke being gone.

Then taking the opportunity of a lull, let go the anchor and put the helm down, trying to club-haul her, and get her round on the other tack, but the hawser catching the heel of the rudder, carried it away. All we had to trust to then was our anchors. We immediately sent two watches below to arrange the cables, and kept one watch on deck to strike lower yards and top-masts; finding we had only 12 fathom, let go the S. bower, and by the time the best bower was gone, she struck. This was between five and six of the morning of the 24th; orders were then given to cut away the masts, and sent hands down to the pump; but finding she gained so much water, all hands were obliged to fly to the poop, where they continued from the 24th, till we left the ship on the 25th, when the whole that remained were either dead, or dying very fast. We looked in vain for boats coming to our assistance; the sea ran so high it was impossible for boats to live: two yards being all we had left, we contrived to make a raft of them alongside; we then got on it, some lashed and some not, those who were not were swept off by the first sea.

The Admiral remained in his cabin till the 24th; when the sea came in he was obliged to be hoisted through the skylight on the poop, where he and the captain (Guion) lay close to each other; at half-past three on the 25th he died, the captain lying alongside of him.

Those who were lashed, myself and three others, got on shore, but so weak as not to be able to get off the raft without assistance. Seven men got on shore afterwards, on planks or pieces of the wreck, as the ship broke up. On coming to our senses we could only muster eleven hands.

(signed) JOHN ANDERSON"

Negro Navigators
From 'Naval Anecdotes.' XXVII 9-16

The following is an extract of a letter from Liverpool:

"There is at present here a singular phenomenon. The brig *Traveller* is just arrived from Sierra Leone, and is owned and commanded by Paul Cuffee, the son of "Cuffee", a negro slave imported into America. Her mate, and all her crew, are negroes, or the immediate descendants of negroes. Captain Cuffee is about 56 years of age; has a wife (a negress) and six children living at New Bedford, Massachusetts, of which state he is a citizen.

When Captain Cuffee's father (who had acquired his freedom) died, he left a family almost unprovided for; but the son laboured hard to support his mother, his brethren,

View of Liverpool, taken by Mr. Pocock, as it appeared when coming up the Mersey, at about a mile distance: a Marble-Head schooner introduced in the foreground. Plate 24

and his sisters. He began trade in a small boat; and after a while almost by himself, built a larger vessel, in which he worked some years with assiduity. Having providentially met a person capable, and willing to impart some knowledge of navigation, his ideas were enlarged, and with his prospects he enlarged his efforts to succeed. Happily for him, and his family, his mind received religious instruction from the Society of Friends (Quakers), and he attached himself to that respectable body, adopted their dress and language, and is now a very respectable member of that community.

When Clarkson's History of the Abolition of the Slave Trade fell into his hands, it awakened all the powers of his mind to the consideration of his origin, and the duties he owed to his people; and, coupled with the sense of duty which his religious information had given him, he longed to impart to the negro race the blessings which British-Christian benevolence had been roused to confer on Africa. This became the ruling desire of his mind. The Directors of the British African Institution, having heard of this singular event, and that Captain Cuffee (his negroe, and therefore his favourite name) was about to sail with his negro crew, applied to this government for a licence, for his coming to England, hoping much from his co-operation and instrumentality.

The zeal Captain Cuffee felt for the African cause, determined his noble mind to forego all prospects of mercantile profit, even the natural desire to return to his wife and children; and he came directly to England, bringing with him a native of Sierra Leone, whose father (a negro) is of considerable property, and in a large way of business. The captain brought him from Sierra Leone, at the express wish of the colonists, to learn navigation; and it is but justice to the diligence and intellect of this young man to say, that, in the short voyage to England, he has learned most surprising fast, and shews that intellect is by no means controlled by the colour of the skin, and that the Blacks are worthy of being the brethren of the fortunately more cultivated whites.

Captain Cuffee is of a very pleasing countenance, and his physiognomy truly interesting; he is both tall and stout, speaks English well, dresses in the Quaker style, in a drab-coloured suit, and wears a large flapped white hat.

It is supposed that the *Traveller* will return to Sierra Leone. We hear that the captain is going to London, to confer on his favourite topic with the Directors of the African Institution."

From the 'Naval History of the Present Year,' 1811-1812
December-January. XXVII 65-66

Rupture Expected Between France and Russia, Sweden Arming

Great expectations are again entertained, of a rupture between France and Russia. - Sweden has assumed a very hostile aspect, and, certainly, is not on amicable terms with France. The reigning Sovereign has ordered an army of 60,000 men to be embodied, for the *defence*, as it is alleged, of the country. - Some of the recent proceedings of the American Senate breathe a more than ordinarily violent and war-disposed spirit against England.

French Forces in Java Capitulate

On the 19th of January, Government received despatches from the Mauritius, containing the intelligence, that, in consequence of the farther operations of the British troops under Lieutenant-general Sir S. Auchmuty, General Jansens and the remainder of the French forces in the Island of Java, had capitulated on the 17th of September, and that by a treaty signed the same day, all the country eastward of Samarang (not previously subject to the British arms) had been surrendered to his Majesty. - All the positions, occupied by the Gallo-Batavian army, fell in succession on the approach of our frigates, and the landing of seamen and marines; and after a few slight skirmishes, Jansens capitulated, with the whole of his Frenchmen, as prisoners of war. Several wagon loads of money were taken, and a vast quantity of coffee, pepper, and spices. Our loss is very trifling, but sickness had made its appearance among the troops, and particularly the marines, who were actively employed on shore.

Boats Lost in Basque Roads Operation

An unfortunate occurrence lately took place in Basque Roads; the particulars of which are thus given, by an officer on that station:

"On the 27th *ult.* (Dec.) the boats of the *Colossus* and *Conquestador*, under the command of Lieutenant Stackpole, of the latter vessel, and Lieutenant Soady of the former, attacked an enemy's convoy passing along shore from the northward, and would have accomplished its capture or destruction, had not the wind suddenly shifted from N.W. to W.S.W. just as the boats were to the southward of Chatillon reef. This shifting of the wind enabled the ships escorting the convoy, viz. three gun-brigs, an armed lugger, and several pinnaces, to attack the boats, the crews of which made several gallant attempts to board their opponents, and particularly the lugger, in two instances: but the superiority of numbers on the part of the enemy rendered every attempt ineffectual. Undaunted by this superiority, or the galling fire from several batteries and the vessels around them, our noble tars, disdaining to surrender to the gun-brigs, pulled coolly towards the shore, where they were taken prisoners (being 104 in number), except those in the boat with Lieutenant Soady, which most miraculously escaped. The *Conquestador*, and *Piercer* gun-brig, were under weigh near the scene of action, and witnessed every part of it, without being able to give our noble fellows the least assistance. Soon afterwards the weather moderated, when a flag of truce was sent into the French commodore (Jacobs), to request that he would allow cloths, &c. to be sent to the prisoners, and give information as to the number of men killed and wounded. The commodore politely replied, that he had no objection to the clothes, &c. being sent, and was happy to say that no more than four or five had fallen, amongst whom was a master's mate, commanding one of the boats. He, at the same time, expressed his astonishment that so few should have fallen; and intimated that the prisoners were in the hands of Frenchmen, who would treat them well, in consequence of the determined bravery they had exhibited. Lieutenant Stackpole was ascertained to be well on the 30th, three days after this unpleasant affair, the result of which must be ascribed solely to the wind frustrating the design in view. A subscription was immediately set on foot in the *Colossus, Conquestador,* and *Arrow* schooner, by which a considerable sum was raised, and sent in with the clothes to Rochelle."

[Further letters and accounts of this action were published in Vol. XXVII, pp105-107.]

Lloyd's Posts Warning about French Privateers

From 'Naval Anecdotes.' XXVII 101-111

The following memorandum has been posted up at Lloyd's:

"The Committee have received information from the first authority, that the privateers fitted out from the ports of St. Maloes, Dieppe, Boulogne, Calais, and Dunkirk (those of St. Maloes are of a large class, the others are small light luggers, with from 50 to 100 men each), commonly sail with the wind from N.W. to N.E., and seldom or never put to sea with the wind from the southward. It is well known, that during five months last autumn and winter, the privateers were principally successful in making captures (between Fecamp and Calais) of armed merchant ships, which being too indifferently manned to resist them, were almost invariably carried by boarding. And there is every reason to believe, from the intelligence obtained, that they will continue to act upon the same plan, being well informed of the equipment of running ships."

From the 'Naval History of the Present Year,' 1812
January-February. XXVII 162-163

Political Affairs

The Regency Restrictions expired on Tuesday, the 18th of February. The ministerial changes, in consequence of this event, have, as yet, been but few. Indeed, very little is, with certainty, known, excepting that Mr. Perceval retains his post, as Premier; that the Marquis Wellesley has resigned the seals of office, not choosing, as it is said, to act *under* Mr. Perceval; and that Lord Castlereagh is to succeed the Marquis Wellesley, as Secretary of State for the Foreign Department. Whether Mr. Yorke retires from the Admiralty is not yet known. . . .

Russia

A war between France and Russia still seems to be fully expected on the continent. - Great activity is said to prevail in the Russian dock-yards, in building and equipping vessels of war - several Ukases have been published for the transport of carpenters and their families from the interior of the empire; a ship of the line, and a 36-gun frigate were launched at Nostolajew, in December.

French Seize Pomerania

The French have seized upon the province of Swedish Pomerania; Buonaparté and Bernadotte are understood to be decidedly at variance; and, according to report, proposals for peace, between Great Britain and Sweden, have been formally made by the Swedish Government.

Abdication of King of Sicily Heralds Pro-British Policy

Despatches, of a very gratifying nature, have been received from Lord Wm. Bentinck, the British minister at the court of Palermo. They announce, that a total change has taken place in the government of Sicily; the King having abdicated his throne in favour of the Hereditary Prince, who has been appointed Regent, with the title of Vicar General. Certain noblemen, who had been exiled for protesting against an unpopular tax, have been recalled, and the tax has been repealed. Lord Bentinck is to have the command in chief of the Sicilian army, with a seat in the cabinet; and a British garrison is to be admitted into Palermo. Report adds, that, previously to the abdication of the King, his Majesty issued a proclamation, forbidding his subjects from holding any correspondence with the Queen, on pain of death.

Earl St Vincent
From 'Naval Anecdotes.' XXVII 191-200

On the 28th of February, Earl St. Vincent met with an accident of a very serious nature, at Rochetts. His Lordship was sitting by himself; and, having occasion to reach forward, he unfortunately fell upon the grate. His head came in contact with one of the spikes which were placed on the top of the grate for the security of the wood; and it was with some difficulty that he forced himself back from the fire, before he sustained any injury from the heat. His servants, on entering, found him covered with blood, from a severe laceration occasioned by the spike. His Royal Highness the Prince Regent was particularly attentive in his inquiries on this occasion; and his Lordship has, happily, recovered from the effects of the accident.

Court Martial on Charges of Cruelty
Marine Law. XXVII 248-250

October 17 1811. A Court Martial was holden on board H.M.S. *Gladiator*, on Captain

Robert Preston, of H.M.S. *Ganymede*, which was continued by adjournment till the 23d.

> Members of the Court:
> Captain Paterson, President
> Captain Bissett,   Captain Halliday
>   - R. Hall   - Honourable Captain Rodney
>   - Phillimore   - Captain R. Elliott
>   - Rushworth   - Lumley
>   - P. Browne   - Sneyd
> M. Greetham, Esq. Judge Advocate

Upon charges exhibited by the Admiralty, of cruelty, tyranny, and oppression, contained in the following letter, which had been forwarded to their Lordships by the Ship's Company of the *Ganymede*:

Portsmouth Harbour, 23 September 1811
"For the Right Honourable the Lords Commissioners of the Admiralty, the petition of the *Ganymede* Ship's Company.
Humbly sheweth,
That your petitioners, from grievances which they labour under, through the cruel treatment they receive from the captain and officers belonging to the said ship, we your petitioners humbly solicit your lordships, that you will be pleased to remedy the same, by a change of ship or officers; as your petitioners wish to be true to their King and Country, and are willing to serve in any ships your Lordships may think proper. Honourable Sir, in granting this your petitioners will every pray. Your Lordships most obedient humble servants at command."

It appeared to the Court, that, upon the receipt of the above letter, the Lords of the Admiralty directed a Court of enquiry to be held on board the *Ganymede*, to ascertain the authenticity of the letter. This Court consisted of Admiral Hargood, Captains Otway and Halliday. Upon turning up the hands, the letter was unanimously declared to have been written with the consent of the whole ship's company; and a seaman (McGowrie) delivered another letter to this Court, which was to the same effect.

The Court of Inquiry expressed a wish, that any twelve of the crew would step forward as prosecutors in the charge. This, however, they declined; and, in a letter they afterwards wrote to Admiral Hargood, signed by nearly all the ship's company, they stated their wish to prosecute in a body.

Upon the above documents and recital appearing before the Court Martial, Admiral Hargood and Captains Otway and Halliday were called, and proved their truth.

John McGowrie, William Lowrie, George Townsend, and 17 other seamen were examined in support of the allegations contained in the above letter. Their evidence went to prove, that Captain Preston was more in the habit of adopting the summary punishment of *starting*, than the witnesses had known to have ever prevailed on board other ships; and to have frequently uttered very intemperate language.

Captain Senhouse, being ordered to proceed to sea, was examined, and deposed that Captain P. had been his most intimate friend and messmate; that he was possessed of gentlemanly manners, not habituated to blasphemous expressions, nor inclined to cruel, or oppressive, or tyrannical manners.

Sir Home Popham sworn. - Captain P. asked: As you have commanded several of H.M. ships, and been many years in the navy, and frequently entrusted with distinguished and most important services, I would beg leave to ask, whether you have not found it generally both expedient and salutary to the service, in the exercise of your own discretion, as a summary punishment, to give four dozen lashes, and sometime more, and to what extent, at the gangway, for offences contrary to the discipline and subordination of your ship; and whether such punishments have not been essentially necessary for the good of H.M. service.

The Court was cleared, and agreed, that, as the information required by questions like the above was irrelevant to the charges, and contained matters of opinion unnecessary to the Court, for the purpose of forming their judgment, the above question should not be put to the witness.

The prosecution being closed, Captain P. begged the indulgence of the Court till the next day, to make his defence: when Mr. Minchin having been taken ill, Mr. Weddell, Solicitor, read it. Captain P. lamented that the Lords of the Admiralty should have brought him before the present Court, upon charges which were anonymously asserted, and equally directed against his officers as himself. When he assumed the command of the *Ganymede*, he found his crew in a bad state; he had to restore them to that degree of discipline and subordination so essential in ships of war; he had certainly practised a summary mode of punishment (that of starting), but there was no degree of severity mixed with it, and he conceived he was justified in the practice, by the custom in all other ships, and by the salutary effects it produced in all delinquents: he never punished from caprice, nor from any feeling but that of the good of the service. When men properly conducted themselves, he was their friend and benefactor: in sickness, they often had had his personal attention, were fed from his table, and participated in all the indulgences the service will admit of.

Lieutenant Sparshot, Mr. Telfer, Surgeon; Mr. Rian, Boatswain; Lieutenant Waring, R.M. and several other officers, were sworn, who deposed, that they knew of no instance in Captain P.'s conduct which could be designated tyrannical or oppressive.

The Court, after deliberating some considerable time, agreed – "That the charges had not been proved against the said Captain Robert Preston, and did adjudge him to be *Acquitted*; but the Court, however, further agreed, that they could not help feeling it their duty, to express their sense of the singularity of the punishment, in many instances, on board the *Ganymede*, and strongly to recommend to Captain Preston, a future change of conduct in that respect."

[A number of important papers on attitudes to discipline are placed in Appendix 6 on Naval Discipline, Volume III, pp338-357.]

From the 'Naval History of the Present Year,' 1812
February-March. XXVII 253-254

Buonaparte to Take Command of the Army in the North; A Russian War Appears Inevitable

Each successive arrival from the North of Europe more strongly impresses the expectation, that a war of the most serious nature is on the eve of bursting forth in that part of the world. Buonaparte remained at Paris as late as the 19th of March; but it was understood that he would leave that capital in the course of a few days, for the purpose of taking the command of the army of the north. He is said to have a force of from 250,000 to 300,000 men, ready to fall upon Russia and Sweden. A treaty of alliance, offensive and defensive, was signed between Prussia and France, on the 3d of March; one of the articles of which stipulates, that the former is to supply the latter with 25,000 troops. In Paris, a *Senatus Consultum* has been agreed to, the object of which, by a sort of new conscription, is, greatly to increase the effective and disposable force of France; in fact, to enable Buonaparte to draw forth nearly all the military strength of the empire. - Sweden, it is expected, will solicit a subsidy from this country. The French have refused to suffer the Swedish troops which were in Stralsund to leave that town; consequently they may be regarded in the same light as prisoners. - Of the precise line of conduct which the Emperor of Russia means to pursue, scarcely any thing seems to be known; but, of his decided hostility towards Buonaparte, no doubt is to be entertained. The Imperial Guards have left St. Petersburg for the frontier; a circumstance strongly denoting war.

Turks and Russians at War

Hostilities have recommenced between the Turks and Russians.

Trade With France Booming

In consequence of a great extension of the licensing system, the intercourse between this country and France is now unusually free and active. Licenses have been sent in great abundance, it is said, to every French port. The French merchants regard this unexpected liberality as a certain indication of a war in the North. They say that the Emperor always relaxes his commercial restrictions, when he is about to undertake any great military expedition, and besides, that the duties on imports are, at such a crisis, of great importance to him, as they produce a supply of ready money to his treasury. It is expected that he will impose new duties on the articles, the importation of which he has allowed.

Battle-Squadron Breaks Out of Lorient

On the night of the 9th of March, a squadron of four or five line-of-battle ships escaped out of L'Orient. Chase was immediately given, but, unfortunately, without effect. The *Nyaden* frigate, on the 14th, on her passage from Portugal, fell in with them, and was so near as to exchange shots. Three large ships, which proved to be homeward-bound Indiamen, were at that time in sight; and, had it not been for the signals which were made by the *Nyaden*, they must inevitably have been captured. They escaped, and have arrived safe at Portsmouth. No satisfactory account has yet been received respecting the enemy's squadron.

Cherbourg

We have received a letter from a correspondent, who informs us, that Cherbourg was reconnoitred by our ships on the night of the 11th of March. The enemy had then there, two sail of the line, one bearing a rear-admiral's flag, one large frigate, one small ditto, all with sails bent. There were also observed a praam, two brigs of war, a lugger, and a cutter; with one frigate with her top-masts on end, in the basin, and one building.

Lord Melville Replaces Yorke at Admiralty

Lord Melville took his seat at the Admiralty Board, as the successor of Mr. Yorke, on the 25th of March. The names of the new Lords Commissioners will be found under the head of *Promotions and Appointments*. . . .

Execution of Traitors

On the 16th of March, William Cundell, and John Smith, two of the unfortunate men, whose trials for high treason, in deserting to the enemy, at the Isle of France, are recorded in a preceding sheet, suffered the sentence of the law at Horsemonger-lane. [They were hanged, drawn, and quartered.] The remainder of the prisoners received the royal pardon.

New Naval Uniform

Copied from the London Gazette of 28th March, 1812

From 'Naval Anecdotes.' XXVII 308-309

Admiralty-Office, March 23d, 1812
His Royal Highness the Prince Regent hath, in the name and on the behalf of the King, signified to my Lords Commissioners of the Admiralty, the Royal pleasure, that the uniform clothing at present worn by the flag officers, captains, commanders, lieutenants, master's-mates, and midshipmen of his Majesty's Royal Navy, shall be altered in the manner undermentioned, namely:

Admiral of the Fleet. - *Full Dress* - Coat of blue cloth, blue cloth collar, white cloth lapels and cuffs, with five laces round the cuffs: laced as at present, with the addition of a crown over the anchor.

Undress - Blue cloth, blue cloth collar, white lapels and cuffs with five laces; laced round the collar and lapels to the end of the skirts; flag and frame, hips and back skirts laced; twist button holes in the lapels and flaps as at present; epaulettes and buttons same as in the dress uniform.

Admirals - *Full Dress* - The same as the Admiral of the Fleet, with only four laces on the cuffs.

Vice-Admirals - The same, with only three laces on the cuffs.

Rear-Admirals - The same, with only two laces on the cuffs.

The epaulettes, with the respective distinctions of three, two, and one star, the same as at present. - Buttons as at present, with the addition of a crown over the anchor.

The undress or frock uniform of Flag Officers, except the Admiral of the Fleet, to be the same as at present, with the alteration only of the button.

The captain to the admiral of the fleet, and first captains to commanders-in-chief (if not flag-officers), to wear, while so employed, the undress or frock uniform of rear-admirals.

Captains and commanders of his Majesty's fleet to wear uniforms of the same pattern.

The full dress to be similar to that in use, excepting that the lapels and cuffs are in future to be white, laced as at present, with a crown over an anchor on the button.

Captains and commanders are both to wear two epaulettes, of the same pattern as at present, with only the following distinctions:

The epaulettes of captains three years post, to have an addition of a silver crown over a silver anchor.

The epaulettes of captains under three years post, to have the silver anchor without the crown.

The epaulettes of commanders to be plain.

Lieutenants of his Majesty's fleet to wear a dress uniform of the same pattern as captains and commanders, but without any lace, and with one plain epaulette (similar to that now worn by captains and commanders) on the right shoulder; buttons of the same patterns as for captains.

The undress or frock uniform of captains, commanders, and lieutenants, respectively, to be the same as at present, with the addition of the epaulettes and button, which are to be worn the same as in the full dress.

The whole of the commissioned officers of his majesty's fleet to have the linings of their dressed uniforms white. The flag officers only to have the linings of their dressed uniforms white silk.

Master's-mates, and midshipmen, to wear the same uniform as at present, with the alteration of the button only, which is to be of the same pattern as that of the captains and lieutenants.

Their lordships do hereby give notice thereof to all flag officers, captains, commanders, lieutenants, master's-mates, and midshipmen, and require and direct them strictly to conform thereto. The said alterations being to take effect generally on the 12th of August, 1812; but such officers of the Royal Navy as may have occasion, before that period, to make up new uniforms, are at liberty to have them made up according to the new patterns.

J.W. CROKER

N.B. The several patterns may be seen at this office.

From the 'Naval History of the Present Year,' 1812
March–April. XXVII 337-338

Wellington's Army Storms Badajoz

Badajoz, the fortress of which was invested by the Earl of Wellington, on the 16th of March, was stormed and taken on the night of the 6th of April. The French garrison originally consisted of 5,000 men, of which 1,200 were killed during the siege, 800 fell in the assault, and 3,000 were taken prisoners. From the commencement of the operation, till the close, the allied army had upwards of 1,000 men killed, and nearly 4,000 wounded. - Seville is reported to have been taken possession of by Ballasteros; and it is expected that the French will be compelled to raise the siege of Cadiz.

French Advance on Russia

Buonaparté is not yet known to have left Paris; but a very formidable army, under Bacoust and Odinot, has marched towards Russia. Buonaparté has offered Finland and part of Russia, as far as the Lake Ladaga, to Sweden, on condition of her bringing 35,000 men to join the French armies. - Sweden, it is added, has declined the offer. - A treaty of alliance, offensive and defensive, to which England is a party, is understood to have been signed between Russia and Sweden.

A Russian Commercial Decree was passed in January, confirming that of 1811, and adding to the list of articles allowed to be imported under the latter, a considerable number of others, of British manufacture, coming under the denomination of hard goods. The Decree does not admit any colonial produce but raw sugar; yet fine cottons of all colours are allowed to be imported: both are subject to an advance of duty; but the commercial facilities are expected to be soon greatly enlarged.

Government Rejects French Proposal for Repeal of Orders in Council

On Sunday, the 19th of April, a flag of truce arrived at Dover, with despatches from the French Government, which were immediately forwarded to London. A Cabinet Council was holden on the Tuesday following; and, on the succeeding day, a Declaration was published by Government, in answer, it may be considered, to the report which was made by the French minister to the Conservative Senate, on the 10th ult. relating to the British Orders in Council. This document bears the date of April 21, the day on which the Cabinet council sat; from which it is inferred, that the French despatches contained some proposal for a repeal, or codification, of the Orders in Council. The British declaration, which must be regarded as a paper of considerable importance, expresses the determination of Government, to defend and maintain the maritime rights and commercial interests of the nation: and it also refutes the appeal, made by the French minister to the Treaty of Utrecht. By this instrument, a solemn engagement is entered into, by the British government, to revoke the Orders in Council, immediately on the actual and unconditional repeal of the Berlin and Milan Decrees, as retaliatory measures against which they were originally issued.

Catholic Question

The Catholic Question was negatived, in the House of Lords, on the 22d of April, by 174 against 102; and, in the House of Commons, on the 24th of April, by 300 against 215.

Lorient Squadron in Brest

The French squadron, whose escape from L'Orient was mentioned at page 254, got into Brest on the 29th of March, without effecting any thing but the capture of a schooner!

Fane Takes Newly Developed Incendiary to US

From 'Correspondence.' XXVII 406-407

J. Robinson to the Editor, Lloyd's Coffee-house, May 8, 1812
Mr. Editor, About six weeks ago, having some transactions with the American Minister and Consul, I, and others of my acquaintance, frequently met Mr. Fane with these gentlemen, which naturally created suspicion that some correspondence was carrying on relative to his fire shot, for the distress of shipping. [See Appendix 8 on Gunnery, Volume IV, p362.] It is needless for me to enter into a description of those very destructive engines, as there are many gentlemen and captains of the navy, &c. here, who, having witnessed their effects, firmly assert, that a fast sailing schooner would destroy every ship in the British navy, by using the fire shot. We of course communicated the circumstance to Lord Melville and the Lords of the Admiral, supposing at least Mr. Fane would have been detained, but, to our utter astonishment, we find he left this kingdom for America, on Monday last. I merely give this statement now, that the people of England may know government were apprized of Mr. Fane's destructive productions, and also from their inattention to him, his determination to leave England.

View of the Northern Part of Port Royal Harbour, Jamaica. Engraved by Baily, from
a drawing by J.E. 1806. [Plate 464]

1812 – The Capture of Batavia

THE HERO OF THE EXPEDITION to Batavia was Lieutenant-General Sir Samuel Auchmuty who, understanding the perilous situation in which he found his soldiers, and the need to act quickly before they were overcome by tropical diseases, obtained a victory against odds, effectively destroying the French garrison. In the final defeat of the French the transport provided by the squadron commanded by Rear-Admiral Stopford was essential.

Letters on Service
Admiralty Office, December 16, 1811. ^{XXVI 501-512}

Captain [Edward] Stopford of the Royal Navy, arrived to-day at this office with despatches, of which the following are copies and extracts, addressed to John Wilson Croker, Esq. by Rear-Admiral the Honourable Robert Stopford, Commander in Chief, of H.M.S. and vessels at the Cape of Good Hope, and Commodore Broughton, late senior officer of H.M.S. in the East Indies.

H.M.S. Scipion, Batavia Roads, August 28, 1811
Sir, I shall confine myself, in this letter, to the relation of the circumstances attending the naval co-operation with the army, in the attack upon the island of Java; and I have to request you will acquaint my Lord Commissioners of the Admiralty, with the unconditional surrender of the capital city of Batavia, on the 8th instant, and the destruction or capture of the greatest part of the enemy's European troops, by a successful assault made upon a strongly entrenched and fortified work, called Muster [or Meester] Cornelis, on the morning of the 26th, by the troops under the command of Lieutenant-General Sir Samuel Auchmuty, who had also with him the Royal Marines of the squadron.

Previous to this important and decisive advantage, the General had caused batteries to be erected, consisting of twenty eighteen-pounders, which were entirely manned by five hundred seamen, from H.M. ships under the direction of Captain Sayer, of H.M.S. *Leda*, assisted by Captains Festing, acting captain of the *Illustrious*; Mansell, of the *Procris*; Reynolds, of the *Hesper*; and Captain Stopford, who volunteered his services from the *Scipion*, where he was waiting for his ship, the *Otter*.

The enemy was enabled to bring thirty-four heavy guns, eighteen, twenty-four and thirty-two pounders, to bear upon our batteries; but from the superior and well-directed fire kept up by the British seamen, the enemy's guns were occasionally silenced, and on the evening of the 25th completely so; their front line of defence also appeared much damaged, and many of their guns were dismounted.

So favourable an opportunity was, therefore, seized by the General, and the fortunate result of the assault, on the morning of the 26th, followed, as before mentioned.

The fatigue of the seamen was great, and much increased, by being exposed to the hot sun of this climate, for three successive days, during which time the fire was kept up with little interruption, but it was borne with their characteristic fortitude, Captain Sayer, and the officers above-mentioned setting them noble examples. . . .

I herewith enclose a list of the killed and wounded; and it is with much regret I add the name of Captain Stopford, who had his right arm carried off by a cannon shot whilst actively employed in the batteries; he is however doing well, and I hope soon to get him removed to a better climate.

Lieutenant-General Sir Samuel Auchmuty being desirous of transmitting an account of his success to England, I send this despatch by the *Caroline*, which ship was previously under order to go home; and I am happy to avail myself of so good an opportunity as is offered by Captain Cole, who has had a large share in every thing relating to this expedition, and from his knowledge of all the parts of the operations, can communicate to their Lordships the fullest account of them.

I have the honour to be, &c.

ROBERT STOPFORD, Rear-Admiral

John W. Croker, Esq.

Admiralty-Office, January 20, 1812. *XXVII 73-75*

Captain Harris, of H.M.S. *Sir Francis Drake*, arrived at this office last night, with despatches from the Honourable Rear-Admiral Stopford, commander-in-chief of H.M. ships and vessels at the Cape of Good Hope, addressed to John Wilson Croker, Esq. of which the following are copies and extracts.

H.M.S. Scipion, off Sourabaya, September 29th, 1811
Sir, In my letter to you from Batavia Roads, under date the 30th of August, I acquainted you, for the information of my Lords Commissioners of the Admiralty, that it was my intention to proceed in the *Scipion* to the Isle of France, in consequence of the principal part of the enemy's force having been captured or destroyed in the successful assault of their work[s], by the British troops on the 26th of that month.

On communication of this my signal to his Excellency the Governor-general of India, who was residing at Batavia, and to Lieutenant-general Sir Samuel Auchmuty, the commander-in-chief of the forces, I was informed by these authorities that the future resources of the enemy were yet unknown, and that they considered it requisite to use all means to bring the contest to as speedy a conclusion as possible, hoping that I would not diminish any part of the British force by my departure.

Upon these suggestions I waived my first intention of quitting the station, and prepared for immediately proceeding to Sourabaya.

In pursuance of my former arrangement, the *Nisus, President, Phoebe*, and *Hesper* (sloop), sailed on the 31st of August to Cheribon, for the purpose of intercepting the enemy's retreat from Meester Cornelius to the eastward. As no troops were ready for embarkation, I relied upon the marines of these ships (to which the party of H.M.S. *Lion* was added) for performing this service, and they fully answered my expectation. Captain Beaver, of H.M.S. *Nisus*, having summoned the place to surrender, took possession of it without opposition; Captain Warren, the bearer of the summons, having hoisted the British flag, received information that the commander-in-chief of the French troops (General Jamelle) had just arrived, and was changing horses to proceed to the eastward. Captain Warren, with his gig's crew, immediately made him his prisoner, and secured him; many other officers and privates were also made prisoners, as their lordships will observe by Captain Beaver's report to me of his proceedings, with Captain Hillyar's account of the surrender of Taggall, both forwarded by this opportunity. The services performed by these ships were of the greatest importance to the ultimate result of the campaign.

On the 4th September, I detached Commodore Broughton, in the *Illustrious*, with the *Minden*, *Lion*, and *Leda*, to rendezvous off the entrance of Gressie: on board these ships were embarked the 14th and part of the 78th regiments of foot, with field-pieces. The *Modest* sailed on the 5th with Lieutenant-general Sir Samuel Auchmuty, and I sailed in the *Scipion* on the 6th, having on board two companies of artillery, and four field-pieces. The transports, with the remainder of the troops, were directed to sail as soon as they were ready.

On the 8th September I received a despatch from Sir Samuel Auchmuty, acquainting me that he had received information of General Jansens' intention of assembling his forces and making a stand at Samarang, and requesting I would proceed there, and collect as many troops as possible. Measures for this purpose were accordingly taken. On the 9th I anchored off Samarang, and on the 10th was joined by Commodore Broughton, with the ships under his orders, and some few transports. On the same day the general, in conjunction with me sent a summons to General Jansens, which was rejected. On that night, I directed the armed-boats of the squadron to take or destroy several of the enemy's gun-boats, lying in-shore, with French colours: this service was completely executed under the direction of Captain Maunsell, acting captain of the *Illustrious*.

The general being in possession of a plan of the town of Samarang, which marked it as strongly fortified, and being unacquainted with the number of the enemy's troops, did not think it advisable to land the nine hundred troops which were collected, but waited for reinforcements from Batavia; nothing was, therefore, attempted until the 12th, when, having learned that the enemy had quitted the town of Samarang, and retired into the interior, a party of troops was landed and took possession of the town without opposition. On the 13th the whole of the troops were landed, which now amounted to fifteen hundred men, preparatory to an attack upon the enemy's position, on an eminence about seven miles from Samarang, where some guns were placed, and a work hastily thrown up.

Concluding that the final retreat of the enemy would be towards Sourabaya, I represented to the general the necessity of being before hand with the enemy, and immediately occupying that post; I accordingly sailed for this purpose on the 15th, with the *Scipion, Lion, Nisus, President, Phoebe,* and *Harpy* (the four last having joined me on the 14th): I intended to collect on my passage such transports, with troops, as had proceeded under the original intention of going to Sourabaya, and had not received the counter order to go to Samarang.

On the 17th I anchored with the squadron, off the town of Ledayo, on the Java shore, leading to Gressie, and was joined by three transports, having two hundred effective Sepoys, and fifty European cavalry; to these were added the marines of the squadron, making a force of nearly four hundred and fifty men.

On the 18th, Captain Harris, of H.M.S. *Sir Francis Drake,* came on board the *Scipion* from the island of Madura. For the previous proceedings of this meritorious officer, whom I had detached from Batavia on the 12th of August, to take possession of the French fortress at Samanap, in which he was eminently successful, and for the subsequent master-stroke of policy, in drawing the Sultan of Madura from the French alliance, and attaching him to the British interest, I beg leave to refer their lordships to my letter, containing Captain Harris's report of his proceedings, and the able and spirited assistance he received from Captain Pellew, of H.M.S. *Phaeton.*

As there was no field-officer of the army with me, I directed Captain Harris to take command of the troops which were landed on the 19th, and to march to Gressie. On the 20th, the place was in our possession, some parties of the enemy with guns having been put to flight.

On the approach of the troops to Sourabaya on the 22d, articles of capitulation were agreed upon between Captain Harris and the commandant (a colonel in the French service), for the surrender of the place. When these terms were on the point of being signed, intelligence was received of the capitulation for the surrender of Java and its dependencies having been concluded on the 18th; Sourabaya was therefore taken possession of, and fell under the general terms of the capitulation.

The general's letter having nearly at the same time reach me, I sent an officer to take possession of fort Ludowick, a place of great strength towards the sea, and completely defending the northern entrance towards Gressie. The fort was in excellent order, containing 98 pieces of heavy cannon, chiefly brass. I had, however, previously marked out the ground for erecting a mortar battery upon the island of Menare, from which it might have been effectually bombarded.

I have the honour to be, &c.

ROBERT STOPFORD, Rear-Admiral

To John Wilson Croker, Esq., Admiralty

[A proclamation was published by Lord Minto prior to his departure from Java, which attempted to reconcile the needs of the Dutch settlers and the British merchants coming in the wake of the armed forces. *The Naval Chronicle* considered it 'remarkable': 'the provisions thereby established for the new subjects of the Crown, would seem to require some explanation to reconcile a British mind to the modifications described in this curious paper, insomuch as they regard the natural-born subjects of Great Britain!' (Vol. XXVII, pp131-133).]

Java Prize-Money, etc
From 'Naval Anecdotes.' *XXVIII 192*

The coffee found in the store-houses at Java is estimated at 40,000 tons. The quantities of rice, sugar, pepper, and other spices, are also very large. Subalterns' shares of prize-money had sold as high as £400 each; and a captain's was estimated to be worth £750. The beautiful country mansion of former Dutch governors at Burtenzorg, including a large and profitable estate, has been purchased by Mr. Raffles, for a lack [lakh] of rupees.

1812 – Operations on the Coast of Catalonia

WHILE WELLINGTON'S ARMY was campaigning successfully in western Spain, British resources in the Mediterranean were inadequate to have a major impact on the course of events. In January Valencia was forced to capitulate. It did prove possible, however, to send Colonel Skerritt from Gibraltar with 12,000 men to reinforce the garrison of Tarifa in the extreme south of Spain to prevent it suffering a similar fate, and later General Maitland was landed at Alicante with a force composed of British, Neapolitan and Spanish soldiers from Majorca. There it was forced to stay, unable to influence events in the north.

The Mediterranean fleet was actively engaged in support of operations ashore. Especially interesting is Captain Codrington's account of the naval support provided to the Spanish regular and irregular forces attempting, unsuccessfully, to recover Tarragona. The guns of his squadron were used, when the February gales did not prevent, to command the coastal road, forcing the French to move slowly through broken country away from the sea where they were vulnerable to guerrilla attacks. Gunfire was also used to make unsafe the coastal towns occupied by the French.

In June Captain Sir Home Popham undertook similar operations around Bilbao, but *The Naval Chronicle* was reduced to publishing a précis of his letters, the first dated 25 June, and gazetted on 14 and 28 July. As space is far more limited in this Consolidated Edition, the précis has been omitted (Vol. XXVIII, pp78-79).

Codrington's Report of his Operations on the Coast of Spain

Letters on Service
Admiralty-Office, March 28, 1812. XXVII 338-342

Extract of a Letter from Vice-Admiral Sir Edward Pellew, Bart. Commander-in-chief of H.M. Ships and Vessels in the Mediterranean, to John Wilson Croker, Esq. dated on board H.M.S. Caledonia, at Port Mahon, the 8th of February, 1812
I have the honour to transmit to you herewith, to be laid before my Lords Commissioners

of the Admiralty, copies of two letters from Captain Codrington, of the *Blake*, dated on board that ship off Mataro, the 26th of January and 2d of February last, which will acquaint their Lordships of the situation of affairs in that principality, according to the latest information.

Throughout the whole of the contest the zeal and judgment with which the aid of His Majesty's naval force has been applied to the patriot cause, is deserving their Lordships' approbation. The officers and men have not only sought every opportunity to distinguish themselves, but have submitted with the greatest cheerfulness to fatigue and privation, shewing the greatest humanity towards the suffering inhabitants.

Blake, off Villa Nueva, January 26, 1812
Sir, An easterly gale of wind prevented our gaining any communication with the coast until the 11th, when I joined the *Invincible* in Salon Bay: shortly afterwards Captain Adam came on board with General Lacy from Reus, and acquainted me with a mediated attack upon Tarragona, by the division of the Baron d'Eroles, previously to their intended march into Arragon, as a diversion in favour of Valencia.

On the morning of the 19th I went to Reus, by desire of General Lacy, to be present at the final arrangement for the attack upon Tarragona that night: I found the commanding officers belonging to the different corps assembled; and the order of attack was scarcely made known to them, before an aide-du-camp of the Baron d'Eroles announced the actual arrival of the French at Cambrills from Tortosa (having left Valencia after its surrender), amounting, according to a letter previously received, to about three thousand men. "Alas armas," cried the Baron d'Eroles, with an animation which seemed to have a suitable effect on all the officers present; and I do not believe more than half an hour had elapsed, before the whole of the Division, consisting of between five and six thousand men, were on the ground, and ready to march. As I had ordered a boat to Salon, with twenty barrels of powder for the army, and as I was anxious to render what assistance might be in my power, I made an attempt to regain my ship, accompanied by an orderly dragoon; but, after proceeding about three miles, we were chased back by a party of French cavalry, which we met with at the crossing of the road.

Upon my return I found the troops advancing on the road to Tarragona, in order to cut the enemy's line of march, the Baron d'Eroles putting himself at the head of about seventy cuirassiers, to reconnoitre their strength and position, while General Lacy directed the movements of the respective corps, in readiness for the intended attack. We had scarcely reached the road from Cambrills to Tarragona, when the Baron brought in prisoners two French cuirassiers, who stated that their General (Lafond) had reached the latter place in safety, accompanied by some dragoons, leaving the infantry amounting to about eight hundred, just by in Villa Suca. General Lacy ordered the Regiment of Buca to attack them immediately, and directed other corps to surround the town, and prevent their escape. The enemy being advantageously posted behind the walls of the village, and that single regiment being much inferior to them in numbers, after a considerable loss in killed and wounded, including amongst the latter, and very severely, their gallant Colonel, Reding, they were obliged to retire; but the regiment intended for their support coming up, forced the French, who had advanced in a compact body, to retire in their turn, and being attacked in their rear by the Baron, they could never effectually rally, notwithstanding the effort they made, accompanied by a general cheer; despair was now visible in their conduct; and one or two discharges from a field-piece, which just then reached the ground, occasioned the surrender of all who remained alive, amounting to above six hundred; - I judge the number of the enemy, dead and dying, which I saw in the field, to amount to two hundred, that of the Spaniards bearing no proportion whatever. It seems, that having information from some spy of our landing, at the time one party of the dragoons chased men, another proceeded to Salon, where they made prisoners of Captain Pringle and Flin, who were walking near the beach, and of Lieutenant Cattle, belonging to this ship, who was waiting on shore with the powder, the boats and boats' crews having effected their escape. These officers, who were guarded close in the rear of the French during the whole of the battle, after being plundered of even part of their clothes, bear witness to their extreme pusillanimity on the approach of disaster, and to their severe loss both in the field and in the houses, in which they sought refuge, owing to the superior dexterity of the Spanish fire. I have given you this little affair in detail, because it evinces considerable improvement in the discipline and organization of the Catalan army; and I can vouch for the cheerfulness with which they proceeded to the attack, under belief of the enemy's force being much nearer their equivalent in numbers. The arrangements made by General Lacy appeared to me well calculated to keep up the mutual support requisite on such an occasion; and the whole conduct of the Baron d'Eroles particularly animating and exemplary; nor shall I readily forget the delight he expressed upon liberating my brother officers from the grasp of our mutual enemy.

Notwithstanding the fatigue of the troops, the General still expressed his intention of attacking Tarragona on that night, and we were therefore escorted to our ships about five o'clock, and weighed immediately. I stationed the *Sparrowhawk* off the Mole to keep up the communication with the army on that side, and the *Merope* to the eastward, for the same purpose, whilst the *Blake* was to occupy the attention of the enemy opposite the Melagro. We had scarcely reached the town, and opened our fire, when the wind increased to a gale at N.W., and prevented all communication by boats with the shore. We persevered, however, under a press of sail, standing off and on, so as to keep up the bombardment until day-light; but the assault was not made, nor could we see any of the Spanish troops in the neighbourhood in the morning. Anxious to afford every encouragement in an enterprize which, besides being of material service to the general cause, would, if successful, have produced me, individually, such particular satisfaction, we continued to work up under as much sail as we could carry the next day, in order to communicate, if possible, with the army, until at length, by the mainsail blowing entirely out of the bolt-rope, other sails splitting, and the barge sinking before we could get the carronade and ammunition out of her, I was driven to the necessity of anchoring for shelter just without range of shot to the eastward of the town. I am still uninformed of the particular cause which prevented the attack being made, either on the 19th or the following night, having had no direct communication with any of the chiefs, but by short requests for assistance, circuitously conveyed, in consequence of the arrival of various divisions of the enemy in those parts, amounting to seven thousand men.

A few lines from General Lacy, which I received on the 23d, induced me to push for Mataro, which I had nearly reached on the 24th, when a very severe gale from the N.E. necessarily reduced me to storm staysails; and whilst persevering off Barcelona, in an endeavour to hold our own, by keeping the ship's head to the eastward, she was struck by a sea, which has started all the timbers and rail of the head, ledges and earlings, bent the iron rail close into the bowsprit, drew the chock in the stern which received the bolt for the bumkin shroud, carried away the round-house and head door, and filled the main deck with water, so that the officers were up to their knees in the ward room, although both our spars and ropes stood this severe trial without injury. I bore up for shelter at Villa Nueva, where we were about to anchor at four P.M. on the 25th, in company with the *Sparrowhawk* and *Merope*, which I had left to assist the Baron d'Eroles, when the latter, which had just weighed, made the signal for the enemy upon the road to the westward, and shortly afterwards opened her fire on them. The gale being over, and the wind light, we made all sail, and soon commenced firing also. We observed three wagons disabled and abandoned, and considerable discomfiture among the troops, notwithstanding the difficulty we were under from a heavy swell setting directly on shore. Arriving opposite Vendrell we perceived another party coming from the westward, with cavalry, artillery, &c. amounting to some thousand men, which directed their course inland upon our approach. We were however enabled, by giving the guns the greatest elevation, to discharge two or three broadsides before dark, which I trust, did them material damage. Since this they have never appeared upon any part of that coast; and I know nothing more of the movements of either army than from the reports of desperate battles having taken place, the result of which is so variously stated, that it is impossible to venture an opinion without more authentic intelligence.

Blake, off Mataro, February 2, 1812
Passing Barcelona on the night of the 26th, Captain Guion brought me communications from Captain Tower, respecting the services of the *Curaçoa*, *Rainbow*, and *Papillon*, in harassing a division of the enemy which was marching along the coast from the eastward, and in finally obliging them to retire, and proceed towards Barcelona by a more circuitous route. And I beg to assure you, that their unremitting exertions on all occasions, in aiding our ally on the one part, and checking the progress of the enemy on the other, fully entitled them to your approbation.

On the 29th, whilst watering at Arens, I received information that the whole French force, which had lately traversed this principality, amounting to seven thousand men (four thousand of which were collected from the Ampurdam, and the other three thousand from the garrison of Barcelona), were about to make a movement along the coast, I therefore directed Captain Tower, instead of returning immediately to the Medas, which he had lately supplied with provisions and water, and which could not well be in any other danger whilst the whole of the army was in this quarter, to proceed with the *Merope* to Mataro, and concert with the governor, Colonel O'Ryan, the most advisable means for its defence. On the morning of the 30th, the *Curaçoa* making the signal that the enemy were advancing, the *Rainbow* opened her fire upon them near Vilasar, as did the *Curaçoa* and *Merope* upon their approach to Mataro. I weighed immediately, and worked up to that place, accompanied by the *Papillon*, which just then joined me, having been driven, in company with the *Triton* transport, off the coast in the late gale.

The French appearing determined to occupy the town, and the inhabitants having had notice of their approach on the preceding evening, and consequently sufficient time to remove their valuable effects, I felt myself called upon to comply with the desire of the Captain-General, repeated by Colonel O'Ryan, and opened the fire of the squadron upon such parts of the town as appeared to be most occupied by the enemy, and which was suffering by indiscriminate plunder. The tops of the mountains were covered as usual by the irregular Spanish forces acting in Guerilla; and I was in hopes that our united efforts had inclined the enemy to quit the place. They returned, however, at night, and have continued to occupy the town partially ever since, as I judge by their movements, giving each part of the army an opportunity to plunder in its turn. It being impossible to continue the great expense of ammunition, by persevering according to the tenor of Colonel O'Ryan's letter, our fire has only been repeated at intervals, so as to keep the enemy in constant trouble and alarm.

We have reports from Arens of their having lost six hundred men; and the evident effects of our shot upon the houses in the parts to which they have been directed, induces me to give credit to that assertion.

I sent the *Curaçoa* and *Papillon* to Arens, in consequence of a report that another French division was about to enter that town, intending the former should return to the Medas the moment her services could be dispensed with, and I have sent Captain Tower eleven thousand five hundred cartridges, to supply the demands lately made on me by the Patriots, and have directed him to furnish them with such proportion of biscuit as they have required, to enable them to maintain the position they occupy upon the mountains at the back of this town. Yesterday evening the *Curaçoa* telegraphed "the enemy entering Catilla, St. Paul, and Canet; but want of wind has prevented that ship and the *Papillon* hitherto from attacking them, except by their boats."

This narrative added to my preceding letter will afford you the best means I can procure to enable you to judge of the critical state of affairs in this principality.

It appears to me, however, that the Spanish army has increased its exertions in proportion to the difficulties it has had to contend against; and I therefore supplicate that you will be pleased to send me all the means you can spare for clearing the coast of the enemy, and furnishing it with such supplies as may be necessary for keeping up the energy and resolution by which it is at present characterised. General Sarsfield I am told was actually taken prisoner, a few days ago, but was rescued by a Swiss grenadier of the regiment of Bosa, who killed the Frenchman that had got possession of him, and recovered even the sash, which he had just stripped from him; and amongst the losses which they have suffered in the late battles, I am sorry to find the names of some of those rising young men, most distinguished for their gallantry; besides Colonel Reding, severely wounded on the 19th, Colonels Villamil, and De Creuft, also of the division of Eroles, were wounded in the hard fought battle of the 24th, in which the French are said to have left six hundred dead on the field; and Colonel Jalon, who has so often distinguished himself with the Cuirassiers, and was left at Mataro to recover from an accidental wound he received at Belpuig, was killed at the head of a Guerilla party on the 31st.

I have now to inform you that the enemy broke up from Mataro this morning before day-light, and seeing this ship weigh for the purpose of watching their movements, they took a line through the vineyards, out of gun-shot, which made their march so very tedious and fatiguing, that they did not reach Arens de Mar, until three o'clock, and after being somewhat harassed upon their approach to that place by the Spanish irregular troops upon the mountains. Seeing them halt upon the hills, I anchored here, and jointly with the *Curaçoa*, *Papillon*, and boats, threw a few shot over this town to deter them from entering it. But as we observed a few of them approach the place just before dark, I have ordered the boats to scour the street which runs down to the sea, to check their plundering the houses, during the night, as much as possible.

I have the honour to be,

E. CODRINGTON

Sir Edward Pellew, Bart.
Vice-Admiral of the Red

1812 – War with the United States

THE ECONOMIC DISTRESS CAUSED BY THE WAR, more than the diplomatic protests from the United States, forced the Government to agree to the establishment of a Parliamentary committee to examine the working of the Orders in Council controlling trade, and it began to hear evidence on 29 April. However, on 11 May the Prime Minister, Perceval, was assassinated in the House of Commons by a man who had been ruined by the seizure of his property in Russia and held the Government to blame for not supporting his claim. This created a cabinet crisis. The Prince of Wales found it difficult to form an administration because of the contentious issue of the emancipation of Catholics, but eventually Lord Liverpool agreed to take over the Government. Lord Melville remained at the Admiralty.

As part of his preparations for the Russian campaign Napoleon Buonaparte, in April, made peace feelers to Britain. There was plenty of reason to suspect his motives, and in the reply it was made clear that Britain would not accept as a condition of peace the recognition of Joseph Buonaparte as king of Spain. That was the end of that.

In response to the domestic distress, and to the attitude of the United States, the Orders in Council were repealed on the American government presenting a copy of what purported to be a French declaration putting an end to the Berlin and Milan decrees. However, five days earlier, the United States had declared war on Britain. The continued irritation of naval impressment was a contributing cause of war, and named in the declaration, so the repeal of the Orders in Council did not lead to a restoration of peace. Another contributing cause, or excuse, was the ill-advised action of the Governor of Canada, Sir James Craig, in sending an agent, Captain Henry, to the United States on a secret mission which may have included instructions to encourage the possibility that the New England states would prefer the break-up of the Union. An entirely spurious claim was added, that the British authorities were supporting

84

the resistance of aboriginal Americans to American western expansion. Probably the most important reason was the ambition in some quarters of the United States to incorporate Canada in the American union, but that was not mentioned.

The Naval Chronicle's reporting of the road to war with the United States included publication of the texts of Napoleon's alleged repeal of the Berlin and Milan decrees, and President Madison's address to Congress of 1 June to which was attached an 'Act Declaring War'. It also published a proclamation issued by Major-General Issac Brock on 22 July preparing the Canadian settlers for the imminent American invasion, a proclamation issued by Admiral Warren at Halifax on 5 October urging British seamen to serve in the navy, and also a proclamation dated 26 October threatening British seamen who served in the American forces with death. Finally it published the Prince Regent's speech on the opening of Parliament on 30 November in which, having reviewed the satisfactory course of the war in Europe, he spoke in conciliatory terms about the possibility of re-establishing peaceful relations with the United States, but noted that there was no sign of a settlement being reached. The text of an announcement that Russia, Sweden and Great Britain had agreed to resolve all their difficulties was also published. The British Government's declaration outlining the 'Causes of the War' was not published until early in 1813 when any immediate hope of a peaceful settlement had been exhausted. It is printed below on pages 132-140.

News of naval action included an account of the destruction of two French frigates and a brig at Isle Grouais by Captain Henry Hotham of the *Northumberland*, but inevitably more attention was paid to the unprovoked attack by an American squadron on HMS *Belvidera*, which she was able to escape, and the capture of the *Guerriere* by the USS *Constitution*. This started considerable discussion of the nature of the American super-frigates which were built on hulls the size of a British second rate. The controversy became even more heated when the USS *United States* captured HMS *Macedonian* after a battle of more than two hours' duration.

Other naval news included another report of a woman serving in the fleet, this one the wife of a sailor. Husband and wife were both killed in an action, and their baby was adopted by the surviving crew. On a more cheerful note, it was reported that the great engineering work to build a mole protecting Plymouth harbour was progressing rapidly.

From the 'Naval History of the Present Year,' 1812
April–May. XXVII 431-432

Prime Minister Assassinated! Cabinet Crisis

On the afternoon of Monday, the 11th of May, as the Right Honourable Spencer Perceval was passing through the lobby, or the entrance to the House of Commons, he was shot through the heart by a man of the name of John Bellingham, who had stationed himself there for the horrible purpose. Mr. Perceval almost instantly expired. The assassin was taken into custody, tried at the Old Bailey, on Friday, the 15th, found guilty of the murder, and executed on Monday, the 18th May. - Bellingham, it appeared, had sustained some pecuniary losses, from mercantile concerns, in Russia; and as he could not obtain the redress to which he conceived himself to be entitled, from the British government, he resolved upon the dreadful crime here recorded. Upon investigation, however, it did not appear that he had the slightest claim upon ministers, beyond what he actually received. On his trial, the plea of insanity was set up by his counsel, but was over-ruled.

This lamented event has necessarily deranged the concerns of the cabinet. Overtures were made to the Marquis Wellesley, and to Mr. Canning, to come into office; but they declined the proffered honour, in consequence of their differing in opinion from his Majesty's ministers, respecting the claims of the Catholics, and the mode of conducting the war in the Peninsula. An attempt was then made to go on with the old cabinet, newly modified. Mr. Vansittart was appointed Chancellor of the Exchequer; and Lord Liverpool, it was understood, was to be First Lord of the Treasury. On the 21st of May, however, Mr. S. Wortley made a motion in the House of Commons, for an address to the Prince Regent, praying his Royal Highness to adopt measures for the forming of a more vigorous and efficient ministry. The motion having been carried, by 174 against 170, an address was accordingly presented to the Prince Regent, who was pleased to return an answer, "that he would take it into his serious and immediate consideration." Negotiations have, in consequence, been going forward ever since; but down to the 28th of May, they had been all unsuccessful, and not even the basis of a new ministry had been formed. The most probable expectation then was, that Lord Moira would be Prime Minister; and that, in farther addition to the Earl of Liverpool and his friends, the Marquis Wellesley, Mr. Canning, and Mr. Huskisson, would come in. . . .

US President Accuses Britain of Seeking to Break Up the Union

On the 9th of March, Mr. Madison, the President of the United States, sent a message to Congress, charging the British government with having employed a secret agent (a Captain Henry) to intrigue with the disaffected, with the view of dissolving the union of the American States, and, eventually, in concert with a British force, to form the eastern part thereof into a political connexion with Great Britain. Ministers have positively denied the serious part of the charge; and the conduct of Mr. Madison, in giving publicity to the affair, is regarded as an electioneering trick. Henry's treachery, in disclosing his instructions, &c. is supposed to have been largely paid for out of the American treasury. - An embargo, for 90 days, has since been laid on in all the ports of the United States; to allow time, as it is said, for the *ultimatum* of the American government to be sent to England, and for an answer thereto to be returned.

Buonaparte to Join Army of the North

Buonaparte left Paris, early in May, to join his army in the north. The Emperor Alexander also left his capital, as far back as the 21st of April, to take the chief command of his army. - The British government is said to have refused to grant a subsidy of £100,000 per month, to Sweden, but has offered, to a certain extent, to supply the Swedish troops with clothes, arms, and ammunition.

French Declaration of the Repeal of the Berlin and Milan Decrees

State Papers. *XXVII 471-472*

Palace of St. Cloud, April 28, 1811
Napoleon, Emperor of the French, King of Italy, Protector of the Confederation of the Rhine, Mediator of the Swiss Confederation.

On the Report of our Minister for Foreign Affairs,

In consequence of the Act of the 2d of March, 1810, by which the Congress of the United States have enacted exemptions from the provisions of the Non-Intercourse Act, which prohibit the entrance into the American ports of the ships and goods of Great Britain, of its colonies, and dependencies;

Considering that the said law is an act of resistance to the arbitrary pretensions consecrated by the British Orders in Council, and a formal refusal to adhere to a system derogatory to the independence of neutral powers, and of their flag;

We have decreed, and decree as follows:

The Decrees of Berlin and Milan are definitively, and from the date of the 1st of November last, considered as never having taken place (*non avenues*) with regard to American vessels.[1]

(signed) NAPOLEON
By order of the Emperor, The Minister and Secretary for Foreign Affairs
(signed) THE COUNT DARU

From the 'Naval History of the Present Year,' 1812
May-June. *XXVII 500-501*

Liverpool to Head Cabinet

Very extraordinary difficulties arose in the formation of a new cabinet. Subsequently to the Address of the House of Commons, praying his Royal Highness the Prince Regent to adopt such measures as might tend to the establishment of an efficient ministry, the Marquis Wellesley received a commission for that purpose. His efforts, however, were unsuccessful. The Liverpool party refused to act with him; and, with the Greys and the Grenvilles, a sufficiently explicit understanding could not be obtained. Lord Moira next received the royal authority to form a new cabinet; but he also failed, in consequence of some difficulties arising, respecting the wished-for removal of the officers of the Household, on the part of the opposition. Lord Liverpool was then, from necessity, as it would appear, appointed First Lord of the Treasury, and Mr. Vansittart Chancellor of the Exchequer. Lord Sidmouth succeeds Mr. Ryder, as Secretary of State for the Home Department; and Earl Bathurst, the Earl of Liverpool, as Secretary for the War and Colonial Department. These are the only changes of note. Lord Melville retains his seat at the head of the Admiralty Board.

---

1 In a conversation which took place in the House of Commons, on the 22d of May, between Mr. Brougham and Lord Castlereagh, respecting the above declaration, Lord Castlereagh treated it as one of those diplomatic documents, which so often disgraced the French Government. It bore, he said, internal evidence of having been drawn up as an answer to the Declaration of the Prince Regent, of April 21, 1812; and the date which had been given to it proved nothing but the fraud of the transaction, which, in every view, would disgrace the government of any civilized country.

Concessions to be Made to Americans

The dissolution of the Perceval administration, however, has already led to some great and important changes in our domestic policy. The Orders in Council have been given up, as far as they relate to America. America, it appears, is to be coaxed into conciliatory measures, and France is to be coaxed through America. So much for vigour and perseverance! Yet America, it should be observed, maintains the most bitter animosity against this country; and at the present moment, after passing a most sanguinary decree, relative to the impressment of seamen, it is doubtful whether she may not actually have declared war against us.

Catholic Question to be Reconsidered

The situation of the Catholics is also to be investigated. Mr. Canning's motion, on the 22d of June, that their case should be taken into consideration, early in the ensuing session of Parliament, was agreed to, on a division, by 235 against 106. The Ministers of the Crown, though refusing to consider it as a cabinet question, all yielded their assent to the proposition, with the greatest facility imaginable.

Buonaparte Heads for St Petersburg

Buonaparte and the Emperor Francis, passed some time together, at Dresden, the latter end of May. Buonaparte has since proceeded towards the Russian frontier; with a threat, as it is said, that he would be at St. Petersburg early in July, to point out to the Emperor Alexander the real confines of his empire.

Fire at Plymouth Dockyard

On the morning of Monday, June the 8th, a fire broke out in three places at once, in the rope-house at Plymouth dock-yard. It raged furiously for several hours, and did considerable mischief. A most rigid investigation has ever since been taking place, as the fire is generally supposed to have been the act of an incendiary.

US Ships Leaving British Ports

Instructions have been given by the American Consul-General, in London, to all masters of ships under the Republican flag, to accelerate the departure of their vessels. Mr. Foster has also written to our Consul-General at New York, to prepare himself to quit the United States, as he may receive only the shortest notice. The *President* and another frigate have sailed from New York, and it is understood with directions to commit acts of aggression against the British flag, not only in the American waters, but, under circumstances explained, beyond that limit.

Remaining Isle de France Traitors Pardoned

The law having been put in execution against several of the men found in arms against their country, at the Isle of France, those on board the *Royal William*, at Spithead, from among whom the worst cases were selected, have been pardoned, and released from confinement; previously receiving an impressive admonition from Sir Richard Bickerton.

Destruction of Two French Frigates and a Brig at Isle Grouais

Letters On Service
Admiralty Office, May 30, 1812. ^XXVII 509-511^

Captain Henry Hotham to Rear-admiral Sir Harry Neale, Bart.
Northumberland, off the Penmarks, Wind S.S.W.
Light Breeze, and Fine Weather, May 24, 1812

Sir, I have the honour to inform you the object of the orders I received from you on the 19th instant, to proceed off L'Orient for the purpose of intercepting two French frigates and a brig, lately seen at sea, has been accomplished by their total destruction, at the entrance of that port, by his Majesty's ship under my command, (the *Growler* gun-brig being in company) under the circumstances I beg leave to relate to you.

On Friday the 22d instant, at a quarter after ten, A.M. the N.W. point of the Isle Groa [Grouais][2] bearing from the *Northumberland* north by compass, ten miles distant, and the wind very light from W. by N. they were discovered in the N.W. crowding all possible sail before it for L'Orient. My first endeavour was to cut them off to windward of the island, and a signal was made to the *Growler* (seven miles off in the S.W.) to chase, but finding I could not effect it, the *Northumberland* was pushed by every exertion round the S.E. end of Groa, and, by hauling to the wind as close as I could to leeward of it, I had the satisfaction of fetching to windward of the harbour's mouth, before the enemy's ships reached it. Their commander, seeing himself thus cut off, made a signal to his consorts and hauled to the wind on the larboard tack to windward of Point Taleet, and they appeared to speak each other. I continued beating to windward between Groa and the continent, to close with them, exposed to the batteries on both sides, when I stood within their reach, which was unavoidable. The wind had by this time freshened considerably, and was about W.N.W.: at 49 minutes after two P.M. the enemy (in force as above described) bore up in close line a-head, and under every sail that could be set, favoured by the fresh wind, made a bold and determined attempt to run between me and the shore, under cover of the numerous batteries with which it is lined in that part. I placed the *Northumberland* to meet them as close as I could to the Point de Pierre Laye, with her head to the shore, and the main-top-sail shivering, and made dispositions for laying one of them alongside; but they hauled so very close round the point, following the direction of the coast to the eastward of it, that, in my ignorance of the depth of water so near the shore, I did not think it practicable, consistent with the safety of his Majesty's ship (drawing near twenty-five feet) to prosecute that plan. I, therefore, bore up and steered parallel to them at the distance of about two cables' length, and opened the broadside on them, which was returned by a very animated and well-directed fire of round grape, and other descriptions of shot, supported by three batteries for the space of twenty-one minutes, and was very destructive to our sails and rigging. My object, during that time, was to prevent their hauling outside the dry rock, named Le Graul, but in steering sufficiently close to it to leave them no room to pass between me and it, and at the same time to avoid running on it myself, the utmost difficulty and anxiety was produced by the cloud of smoke which drifted ahead of the ship, and totally obscured it. However, by the care and attention of Mr. Hugh Stewart, the Master, the ship was carried within the distance of her own length on the south west side, in quarter less

---

2 Grouais, erroneously written Groa, is an island on the west coast of France, in latitude 47°38'4"N. longitude 3°26'8" W. from Greenwich.

seven fathoms, and the enemy were, in consequence, obliged, as their only alternative, to attempt passing within it, where there was not water enough, and they all grounded, under every sail, on the rocks between it and the shore.

The sails and rigging of the *Northumberland* were so much damaged, that I was obliged to leave the enemy to the effects of the falling tide, it being only one quarter ebb, while I repaired the rigging and shifted the fore-top-sail, which was rendered entirely useless; working to windward during that time under what sail I could set, to prevent falling to leeward; in which interval, at five o'clock, the *Growler* joined, and fired on the enemy occasionally. At 28 minutes after five, I anchored the *Northumberland* in six and a half fathoms water, Point de Pierre Laye bearing N.W. half N. the citadel of Port Louis[3] E. three quarters N. and the rock named Le Gaul N. half E. two cables' length distance, with her broadside bearing on the enemy's two frigates and brig, at a point blank range, all of them having fallen over on their sides next the shore as the tide left them, and exposed their copper to us, and the mainmast of one frigate and the brig were gone, and from 34 minutes after five till 49 minutes past six (which was near the time of low water), a deliberate and careful fire was kept up on them, at which time, believing I had fully effected the object of my endeavours, the crews having quitted their vessels, all their bottoms being pierced by very many of our shot, so low down as to ensure their filling on the rising tide, and the leading frigate being completely in flames, communicated to the hull from a fire which broke out in her foretop, I got under sail. Three batteries fired at the ship during the whole time she was at anchor, and although the position was so far well chosen that she was out of the range of two of them, the other (to which the enemy's vessels were nearest) reached her, and did so much execution in the hull, as all the fire she had been exposed to before.

I directed the Commander of the *Growler* to stand in and fire, to prevent the enemy from returning to their vessels after I had ceased.

At five minutes before eight, the frigate on fire blew up with an awful explosion, leaving no remains of her visible. At the close of day I anchored for the night, out of reach of the batteries on both sides, Point Taleet bearing N.N.W., half W. S.E. point of Groa S.S.W. half W., the enemy's vessels N. by E. At ten, the other frigate appeared to be on fire also (some smoke having been seen on board her from the time the firing ceased), and at half-past eleven, the flames burst forth from her ports and every part with unextinguishable fury, which unlooked for event leaving me nothing more to attempt in the morning, the brig being quite on her beam ends, and very much damaged by our shot in every part of her bottom, even very near her keel, I weighed anchor at midnight, with a very light air from the northward, with the *Growler* in company, profiting by the brightness of the moon to get to sea; but it was so near calm that I made very little progress, and therefore saw the frigate burning from head to stern all night, and explode at thirty-five minutes after two in the morning of yesterday, leaving a portion of her after-part still burning, till it was entirely consumed; and in the course of the day I had the satisfaction to see, from off the N.W. point of Broa, a third fire and explosion in the same spot, which could have been no other than the brig.

During the time of firing on the enemy's vessels, a seaman, who states himself to be a native of Portugal, captured in the ship *Harmony*, of Lisbon, by the frigates, on the 22d of February, swam from one of them to the *Northumberland*, by whom I am informed their names were *L'Arianne* and *L'Andromache*, of forty-four guns and four hundred

3 Port Louis is situated in latitude 47°42'47"N. longitude 3°20'15"W. from Greenwich.

and fifty men, and the *Mameluke* brig, of eighteen guns and one hundred and fifty men; that they sailed from the Loire in the month of January, had been cruising in various parts of the Atlantic, and had destroyed thirty-six vessels of different nations, (Americans, Spaniards, Portuguese, and English), taking the most valuable parts of their cargoes on board the frigates (and they appeared very deep for ships so long at sea), and one vessel they sent as a cartel to England, with about two hundred prisoners.

I am happy to have now the gratifying duty to discharge, of bearing testimony to the creditable conduct of every officer and man I had the honour to command . . .

I have the honour to be, &c.

H. HOTHAM, Captain

Rear-Admiral Sir Harry Neale, Bart., &c.

Commercial Licenses for Trading with the Enemy

From 'Naval Anecdotes.' XXVIII 48-51

The following account of the number of Commercial Licenses, granted during the last ten years, distinguishing the years, has been published by order of the House of Commons: - 1802, 68; 1803, 836; 1804, 1141; 1805, 791; 1806, 1620; 1807, 2606; 1808, 4910; 1809, 15,226; 1810, 18,356; 1811, 7602.

[These licenses were used to channel trade with occupied Europe into British hands. Accordingly, unlike the licenses Napoleon issued, which undermined his Berlin and Milan decrees, the British licenses were an effective part of the commercial control instituted by the notorious 'Orders in Council'. Their number was a measure of British success, and provided the economic support for Britain's subsidies to the people resisting Napoleon's despotism, but of course they were also an impediment to American profiteering from the war and hence a cause of friction between Britain and the United States.]

Naval Conjugal Correspondence

The following is given in a Cornwall paper, as a correct copy of a letter received some time since by a woman in Truro, from her husband, a seaman on board the *Edgar*, then lying at Plymouth:

H.M.S. Edgar, at Plymouth Dock
My Dear Grace, This coms with my kind love, hopine it will find you as it leves me. I hope if the child is a boy, you will cale it after my nam for may sak, and as i dozen intend never to see you agen, you may be married as son as you wil, for I shall be married as son as I can. - So no mor at present from your afectinate husbant.
To Mrs. G—, in the Work-House

From the 'Naval History of the Present Year,' 1812
June-July. XXVIII 73-74

War Appears Certain with the United States

The American Senate has passed a resolution for declaring war against Britain; and circumstances have transpired which strongly indicate, that that resolution has been sanctioned by the President of the United States. - On the 25th of July, as we learn from the "*Hampshire Telegraph*," the *Mackarel* schooner arrived at Portsmouth, from Halifax, with despatches from Admiral Sawyer, relating, that, on the 24th of June, the *Belvidera* frigate, commanded by Captain Richard Byron (one of the ships under his command), was cruising off Sandy Hook, but not in sight of land, when she fell in with an American squadron, consisting of the *President, United States, Congress,* and *Essex* frigates, and *Hornet* sloop of war, which ships, as soon as they were within point blank shot, *without previous communication with the Belvidera*, immediately commenced firing upon her. - The *Belvidera*, of course, made sail from so very superior a force, and the Americans pursued her, maintaining a running fight with her, as long as she was within reach of shot; in the course of which she had two men killed, and Captain Byron was hurt in the thigh, by a gun falling upon him. The *Belvidera*, made her way to Halifax, to acquaint Admiral Sawyer of the transaction, and repair her damages. On her arrival there Admiral Sawyer sent Captain Thompson, in the *Colibri* sloop of war, *with a flag of truce,* to New York, to request an explanation of the matter; despatched the *Rattler* to Bermuda, and the different cruising stations, to order all his squadron to assemble at Halifax; and sent Captain Hargrave in the *Mackarel* to England, with despatches for Government. - Captain Byron is said to have captured three American vessels, on his way to port, but Admiral Sawyer released them. [Particulars of the action, by an officer on board the *Belvidera*, were published in Vol. XXVIII, pp104-105.]

Our Government has expressed an opinion, that the attack made upon the *Belvidera* had neither resulted from any new orders of the American Government, nor was any proof that war had been decided on. The American frigates, it was thought, had acted in conformity to a previous order of the Government of the United States, not to permit vessels of war belonging to foreign powers to cruise within their waters.

Buonaparte Crosses Niemen

Buonaparte has crossed the Niemen, and, according to the latest accounts, was proceeding on his route towards St. Petersburg, the Russian army retreating before him.

Tripoli Declares War on Spain

The Regency of Tripoli has declared war against Spain. It has transpired, from the French papers, and the truth of the statement has been acknowledged in Parliament, that when the intercourse took place between the British and French Governments, in the month of April last, a proposition for peace was made, on the basis that the reigning dynasty should be acknowledged Sovereign of Spain (the integrality of the Spanish dominions to be guaranteed in his family, which is termed "the present, or actual dynasty:") that Naples should remain in the hands of Murat, and Sicily in that of its legitimate Sovereign; and that each power should retain the portion, of which the other could not deprive it by war. To this proposition Lord Castlereagh replied, that ministers had no objection to treat of a peace; but, with respect to the proposed basis, he wished to be informed, whether, by the "actual dynasty" were really meant Joseph and his kin; as, if so, the obligations of good faith did not permit the Prince Regent to attend to the proposition. Buonaparte offered no explanation, and thus the correspondence terminated.

Message of the President of the United States to Congress

State Papers. XXVIII *132-138*

... Not content with these occasional expedients [i.e. blockades] for laying waste our neutral trade, the Cabinet of Great Britain resorted, at length, to the sweeping system of blockades, under the names of Orders in Council, which has been moulded and managed as might best suit its political views, its commercial jealousies, or the avidity of British cruisers.

To our remonstrances against the complicated and transcendent injustice of this innovation, the first reply was, that the Orders were reluctantly adopted by Great Britain, as a necessary retaliation on decrees of her enemy, proclaiming a general blockade of the British Isles, at a time when the naval force of the enemy dared not to issue from his own ports. She was reminded, without effect, that her own prior blockades, unsupported by an adequate naval force actually applied and continued, were a bar to this plea; that executed edicts against millions of our property could not be retaliated on edicts confessedly impossible to be executed; that retaliation, to be just, should fall on the party setting the guilty example, not on an innocent party, which was not even chargeable with an acquiescence in it.

When deprived of this flimsy veil for a prohibition of our trade with Great Britain, her Cabinet, instead of a corresponding repeal, or a practical discontinuance of its Orders, formally avowed a determination to persist in them against the United States, until the markets of her enemy should be laid open to British products; thus asserting an obligation on neutral power to require one belligerent to encourage, by its internal regulations, the trade of another belligerent; contradicting her own practice towards all nations in peace as well as in war; and betraying the insincerity of those professions which inculcated a belief, that, having resorted to her Orders with regret, she was anxious to find an occasion for putting an end to them.

Abandoning still more all respect for the neutral rights of the United States, and for its own consistency, the British Government now demands as pre-requisites to a repeal of its Orders, as they relate to the United States, that a formality should be observed in the repeal of the French Decrees, no wise necessary to their termination, nor exemplified by British usage; and that the French repeal, besides including that portion of the Decrees which operates within a territorial jurisdiction, as well as that which operates on the high seas against the commerce of the United States, but should be extended to whatever other neutral nations unconnected with them may be affected by those Decrees.

And as an additional insult, they are called on for a formal disavowal of conditions and pretensions advanced by the French Government, for which the United States are so far from having been themselves responsible, that, in official explanations which have been published to the world, and in a correspondence of the America Minister at London, with the British Minister for Foreign Affairs, such a responsibility was explicitly and emphatically disclaimed.

It has become, indeed, sufficiently certain, that the commerce of the United States is to be sacrificed, not as interfering with the belligerent rights of Great Britain - not as supplying the wants of their enemies, which she herself supplies - but as interfering with the monopoly which she covets for her own commerce and navigation. She carries on a war against the lawful commerce of a friend, that she may the better carry on a commerce with an enemy - a commerce polluted by the forgeries and perjuries which are for the most part the only passports by which it can succeed. . . .

We behold our seafaring citizens still the daily victims of lawless violence, committed on the great and common highway of nations, even within the sight of the country which owes them protection. We behold our vessels freighted with the products of our soil and industry, or returning with the honest proceeds of them, wrested from their lawful destinations, confiscated by prize courts, no longer the organs of public law, but the instruments of arbitrary edicts, and their unfortunate crews dispersed and lost, or forced or inveigled in British ports into British fleets; whilst arguments are employed in support of these aggressions, which have no foundation but in a principle equally supporting a claim to regulate our external commerce in all cases whatsoever. . . .

Having presented this view of the relations of the United States with Great Britain, and of the solemn alternative growing out of them, I proceed to remark, that the communications last made to Congress on the subject of our relations with France, will have shewn, that since the revocation of her Decrees, as they violated the neutral rights of the United States, her Government has authorized illegal captures by its privateers and public ships; and that other outrages have been practised on our vessels and our citizens. It will have been seen, also that no indemnity had been provided, or satisfactorily pledged, for the extensive spoliation committed under the violent and retrospective order of the French government against the property of our citizens, seized within the jurisdiction of France.

I abstain at this time from recommending to the consideration of Congress definitive measures with respect to that nation, in the expectation, that the result of the unclosed discussions between our Minister Plenipotentiary at Paris, and the French Government, will speedily enable Congress to decide with greater advantage, on the course due to the rights, the interests, the honour of our country.

JAMES MADISON

Washington, June 1, 1812

[Madison also charged the British government with fomenting 'the warfare just renewed by the savages on one of our extensive frontiers; a warfare which is known to spare neither age nor sex, and to be distinguished by features particularly shocking to humanity,' but made no mention of the aggressive lobby seeking to extend American jurisdiction over British North America, and passed over the preference of the trading interests of New England for continued peace with Britain as the work of British agents. The British government was certainly 'sacrificing' the commerce of the United States 'as interfering with the monopoly which she covets for her own commerce,' but of course the motive was to use the financial resources of trade to defeat the Buonapartist tyranny which had conquered most of Europe. Subjoined to Madison's address was published: An Act Declaring War between the United Kingdom of Great Britain and Ireland, and the Dependencies thereof, and the United States of America, and their Territories. In latter pages was published 'An Act to prohibit American Vessels from proceeding to our trading with the Enemies of the United States, and for other Purposes.' (Vol. XXVIII, pp224-225)]

[On 1 August 1812 the Admiralty revoked all licenses for 'vessels to sail without convoy' to ports in North America and the West Indies. (Vol. XXVIII, p139)]

Peace Between Great Britain, Russia and Sweden

State Papers. XXVIII 139-140

From the 'London Gazette. Extraordinary,' July 31, 1812

Foreign Office, Downing-Street, July 31, 1812
Viscount Castlereagh has this day received, by Lieutenant Dobree, of H.M.S. *Victory*, despatches from E. Thornton, Esq. his Majesty's Plenipotentiary in Sweden, transmitting a Treaty of Peace and Friendship between his Majesty and the Emperor of all the Russias; and a Treaty of Peace and Friendship between his Majesty and the King of Sweden, signed at Orebro, by Mr. Thornton, and the respective Plenipotentiaries of the two Powers, on the 18th instant.

[The text of the treaty with Sweden was published in Vol. XXVIII, pp300-301, and that with Russia on pp418-419. The fortunate timing of the Russian defection from Buonaparte's 'Continental System' was important in enabling Britain to survive the American war.]

From the 'Naval History of the Present Year,' 1812
July-August. XXVIII 157-157

British Envoy Leaves New York

In consequence of the hostile conduct of the American Government, towards Great Britain, Mr. Foster, our Envoy, left New York on the 14th of July, in the *Atalanta* sloop of war, and arrived at Portsmouth on the 19th of August. Mr. Baker, Secretary to the Envoy, remained at Washington, to act as occasion might require.

American War Not in National Interest - Editorial

A large portion of the daily press in England has been engaged in promulgating errors with regard to America; by which the public has been induced more or less to approve of the measures which have now produced so serious a calamity as a new war. We have been persuaded to believe that our hostile system was useful, and that the American government had not the power, if it had the spirit, to resent provocation. The state of affairs between the two countries now stands thus: There have existed disputes on our celebrated Orders in Council; on the impressment of American seamen; and on certain points relating to Florida. Of these the first only has been settled by the revocation which took place on 23d June, and that step was too late in its adoption to prevent war, which was in fact declared on 18th June by America, who had been preparing many months. In consequence of which, an Order in Council was issued on 31st July, for an embargo on American vessels in our ports, and also for detaining them at sea. The next question now appears to be, whether, when that government hears of our repeal, they will revoke their declaration. On this momentous point the same sort of infatuation appears still to prevail in some degree. The writers who are instrumental thereto seem to forget, that two important points of difference, out of three, still remain at issue: that the declaration of war in America is a legislative act, and that to do away its effect another act must pass: that it is the people, and not merely the government of the United States, who have declared war; and that the people must be consulted before that declaration can be annulled. In short we are, contrary to all political prediction, at war with America; and before we can have peace again we must have a treaty. This is a question in which hundreds of thousands are interested, and relative to which we have felt it our duty to lend our aid towards dispelling deception, by stating the case distinctly and fairly.

Respecting the justness, policy, or probable success of the war, there is, in America, much difference of opinion. Various resolutions, and counter-resolutions, have been passed upon the subject. In an address for a public meeting, in the state of New York, are the words: "Disguise it as they may, one fact is too palpable for denial: the Rulers of our Government are compelling a free people to connect their destinies with those of the French Empire, and to unite in war with the Tyrant of Europe, for the destruction of England." - It may also be mentioned, that, while the House of Representatives of the State of Massachusetts have addressed their constituents in disapprobation of the war with England, the Senate of the same State have issued a counter-declaration in favour of the war.

The latest intelligence we have from America is by the *Bloodhound* gun-brig, which sailed from Annapolis, on the 24th of July, with Mr. Schaw the messenger, on board, who is returned to England, after delivering despatches to Mr. Baker, the British Secretary of Legation at Washington. At the departure of the *Bloodhound*, no intimation had been received at the seat of Government in America, of the revocation of the Orders in Council, or of any intention to that effect on the part of the British Government. We have still, therefore, to learn what effect may have been produced in America, by the arrival of the *Gleaner*, or any other vessel that took out accounts of the repeal of the Orders in Council. In the mean time, the Americans were making preparations for war according to their means, particularly in fitting out a number of privateers, by which they hoped to annoy the trade of this country. It was said to be a favourite scheme of the American Government to seduce British seamen who may happen to be made prisoners, to enter the American navy. For this purpose it had agents employed at the different ports where captured vessels were likely to arrive; and it is said, that upwards of 30 of the *Bloodhound*'s crew had been induced to desert.

Jamaica Fleet Safe

Great expectations were formed in America of Commodore Rodgers falling in with the Jamaica fleet, and capturing the greater part of it. H.M.S. *Thetis*, however, and the whole of the convoy, from Jamaica, arrived in the Downs on the 24th of August. On the 6th, Commodore Rodgers's squadron hove in sight of the convoy, upon which the *Aeolus*, the *Shannon*, and the *Belvidera* frigates, which were escorting it across the Atlantic, parted company, in chase of the enemy.

Admiral Warren Sails for American Waters

On the 14th of August, Admiral Sir J.B. Warren sailed from Portsmouth, in the *San Domingo*, 80, Captain Gill, for the coast of America. - The *Poitiers*, 74, Sir John Poo Beresford; *Sophie*, Captain Lockyer; *Magnet*, Captain Maurice; and *Mackarel* schooner, sailed with him. The *Tenedos*, Captain Hyde Parker; and the *Niemen* (frigates), Captain Pym, were to follow as soon as possible. - Sir John, we understand, is gone out with powers to negotiate, as well as to act offensively with the ships under his orders; but proposals of conciliation are, in the first instance, to be made. He goes direct to Halifax, and from thence to New York with his squadron. He was spoken with by the *Marlborough* packet, from Lisbon, on the 19th of August, in lat. 46°50'N. long. 8°25'W.

Victory in Spain

On the 22d of July, Lord Wellington obtained a signal victory over Marmont, in the neighbourhood of Salamanca. Marmont himself was severely wounded, and is since dead; in killed, wounded, and prisoners, the enemy lost from 16 to 18,000 men; and King Joseph, who had left Madrid, with a corps of 15,000 men, for the purpose of reinforcing Marmont, very narrowly effected his escape, by flight. For his services on this occasion, Lord Wellington has been raised to the dignity of a Marquis of the United Kingdom. - Sir Home Popham, for his exertions on the North coast of Spain, has been honoured with Lord Wellington's particular approbation.

Russia

There has been much severe fighting, but no general action, between the French and the Russians. At the date of the latest accounts (August 4th) the French had gone into quarters of refreshment, in consequence, as it was said, of the great heat of the weather. The army was then at Witepsk, in the direction of Moscow. - The English Admiral, Martin, remains at Riga, and, by his judicious disposition of the gun boats, &c. has contributed greatly to the defence of that City.

Naval Promotion

The birth-day of his Royal Highness the Prince Regent was distinguished by a Naval Promotion which then took place. . . .

From 'Naval Anecdotes.' XXVIII 193-204

State of New South Wales

Letters from New South Wales, of the 20th of May, state, that great improvements have taken place in that colony since the accession of Colonel Macquarrie to the government. The town of Sydney is laid out in regular street, and divided into districts, with headboroughs, sub-constables, watchmen, &c. Mr. D'Arcy Wentworth has been appointed to the head of the police. Five townships have been laid out on the Hawkesbury and George Rivers, to be called Windsor, Richmond, Wilberforce, Pitt, and Castlereagh. The roads from Sydney to Paramatta and Hawkesbury, which were scarcely passable, have been repaired, bridges thrown over the steams, and turnpikes established. No fears of a scarcity of provisions were to be apprehended, vast quantities of cattle being reared, and the storehouses filled with grain. - Butchers' meat was from 1s to 1s 3d per lb. and the supply equal to the consumption, without assistance from the mother country. Wool was to be their first staple commerce. Settlers of good character were furnished with live stock, from the government stores, in consideration of paying the value, in money or grain, in 18 months. The population of Sydney is estimated at 10,000, of which 8,000 have been sent from England as convicts. Governor Macquarrie was indefatigable in reforming public morals, and in checking drunkenness, concubinage, and other vices.

View of the entrance into Halifax Harbour, in Nova Scotia. Engraved by Wells,
from a drawing by Dominic Serres.
  Halifax, a town of Nova Scotia, in North America, is commodiously situated on
Chebucto Bay, 789 miles N.E. of New York, in longitude 63° 30' W. latitude 44° 45'
N. The harbour, of which we have presented an accurate view, is a very fine one,
with safe anchorage, and sufficiently large to shelter a squadron of ships throughout
the winter.
  The building of the town of Halifax commenced in the year 1749, at which period
three thousand families were transported from England, at the expense of
government, for the purpose of forming a settlement. . . . The climate is healthful,
but is somewhat subject to fogs; the winter is long and cold, and the summer is
intensely hot. [Plate 136]

Melancholy and Interesting Narrative –
An Officer's Account of the Action of the Swallow, off Frejus
June 16, 1812, with Two French Frigates

The affecting little story here related, is from one of the officers of the *Swallow*:
  In the gallant and sanguinary action . . . there was a seaman named Phelan, who
had his wife on board: she was stationed (as is usual when women are on board in time
of battle) to assist the surgeon in the care of the wounded. From the close manner in
which the *Swallow* engaged the enemy, yard-arm and yard-arm, the wounded, as may
be expected, were brought below very fast: amongst the rest, a messmate of her husband's
(consequently her own), who had received a musket-ball through the side. Her exertions
were used to console the poor fellow, who was in great agonies, and nearly breathing his
last: when, by some chance, she heard her husband was wounded, on deck: her anxiety

and already overpowered feelings could not one moment be restrained; she rushed instantly on deck, and received the wounded tar in her arms; he faintly raised his head to kiss her - she burst into a flood of tears, and told him to take courage, "all would yet be well," but scarcely pronounced the last syllable, when an ill-directed shot took her head off. The poor tar, who was closely wrapped in her arms, opened his eyes once more - then shut them for ever. What renders the circumstance the more affecting was, the poor creature had been only three weeks delivered of a fine boy, who was thus in a moment deprived of a father and a mother. As soon as the action subsided, "and nature began again to take its course," the feelings of the tars, who wanted no unnecessary incitement to stimulate them, were all interested for poor Tommy (for so was called); many said, and all feared, he must die; they all agreed he should have a hundred fathers, but what could be the substitute of a nurse and a mother? However, the mind of humanity soon discovered there was a Maltese goat on board, belonging to the officers, which gave an abundance of milk; and as there was no better expedient, she was resorted to, for the purpose of suckling the child, who, singular to say, is thriving and getting one of the finest little fellows in the world; and so tractable is his nurse, that even now she lies down when poor little Tommy is brought to be suckled by her. Phelan and his wife were sewed up in one hammock, and, it is needless to say, buried in one grave.

From the 'Naval History of the Present Year,' 1812
August-September. XXVIII 246-249

Wellington Rolls Back French Forces in Spain

The Marquis of Wellington's victory at Salamanca, announced at page 159, has produced very important results. His Lordship entered Madrid on the 12th of August, Joseph Buonaparte precipitately retreating towards Valencia. Having left a considerable force in Madrid, Lord Wellington was at Valladolid on the 8th of September, and the French had retreated in the direction of Burgos. - The siege of Cadiz, which had lasted upwards of two years and a half, was abandoned on the night of the 24th of August; Marshal Suchet leaving behind him a considerable quantity of stores, ammunition, &c. The allied troops, under the command of General Cruz and Colonel Skerrett, subsequently took the town of Seville by assault, sustaining scarcely any loss. Suchet continued his retreat. - Sir Home Popham continues his exertions on the north coast of Spain. . .

Russia

As the Russians continued to retreat, Buonaparte, according to the latest advices from the seat of war on the North, expected to approach near to Moscow about the 6th or 7th of September. The Russians had established lines in front of Moscow, and were also forming an entrenched camp at Mojaisk. - An armament, composed of 50,000 Swedes, and 40,000 Russians, was expected to sail from Gottenburg, about the 20th of September, for the purpose of acting upon the rear of the French army. . . .

East Indies

An expedition, under the command of Captain Owen, of the *Cornelia* (brother of Commodore Owen), sailed from Batavia on the 16th of February last, to take possession of Palembang, in the island of Banker.

Third Battalion for Marines

A third battalion of Royal Marines is to be immediately formed for actual service, the command of which, it is said, will be given to Major Timins. About 300 are arrived from Anholt, who are to constitute a part of the force. The island is now garrisoned by one of the garrison battalions. . . .

Honour Awarded – by Admiralty

Captain Talbot, of the *Victorious*, 74, has been presented by the Board of Admiralty with a gold medal, to be worn with his full uniform, suspended by a ribbon from the fourth button-hole, on the left side of the lapel, for his gallant conduct in capturing the *Rivoli*, of 80 guns, in the Adriatic Gulph. – We thought it belonged only to the Crown to bestow *honours* on its *Officers* and *servants*. . . .

Scheldt Sailors Sent to Join Army in Russia

A letter from on board H.M.S. *Royal Oak*, dated the 6th September off Flushing, contains the following particulars concerning the enemy's fleet in the Scheldt: – "The French fleet here consists of twenty-one sail of the line, nine frigates, and four brigs. We have seventeen sail of the line, five frigates, and four brigs. It is not expected that the enemy's fleet will attempt putting to sea this year, as there were lately 2,000 of their best sailors marched off to join their army on the frontiers of Russia." . . .

From 'Naval Anecdotes.' XXVIII 280-284

The Health of French Prisoners of War

As a proof of the good treatment of the prisoners of war in this country the following comparative statement of those sick and in health will be the best answer to the calumnies of the *Moniteur*:

Thursday, August 20 1812	*In health*	*Sick*
On board prison ships in Hamoaze	6,100	61
In Dartmoor dépôt	7,500	74

This small proportion of sick is less than the common average of persons not confined as prisoners of war. At Dartmouth dépôt, 500 prisoners, such as labourers, carpenters, smiths, &c. are allowed to work from sun-rise to sun-set; they are paid 4d and 6d per day, according to their abilities, and have each their daily rations of provisions, *viz.* a pound and a half of bread, half a pound of boiled beef, half a pound of cabbage, and a proportion of soup and small beer. They wear a tin plate in their caps, with the name of the trade they are employed in, and return every evening to the dépôt to be mustered.

Early in the month of September, the prisoners at Dartmoor exhibited alarming symptoms of riot. The alleged reason was, their being deprived of their pound and a half of soft bread, and having a pound and a half of biscuit in lieu thereof; the reason of which was, that the bakehouse and all the ovens had been destroyed by fire in the preceding week, and the contractors had not rebuilt them. In consequence of this turbulent behaviour, a detachment of the Cheshire Militia, and of the South-Gloucester

Regiment, was drawn up on the walls surrounding the prison; but, although they had loaded their pieces with ball, the prisoners appeared undaunted, and insulted them in the grossest terms. A sentinel on duty had his bayonet wrenched off his piece, yet nobly reserved his fire; an officer, however, followed the Frenchman, struck him over the shoulder with his sword, and brought off the bayonet. The Frenchmen even bared their breasts to the troops, and seemed regardless of danger. The number of prisoners is about 7,500; and so menacing was their conduct, that an express was sent off to Plymouth-dock, at eleven o'clock on a Sunday night, soliciting immediate assistance. Three pieces of artillery were in consequence sent off early on Monday morning; and on their arrival at the principal gate, the bars of which, of immense size, had been previously broken by stones hurled against them by the insurgents, they were placed in such directions as completely to command the whole of the prison. This had the desired effect, and order was restored. It is to be noticed, that the allowance of bread at which these men so indignantly spurned, is precisely the same as that which is served out to our own sailors and marines.

Americans Tar and Feather British Seamen

The *Tyne Mercury* presents the following statement relating to the man who, as described at a preceding page, was tarred and feathered, by the crew of the American frigate *Essex*, to which he belonged, for avowing himself an Englishman, and refusing to fight against his country:

"By a New York Paper of the 27th of June, it appears, that a seaman, named Erring, a native of this town, was tarred and feathered by the crew of the *Essex* frigate, Captain Porter, for refusing to fight against his country. This base conduct excited much indignation at New York, and a statement was published from the man's own deposition, to clear the city from any participation in the affair. The deposition states, that 'John Erring was born in Newcastle-upon-Tyne, England, that he has resided within the United States since 1800, and has never been naturalized; that on the 14th of October, 1811, he entered on board the *Essex*, and joined her at Norfolk; that Captain Porter, on the 26th of June, caused all hands to be piped on deck, to take the oath of allegiance to the United States, and gave them to understand, that any man who did not choose to do so should be discharged; that when deponent heard his name called, he told the captain, that being a British subject, he must refuse taking the oath; on which the captain spoke to the petty officers, and told them they must pass sentence on him; that they then put him in the petty launch which lay alongside the frigate, and there poured a bucket of tar over him, and then laid on a quantity of feathers, having first stripped him naked from the waist; that they then rowed him ashore stern foremost, and landed him. That he wandered about from street to street, in this condition, not knowing where to go, until Mr. Ford took him into his shop, to save him from the crowd then beginning to gather; that he stayed there until the police magistrate took him away, and put him in the city prison for protection, where he was cleansed and clothed. None of the citizens molested or insulted him. He says he had a protection, which he bought of a man in Salem, of the same name and description with himself, for 4s 6d which he got renewed at the Custom-house, Norfolk. - He says he gave as an additional reason to the captain, why he did not choose to fight against his own country, that if he should be taken prisoner he would certainly be hung.' - This story shall be closed by asking the reader a simple question: suppose the captain of an English frigate should suffer his men to tar and feather an American sailor in the port of London, because he would not join in a cruise to fight against his own country, what would you think and say of such an action?"

Proclamation on the Determination of Upper Canada to Resist American Attack

State Papers. XXVIII 301-303

The unprovoked declaration of war by the United States of America, against the United Kingdom of Great Britain and Ireland, and its dependencies, has been followed by the actual invasion of this province in a remote frontier of the western districts, by a detachment of the United States. The officer commanding that detachment has thought proper to invite his Majesty's subjects, not merely to a quiet and unresisting submission, but insults them with a call to seek voluntarily the protection of his government.

Without condescending to repeat the illiberal epithets, bestowed in this appeal of the American commander to the people of Upper Canada, on the administration of his Majesty, every inhabitant of the province is desired to seek the confutation of such indecent slander in the review of his own particular circumstances. Where is the Canadian subject, who can truly affirm to himself that he has been injured by the government in his person, his property, or his liberty? Where is to be found, in any part of the world, a growth so rapid in prosperity and wealth as this colony exhibits? Settled not thirty years by a band of veterans, exiled from their former possessions on account of their loyalty, not a descendant of these brave people is to be found, who, under the fostering liberality of their Sovereign, has not acquired a property and means of enjoyment, superior to what were possessed by their ancestors. This unequalled prosperity would not have been attained by the utmost liberality of the government, or the persevering industry of the people, had not the maritime power of the mother country secured to its colonies a safe access to every market where the produce of their labour was in request. The unavoidable and immediate consequence of a separation from Great Britain, must be the loss of this inestimable advantage, - and what is offered to you in exchange? To become a territory of the United States, and share with them that exclusion from the ocean which the policy of their government enforced; you are not even flattered with a participation of their boasted independence; and it is but too obvious, that once exchanged from the powerful protection of the United Kingdom, you must be re-annexed to the dominion of France, from which the provinces of Canada were wrested by the arms of Great Britain at a vast expense of blood and treasure, from no other motive than to relieve her ungrateful children from the oppression of a cruel neighbour; this restitution of Canada to the empire of France, was the stipulated reward for the aid afforded to the revolted colonies, now the United States; the debt is still due, and there can be no doubt but the pledge has been renewed as a consideration for commercial advantages, or rather for an expected relaxation in the tyranny of France over the commercial world. Are you prepared, inhabitants of Canada, to become willing subjects, or rather slaves, to the despot who rules the nations of Europe with a rod of iron? If not, arise in a body, exert your energies, co-operate cordially with the King's regular forces, to repel the invader, and do not give cause to your children, when groaning under the oppression of a foreign master, to reproach you with having too easily parted with the richest inheritance of this earth - a participation in the name, character, and freedom of Britain. The same spirit of justice which will make every reasonable allowance for the unsuccessful efforts of zeal and loyalty, will not fail to punish the defalcation of principle. Every Canadian freeholder is by deliberate choice bound, by the most solemn oaths, to defend the Monarchy as well as his own property; to shrink from that engagement is a treason not to be forgiven. Let no man suppose, that if in this unexpected struggle, his Majesty's arms should be compelled to yield to an overwhelming force, that the province will be eventually abandoned; the endeared relation of its first settlers, the intrinsic value of its commerce, and the pretensions of its powerful rival to re-possess the Canadas, are pledges that no peace will be established between the United States and Great Britain and Ireland, of which the restoration of these provinces does not make the most prominent condition.

Be not dismayed at the unjustifiable threat of the commander of the enemy's forces to refuse quarter, should an Indian appear in the ranks. The brave bands of natives which inhabit this colony, were, like his Majesty's subjects, punished for their zeal and fidelity, by the loss of their possessions in the late colonies, and rewarded by his Majesty with lands of superior value in this province.

The faith of the British Government has never yet been violated; they feel that the sod they inherit, is to them and their posterity protected from the base arts so frequently devised to over-reach their simplicity. By what new principle are they to be prohibited from defending their property? If their warfare, from being different to that of the white people, is more terrific to the enemy, let him retrace his steps - they seek him not, and cannot expect to find women and children in an invading army; but they are men, and have equal rights with all other men to defend themselves, and their property when invaded, - more especially when they find in the enemy's camp a ferocious and mortal foe, using the same warfare which the American commander affects to reprobate.

This inconsistent and unjustifiable threat of refusing quarter, for such a cause as being found in arms with a brother sufferer, in defence of invaded rights, must be exercised with the certain assurance of retaliation, not only in the limited operations of war on this part of the King's dominions, but on every quarter of the globe, for the national character of Britain is not less distinguished for humanity than retributive justice, which will consider the execution of this threat as deliberate murder, for which every subject of the offending power shall make expiation.

ISAAC BROCK, Major-General and President

Head Quarters, Fort George, July 22, 1812

By order of his Honour the President, J.B. GLEGG, Captain.
God save the King.

From the 'Naval History of the Present Year,' 1812
September-October. XXVIII 343-345

Reprisals Ordered Against United States

Ever since the 18th of June have the United States of America been at war against England. But it is only since the 13th of October that we have been placed in a corresponding attitude towards that commonwealth, by an order in council; wherein general reprisals are granted against the ships, &c. of the United States, except any vessels sailing under license or special release from embargo: and recognition is explicitly made of a pacific declaration which the English commander-in-chief of the American station has been previously authorized to issue to that government. The former document alluded to is given at length in another part of this volume.

[At a Court at Carlton House, 13 October 1812, His Royal Highness the Prince

Regent in Council ordered 'that general reprisals be granted against the ships, goods, and citizens of the United States of America.' (Vol. XXVIII, pp304-306)]

The Prince Regent's declaration of war shews in its concluding paragraph an anxious and laudable readiness to seize the first honourable means of reconciliation. Let a similar spirit animate a majority of the American people, and an opening will soon be afforded to accommodate all differences between us, and to save the American people from that worst of dangers, - French connection. Meanwhile, the first campaign of these lamentable hostilities has been marked by events on land and at sea each respectively diametrically opposite to the public expectation: at least certainly so to the speculations we had formed - One of the continental armies destined for the invasion of Canada, hardly passed the frontiers 'ere it found itself under the necessity of laying down its arms before the small English force that could be hastily assembled for the defence of that province, as much inferior upon paper as it proved itself superior in the field. And for which it has been rewarded in the person of its commanding officer, Major General Isaac Brock, who has been promptly and deservedly named an *extra* knight of the most honourable military order of the Bath. - "The cheap defence of nations!" The unlooked for reverse of the medal is the capture of one of our stoutest frigates, the *Guerriere*, by a single opponent of the same class of ship, commanded by a nephew, bearing the same name, of the invading general against whom the fortune of war proved so adverse in the back-settlements. Disasters of this kind are so rare in our naval annals, that it is not to be wondered at if such a result of a single-ship action, fought under such peculiar circumstances, should have aroused a more than common feeling. The character of the service is so far compromised by it, that we feel ourselves called upon to contribute our humble endeavours to make this event better understood than it seems hitherto to have been. The reader will perhaps attend to the following statement of one jealous of his country's honour.

Dealing With American 44-Gun Frigates

An English frigate, rated 38 guns, should undoubtedly (barring extraordinary accidents) cope successfully with a 44-gun ship of any nation: but if that 44, by advantage of wind and superior sailing, should be able to choose her position, and vary her distance as may suit her convenience, it becomes problematical whether an English 38 could conquer her adversary under such circumstances; which seem to have been those attending this action. If, in addition to these advantages, the enemy should have a much more numerous crew, and so superior a weight of metal as the American possessed; then we have little doubt, that unless some critical accident should befall the enemy, such as a shot in the rudder, or the loss of a mast, neither valour nor seamanship can obtain a victory. In this case, it is to be remembered, the accident last mentioned fell to the lot of the English frigate in a triple proportion. It will be found, by multiplying the number of guns on board the respective ships, by the weight of their shot, that at every broadside the *Constitution* discharged 777 lbs of metal, and that the *Guerriere* discharged but 526 lbs. The proportion is as 3 to 2: consequently, if the *Guerriere* had mounted 48 guns of one calibre, the *Constitution* was armed with the equivalent of 72 similar guns. With this overwhelming superiority of artillery, manned by a crew nearly double to that of the *Guerriere*, affording the means of employing a numerous musketry, with the power of choosing a position, which enabled her to apply her fire in the most destructive direction, it may well be asked whether there was a rational possibility of our countrymen effecting any thing, even if their masts had not gone so early. Had the *Constitution* been the English frigate, we are confident (without meaning to cast invidious national reflections, particularly in a case where the victors have displayed both bravery, and its usual concomitant, humanity), that in half an hour the *Guerriere* would have been ours, or at the bottom.

Such of our countrymen as are ill-informed of Yankee prowess should remember, that Captain Bingham defended a contemptible brig (*Little-belt*) against the sister ship of the *Constitution* (*President*). At the same time considering that these immense frigates are equal in weight of metal and complement of men to our two-decked fifties, being actually laid down on the keels of seventy-fours; the public must make up its mind to hear before long of some farther misfortunes, similar to that of the *Guerriere*, without feeling that any tarnish has been left upon the national Trident. Above all, let not any premature uncharitable censure be case upon an officer, who, like Captain [Richard] Dacres, has valiantly defended his flag, who, in yielding to irresistible strength, has presented no durable trophy to the enemy, and who has yet to justify his conduct before the proper tribunal.[4]

Buonaparte in Moscow! - Russians Torch City

Buonaparté, after much sanguinary fighting, entered Moscow, the ancient capital of Russia, on the 14th of September. It did not enter into the plan of the Russians, that Moscow should be taken; but, when they found that that event was inevitable, they adopted the most prompt and decisive means, for its destruction, by fire. Every thing having been removed, that time would permit, the city was set fire to in many places at the same moment; and, according to the French statement, about 1600 churches, 1000 palaces, and 30,000 sick and wounded Russians, in the hospitals, perished in the flames! The disappointment of the French ruler is, consequently, great; and his head quarters, should he remain at Moscow during the winter, will be far from commodious.

This dreadful calamity, instead of depressing the spirits, or striking a panic into the mind of, the Russian Emperor, seems to have inspired him with more determined resolution, to hold out to the last, and to reject every proposal for accommodation. - Buonaparte remained at Moscow on the 30th of September; at which time, the Russians were understood to hold very strong positions in its neighbourhood.

Sweden

The Swedish expedition, respecting which so much has been said, has not yet commenced its operations.

Proclamation,
Issued by Admiral Sir J B Warren, on his Arrival at Halifax. XXVIII 420

Whereas many British seamen are now in the U.S. of America and several of them by various means have been seduced to serve on board the American ships at war with the United Kingdom of Great Britain and Ireland, and others who have deserted from his Majesty's service have been forced to serve against their native country; I therefore call

---

4 Since this was prepared for the press, accounts have been received of the trial, and honourable acquittal of Captain Dacres. The loss of the *Guerriere*'s masts is attributed more to their *"defective state,"* than to the fire of the enemy.

The annexed plate exhibits a view of the Commissioner's House in the Naval Yard, Halifax. It was built during the peace before the last, while the present Deputy-Comptroller of the Navy was the the head of Halifax yard [Sir A.S. Hamond].

To the Editor of the Naval Chronicle
July 3, 1803
Sir, The enclosed view was taken from the moorings in Halifax harbour, south-east of the navy yard. The yard is on the western shore of this safe and capacious harbour, about a mile from the centre of the town of Halifax. Here our largest men of war heave down, shift their masts, and undergo every repair but that of docking, with ease and security. About a quarter of a mile higher up the harbour on the same shore, is the naval hospital, a large and commodious building. Alongside the yard, under the sheers, a line-of-battle ship is introduced, and in the fore-ground, the Commissioner's yacht, and an indian bark canoe.

Hoping the above sketch may be the means of your receiving more particular information on the subject, I am
Your humble servant,   "Half-Pay." Plate 145

upon all British seamen and others, in the present state of war, and before it may be too late to join the British colours, under which many of them have obtained glory and honour, to repair to any of his Majesty's provinces, garrisons, ships or vessels: and upon giving themselves up, and declaring their sense of error, I pledge myself to obtain for them H.R.H. the Prince Regent's free pardon and forgiveness; and to those who are willing to enter into the British navy, every encouragement they could wish. I trust that every British seaman will unite in supporting the noblest cause that ever called for the efforts of man, - the preservation of the liberties, independence, religion, and laws of all the remaining nations of the world, against the tyranny and despotism of France; and to defend the honour of the British flag upon the seas, at a moment when Providence has blessed her army with success in sustaining the cause of injured Spain and Portugal.
(signed) J.B. WARREN

Dated 5th of October, 1812

From the 'Naval History of the Present Year,' 1812
October-November. XXVIII 425-427

Buonaparte Retreats From Moscow

Buonaparte has abandoned Moscow, and retreated, with the whole of his army, towards Poland. The state of the war is generally considered as very favourable towards Russia.

Sidney Smith Second in Command in Mediterranean

The Mediterranean station has received the accession of a new second-in-command by the arrival of Vice-admiral Sir Sidney Smith, who joined the squadron cruising off Toulon early in October, and shifted his flag from the *Tremendous* to the *Hibernia*. . . .

Plymouth Breakwater in Forwardness

As our navy is the dearest object of national solicitude, whatever tends to its preservation and safety merits approbation, not only upon principles of patriotism, but from motives of affection to those who are more immediately to derive benefit from thence. It is with pleasure, therefore, that we announce the promising state of the breakwater in Plymouth harbour, and assign the small portion of honour which it is in our power to confer, on all those whose skill or industry have contributed in their respective stations to the advancement of so useful an undertaking. The Navy Board is taking the most effectual means for the completion of this great national work; and by the zeal and indefatigable exertions of Mr. Whidbey, to whom the superintendence thereof is confided, the proposed pier-head has already been raised ten feet from the bottom. We are happy, also, to be in some degree able to announce the ultimate success of the plan, by the proofs which it has already afforded of its efficacy; for, during the late tremendous gales of wind, it was observed from shore, that the structure, even in its present state, broke the force of the sea; so that the ships of war, which were moored nearest to it, rode out the gales much more easily than those which were farther in shore. A correspondent, however, has suggested the propriety of displaying floating lights, every dark night, along the line of this undertaking.

The Prince Regent's Speech on the Opening of the New Parliament

November 30, 1812
State Papers. XXVIII 487-491

My Lords, and Gentlemen
It is with the deepest concern that I am obliged to announce to you, at the opening of parliament, the continuance of his Majesty's lamented indisposition, and the diminution of the hopes which I have most anxiously entertained of his recovery.

The situation of public affairs has induced me to take the earliest opportunity of meeting you after the late elections. I am persuaded you will cordially participate in the satisfaction which I derive from the improvement of our prospects during the course of the present year.

The valour and intrepidity displayed by his Majesty's forces, and those of his allies, in the Peninsula, on so many occasions during this campaign, and the consummate skill

PLYMOUTH SOUND with the Projected BREAK-WATER

Reduced from the Chart ordered by the HOUSE OF COMMONS to be printed 1812.

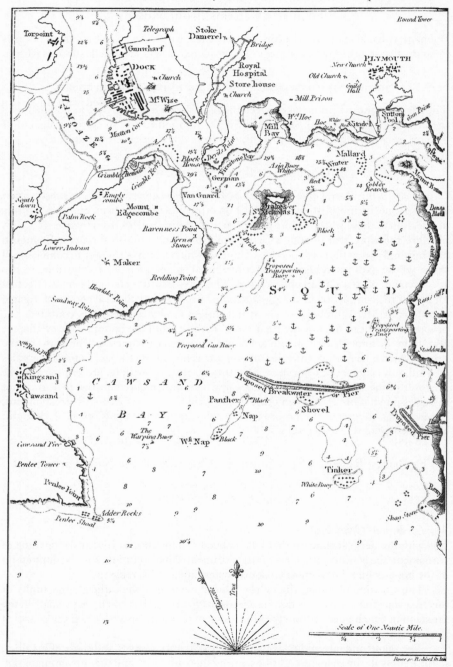

and judgment with which the operations have been conducted by General the Marquess of Wellington, have led to consequences of the utmost importance to the common cause.

By the transferring the war into the interior of Spain, and by the glorious and ever-memorable victory obtained at Salamanca, he has compelled the enemy to raise the siege of Cadiz; and the southern provinces of that kingdom have been delivered from the power and arms of France.

Although I cannot but regret that the efforts of the enemy, combined with a view to one great operation, have rendered it necessary to withdraw from the siege of Burgos, and to evacuate Madrid, for the purpose of concentrating the main body of the allied forces; these efforts of the enemy have, nevertheless, been attended with important sacrifices on their part, which must materially contribute to extend the resources, and facilitate the exertions of the Spanish nation.

I am confident I may rely on your determination to continue to afford every aid in support of a contest which has first given to the continent of Europe the example of persevering and successful resistance to the power of France, and on which not only the independence of the nations of the peninsula, but the best interests of his Majesty's dominions, essentially depend.

I have great pleasure in communicating to you, that the relations of peace and friendship have been restored between his Majesty and the Courts of St. Petersburg and Stockholm.

I have directed copies of the treaties to be laid before you.

In a contest for his own sovereign rights, and for the independence of his dominions, the Emperor of Russia has had to oppose a large proportion of the military power of the French government, assisted by its allies, and by the tributary states dependent upon it.

The resistance which he has opposed to so formidable a combination, cannot fail to excite sentiments of lasting admiration.

By his own magnanimity and perseverance, by the zeal and disinterestedness of all ranks of his subjects, and by the gallantry, firmness, and intrepidity of his forces, the presumptuous expectations of the enemy have been signally disappointed.

The enthusiasm of the Russian nation has increased with the difficulties of the contest, and with the dangers with which they were surrounded. They have submitted to sacrifices of which there are few examples in the history of the world; and I indulge the confident hope, that the determined perseverance of his Imperial Majesty will be crowned with ultimate success; and that this contest, in its results, will have the effect of establishing, upon a foundation never to be shaken, the security and independence of the Russian empire.

The proof of confidence which I have received from his Imperial Majesty in the measure which he has adopted of sending his fleets to the ports of this country, is in the highest degree gratifying to me; and his Imperial Majesty may most fully rely on my fixed determination to afford him the most cordial support in the great contest in which he is engaged.

I have the satisfaction further to acquaint you, that I have concluded a treaty with his Sicilian Majesty, supplementary to the treaties of 1808 and 1809.

As soon as the ratifications shall have been exchanged, I will direct a copy of this treaty to be laid before you.

Plymouth Sound, with the projected Break water. Reduced by Rowe, from the Chart ordered by the House of Commons to be printed, 1812. Plate 372

My object has been to provide for the more extensive application of the military force of the Sicilian government to offensive operations; a measure which, combined with the liberal and enlightened principles which happily prevail in the councils of his Sicilian Majesty, is calculated, I trust, to augment his power and resources, and at the same time to render them essentially serviceable to the common cause.

The declaration of war by the government of the United States of America, was made under circumstances which might have afforded a reasonable expectation that the amicable relations between the two nations would not long be interrupted. It is with sincere regret that I am obliged to acquaint you, that the conduct and pretensions of that government have hitherto prevented the conclusion of any pacific arrangement.

Their measures of hostility have been principally directed against the adjoining British provinces, and every effort has been made to seduce the inhabitants of them from their allegiance to his Majesty.

The proofs, however, which I have received of loyalty and attachment from his Majesty's subjects in North America, are highly satisfactory.

The attempts of the enemy to invade upper Canada have not only proved abortive, but by the judicious arrangements of the governor-general and by the skill and decision with which the military operations have been conducted, the forces of the enemy assembled for that purpose in one quarter, have been compelled to capitulate, and in another have been completely defeated.

My best efforts are not wanting for the restoration of the relations of peace and amity between the two countries; but until this object can be obtained without sacrificing the maritime rights of Great Britain, I shall rely upon your cordial support in a vigorous prosecution of the war.

From the 'Naval History of the Present Year,' 1812
November–December. XXVIII 507-509

Chesapeake Blockade

The *London Gazette* of December 26 contained an official notice, that the necessary measures had been taken, by the command of his Royal Highness the Prince Regent, for the blockade of the ports and harbours of the bay of the Chesapeake, and of the river Delaware . . .

Macedonian Captured

It is our painful duty to announce the capture of another British frigate by the Americans. In latitude 29° N. longitude 29° 30' W. the *Macedonian*, of 38 guns and 300 men, commanded by Captain Carden, was fallen in with, on the 25th of October, by the *United States*, American frigate, of 55 guns and 478 picked men, commanded by Commodore Decatur; and, after a sanguinary action of two hours and ten minutes, in which she had 36 men killed, 36 severely, and 32 slightly wounded, she was compelled to surrender.

Frolic Retaken

H.M.'s brig *Frolic*, which was captured by the American sloop of war *Wasp*, has been retaken, together with the *Wasp*, by H.M.S. *Poitiers*.

Baltic Fleet News

It is with regret we state the loss of the *Belette* sloop of war, Captain Sloane. She was appointed to lead the Russian ships through the S.W. passage of Anholt, when she unfortunately got on shore on the rocks, off the Island of Lessoe (in the Kattegat), and all the officers and crew perished, except five men.

By letters received from the masters of vessels bound for this country, but detained at Matwyck for want of convoy, we learn, that the admiral commanding the last division of the Russian fleet, and the minister of marine, had both agreed that the whole of the homeward-bound vessels remaining in Kronstadt should be convoyed home by the former. The captain of H.M.S. *Snipe*, however, on learning this circumstance, positively forbade any of these vessels to avail themselves of the protection thus generously conceded. They are in consequence wintering at Matwyck and Karlscrona. . . .

Fir Frigates to be Built

Government have ordered twelve new frigates to be immediately built of fir timber; some to be ready in twelve months, and named as follows: *Hebros* [*Hebrus*], *Pactolus*, *Eurydanus* [*Eridanus*], *Niger, Tagus, Tiber*, &c. &c. Of these, five are to be built at Blackwall, one at Deptford, one at Northfleet, one at the Isle of Wight, and two at Limehouse.

1812 - USS Constitution and HMS Guerriere

THIS WAS THE FIRST ENGAGEMENT between a British frigate and an American super-frigate, the USS *Constitution*. Built on the hull of a large third rate, or second rate, and carrying nearly double the armament and number of men as were the complement of British frigates of the larger size, the *Constitution* was quite a shock to the Royal Navy.

Admiral Sawyer's Report
Letters on Service
Admiralty Office, 10 October 1812. XXVIII 346-348

Copy of a Letter from Vice-admiral Sawyer to John Wilson Croker, Esq. dated on board H.M.S. Africa, at Halifax, the 15th September 1812

Sir, It is with extreme concern I have to request you will be pleased to lay before the Lords Commissioners of the Admiralty the enclosed copy of a letter from Captain Dacres, of H.M. late ship *Guerriere*, giving an account of his having sustained a close action, of near two hours, on the 19th ult. with the American frigate *Constitution*, of very superior force, both in guns and men (of the latter almost double), when the *Guerriere* being totally dismasted, she rolled so deep as to render all further efforts at the guns unavailing, and it became a duty to spare the lives of the remaining part of her valuable crew, by hauling down her colours. The masts fell over the side from which she was about to be engaged, in a very favourable position for raking by the enemy. A few hours after she was in possession of the enemy, it was found impossible to keep her above water; she was, therefore, set fire to and abandoned, which I hope will satisfy their Lordships she was defended to the last.

Captain Dacres has fully detailed the particulars of the action, as well as the very gallant conduct of, and the support he received from, the whole of his officers and ship's company, and I am happy to hear he is, with the rest of the wounded, doing well; they have been treated with the greatest humanity and kindness, and an exchange having been agreed on, I am in daily expectation of their arrival here. ...

I have the honour to be,

H. SAWYER, Vice Admiral

[Unfortunately it has not been possible to include Captain Dacres' letter, nor other officers' letters, describing a hard fought but unequal action. The only matter of tactical interest they provided was the account of the early loss of *Guerriere*'s mizzen mast, which made her unmanageable. (Vol. XXVIII, pp370-371, 426)]

Court Martial of Captain Richard Dacres, Formerly of HMS Guerriere [XXVIII 422-424]

Captain Dacres' Defence

Mr. President and Gentlemen of the Court. - By my letter to Admiral Sawyer, and the narrative of the principal officers, I trust that you will be satisfied that every exertion was used in defending the ship, as long as there was the smallest prospect of resistance being of any use. In my letter, where I mention the boarders being called, it was my intention, after having driven back the enemy, to have boarded in return; and in consequence I ordered down the first lieutenant on the main-deck to send every body up from the guns; but finding his deck filled with men, and every preparation made to receive us, it would have been almost impossible to succeed. I ordered the men down to their quarters, and desired Mr. Kent to direct part of his attention to the main-deck, the lieutenant being killed. The main-mast fell without being struck by a single shot, the heart of the mast being decayed, and it was carried away solely by the weight of the foremast; and though every thing was done, we could not succeed in getting the ship under command; and on the enemy wearing round to take us, without our being able to make any resistance, and after having used every exertion, to the best of my abilities, I found myself obliged to order the colours to be struck; which nothing but the unmanageable state of the ship (she lying a perfect wreck) could ever have induced me to do, conceiving it was my duty not to sacrifice uselessly the lives of the men, without any prospect of success, or of benefit to their country.

On the larboard side about thirty shot had taken effect; about five sheets of copper down, and the mizen-mast had knocked a large hole under her starboard counter, and she was so completely shattered, that the enemy found it impossible to refit her sufficiently to attempt carrying her into port, and they set fire to her as soon as they got the wounded out. What considerably weakened my quarters was, permitting the Americans belonging to the ship to quit their quarters, on the enemy hoisting the colours of that nation, which, though it deprived me of the men, I thought it was my duty.

I felt much shocked, when on board the *Constitution*, to find a large proportion of this ship's company British seamen, and many of whom I recognised as having been foremost in the attempt to board.

Notwithstanding the unlucky issue of the affair, such confidence have I in the exertions of the officers and men who belonged to the *Guerriere*, and I am so aware that the success of my opponent was owing to fortune, that it is my earnest wish, and would be the happiest period of my life, to be once more opposed to the *Constitution*, with them under my command, in a frigate of similar force to the *Guerriere*.

I cannot help noticing, that the attachment of the ship's company in general to the service of their King and Country, reflects on them the highest credit; for though every art was used to encourage them to desert, and to inveigle them in to the American service, by high bounties and great promises, by the American officers, in direct contradiction to the declaration to me, that they did not wish such a thing; only eight

Englishmen have remained behind, two only of which number have volunteered for their service. . . .

[Verdict:] The Court do, therefore, unanimously and honourably acquit the said Captain Dacres, the officers, and crew, of H.M.'s late ship *La Guerriere*; and they are hereby honourably acquitted accordingly. - The Court, at the same time, feel themselves called upon to express the high sense they entertain of the conduct of the ship's company in general, when prisoners, but more particularly of those who withstood the attempts made to shake their loyalty, by offering them high bribes to enter into the land and sea service of the enemy, and they will represent their merit to the commander-in-chief.

From 'Correspondence.' XXVIII 378-379; XXIX 12-13

The Government's Obligation to Provide for Returning British Seamen

"FABER" to the Editor
Dover, 2 November, 1812
On the 26th of October there issued from the court at Carlton-house, a proclamation of the Prince-regent, declaring the punishment of death, and all other pains and penalties of high treason and piracy, against all British mariners, &c. who shall enter, or serve, or be found on board any ship or vessel belonging to the United States of America. There is no doubt of this being the law of the land, and applicable to existing circumstances. But on ruminating what I had just been reading, connected with recent trials for similar offences detected at the Isle of France, certain doubts and queries arose in my mind, which I should wish to have settled through the medium of your impartial publication.

It is taken for granted, that if a British subject, and his property, were in the hands of the enemy, our laws would hold him guilty, if to preserve it he consented to serve against his native country; to which I do not make objection: - but I ask in what manner a subject so situated ought to be treated on his return home, supposing he had contrived to escape, after sacrificing all he possessed sooner than contract any such dishonourable or illegal engagement? and whether, if he applied to government for aid, the first question would not be, are you not an emigrant? We know the consequence of the answer to that question: still we expect loyalty and attachment, in short, every thing on one side, and nothing on the other.

The American Super-Frigates

"R" to the Editor, October 13, 1812
Mr. Editor,   The loss of H.M. frigate *Guerriere* is no doubt much to be regretted; but she is not in possession of the enemy, she is not a trophy of victory - not a tarnish is to be found upon the trident of the seas - it was nobly wielded by Captain Dacres and his bold companions in arms, and if they did not conquer, they nobly fell. Why, then, should a certain newspaper trace such a sentiment as the following: "We do not say Captain Dacres deserves to be punished; but this we dare assert, that there are captains in the British navy, who would rather have gone to the bottom, than have struck their colours." Is the editor of the paper alluded to ignorant of the force of the *Constitution*? Does he know that she is as heavy as an English sixty-four? Has any person informed him that the upper deck of the *Constitution* is flush fore and aft, and that she thereby

mounts a double tier of guns, like a line-of-battle ship? Does he not feel, does his conscience not tell him, that when a ship has been fought to the last extremity, until resistance is impotent, and perseverance vain, that the captain is responsible for the lives of his crew; and that had Captain Dacres obstinately persisted longer, the blood of every forfeited life would have been upon him, and their valuable services would have been taken from their country, to deck the funeral of the commander? - Had the *Guerriere* gone down from such obstinacy as the editor alluded to requires, Captain Dacres would have been an executioner. The man who gives no quarter to the wounded, is not worse, than the man, who, to add to his posthumous fame, sacrifices the lives of his vanquished followers. The British admiral's letter is quite satisfactory. But I would advise the said editor to speculate in a privateer; or, if he has a strong imagination, let him fancy himself commanding a frigate in battle - a much larger ship bears down upon him, he fights nobly - but the die of fortune turns against him. He is overpowered by the strength of his antagonist; he is wounded and in agony; yet he fights bravely on; he struggles to the last; resistance becomes incapable of exertion, and hope expires; why then should he not save the remaining lives of his defeated companions; why should he not do as the late captain of the late *Guerriere* has done, surrender his wreck to the flames of irresistible strength? I am not acquainted with Captain Dacres, or his officers, but in justice to the British navy and its courageous men, I request this letter may be inserted in the *Naval Chronicle.*

Operational Deployments Questioned

"Oceanus" to the Editor, December 1. 1812
Mr. Editor, Though I am convinced that clever men are selected to form the board of Admiralty, I am at a loss to determine their motive for not employing our largest frigates on the American station. Had common precaution been taken, previously to the declaration of war against us, we should, in all probability, have been spared the mortification that was felt at the loss of the *Guerriere.* The size and force of the American frigates, with the great number of men they carry, were made known to government long before any difference took place between the two countries:[1] why, therefore, did they not provide against the chance of our ships falling a prey to the enemy, from inferiority of force? and why, now the misfortune has occurred, do they not endeavour to prevent it in future? It is true, that, after the *Little Belt*'s action with the *President*, the *Spartan* and *Shannon* were sent out to relieve two ships of smaller class; but either of these ships, with eighteen-pounders and an inferiority of men, is as little able to sustain an action with an American frigate, as the *Guerriere* was.

Commodore Rodgers' Cruise XXVIII 384-386

Mr. Editor, The American *National Intelligencer* has furnished the following *Extract from the Journal of Commodore Rodgers.* "T"
June 23d - Pleasant breezes from N.W. to W.S.W. at three A.M. spoke an American

---

1 Twelve years ago, regular information was given to the Admiralty Board, that the Americans, with great nautical skill, were about to build frigates of the size and form which now annoy us. And about the same time, an excellent officer, Admiral Blanket, shewed in a clear and well-written paper, that the frigates of our own size were under-manned - for there never was a sufficient complement to allow of number to be stationed in the tops, &c. with small arms and for boarding.

brig from Madeira, bound to New York, the master of which informed me, that four days before, in lat. 36° long. 67° he passed a fleet of British merchantmen, under convoy of a frigate and a brig, steering to eastward: I now perceived, that this was the convoy of which I had received intelligence, prior to leaving New York, and shaped our course east in pursuit of them. At six A.M. Nantucket Shoal, bearing N.E. distant 35 miles, saw a large sail in N.E. standing to S.W. which was soon discovered to be a frigate. The signal was made for a general chase, when the several vessels of the squadron took in their studding sails, and made all sail by the wind, on the starboard tack, in pursuit. At a quarter before seven, the chase tacked, made all sail, and stood from us, by the wind on the same tack. At half past eight, he made signals, when, perceiving we were coming up with him, he edged away a point or thereabouts, and set his top-gallant studding sails. At 11, cleared ship for action, in the expectation that we would soon be up with the chase; the breeze about this time, however, began to incline more to the westward, and became lighter, which I soon discovered was comparatively an advantage to our opponent. At a quarter past one P.M. the chase hoisted English colours. At two, the wind veered to the W.S.W., and became lighter. At 20 minutes past four, having got within gun-shot of the enemy, when, perceiving that he was training his chase guns, and in the act, as I supposed, of firing, that the breeze was decreasing, and we now sailed so nearly alike, that to afford him an opportunity of doing the first injury to our spars and rigging, would be to enable him to effect his escape, I gave orders to commence a fire with the bow-chase guns, at his spars and rigging, in the hope of crippling one or the other, so far as to enable us to get alongside. The fire from our bow-chase guns he instantly returned, with those of his stern, which was now kept up by both ships without intermission, until 30 minutes past four P.M. when one of the *President*'s chase guns burst, and killed and wounded sixteen persons, among the latter myself. This was not, however, the most serious injury, as, by the bursting of the gun, and the explosion of the passing box, from which it was served with powder, both the main and the forecastle decks, near the gun, were so much shattered, as to prevent the use of the chase gun, on that side, for some time. Our main-deck guns being single shotted, I now gave orders, to put our helm to starboard, and fire the starboard broadside, in the expectation of disabling some of her spars, but did not succeed, although I could discover that his rigging had sustained considerable damage, and that he had received some injury in the stern.

I now endeavoured, by altering course half a point to port, and wetting our sails, to gain a more effectual position on his starboard quarter, but soon found myself losing ground. After this, a similar attempt was made at his larboard quarter, but without any better success, as the wind, at this time, being very light, and both sailing so nearly alike, that, by making an angle of only half a point from the course he steered, enabled him to augment his distance. No hope was now left of bringing him to close action, except that derived from being to windward, and the expectation the breeze might favour us first. I accordingly gave orders to steer directly after him, and to keep our bow-chase-guns playing on his spars and rigging, until our broadside would more effectually reach him. At five, finding from the advantage his stern guns gave him, that he had done considerable injury to our sails and rigging, and being within point blank shot, I gave orders, to put the helm to starboard, and fire our main deck guns; this broadside did some farther damage to his rigging, and I could perceive that his foretop-sail-yard was wounded, but the sea was so very smooth, and the wind so light, that the injury done was not such as materially to affect his sailing. After this broadside, our course was instantly renewed in his wake, under a galling fire from his stern-chase guns, directed at our spars and rigging, and continued until half past six; at which time, being within reach of his grape, and finding our sails, rigging, and several spars, particularly the main-yard, which had little to support it except the lifts and braces, much disabled, I again gave orders to luff across his stern, and gave him a couple of broadsides.

The enemy, at this time, finding himself so hard pressed, and seeing, while in the act of firing, our head-sails to the left, and supposing the ship had in a measure, lost the effect of her helm, he gave a broad yaw, with the intention of bringing his broadside to bear; finding the *President*, however, answered her helm too quick for this purpose, he immediately reassumed his course, and precipitately fired his four after main-deck guns on the starboard side, although they did not bear upon us at the time, by 25 or 30 degrees, and he now commenced lightening his ship, by throwing overboard all his boats, waste anchors, &c. and by this means, was enabled, by a quarter before seven, to get so far ahead, as to prevent our bow-chase guns doing execution, and I now perceived, with more mortification than words can express, that there was little or no chance left of getting within gun-shot of the enemy again. Under every disadvantage of disabled spars, sails, and rigging, I, however, continued the chase with all the sail we could set until half-past eleven, P.M. when perceiving he had gained upwards of three miles, and not the slightest prospect left of coming up with him, I gave up the pursuit, and made the signal to the other ships as they came up to do the same.

During the first of the chase, while the breeze was fresh and sailing by the wind, I thought the whole of the squadron gained upon the enemy. It was soon discoverable, however, the advantage he acquired by sailing large, and this I conceived, he must have derived in so great a degree by starting his water, as I could perceive upwards of an hour before we came within gun-shot, water running out of his scuppers.

While in chase, it was difficult to determine whether our own situation, or that of the other vessels of the squadron, was the most unpleasant. The superior sailing of the *President* was not such, off the wind, as to enable us to get upon the broadside of the enemy. The situation of the others was not less irksome, as not even the headmost, which was the *Congress*, was able at any time, to get within less than two gun-shots distant, and even at that but for a very little time.

1812 – Defeat of
HMS Macedonian

ON 25 OCTOBER 1812 the 38-gun frigate *Macedonian* encountered the USS *United States* in latitude 29° north and longitude 29°30' west. The only advantage possessed by the *Macedonian* lay in point of speed, but Captain Carden had not heard of the loss of the *Guerriere*, and consequently underestimated his enemy. With an armament and crew nearly double that of the British ship, Commodore Decatur easily won the subsequent engagement. Captain Carden's service letter reporting the loss of the *Macedonian* was published in Vol. XXIX, pp77-79. Here we include the verdict of the court martial on his engagement.

Marine Law XXX 159

A court martial assembled on board the *San Domingo*, at Bermuda, on the 27th, and continued by adjournment to the 31st of May [1813], to inquire into the conduct of Captain John Surman Carden, the officers and crew, of H.M. late ship *Macedonian*, on the capture of that ship by the American ship *United States*, and to try them for the same. The Court have most strictly investigated (during its sitting of four days) every circumstance, and examined the different officers, and many of the crew, and having very deliberately and maturely weighed and considered the whole and every part thereof, was of opinion,

"That, previous to the commencement of the action, from an over anxiety to keep the weather gauge, an opportunity was lost of closing with the enemy; and that, owing to this circumstance, the *Macedonian* was unable to bring the *United States* to close action, until she had received material damage; but as it does not appear that this omission originated in the *most distant wish* to keep back from the engagement, the Court is of opinion, that Captain John Surman Carden, the officers, and ship's company, *in every instance throughout the action, behaved with the firmest and most determined courage, resolution, and coolness*, and that the colours of the *Macedonian* were not struck until she was unable to make farther resistance. The Court does, therefore, most honourably acquit Captain Surman Carden, the officers and remaining company of his Majesty's late ship *Macedonian*; and they are most honourably acquitted accordingly.

The Court observed, it could not dismiss Captain Carden, without expressing its

118

admiration of the uniform testimony which has been borne to his gallantry and good conduct throughout the action; nor Lieutenant David Hope, senior lieutenant, the other officers, and ship's company, without expressing the highest approbation of the support given by him and them to their captain, and of their courage and steadiness during the contest with an enemy of very superior force; a circumstance, that whilst it reflects high honour on them, does no less credit and honour to the discipline of the *Macedonian*. The Court also feels it a gratifying duty to express its admiration of the fidelity to their allegiance, and attachment to their King and Country, which the remaining crew appear to have manifested, in resisting the various insidious and repeated temptations which the enemy held out to seduce them from their duty, and which cannot fail to be fully appreciated."

Commodore HENRY HOTHAM, Captain of the Fleet, President

The President, on returning Captain Carden his sword, in a most elegant and animated speech, highly extolled the distinguished valour displayed by Captain Carden, and concluded by saying, that whenever the honour of the British flag should be entrusted to him, he would crown it with additional honours.

1813 - Fleet Strengths

Review of the Maritime Forces of Europe ^{XXIX 32-38}

The subjoined estimate will, it is believed, be found to present a tolerably correct view
of the naval force of the respective powers to which it relates:

The British Navy

Abstract of the British naval force up to the 1st of January, 1813: - At sea, 79 ships of
the line; nine from 50 to 44 guns; 122 frigates; 77 sloops and yachts; four bombs, &c;
161 brigs; 54 cutters; 52 schooners, &c. In port and fitting - 39 of the line; 11 from 50
to 44 guns; 29 frigates: 18 sloops; four bombs, &c.: 36 brigs; six cutters; 11 schooners,
&c. Hospital-ships, prison-ships, &c. - 28 of the line; 2 from 50 to 44; two frigates; one
yacht. - Ordinary and repairing for service, 77 of the line; 10 from 50 to 44 guns; 70
frigates; 37 sloops; three bombs; 11 brigs; one cutter; two schooners. - Building, 29 of
the line; four from 50 to 44 guns; 15 frigates; five sloops, &c; three brigs.

Total at sea	536
- in commission	740
- building, repairing, and in ordinary	267
Grand Total	1,545

The Russian Navy

The navy has long been an object of peculiar attention in Russia; and, during the reign
of the Emperor Alexander, a number of important alterations and improvements have
been made in the sea-service.

The mode of balloting for the promotion of officers, introduced by Peter the First,
has been modified by an ordinance which limits it to the ranks from lieutenant to rear-
admiral. By this alteration the minister has acquired the means of recompensing
extraordinary merit.

A school for pilots has been created, and their condition on board has been
meliorated; that of the sailors has also been greatly improved. They are divided into
two classes; that of recruits, and that of men who have already served. For recruiting,
those provincial governments are selected which have many lakes, great rivers, or which
border on the sea. The age of recruits was fixed at twenty-five years; but since 1803,
boys from twelve to twenty, are received in the provinces of the Baltic.

The above engraving, from a drawing by Pocock, represents a view of the *Lady Banks*, a ship built for the East Country Trade, at Boston, Lincolnshire, taken from a sawpit in the builder's yard. Boston steeple in the distance. From a drawing by W. Brand, Esq. of Boston. [sic] Plate 6

The number of marines on board has been diminished, and that of sailors augmented. The corps of marine cadets has undergone several improvements. Much attention has been paid to the construction of ships after models from England. The Admiralty is engaged in procuring translations into the Russian language, of the best works on the nautical art, and in the compilation of manuals for learners. The emperor has approved of a committee for drawing up a system of nautical sciences; and very considerable progress has been made in the work. The Marine Geography has been some time published. The organization of the Admiralty has been simplified, and the officers and sailors have received permission to enter into the merchant service when their services in the Imperial navy can be dispensed with.

The port of Kronstadt, which is the centre of the Baltic fleet, has been improved. At Revel, the old harbour is left for commerce, and a new one is constructing for twenty-five ships of the line. This port, as well as Riga, has been strongly fortified on the land side, since the invasion of Russia by the French. On the Black Sea, ships of war are constructed at Kerson and Nicolaief, fitted out at Orshakoff, and stationed at Achtiar or Sebastopol. Ships of the line lie in safety in the road of Odessa. There are usually four admirals under the minister of marine, who have the inspection of the naval ports.

The following is an abstract of a late report made by the Russian minister of marine, of the amount and disposition of the Imperial navy:

1st,   The great fleet of the Baltic, consisting of 59 vessels, and
          carrying 2,260 guns, *viz.*

20 ships of the line	1,518 guns
14 frigates	426
6 cutters	130
19 smaller vessels	116

2nd,   Baltic galley fleet, 41 sail, 705 guns, *viz.*

20 galleys	220 guns
25 batteries	160
81 gun-boats	162
63 yawls	163

3d,   Black Sea fleet, 41 sail, 1,225 guns

12 ships of the line	918 guns
4 frigates	162
7 brigs	54
18 small armed vessels	91

4th,   Rowing fleet of the Black Sea, 40 gun-boats, carrying 52 guns,
          and 30 falconets.

5th,   The flotilla in the Caspian Sea, 6 vessels, carrying 70 guns.

6th,   The flotilla of Ochozk, on the coast of Siberia, 11 vessels,
          carrying 36 guns.

7th,   At sea, 11 ships of the line, carrying 70 guns, the precise
          stations of which are not mentioned, neither are the smaller
          vessels particularized.[1]

8th,   Building, 10 sail of the line.

Total -   53 sail of the line; 34 frigates; 59 cutters, brigs, &c; smaller
          vessels 226, carrying in all 4,428 pieces of cannon.

In this estimate are included imperial ships of every class and condition, from a first-rate to a gun-brig; those that are building, under repair, and laid up in ordinary as unserviceable, as well as those that are in commission and fit for immediate service. Several of the ships that remain in the Baltic, and, we have heard, all that were under the command of Admiral Seniavin, in the Tagus, and which were by convention delivered up to Admiral Sir C. Cotton, and by him sent to England, to remain as a deposit, are fit only for condemnation. The fleet that arrived at Chatham, about the middle of December, 1812, are in a state of efficiency. With such repairs as might be deemed requisite, and the transfer of a competent number of hands from the smaller vessels, Russia might have in a few weeks 36 sail of the line, and 23 frigates, ready for sea, and fit for service on any station, *viz.*

1 The Russian fleet, consisting of nine sail of the line, and one frigate, under Admiral Seniavin, in the Tagus, and subsequently sent to England by Admiral Sir C. Cotton, is probably part of the ships here stated to be "at sea", yet it is not easy to reconcile this conjecture with the aggregate number of guns on board eleven ships of the line. *Vide* N.C. XX 245, 246, 364, 367; XXI 234 to 242; XXVII 386.

At Chatham	15 sail of the line	6 frigates
In the Baltic	11	7
In the Black Sea	10	10
	36	23

The Swedish Navy

The Swedish fleet consists of 12 sail of the line, eight frigates, besides cutters, gunboats, &c and there are two ships of the line and three frigates building.

The Navy of Portugal

The Portuguese were, at one period, esteemed the most adventurous and scientific navigators in the world, and their navy formidable; but the incursions of the French, which have desolated the Peninsula, and forced the ancient family of Braganza to seek an asylum in their trans-atlantic dominions, have proved equally injurious to the fleet and maritime interests of our faithful and ancient ally. The subjoined is the latest and most correct list of the navy of Portugal that we have been able to procure:

At Brazil:

Names	Guns	Names	Guns
Principe Real	84	*Minerva*	44
Rainha de Portugal	74	*Golfinho*	36
Conde Henrique	74	*Urania*	32
Medusa	74	*Voador*	22
Alfonso de Albuquerque	64	*Vingonea*	20
D'Joso de Castro	64	*Le Bre*	22
Principe de Brazil	74	*Escuna Cunoza*	12
Martin de Freitos	64		

In the Port of Lisbon:

St. Sebastian	In want of great repair
Maria Prima	Ditto.
Vasco de Gama [sic]	In bad condition
Princessa de Brisa	Fit only for condemnation
Fenix	Wants repair
Amazon	Ditto
Perola	Ditto
Tritico	Very bad
Venus	The same

The French Navy

	Line	Frigates		Line	Frigates
In the Texel	9	4	Fitting	1	4
In the Scheldt	19	14	and	9	1
Other Dutch ports	1	6	Building	3	2
Cherbourg	2	5		2	2
Brest	5	6		2	1
L'Orient	1	1		2	2

Rochefort	5	3	5	2
Toulon	18	14	3	0
In the minor ports of France	0	2	0	4
Genoa	1	1	0	2
Naples	1	2	1	3
Venice	3	3	4	3
Making a total of	65	61	32	26

Ready for sea, and in such a state of forwardness, that in the course of the present year we shall have opposed to us under French colours a numerical force of 97 sail of the line, and 87 frigates; but even the ships which are pretended to be ready for a start, particularly those in the Scheldt, are very badly manned, an evil for which the enemy does not possess any practicable remedy.

The Danish Navy

By the capitulation of Copenhagen, September 7, 1807, 18 ships of the line, 15 frigates, six brigs, and 25 gun-boats, were delivered up to his Majesty's force, and all, we believe, were brought to England. In the interval the Danes have not made much progress in regenerating their navy, their maritime operations being carried on wholly by flotillas of gun-brigs, which carry heavy metal, are well manned, manoeuvred, and well fought; and in a calm are formidable even to ships of war. The present naval force of Denmark consists of four ships of the line, two frigates, and about 120 gun-boats. There are two ships of the line, and three frigates on the stocks, but owing to the annihilation of commerce, and the embarrassments of the government, scarcely any progress is made in the construction of them.

The Naval Force of the United States of America, November 1, 1812

FRIGATES

Ships	Rated	Mounting	Commanders
Constitution	44	58	Captain Hull
United States	44	58	- Decatur
President	44	58	Commodore Rodgers
Chesapeake	36	44	Ordinary
New York	36	44	Ditto
Constellation	36	44	Captain Bainbridge
Congress	36	44	- Smith
Boston	32	-	Ordinary
Essex	32	-	Captain Porter

CORVETTES

John Adams	-	-	Prison Ship

SLOOPS, Called by the Americans Ships of War

Wasp [2]	16	18	Captain Jones
Hornet	16	18	- Lawrence

2 The *Wasp* was captured on the 18th of October, by H.M.S. *Poitiers*, Captain Beresford, and carried into Bermuda. - *Vide* Letters on Service, in subsequent pages.

BRIGS

Syren	16	–	Lieutenant Carrol
Argus	16	–	–
Oneida	16	–	Lieutenant Walsey

SCHOONERS

Vixen	12	–	– Godsden
Enterprise	12	–	– Blakeley
Viper	12	–	– Bainbridge

GUN-BOATS

170 stationed at New Orleans.

BOMBS

Vengeance, Aetna, Vesuvius, and *Spitfire*.

The subjoined table of the comparative dimensions of British and American ships, will enable the reader to appreciate the heroism with which our officers and seamen have defended themselves in the recent actions with our trans-atlantic descendants.

Name	Rate	Length on Gundeck	Breadth for tonnage		Tons
President	44	180 ft.	45 ft 10 in		1630
Constitution					
United States					
Acasta	40	154	40	5	1127

– This is the largest frigate we have on the American station.

Arethusa	38	141 1/2	39	1/2	248
Tigre	50	151	41	0	1114
Africa	64	160-10	44	9	1415

– Admiral Sawyer's ship.

Average of 12:	64	159-6	44	5	1383
Dragon	75	178	48	0	1798

– This an extraordinary large 74, built by Sir W. Rule, 1798.

Average of 12:	74	171-3	47	7	1628
Atlas	98	177-6	50	2	1950
Average of 12:	98	177-6	50	3	1938
Britannia	110	178	52	1/2	2091

By this table it will be seen, that these American *frigates* are longer than an English first-rate; that they are longer than, and of nearly equal tonnage with, our modern large seventy-fours, and of greater tonnage than our old seventy-fours; that they are longer, broader, and of greater tonnage than any of our sixty-fours; and that they exceed in tonnage our fifties, in the proportion of nearly three to two; and our thirty-eights in the proportion of seven to four. Is not the term frigate most violently perverted, when applied to such vessels? As well might we call the *Ville de Paris* a fifty, or the *Caledonia* a sixty-four; or as well might we call the one a jolly-boat and the other a yawl.

These frigates carry long 24-pounders on the main-deck, when even the largest first-rates in our service carry on the main-deck only long eighteens. Their quarter-deck and forecastle guns are 44-pound carronades; and no vessel of any description in our navy carries on either of these decks a heavier gun than a 32. Now, the vast superiority a ship derives from heavy metal, was pretty well illustrated by Sir H. Trollope's action last war, in which that celebrated officer was able to beat off a French *squadron*, in consequence of his ship (the *Glatton*) carrying carronades.[3]

To all these advantages, we must add the consideration of the numbers of their crews. The complement of an English 74 is 500 men, but seldom is there on board, even on the home stations, more than from 460 to 480 men, and of these generally about 30 are foreigners, and about 60 are boys. The *United States*, in the recent engagement with the *Macedonian*, had a complement of 478 men; that is, 12 less than the *nominal* complement of our 74's, and at least equal to the number that any 74 actually has on board. But a consideration of by far greater consequence than the quantity of men is their quality. From the extended state of the British navy, it is impracticable to man our fleets entirely with seamen. About 6/7ths of every ship's company are landsmen; and thus, in a 74, there are seldom more than 70 hands that can be put upon the forecastle, or rated as able seamen. Now the Americans, having but few national vessels, are able to man their ships not only entirely with *sailors*, but with picked, choice sailors; and they have been but too successful in enticing some of our ablest hands to become their petty officers.

[The report of the 'Committee appointed on that part of the President's Message which relates to the Naval Establishment,' with several papers expressing the relative merit of building ships of the line, and part of the text of 'An Act, to increase the Navy of the United States,' dated 2 January 1813, giving the wartime establishment of American 74-gun ships, four of which were to be built 'as soon as suitable materials can be procured,' was published in Vol. XXIX, pp238 and 454-464.]

3 Reported in N.C. XVIII 357.

1813 – Naval News

THE CONSOLIDATED EDITION of *The Naval Chronicle* for 1813 begins with President Madison's report to Congress on the first campaign of the war, which, apart from the frigate action with *Macedonian*, and subsequently, at the end of the year, with *Java*, had gone badly for the United States. American military defeats in Canada were blamed on the British use of aboriginal warriors. Madison admitted to the fact that the United States had moved forces into Michigan prior to the outbreak of war, ready to strike, but did not remark on the earlier campaign to 'pacify' the aboriginals which had driven them into alliance with the British. The fact that Britain had rescinded the offending Orders in Council was noted, but as long as Britain continued to use impressment to recruit seamen, Madison could not put reliance on any British undertaking not to impress Americans.

In reply to President Madison is the declaration of the British Government in January 1813 of the 'Causes of the American War'. This was an important review of the French economic strategy against Britain, the 'Continental System', and the British response through Orders in Council designed to oblige the French to trade with Britain. The impact of both on neutral commerce was contrasted. The bias of American retaliatory trade policy was emphasised. The paper reviewed the British response, the repeal of the Orders in Council when the American government produced what purported to be notification of the French abandonment of the Continental System. Madison's additional demands that Britain stop searching merchant vessels for British deserters, and stop employing impressment, had not formed a part of prewar discussions, and could not be admitted without destroying Britain's ability to support her wartime fleet.

The capture of yet another British frigate, HMS *Java*, by an American super-frigate was the most dramatic naval news of the early part of 1813, and added to the chagrin of the Royal Navy. A correspondent warned that a new American assault on Canada was to be expected. In June, however, the USS *Chesapeake*, a 36-gun frigate fresh out of ordinary and badly manned, was defeated by HMS *Shannon* in fifteen minutes and brought into Halifax. Although this event did nothing to affect the prowess of the American super-frigates, it was a great boost to Royal Navy morale.

From the Baltic, on the other hand, the news was good. In December 1812, a Russian squadron had arrived at Chatham to work with the Royal Navy, but its utility was less than minimal because it was stricken with a malignant fever such as had plagued the Royal Navy before it learnt effective methods of hygiene. In early 1813 news was received that, as a result of the French disaster in Russia, a truce had been reached among France, Russia and Prussia.

Other naval news included the sad affair of Lieutenant Gamage who killed one of the crew of the sloop *Griffon*, and was hanged for it; the efforts of Emma Hamilton to obtain some share of the Government's provision for the Nelson family was also a matter of interest. Following the general election, a list was published of the members of the new Parliament who were naval officers.

State Papers. *XXIX 53-59*

Message of the President of the United States to Congress

Fellow Citizens of the Senate, and of the House of Representatives
On our present meeting, it is my first duty to invite your attention to the providential favours which our country has experienced in the unusual degree of health dispensed to its inhabitants, and in the rich abundance with which the earth has rewarded the labours bestowed on it. In the successful cultivation of other branches of industry, and in the progress of general improvement favourable to the national prosperity, there is just occasion also for our mutual congratulations and thankfulness.

With these blessings are naturally mingled the pressures and vicissitudes incidental to the state of war into which the United States have been forced by the perseverance of a foreign power in its system of injustice and aggression. Previous to its declaration, it was deemed proper, as a measure of precaution and forecast, that a considerable force should be placed in the Michigan territory, with a general view to its security; and, in the event of war, to such operations in the uppermost Canada, as would intercept the hostile influence of Great Britain over the savages; obtain the command of the lake on which that part of Canada borders; and maintain co-operating relations with such forces as might be most conveniently employed against other parts.

Brigadier-general Hull was charged with this provisional service, having under his command a body of troops, composed of regulars and volunteers from the State of Ohio: having reached his destination, after his knowledge of the war, and possessing discretionary authority to act offensively, he passed into the neighbouring territory of the enemy, with a prospect of an easy and victorious progress. The expedition, nevertheless, terminated unfortunately, not only in a retreat to the town and fort of Detroit, but in the surrender of both, and of the gallant corps commanded by that officer. The causes of this painful reverse will be investigated by a military tribunal. A distinguishing feature in the operations which preceded and followed this adverse event,

The Bathing Place, Teignmouth, Devonshire. Engraved by Baily, from a drawing by Richard Speare, Esq. Plate 454

is the use made by the enemy of the merciless savages under their influence. Whilst the benevolent policy of the United States invariably recommended peace, and promoted civilization amongst that wretched portion of the human race, and was making exertions to dissuade them from taking either side in the war, the enemy has not scrupled to call to his aid their ruthless ferocity, armed with the horrors of those instruments of carnage and torture, which are known to spare neither age nor sex. In this outrage against the laws of honourable war, and against the feelings sacred to humanity, the British commanders cannot resort to a plan of retaliation; for it is committed in the face of our example. They cannot mitigate it by calling it a self defence against men in arms, for it embraces the most shocking butcheries of defenceless families: nor can it be pretended that they are not answerable for the atrocities perpetrated, since the savages are employed with the knowledge, and even with menaces, that their fury could not be controlled. Such is the spectacle which the deputed authorities of a nation, boasting its religion and morality, have not been restrained from presenting to an enlightened age.

The misfortune at Detroit was not, however, without a consoling effect. It was followed by signal proofs, that the national spirit rises according to the pressure on it. The loss of an important post, and of the brave men surrendered with it, inspired every where new ardour and determination. In the states and districts least remote, it was no sooner known, than every citizen was eager to fly with his arms at once to protect his brethren against the blood thirsty savages let loose by the enemy on an extensive frontier; and to convert a partial calamity into a source of invigorated efforts. This patriotic zeal, which it was necessary rather to limit than excite, has embodied an ample force from the states of Kentucky and Ohio, and from parts of Pennsylvania and Virginia. It is placed, with the addition of a few regulars, under the command of Brigadier-general

Harrison, who possesses the entire confidence of his fellow soldiers; among whom are citizens - some of them volunteers in the ranks - not less distinguished by their political stations, than by their personal merits.

The greater portion of this force is proceeding on its destination towards the Michigan territory, having succeeded in relieving an important frontier post, and in several incidental operations against hostile tribes of savages, rendered indispensable by the subserviency into which they had been seduced by the enemy; a seduction the more cruel, as it could not fail to impose a necessity of precautionary severities against those who yielded to it.

At a recent date, an attack was made on a post of the enemy near Niagara, by a detachment of the regular and other forces, under the command of Major-general Van Rensselaer, of the militia of the state of New York. The attack, it appears, was ordered in compliance with the ardour of the troops, who executed it with distinguished gallantry, and were for a time victorious; but not receiving the expected support, they were compelled to yield to reinforcements of British regulars and savages. Our loss has been considerable, and is deeply to be lamented. That of the enemy, less ascertained, will be the more felt, as it includes among the killed, the commanding general, who was also governor of the province; and was sustained by veteran troops, from inexperienced soldiers, who must daily improve in the duties of the field.

Our expectation of gaining the command of the Lakes, by the invasion of Canada from Detroit, having been disappointed, measures were instantly taken to provide on them a naval force superior to that of the enemy. From the talents and activity of the officer charged with this object, every thing that can be done may be expected. Should the present season not admit of complete success, the progress made will ensure for the next a naval ascendancy where it is essential, to a permanent peace with, and a control over, the savages.

Among the incidents of the measures of the war, I am constrained to advert to the refusal of the governors of Massachusetts and Connecticut to furnish the required detachments of militia towards the defence of the maritime frontier. The refusal was founded on a novel and unfortunate exposition of the provisions of the constitution relating to the militia. The correspondence which will be laid before you contains the requisite information on the subject. It is obvious that, if the authority of the United States to call into service and command the militia for the public defence can be thus frustrated, even in a state of declared war, and of course under apprehensions of invasion preceding war, they are not one nation for the purpose most of all requiring it, and that the public safety may have no other resource than those large and permanent military establishments which are forbidden by the principles of our free government, and against the necessity of which the militia were meant to be a constitutional bulwark.

On the coasts and on the ocean, the war has been as successful as circumstances inseparable from its early stages could promise. Our public ships and private cruisers, by their activity, and where there was occasion, by their intrepidity, have made the enemy sensible of the difference between a reciprocity of captures, and the long confinement of them to their side. Our trade, with little exception, has safely reached our ports, having been much favoured in it by the course pursued by a squadron of our frigates, under the command of Commodore Rodgers; and in the instance in which skill and bravery were more particularly tried with those of the enemy, the American flag had an auspicious triumph. The frigate *Constitution*, commanded by Captain Hull, after a close and short engagement, completely disabled and captured a British frigate;

gaining for that officer, and all on board, a praise which cannot be too liberally bestowed; not merely for the victory actually achieved, but for that prompt and cool exertion of commanding talents, which, giving to courage its highest character, and to the force applied its full effect, proved that more could have been done in a contest requiring more.

Anxious to abridge the evils from which a state of war cannot be exempt, I lost no time after it was declared, in conveying to the British government the terms on which its progress might be arrested, without waiting the delays of a formal and final pacification: and our chargé d'affaires at London was at the same time authorized to agree to an armistice, founded upon them. These terms required, that the orders in council should be repealed, as they affected the United States, without a revival of the blockades violating acknowledged rules; that there should be an immediate discharge of American seamen from British ships, and a stop to impressment from American ships, with an understanding that an exclusion of the seamen of each nation from the ships of the other should be stipulated, and that the armistice should be improved into a definitive and comprehensive adjustment of depending controversies.

Although a repeal of the orders susceptible of explanations meeting the views of this government had taken place before this pacific advance was communicated to that of Great Britain, the advance was declined, from an avowed repugnance to a suspension of the practice of impressment during the armistice, and without any intimation that the arrangement proposed with respect to seamen would be accepted. Whether the subsequent communications from this government, affording an occasion for reconsidering the subject on the part of Great Britain, will be viewed in a more favourable light, or received in a more accommodating spirit, remains to be known. It would be unwise to release [ie relax?] our measures, in any respect, on a presumption of such a result.

The documents from the department of state which relate to this subject, will give a view also of the propositions for an armistice which have been received here - one of them from the authorities at Halifax and in Canada, the other from the British government itself, through Admiral Warren; and of the grounds upon which neither of them could be accepted.

Our affairs with France retain the posture which they held at my last communication to you.

Notwithstanding the authorized expectation of an early as well as favourable issue of the discussions on foot, these have been procrastinated to the latest date. The only intervening occurrence meriting attention is, the promulgation of a French decree, purporting to be a definitive repeal of the Berlin and Milan decrees. This proceeding, although made the ground of the repeal of the British orders in council, is rendered, by the time and manner of it, liable to many objections. ...

There being reason to believe, that the act prohibiting the acceptance of British licenses is not a sufficient guard against the use of them, for purposes favourable to the interest and views of the enemy; further provisions on that subject are highly important. Nor is it less so, that penal enactments should be provided for cases of corrupt and perfidious intercourse with the enemy, not amounting to treason, nor yet embraced by any statutory provisions.

(signed) JAMES MADISON

Washington, November 4, 1812

The Prince Regent's Declaration on the Causes of the American War XXIX 140-150

The earnest endeavours of the Prince Regent to preserve the relations of peace and amity with the United States of America having unfortunately failed, his Royal Highness, acting in the name and on the behalf of his Majesty, deems it proper publicly to declare the causes, and origin of the war, in which the government of the United States has compelled him to engage.

No desire of conquest, or other ordinary motive of aggression has been, or can be with any colour of reason, in this case, imputed to Great Britain: that her commercial interests were on the side of peace, if war could have been avoided, without the sacrifice of her maritime rights, or without an injurious submission to France, is a truth which the American government will not deny.

H.R.H. does not, however, mean to rest on the favourable presumption to which he is entitled. He is prepared, by an exposition of the circumstances which have led to the present war, to show, that Great Britain has throughout acted towards the United States of America, with a spirit of amity, forbearance, and conciliation; and to demonstrate the inadmissible nature of those pretensions, which have at length unhappily involved the two countries in war.

It is well known to the world, that it has been the invariable object of the ruler of France, to destroy the power and independence of the British empire, as the chief obstacle to the accomplishment of his ambitious designs.

He first contemplated the possibility of assembling such a naval force in the Channel as, combined with a numerous flotilla, should enable him to disembark in England an army sufficient, in his conception, to subjugate this country; and through the conquest of Great Britain he hoped to realize his project of universal empire.

By the adoption of an enlarged and provident system of internal defence, and by the valour of H.M.'s fleets and armies, this design was entirely frustrated; and the naval force of France, after the most signal defeats, was compelled to retire from the ocean.

An attempt was then made to effectuate the same purpose by other means: a system was brought forward, by which the ruler of France hoped to annihilate the commerce of Great Britain, to shake her public credit, and to destroy her revenues; to render useless her maritime superiority, and so to avail himself of his continental ascendancy, as to constitute himself in a great measure the arbiter of the ocean, notwithstanding the destruction of his fleets.

With this view, by the decree of Berlin, followed by that of Milan, he declared the British territories to be in a state of blockade; and that all commerce, or even correspondence with Great Britain, was prohibited. He decreed that every vessel and cargo, which had entered, or was found proceeding to a British port, or which, under any circumstances, had been visited by a British ship of war, should be lawful prize: he declared all British goods and produce, wherever found, and however acquired, whether coming from the mother country, or from her colonies, subject to confiscation: he further declared to be denationalized, the flag of all neutral ships that should be found offending against these his decrees: and he gave to this project of universal tyranny, the name of the continental system.

For these attempts to ruin the commerce of Great Britain, by means subversive of the clearest rights of neutral nations, France endeavoured in vain to rest her justification upon the previous conduct of H.M.'s government.

Under circumstances of unparalleled provocation; H.M. had abstained from any measure, which the ordinary rules of the law of nations did not fully warrant. Never was the maritime superiority of a belligerent over his enemy, more complete and decided. Never was the opposite belligerent so formidably dangerous in his power, and in his policy, to the liberties of all other nations. France had already trampled so openly and systematically on the most sacred rights of neutral powers, as might well have justified the placing her out of the pale of civilized nations. Yet in this extreme case, Great Britain had so used her naval ascendancy, that her enemy could find no just cause of complaint: and in order to give to these lawless decrees the appearance of retaliation, the ruler of France was obliged to advance principles of maritime law unsanctioned by any other authority, than his own arbitrary will.

The pretexts for these decrees were, first, that Great Britain had exercised the rights of war against private persons, their ships, and goods; as if the only object of legitimate hostility on the ocean were the public property of a state, or as if the edicts, and the courts of France itself, had not at all times enforced this right with peculiar rigour; secondly, that the British orders of blockade, instead of being confined to fortified towns, had, as France asserted, been unlawfully extended to commercial towns and ports, and to the mouths of rivers; and thirdly, that they had been applied to places, and to coasts which neither were, nor could be actually blockaded. The last of these charges is not founded on fact; whilst the others, even by the admission of the American government, are utterly groundless in point of law.

Against these decrees, his Majesty protested and appealed; he called upon the United States, to assert their own rights, and to vindicate their independence, thus menaced and attacked; and as France had declared, that she would confiscate every vessel, which should touch in Great Britain, or be visited by British ships of war, his Majesty, having previously issued the order of January, 1807, as an act of mitigated retaliation, was at length compelled, by the persevering violence of the enemy, and the continued acquiescence of neutral powers, to revisit, upon France, in a more effectual manner, the measure of her own injustice; by declaring, in an order in council, bearing date the 11th of November, 1807, that no neutral vessel should proceed to France, or to any of the countries from which, in obedience to the dictates of France, British commerce was excluded, without first touching at a port in Great Britain, or her dependencies. At the same time his Majesty intimated his readiness to repeal the orders in council, whenever France should rescind her decrees, and return to the accustomed principles of maritime warfare; and at a subsequent period, as a proof of his Majesty's sincere desire to accommodate, as far as possible, his defensive measures to the convenience of neutral powers the operation of the orders in council was, by an order issued in April 1809, limited to a blockade of France, and of the countries subjected to her immediate domination.

Systems of violence, oppression, and tyranny, can never be suppressed, or even checked, if the power against which such injustice is exercised, be debarred from the right of full and adequate retaliation: or, if the measures of the retaliating power, are to be considered as matters of just offence to neutral nations, whilst the measures of original aggression, and violence, are to be tolerated with indifference, submission, or complacency.

The government of the United States did not fail to remonstrate against the orders in council of Great Britain. Although they knew, that these orders would be revoked, if the decrees of France, which had occasioned them, were repealed, they resolved at the same moment to resist the conduct of both belligerents, instead of requiring France, in the first instance to rescind her decrees. Applying most unjustly the same measure of resentment to the aggressor, and to the party aggrieved, they adopted measures of commercial resistance against both - a system of resistance, which, however varied in the successive acts of embargo, non-intercourse, or non-importation, was evidently unequal in its operation, and principally levelled against the superior commerce, and maritime power of Great Britain.

The same partiality towards France was observable, in their negotiations, as in their measures of alleged resistance.

Application was made to both belligerents for a revocation of their respective edicts; but the terms in which they were made, were widely different.

Of France was required a revocation only of the Berlin and Milan decrees, although many other edicts, grossly violating the neutral commerce of the United States, had been promulgated by that power. No security was demanded, that the Berlin and Milan decrees, even if revoked, should not under some other form be re-established: and a direct engagement was offered, that, upon such revocation, the American government would take part in the war against Great Britain, if Great Britain did not immediately rescind her orders. - Whereas no corresponding engagement was offered to Great Britain, of whom it was required, not only that the orders in council should be repealed, but that no others of a similar nature should be issued, and that the blockade of May, 1806, should be also abandoned. This blockade, established and enforced according to accustomed practice, had not been objected to by the United States at the time it was issued. Its provisions were on the contrary represented by the American minister resident in London at the time, to have been so framed, as to afford, in his judgment, a proof of the friendly disposition of the British cabinet towards the United States.

Great Britain was thus called upon to abandon one of her most important maritime rights; by acknowledging the order of blockade in question, to be one of the edicts, which violated the commerce of the United States; although it had never been so considered in the previous negotiations; - and although the President of the United States had recently consented to abrogate the non-intercourse act, on the sole condition of the orders in council being revoked; thereby distinctly admitting these orders to be the only edicts, which fell within the contemplation of the law, under which he acted.

A proposition so hostile to Great Britain could not but be proportionably encouraging to the pretensions of the enemy. As, by thus alleging that the blockade of May, 1806, was illegal, the American government virtually justified, so far as depended on them, the French decrees.

After this proposition had been made, the French minister for foreign affairs, if not in concert with that government, at least in conformity with its views, in a despatch, dated the 5th of August, 1810, and addressed to the American minister resident at Paris, stated that the Berlin and Milan decrees were revoked, and that their operation would cease from the first day of November following, provided his Majesty would revoke his orders in council, and renounce the new principles of blockade; or that the United States would cause their rights to be respected; meaning thereby, that they would resist the retaliatory measures of Great Britain.

Although the repeal of the French decrees thus announced was evidently contingent, either on concession to be made by Great Britain (concessions to which it was obvious Great Britain could not submit), or on measures to be adopted by the United States of America, the American President at once considered the repeal as absolute. Under that pretence, the non-importation act was strictly enforced against Great Britain, whilst the ships of war, and merchant ships of the enemy, were received into the harbours of America.

The American government, assuming the repeal of the French decrees to be absolute, and effectual, most unjustly required Great Britain, in conformity to her declarations, to revoke her orders in council. The British government denied that the repeal, which was announced in the letter of the French minister for foreign affairs, was such as ought to satisfy Great Britain: and in order to ascertain the true character of the measures adopted by France, the government of the United States was called upon to produce the instrument, by which the alleged repeal of the French decrees had been effected. If these decrees were really revoked, such an instrument must exist, and no satisfactory reason could be given for withholding it.

At length, on the 21st of May, 1812, and not before, the American minister in London did produce a copy, or at least what purported to be a copy of such an instrument.

It professed to bear date the 28th of April, 1811, long subsequent to the despatch of the French minister of foreign affairs of the 5th of August, 1810, or even the day named therein, viz. the 1st November following, when the operation of the French decrees was to cease. This instrument expressly declared that these French decrees were repealed in consequence of the American legislature having, by their act of the 1st March, 1811, provided, that British ships and merchandise should be excluded from the ports and harbours of the United States.

By this instrument, the only document produced by America as a repeal of the French decrees, it appears beyond a possibility of doubt or cavil, that the alleged repeal of the French decrees was conditional, as Great Britain had asserted; and not absolute or final, as had been maintained by America: that they were not repealed at the time they were stated to be repealed by the American government: that they were not repealed in conformity with a proposition, simultaneously made to both belligerents, but that in consequence of a previous act on the part of the American government, they were repealed in favour of one belligerent, to the prejudice of the other: that the American government having adopted measures restrictive upon the commerce of both belligerents, in consequence of edicts issued by both, rescinded these measures, as they affected that power, which was the aggressor, whilst they put them in full operation against the party aggrieved; although the edicts of both powers continued in force; and lastly, that they excluded the ships of war, belonging to one belligerent, whilst they admitted into their ports and harbours the ships of war belonging to the other, in violation of one of the plainest, and most essential duties of a neutral nation.

Although the instrument thus produced was, by no means, that general and unqualified revocation of the Berlin and Milan decrees, which Great Britain had continually demanded, and had a full right to claim; and although this instrument, under all the circumstances of its appearance at that moment, for the first time, was open to the strongest suspicions of its authenticity; yet, as the minister of the United States produced it, as purporting to be a copy of the instrument of revocation, the government of Great Britain, desirous of reverting, if possible, to the ancient and accustomed principles of maritime war, determined upon revoking conditionally the orders in council. Accordingly, in the month of June last, his Royal Highness the Prince Regent was pleased to declare in council, in the name and on the behalf of his Majesty, that the orders in council should be revoked, as far as respecting the ships and property of the United States, from the 1st of August following. This revocation was to continue in force provided the government of the United States should, within a time to be limited, repeal their restrictive laws against British commerce. His Majesty's minister in America was expressly ordered to declare to the government of the United States, that "this measure had been adopted by the Prince Regent in the earnest wish and hope, either that the government of France, by further relaxations of its system, might render perseverance on the part of Great Britain in retaliatory measures unnecessary, or if this hope should prove delusive, that his Majesty's government might be enabled, in the absence of all irritating and restrictive regulations on either side, to enter with the government of the United States into amicable explanations, for the purpose of ascertaining whether, if the necessity of retaliatory measures should unfortunately continue to operate, the particular measures to be acted upon by Great Britain, could be rendered more acceptable to the American government, than those hitherto pursued."

In order to provide for the contingency of a declaration of war on the part of the United States, previous to the arrival in America of the said order of revocation, instructions were sent to his Majesty's minister plenipotentiary accredited to the United States (the execution of which instructions, in consequence of the discontinuance of Mr. Foster's functions, were at a subsequent period entrusted to Admiral Sir John Borlase Warren), directing him to propose a cessation of hostilities, should they have commenced; and further, to offer a simultaneous repeal of the orders in council on the one side, and of the restrictive laws on British ships and commerce on the other.

They were also respectively empowered to acquaint the American government, in reply to any inquiries with respect to the blockade of May, 1806, whilst the British government must continue to maintain its legality, "that in point of fact this particular blockade had been discontinued for a length of time, having been merged in the general retaliatory blockade of the enemy's ports, under the orders in council, and that his Majesty's government had no intention of recurring to this, or to any other of the blockades of the enemy's ports, founded upon the ordinary and accustomed principles of maritime law, which were in force previous to the orders in council, without a new notice to neutral powers, in the usual form."

The American government, before they received intimation of the course adopted by the British government, had, in fact, proceeded to the extreme measure of declaring war, and issuing "Letters of Marque," notwithstanding they were previously in possession of the report of the French minister for foreign affairs, of the 12th of March, 1812, promulgating anew the Berlin and Milan Decrees, as fundamental laws of the French empire, under the false and extravagant pretexts, that the monstrous principles therein contained, were to be found in the treaty of Utrecht, and were, therefore binding upon all states. From the penalties of this code, no nation was to be exempt, which did not accept it, not only as the rule of its own conduct, but as a law, the observance of which, it was also required to enforce upon Great Britain.

In a manifesto, accompanying their declaration of hostilities, in addition to the former complaints against the orders in council, a long list of grievances was brought forward; some trivial in themselves, others which had been mutually adjusted, but none of them such, as were ever before alleged by the American government to be grounds for war.

As if to throw additional obstacles in the way of peace, the American Congress, at the same time, passed a law, prohibiting all intercourse with Great Britain, of such a tenor, as deprived the executive government, according to the president's own construction of that act, of all power of restoring the relations of friendly intercourse between the two states, so far, at least, as concerned their commercial intercourse, until Congress should re-assemble.

The president of the United States has, it is true, since proposed to Great Britain an Armistice; not, however, on the admission, that the cause of war, hitherto relied on, was removed, but on condition, that Great Britain, as a preliminary step, should do away a cause of war, now brought forward as such, for the first time; namely, that she should abandon the exercise of her undoubted right of search, to take from American merchant vessels, British seamen, the natural born subjects of his Majesty; and this concession was required upon a mere assurance, that laws would be enacted by the legislature of the United States, to prevent such seamen from entering into their service; but, independent of the objection to an exclusive reliance on a foreign state, for the conservation of so vital an interest, no explanation was, or could be afforded by the agent who was charged with this overture, either as to the main principles, upon which such laws were to be founded, or as to the provisions which it was proposed they should contain.

This proposition having been objected to, a second proposal was made, again offering an armistice, provided the British government would secretly stipulate to renounce the exercise of this right in a treaty of peace. An immediate and formal abandonment of its exercise, as preliminary to a cessation of hostilities, was not demanded; but his Royal Highness the Prince Regent was required, in the name, and on the behalf of his Majesty, secretly to abandon, what the former overture had proposed to him publicly to concede.

This most offensive proposition was also rejected, being accompanied, as the former had been, by other demands of the most exceptionable nature, and especially of indemnity for all American vessels, detained and condemned under the orders in council, or under what were termed illegal blockades - a compliance with which demands, exclusive of all other objections, would have amounted to an absolute surrender of the rights, on which those orders and blockades were founded.

Had the American government been sincere in representing the orders in council, as the only subject of difference between Great Britain and the United States, calculated to lead to hostilities, it might have been expected, so soon as the revocation of those orders had been officially made known to them, that they would have spontaneously recalled their "Letters of Marque," and manifested a disposition immediately to restore the relations of peace and amity between the two powers.

But the conduct of the government of the United States by no means corresponded with such reasonable expectations.

The order in council of the 23d of June, being officially communicated in America, the government of the United States, saw nothing in the repeal of the orders in council, which should of itself restore peace, unless Great Britain were prepared, in the first instance, substantially to relinquish the right of impressing her own seamen, when found on board American merchant-ships.

The proposal of an armistice, and of a simultaneous repeal of the restrictive measures on both sides, subsequently made by the commanding officer of his Majesty's naval forces on the American coast, were received in the same hostile spirit by the government of the United States. The suspension of the practice of impressment was insisted upon, in the correspondence which passed on that occasion, as a necessary preliminary to a cessation of hostilities: negotiation, it was stated, might take place, without any suspension of the exercise of this right, and also without any armistice being concluded; but Great Britain was required previously to agree, without any knowledge of the adequacy of the system which would be substituted, to negotiate upon the basis of accepting the legislative regulations of a foreign state, as the sole equivalent for the exercise of a right, which she has felt to be essential to the support of her maritime power.

If America, by demanding this preliminary concession, intends to deny the validity of that right, in the denial, Great Britain cannot acquiesce; nor will she give countenance to such a pretension, by acceding to its suspension, much less to its abandonment, as a basis on which to treat. If the American government has devised, or conceives it can devise, regulations which may safely be accepted by Great Britain as a substitute for the exercise of the right in question, it is for them to bring forward such a plan for consideration. The British government has never attempted to exclude this question from amongst those, on which the two states might have to negotiate: it has, on the contrary, uniformly professed its readiness to receive and discuss any proportion on this subject coming from the American government: it has never asserted any exclusive right, as to the impressment of British seamen from American vessels, which it was not prepared to acknowledge, as appertaining equally to the government of the United States, with respect to American seamen when found on board British merchant ships. But it cannot, by acceding to such a basis, in the first instance, either assume or admit that to be practicable, which, when attempted on former occasions, has always been found to be attended with great difficulties; such difficulties, as the British commissioners, in 1806, expressly declared, after an attentive consideration of the suggestions brought forward by the commissioners on the part of America, they were unable to surmount.

Whilst this proposition, transmitted through the British admiral, was pending in America, another communication, on the subject of an armistice, was unofficially made to the British government, in this country. The agent, from whom this proposition was received, acknowledged, that he did not consider, that he had any authority himself to sign an agreement on the part of his government. It was obvious, that any stipulations entered into, in consequence of this overture, would have been binding on the British government, whilst the government of the United States would have been free to refuse or accept them, according to the circumstances of the moment. This proposition was, therefore, necessarily declined.

After this exposition of the circumstances which preceded, and which have followed, the declaration of war by the United States, his Royal Highness the Prince Regent, acting in the name and on the behalf of his Majesty, feels himself called upon to declare the leading principles by which the conduct of Great Britain has been regulated in the transactions connected with these discussions.

His Royal Highness can never acknowledge any blockade whatsoever to be illegal, which has been duly notified, and is supported by an adequate force, merely upon the ground of its extent, or because the ports, or coasts blockaded, are not, at the same time, invested by land.

His Royal Highness can never admit, that neutral trade with Great Britain can be constituted a public crime, the commission of which can expose the ships of any power whatever to be denationalized.

His Royal Highness can never admit, that Great Britain can be debarred of its right of just and necessary retaliation, through the fear of eventually affecting the interest of a neutral.

His Royal Highness can never admit that, in the exercise of the undoubted and hitherto undisputed right of searching neutral merchant vessels, in time of war, the impressment of British seamen, when found therein, can be deemed any violation of a neutral flag. Neither can he admit, that the taking such seamen from on board such vessels can be considered by any neutral state as a hostile measure, or a justifiable cause of war.

There is no right more clearly established, than the right which a sovereign has to the allegiance of his subjects, more especially in time of war. Their allegiance is no optional duty, which they can decline and resume at pleasure. It is a call which they are bound to obey; it began with their birth, and can only terminate with their existence.

If a similarity of language and manners may make the exercise of this right more liable to partial mistakes, and occasional abuse, when practised towards vessels of the United States, the same circumstances make it also a right, with the exercise of which, in regard to such vessels, it is more difficult to dispense.

But if, to the practice of the United States to harbour British seamen, be added their assumed right to transfer the allegiance of British subjects, and thus to cancel the jurisdiction of their legitimate sovereign, by acts of naturalization and certificates of citizenship, which they pretend to be as valid out of their own territory, as within it, it is obvious that to abandon this ancient right of Great Britain, and to admit these novel pretensions of the United States, would be to expose to danger the very foundation of our maritime strength.

Without entering minutely into the other topics, which have been brought forward by the government of the United States, it may be proper to remark, that whatever the declaration of the United States may have asserted, Great Britain never did demand, that they should force British manufactures into France; and she formally declared her willingness entirely to forego, or modify, in concert with the United States, the System, by which a commercial intercourse with the enemy had been allowed under the protection of licences; provided the United States would act towards her, and towards France, with real impartiality.

The government of America, if the differences between states are not interminable, has as little right to notice the affair of the *Chesapeake*. The aggression, in this instance, on the part of a British officer was acknowledged, his conduct was disapproved, and a reparation was regularly tendered by Mr. Foster on the part of his Majesty, and accepted by the government of the United States.

It is not less unwarranted in its allusion to the mission of Mr. Henry, a mission undertaken without the authority, or even knowledge of his Majesty's government, and which Mr. Foster was authorized formally and officially to disavow.

The charge of exciting the Indians to offensive measures against the United States, is equally void of foundation. Before the war began, a policy the most opposite had been uniformly pursued, and proof of this was tendered by Mr. Foster to the American government.

Such are the causes of war which have been put forward by the government of the United States. But the real origin of the present contest will be found in that spirit, which has long unhappily actuated the councils of the United States: their marked partiality in palliating and assisting the aggressive tyranny of France; their systematic endeavours to inflame their people against the defensive measures of Great Britain; their ungenerous conduct towards Spain, the intimate ally of Great Britain; and their unworthy desertion of the cause of other neutral nations. It is through the prevalence of such councils, that America has been associated in policy with France, and committed in war against Great Britain.

And under what conduct on the part of France has the government of the United States thus lent itself to the enemy? The contemptuous violation of the commercial treaty of the year 1800, between France and the United States; the treacherous seizure of all American vessels and cargoes in every harbour subject to the control of the French arms; the tyrannical principles of the Berlin and Milan Decrees, and the confiscations under them; the subsequent confiscations under the Rambouillet Decree, antedated or concealed to render it the more effectual; the French commercial regulations which render the traffic of the United States with France almost illusory; the burning of their merchant ships at sea, long after the alleged repeal of the French Decrees - all these acts of violence on the part of France produce from the government of the United States, only such complaints as end in acquiesce and submission, or are accompanied by suggestions for enabling France to give the semblance of a legal form in her usurpations by converting them into municipal regulations.

This disposition of the government of the United States - this complete subserviency to the Ruler of France - this hostile temper towards Great Britain - are evident in almost every page of the official correspondence of the American with the French government.

Against this course of conduct, the real cause of the present war, the Prince Regent solemnly protests. Whilst contending against France in defence not only of the liberties of Great Britain, but of the world, His Royal Highness was entitled to look for a far different result. From their common origin - from their common interest - from their professed principles of freedom and independence, the United States were the last power, in which Great Britain could have expected to find a willing instrument, and abettor of French tyranny.

Disappointed in this his just expectation, the Prince Regent will still pursue the policy, which the British government has so long and invariably maintained, in repelling injustice, and in supporting the general rights of nations; and, under the favour of Providence, relying on the justice of his cause, and the tried loyalty and firmness of the British nation, his Royal Highness confidently looks forward to a successful issue to the contest, in which he has thus been compelled most reluctantly to engage.

Westminster, January 9, 1813

From the 'Naval History of the Present Year,' 1813
January-February. XXIX 170

Southampton and USS Vixen Lost

In the *Brazen*, Captain Stirling, which arrived at Portsmouth, on the 9th of February, Captain Sir James Yeo, of H.M.'s late ship *Southampton*, came home passenger. The *Southampton* having captured the United States brig *Vixen*, of fourteen guns, and one hundred and thirty men, was on her passage with her prize to Jamaica, and going through the Crooked Island Passage, on the night of the 27th of November, they both ran on a reef of rock, which extends eight or nine miles from one of the points of Conception Island. The *Southampton* bilged soon after she struck; her prize was under water in a few hours. The crews were all saved. The reef was not known to the Bahama pilots, one of the best of whom was on board the *Southampton*. - A court martial was held on the 13th of February to try Sir James Yeo, for the loss of his ship; when the court agreed, that the loss of the *Southampton* was caused by a strong westerly current driving her on a reef near the Isle of Conception, not laid down in the charts, and very imperfectly known; and that no blame was imputable to Sir James Yeo, his officers and ship's company, for their conduct, and did adjudge them to be acquitted.

Decatur Treats Defeated Macedonians Kindly

Letters received from officers of H.H.'s late ship *Macedonian*, dated New London, Long Island, January 6, 1813, speak in terms of gratitude and admiration, of the humane, generous, and noble conduct of their enemy, Commodore Decatur, who, with the officers of the United States, had treated the remaining crew of the *Macedonian* with the utmost kindness and attention. He had given up all the officers' private property taken in the ship, extending this generosity to even a quantity of wine, which they had purchased at Madeira for their friends in England. They were in daily expectation of being sent in a cartel to Bermuda.

The Sad Affair of Lieutenant Gamage XXIX 25-31

___ *to the Editor*
Mr. Editor, The fate of the unfortunate Lieutenant [Richard Stewart] Gamage, of H.M.'s sloop *Griffon*, which has so recently engaged the attention of the public at large, must by the navy be ever viewed with peculiar interest. The sons of Neptune, doomed by their profession to a rude and boisterous life, amid scenes more calculated to nurture, than to meliorate the stormy passions, have seldom witnessed a scene similar to the melancholy one now adverted to; as it has but very rarely occurred, in the naval annals of this country, that an officer of his rank has suffered the last penalty of the law; and still more rarely, if ever, for the commission of a similar offence. Whilst this may very justly be the subject of our congratulation, God forbid, that any one, from being unacquainted with the true colouring of the incidents leading to the unhappy transaction, should ever push his accusation beyond its deserts. And as the affair may frequently arise in conversation amongst naval men, I transmit the following concise narrative (which your readers may rely on for its authenticity), of the life and services of the late Lieutenant Gamage, previously to the fatal event ...

The general tenor of Lieutenant Gamage's conduct, as first lieutenant of the *Griffon*, was so mild, so forbearing to those under his command, that he secured the affection of the meanest individual. The degree of affection evinced by the ship's company was so fully shewn, in their representation to the court martial, and their subsequent petition to the Regent, that it demands no other evidence, to stamp him a humane and benevolent officer. As a messmate, and as a gentleman, he possessed every qualification to render such a character the object of estimation: he was gentle, friendly, and sincere, abounding in social virtues. The morning of the 20th of October was unmarked by any peculiar event. The forenoon passed with the usual chain of occurrences; and on the officers meeting together in the gun-room, when the ship's company were piped to dinner, Lieutenant G. took his seat with his accustomed smile of good humour and complacency. The crew were turned up at one o'clock, when he went on deck to carry on the public duties of his station. About half-past one, the officers below were roused by a fearful and sudden cry on deck. A hurried footstep immediately descended the companion ladder, and they were struck with dismay, at the intelligence, that, "Gamage had stabbed the serjeant." - They instantly flew on deck, and found the serjeant lying near the main-mast, surrounded by a crowd of sailors. His countenance bespoke approaching dissolution, and in a few minutes he expired. The body was conveyed below. Words cannot express the dreadful and torturing emotions, which at that awful moment racked the heart of Lieutenant Gamage - he remained fixed on the spot, and gazing, in all the agony of unutterable grief on the terrific scene before him, whilst in his attitude and countenance, the terrible conflict of contending passions, the yearnings of pity and remorse, which swelled his bosom almost to bursting, were depicted in the strongest manner -

                . . . He stood,
        Pierd'd by severe amazement, hating life,
        Speechless, and fixed in all the death of woe.

When he recovered himself sufficiently to speak, he called the ship's company together, expressed his deep contrition at the rash act he had committed, and surrendered himself to justice, by giving the command to the second lieutenant.

The circumstances which gave rise to the fatal quarrel, have already been before the public; and as they were most fully and feelingly stated in the Defence of Lieutenant G. on his trial [NC, Vol. XXVIII, p501ff], I shall not here enter into their detail. I trust, however, your readers will excuse the insertion of a summary of the transactions which occasioned the distressing catastrophe, as it is necessary to connect the chain of narrative.

From the evidence, as delivered on oath before the court martial, it appeared that the deceased, Serjeant Lake, had behaved in the most violent and disorderly manner, by threatening to beat the carpenter of the ship, his superior officer, who accordingly lodged a complain with Lieutenant Gamage, then commanding on board, in the temporary absence of the captain; who, after weighing the circumstances, sent for the serjeant, and ordered him to walk the quarter-deck, with a shouldered musket, as a slight and summary punishment, to which he was induced by a prepossession in favour of the serjeant, and a consequent wish, to preserve him from degradation, and severe corporal punishment; which must have been the result, if the steps authorized by the service, had been strictly adopted. The order the serjeant in a peremptory and insulting manner, repeatedly refused to obey. What temper, however stoical, could withstand so flagrant a breach of all rules of discipline, in the eyes of the whole ship's company? Mr. Gamage became violently enraged, and ran below for his sword, certainly not with any intent to use it fatally, but to intimidate, and enforce an obedience to his orders. When he came again on deck, which was instantaneously, the serjeant had so far complied as to hold the musket in his hand; Mr. Gamage struck the musket with his sword, expressed his indignation at the subversive conduct of the serjeant, and ordered him to walk about. He shouldered arms, and appeared to comply, upon which Lieutenant G. *returned his sword to its sheath, and was in the act of walking away,* when, in the same instant, the serjeant threw the musket down, and, with a loud oath, asserted his determination to persist in his disobedience. Lieutenant G. became infuriated again, drew his sword, and made a short thrust. The consequence was fatal. The sword, taking an upward direction, entered into the body of the unfortunate serjeant, and occasioned his almost immediate death! . . .

The court was assembled on the 27th of October, and, assured of the general sympathy he attracted, he appeared before it with a dignified composure, equally remote from confidence or dismay. When the prosecution was closed, which was conduced under an Admiralty order, by Captain Trollope, of the *Griffon,* who on this occasion, as well as during the whole affair, behaved with the greatest delicacy and attention, Lieutenant Gamage was called upon for his defence; which he read himself. The affecting manner of his delivering that appeal to the feelings of the court, frequently broken by excess of agitation, had its full force; and he ended amidst an universal burst of sympathy. The evidence in support of the defence was soon gone through, and the court cleared, the spectators waiting in anxious suspense the decision of the tribunal. Evening approached, before his judges had decided on his fate: when it was announced that the court was ready to pronounce sentence, he shewed some agitation, and taking a friend by the hand, exclaimed, "Now-now," intimating that he should then know his destiny. On re-entering the court, the distressing result of its deliberations was too evidently depicted in the mournful expression which marked the features of every member. Amidst a profound silence, and in a low and tremulous tone of voice, the judge-advocate pronounced the awful sentence of - Death. Lieutenant G. heard no more; he fell into the arms of a friend, and was carried from the court in a state of insensibility, whilst the ejaculations of, "God bless him," resounded from every mouth. The sentence was accompanied by an earnest recommendation of the court to mercy, and every exertion was made for his preservation. The ship's company of the *Griffon* petitioned the Regent, as a further proof of their affection; and his friends and relations were most zealously employed in exerting every possible interest in his behalf. The affair was the subject of long and frequent deliberation with the Lords of the Admiralty, and by them was referred for the opinion of the law officers of the crown. . . .

At length the fatal warrant for his execution arrived, and the dread intelligence was unfolded to him, in the tenderest manner, by Captain Trollope. He seemed greatly shocked! and a sad conflict took place within his then agitated bosom. The ties which bind us to existence, are made, for the wisest purposes, of the most powerful texture, and dreadful must that struggle be which bursts their force.

> For who, to dull forgetfulness a prey,
> This pleasing anxious being e'er resign'd;
> Left the warm precincts of the cheerful day,
> Nor cast one longing, lingering look behind?

The combat in the breast of the unfortunate Gamage was severe, but short; the bright beams of religion soon dissipated the gloom of despair, and pointed to felicity beyond the grave; warmed and supported by that assurance, he quickly attained a heavenly composure of mind, which, with unshaken intrepidity, he maintained unto the last. His temporal affairs were soon arranged, and the intervals of his religious exercises he occupied in writing to his friends his dying benedictions: he frequently conversed on his latter end in a calm and collected manner, and as a mark of his feeling towards the unhappy author of his woes, he requested that he might be interred by his side. [This request was complied with.] On the evening of Thursday, the 19th of November, the nature of his destiny was first intimated to him, and the succeeding Monday was appointed for his execution. As the time drew near, he evinced no symptoms of alarm or dismay; but his fortitude and resignation seemed to accumulate with every hour. Though his mental energies thus increased, he became so debilitated in body as to find some difficulty in supporting himself. On Sunday night he sent for several of the ship's company, and in pathetic terms expressed his gratitude for the affection they had shewn towards him, and bade them a final adieu. The poor fellows, melted by his appearance and manner, shed abundance of tears, and spreading the affecting tale amongst their messmates, the whole ship presented but one scene of commiseration and distress. The residue of the night was spent in serious preparation for his awful and now near approaching change: about one in the morning he fell into a deep sleep, which continued tranquil and unbroken until six: he then arose, and dressed in black, which was deemed more suitable than uniform on this most sad and solemn occasion.

The time from six until nine was employed in earnest devotion. At nine a gun was fired, and the signal for punishment hoisted at the fore-top-gallant-mast head. When this took place, his countenance betrayed no alarm, no anxiety, but heavenly serenity beamed in every feature - he exclaimed to a friend, "Feel me, I do not tremble, death has now no terrors for me; God is with me! my Saviour is with me!" These ejaculations he frequently repeated. As the boats assembled, the hum of voices, and the noise of oars, were distinctly heard in his cabin: they produced no agitation; he looked at the clergymen, and said, "I would now say with my Saviour, in the garden of Gethsemane, If it were possible, that this cup depart from me, but not my will, but thine be done, O Lord!" At a quarter after nine, he was joined in fervent prayer by the officers of the ship, who assembled for that purpose in the gun-room; he then partook of some warm wine, and again retired to his cabin; at a quarter before ten, he heard the dreadful annunciation of, "Readiness;" without the alteration of a single feature, he replied, "I am prepared, my Saviour is with me:" he then ascended the companion ladder, and proceeded along the deck, with a slow but steady step, to the foot of the platform; he there leaned, for a short time, on the shoulder of a friend, looked earnestly on the ship's company, and said, "See how a christian can die." He then mounted the forecastle, surveyed with a scrutinizing eye the fatal apparatus, expressed a hope that all was right, and gave some directions to the provost marshal - he requested permission to look around him, and took his farewell of the sun, which now shone with much brilliancy; his face was covered, he gave his last adieu; the appointed signal was given, and the ill-fated Gamage was hurried into eternity.

Thus died this unfortunate and lamented young man, whose many virtues and excellencies of heart entitled him to a better fate in this world; whose sincere repentance, through the merits of his Redeemer, has, it is sincerely hoped and believed, secured him eternal happiness in the next; and whose memory will ever be cherished by his friends, and all who knew him, as a high example of honour and integrity in prosperity, of piety and resignation in adversity, and of magnanimous intrepidity in death.

From 'Naval Anecdotes'. *XXIX 11; XXX 48-49*

Tristan D'Acunha

Mr. Lambert, the American, who, in 1811, took possession of the island of Tristan d'Acunha, in the Southern Ocean, has recently applied to the governor of the Cape of Good Hope, for the patronage and assistance of the British government and the East India Company. His agent at the Cape has declared that he would endeavour to afford refreshments to whatever vessels might pass in that track of sea; and that whenever the sanction of the British government should be known, the necessary assistance being given him, he would most solemnly declare himself allied to that government; and, by permission, display the British flag on the island, reserving however always to himself the governorship, provided an equivalent could not be agreed upon. Lord Caledon had granted to his agent a small vessel, to carry from the Cape five industrious families, who had requested leave to emigrate thither: also a few black cattle, sheep, goats, &c. with such other small necessaries as might conduce to the growth and production of the island.

Russian Fleet at Chatham

The following has been handed to us, as a correct list of the Russian fleet, which arrived at Chatham in the month of December, 1812:

Ships	Guns	Commanders
Chabroy	110	Commodore Butchensky
Pametgeftavi	74	Rear-Admiral Karopka
		Captain Butchensksy
Smeloy	80	- Ogleby
Prechsvotitel	74	- Rose
Borey	74	- Ratmanof
Severdaja Suezda	74	- Povahehen
Jupiter	74	Commodore Boyle
Orel	74	Captain Durnoff
Miranosetz	74	- Moore
Tshesma	74	- Shishmaneff
Vinera	36	- Heldebrand
Sverburg	36	Admiral Tate; Captain Butchensky
Bustroy	36	Captain Nivetsky
Archipelago	36	- Polozoff
Melpomen	24	- Waselefsky
Germyon	24	- Bojadenoff
Ganz, brig	18	Captain-lieutenant Gefimgef
Nord Agler	74	Vice-admiral Crown
		Captain Hamilton
Netron	74	- Mitkoff
Trocharach	74	- Ternofsky
Svetoslef	74	- Stepanoff
Podedanosctz	64	- Disvowith

Fever in the Russian Fleet

We rejoice to learn that the contagious fever which prevailed in the Imperial Russian Fleet, in the River Medway, has been completely subdued; and that, upon the consequent reduction of the medical establishment, under the superintendence of Doctor Dickson, the Lords Commissioners of the Admiralty have been pleased to testify their approbation, by expressing their favourable opinion of the professional exertions, and merits, of the British medical officers employed on that occasion.

Almost all those so employed, together with the attendants upon the sick, have been attacked with fever; the consequences of which proved fatal to Mr. Alexander Torbitt, surgeon, and to Mr. John Temple, assistant-surgeon.

While we justly lament the honourable fate of the warrior, we would not withhold the feelings of commiseration which are due to those who suffer in the hazardous discharge of a most arduous and painful course of duty, that of opposing the ravages of a malignant disease.

We understand that government, with a laudable attention to the interests of humanity, has directed some French prisoners, who volunteered their attendance upon the sick, to be liberated.

From 'Correspondence.' XXX 405-407

Letter to the Editor on the Contagion in the Russian Fleet

From J. Hall, Surgeon of H.M.S. Jason, n.d.

Mr. Editor, Having just commenced receiving your excellent work, I have seen in the number for July some observations on the contagious fever which lately prevailed in the Imperial Russian fleet at Chatham. You take occasion very pathetically to commiserate the fate of those English officers who suffered by that fever. As I was one of the surgeons who had the honour of being appointed to superintend the Russian sick immediately on the arrival of their ships in the River Medway, I am enabled to offer you a few remarks, which, if you think worthy of publication in your useful work, are at your service. You say, that the Lords Commissioners of the Admiralty have been pleased to testify their approbation of the exertions and merits displayed by the British medical officers employed on that occasion. If their Lordships have done so, I never before heard of it; and rather believe, that their approbation has been signified to the medical department of the Transport Board, or else to Dr. Dickson.

It was not supposed by any of us, that either praise or remuneration would be given, by our own government, for discharging our duty, however hazardous that might be; but certainly, from the well-known generosity of the Russian government, tokens of approbation were expected. Most assuredly, thanks from that quarter were highly merited by all the English medical officers employed on that service, which was peculiarly harassing and laborious; highly unpleasant, from the singularity of its nature; and hurtful to the feelings, from the prejudices and oppositions which were to be combated; difficulties, indeed, less dangerous than the fever, but far more hard to be eradicated. Men who seldom reason, whose ideas on any subject, being once received, and by habit firmly impressed, such reluctantly yield their opinions; and although they may by compulsion be forced to yield to the knowledge of others, yet it rarely happens, but that ignorance and obstinacy, united, long maintain the conflict. From such causes arose numerous impediments and annoyances in the performance of our duty; the more painful to those English medical officers who, from having previously served under the Imperial Flag, possessed a knowledge of the language, which, although it greatly facilitated their duties, yet rendered them sensible of many unpleasant remarks which were unknown to their companions.

On my joining that division of the fleet which had been assigned to me, I found some ships in a very bad state: many men were lying in heaps on the lower deck, notwithstanding two hospital ships, the *Argonaut* and *Trusty*, had been filled with sick from these ships. The nature of that fever, its causes, and successful treatment, will, I doubt not, be ably described by those whom talents and experience have rendered capable of doing it. To Dr. Weir, the inspector of hospitals, is due every praise; particularly from the Russian government. He first adopted, and energetically pursued, those measures which stopped the contagion in the ships, by removing and destroying some of its principal sources. Those unfortunates who were languishing under its dire effects were soon restored to a state of convalescence by the method of treatment which was laid down and insisted on by him; and by his representations, and the generosity of the Transport Board, several articles of nourishment were supplied to the sick.

The mortality was great, as was to be expected, from the number of sick, and the advanced stage of their complaints; and had the Russian fleet been a week longer at sea, one half of its sick would have been consigned to a watery grave. Dr. Dickson had the medical superintendence of the Imperial Fleet a few weeks after its arrival; he fell sick during the exercise of his well-known exertions; but recovered. - To him, to Dr. Douglas, surgeon of the *Argonaut*, and to Mr. Dobson, surgeon of the *Trusty*, are unexceptionably due every praise; not only for their exertions but also for their laborious employments. Among the English medical officers who became sufferers from the discharge of their duties, may be also enumerated Mr. Dobson, Mr. Torbitt, myself, and Mr. Temple, assistant-surgeon; the latter, with Mr. Torbitt, a man of acknowledged talents, fell victims. By the assiduous and humane care and skilful treatment afforded me by Dr. Douglas, I now have the blessing of existence; so far as the exertions of mortals are successful - *Deo juvante.*

I recovered, but witnessed and assisted at the interment of my lamented brother officer, Torbitt. Alas! a sad and gloomy task; but still easier to be accomplished than the one I have assigned to myself: - in rendering to merit tributes, which, although due, may be unacceptable, in standing forth as a witness to the exertions of others, who require not my testimonials, I may unfortunately excite the suspicion of the one, and be accused of arrogance by the other: however, I acquit my heart of a debt, and confirm my mind by reflecting, that

"Nuda nunquam crubescit veritus."

I am, Sir, your most obedient servant,

J. HALL, Surgeon of H.M.S. *Jason*

From 'Naval Anecdotes.' XXIX 110-112; 189-195

Lord Nelson and Lady Hamilton

Lady Hamilton has published a statement of her case, laying claims to a remuneration from the public, for her services at the court of Sicily. - The following anecdote, relative to the codicil of Lord Nelson's will, in which he bequeathed her ladyship to the protection of the country, has not yet been before our readers:

"When Captain Blackwood," says Lady Hamilton, "brought it (the will) home, he gave it to the present Earl Nelson, who, with his wife and family, were then with me, and had indeed been living with me many months - To their son I was a mother; and their daughter, Lady Charlotte, had been exclusively under my care for six years. The Earl, afraid I should be provided for in the sum that parliament was expected to grant, to uphold the hero's name and family, kept the codicil in his pocket until the day £200,000 was voted for that purpose; *on that day* he dined with me in Clarges-street: hearing at table what was done, he took the *codicil out*, threw it to me, and said, with a very course expression, 'that I might now do as I pleased with it:' I had it registered the next day at Doctors' Commons, where it now rests for the national redemption."

Another anecdote related by her Ladyship is as follows:

"When Sir William was recalled from his embassy at Palermo, in 1800, the Queen determined to travel with us as far as Vienna, to see her daughter, then Empress of Germany. Nelson also accompanied us. His Lordship and Sir William were present at my parting with the Queen: at that affecting moment, her Majesty put into my hands a paper, saying it was the conveyance of £1000 a year, that she had fixed to invest for me in the hands of Friez, the government banker at Vienna. This she said, 'lest by any possibility I should not be suitably compensated for the services I had rendered, the monies I generously expended, and the losses I had so voluntarily sustained for the benefits of her nation and her own.' - As I then stood, I thought the acceptance *of* such a reward from the Queen, *circumstanced* as she was, unworthy a British heart; with every expression of respect and gratitude to her Majesty, I destroyed the instrument, saying, England was ever just, and, to her faithful servants, *generous*! - and that I would feel it insulting to my own beloved magnanimous Sovereign, to accept of meed or reward from any other hand."

Naval Members of the Newly Elected Parliament of the United Kingdom

Names	Rank	Places
Sir Edward Buller, Bart.	Vice-Admiral	East-Looe
George Campbell, Esq.	Vice-Admiral	Carmarthen
Lord Cochrane, K.B.	Captain	Westminster
Sir John Thomas Duckworth, K.B.	Admiral	N. Romney
William Johnstone Hope, Esq.	Rear-Admiral	Dumfries-shire
John Markham, Esq.	Vice-Admiral	Portsmouth
Robert Moorsom, Esq.	Rear-Admiral	Queenborough
Sir Harry Neale, Bart.	Rear-Admiral	Lymington
Charles Herbert Pierrepoint, Viscount Newark	Captain	Nottingham-shire
Honourable Charles Paget	Captain	Launceston
Pownell Bastard Pellew, Esq.	Captain	Plymouth
Lord William Stuart	Captain	Cardiff
Sir Thomas Boulden Thompson, Bart.	Rear-Admiral	Rochester
Sir Joseph Sydney Yorke, Knt	Rear-Admiral	Sandwich

The Acasta Frigate

Captain Kerr, placing a due confidence in the largest, the best officered, and best manned frigate in the service, has been roaming about for his prey for several months, and we only wish him fairly alongside the *President, Constitution,* or the *United States.* On receiving the accounts of the capture of the *Guerriere,* Captain Kerr assembled his crew, and addressed them as follows: - "My Lads, it is with a distress which I cannot sufficiently depict to you, that I inform you of the capture of the *Guerriere,* by the *Constitution* American frigate. We are going to sea, and in the largest and best armed frigate in the service. Hear my determination - *I am determined never to strike the colours of the Acasta*- My mind is made up - What say you, my boys?" The exclamation of - "To the bottom!" and three truly British cheers, followed his words, and the anchor was weighed. - From the excellent equipment of the *Acasta,* her great size, weight of metal, and number of men, we are confident that with her there will be no desecration of the seaman's religion - the Flag! The *Acasta* has taken on board 24-pounders on her maindeck - and we may cheerfully trust the national honour to her efforts.

Progress of a Fright

A young tradesman of Plymouth had lately occasion to go on board a man of war in

Hamoaze, on particular business to one of the officers. Just as he reached the gangway, a seaman fell down from the maintop-gallant-yard, and dashed his brains out, near the place where he was standing. The horrible spectacle so affrighted him, that he ran down the main hatchway ladder, and got below into the first berth he could find. He had no sooner entered it, than he was assailed with the groans of a master's-mate's wife, in the pangs of child-birth. He set off again, and rested, to recover himself, on a gun, for some minutes - then ascended the hatchway ladder, to get over the side, into a boat, to go on shore. The first object when he got on deck, which presented itself to his view, was a poor culprit of a seaman (who had been sentenced to death for striking a superior officer), proceeding, with the chaplain and provost-marshal, and a guard of royal marines, along the gangway towards a platform at the forecastle, to be hanged at the fore-yard arm! This completed the climax of his fears and terrors. He got over the side into a shore-boat, and rowed to Northcorner-beach. On landing, he swore he would not go again on board a King's ship for a King's ransom.

From 'Corrsepondence.' XXIX 196-216

A Defiance to the Americans

Frederick Hickey, Captain of H.M.S. Atalante to the Editor
H.M.S. Atalante, Halifax harbour, February 1 1813
Messers. Editors, For the information of the public, and to do justice to the character of the seamen composing the crew of H.M.S. under my command, on whose loyalty and exertions, when called for, I have the most implicit reliance, I beg you will insert the following letter, and its several signatures.

"Sir, Perceiving by the Halifax newspaper, that a scandalous report (far from the character of British seamen) has arise, that the crew of H.M.S. *Orpheus*, and other ships on this station, would not fight in case of falling in with an American frigate, and having read the letter from the crew of the *Orpheus* to Lieutenant Fayrer, for the information of Captain Pigot [protesting against the calumny]; the crew of the *Atalante* do most heartily coincide in their comrades' representation, and their loyal disposition for their King and country: and beg it may be made known also, that should an opportunity occur, the *Atalante* will never surrender, even to a superiority of force; that all on board are loyal and true, and have devoted their lives to the service of their beloved country.

J. Fowler, boatswain's mate.	J. Hear, captain of the after-guard
D. Wilson, J. Wilson,	W. Howell, sail-maker
captains of the maintop	W. Crose, coxswain
T. Smith, W. Dixon,	R. Bishop, quarter-master
captains of the foretop	T. Balfour, quarter-master's mate
R. Hillary, gunner's-mate	J. Stevens, serjeant of marines
S. Shanks, ship's-corporal	H. Boys, ship's-corporal's mate
T. Taylor, quarter-master	W. Armitage, corporal of marines
A. Butlin, yeoman of the powder-room"	

Defence of the Canadian Lakes

"Mentor" to the Editor
Mr. Editor, There is every reason to believe that the Americans intend to renew their

attacks on Canada, as soon as the return of open weather will allow them to act. With this view, it appears they have prepared a considerable naval force on the Lakes, to man which, a large draft of seamen, with some of their best officers, were sent from New York at the end of the year. I am happy to perceive that our board of Admiralty are taking adequate measures to obtain, and preserve, a superiority on those distance waters, by sending some of our sloops of war, of the smallest draft of water, which are to be floated over the shallows, and so conveyed to the Lakes, where they will be immediately serviceable. It is to be hoped that they will be at their destination early in May, when the St. Lawrence will be open; and that an active, enterprising, and experienced officer will be selected for commodore.[1] There can be no doubt that the Americans will strain every nerve to have the superiority; but I hope in this they will be disappointed, and be repelled afloat, as they have been (and I trust will be) ashore, by the brave troops serving under that able and active officer, Sir G. Prevost.

From the 'Naval History of the Present Year,' 1813
February–March. XXIX 242-245

British Interests Prosper in the Baltic

The affairs of the Continent present an eminently favourable aspect. All the ports of Prussia, not actually in the possession of the French, are open to this country. The French authorities have been under the necessity of quitting Hamburg; and the intercourse between that port and England has been restored to its former footing. – It is also generally understood, that an amicable arrangement has been concluded between Great Britain, Denmark, and Sweden, decidedly in opposition to what has been termed the Continental System.

But the Lamentable War with America Continues; HMS Java Captured

We have still, however, to regret the disastrous progress of the naval war between this country and America. Another frigate [HMS *Java*] has fallen into the hands of the enemy! – The subject is too painful for us to dwell upon . . .

Captain Lambert, the commander of the *Java*, had often distinguished himself in action. He commanded the *St. Fiorenzo*, in February, 1805, when that ship captured the French frigate *Psyche*, commanded by the active Captain Bergeret, which officer commanded the *Virginie*, when captured by Sir Edward Pellew. He also commanded the *Iphigenia* frigate, in the attack of the French frigates at Port South East, Isle of France. He was brother to Captain Robert Lambert, of H.M.S. *Duncan*. The supernumerary officers on board were: – one commander, two lieutenants, one marine officer, four midshipmen, one clergyman, one assistant-surgeon.

Sanguinary Frigate Action

The *London Gazette* of the 23d March, contains the official report of one of the most sanguinary conflicts ever maintained by a single frigate, without a decisive termination. The *Amelia*, commanded by Captain Irby, was engaged, on the 7th past, off the coast of Africa, against the French frigate *Aréthuse*, which the English commander had judiciously

1 Sir James Yeo has been mentioned: an appointment, it is presumed, perfectly satisfactory. Ed.

contrived to separate from another called *Rubis*; thus rendering the latter an inactive spectator of the combat. With every disposition to exult in the heroism of our gallant countrymen, we cannot contemplate without pain their exposure to so slaughterous a contest. It is long since any thing like this persevering effort has been witnessed on the part of the French. Is it not obvious that they are stimulated by American triumphs? Does the Admiralty now believe we were wrong in foreseeing a train of ills from the surrender of the *Guerriere*? It is, perhaps, by this time discovered, that there was a plain, and unfortunately too accurate, meaning in our words. The French sailor, who went into battle, with a persuasion, founded on long experience, that his antagonist must be victorious, was already half-conquered. How different when he learns that his dreaded opponent has been beaten, yea, thrice beaten, by a new and inexperienced enemy. Not only does this cure him of superstitious terror, but it substitutes a spirit of emulation, and national rivalry. These are not flattering reflections; but we ought not to shrink from them. The *Gazette* contains a pretty long list of captures and recaptures on the American station: still, however, we are behind-hand, from the petty hesitating system of warfare we adopted at the outset: though it is not by a tedious account of mercantile profit and loss that we should settle such a war as that which we are waging against the United States. The Americans ought to be made to *feel* the real weight of the British trident, when properly wielded; and not be allowed to skulk from their challenge for mastery on the ocean, under the shelter of some compromising special-pleading treaty, till not only our losses have been indemnified, our defeats avenged, but the *spell* be restored. The *Naval Chronicle* stands unconnected with either of the in or out factions who dispute the sway of the state: but on this occasion we cannot refrain from standing forth in behalf of that vital interest of this sea girt isle, to which we are devoted, and protesting against the ministry of clerks. Persons who are advanced to power, after having been nurtured in the routine of offices, do admirably well, as long as things go on in the common track; but when the high roads are broken up, and the waters are out; when a new and troubled scene is opened, and the official file affords neither precedent nor clue; then it is that a greater knowledge of mankind, and a far more extensive comprehension, are required, than ever office gave, or than office ever can give.

Sir Sidney Smith Implicated in 'A Delicate Investigation'

We have heard, but we can hardly believe, that Vice-Admiral Sir Sidney Smith has been recalled from the Mediterranean, on account of the manner in which his name has been so prominently brought in question at home, by what has been recently *published* of the state inquest upon the conduct of the Princess of Wales; an inquest, in our humble opinion, most improperly styled a "delicate investigation." It is rather a remarkable coincidence, that this officer should have happened to be absent on foreign service during the two inquiries set on foot relative to the Princess's domestic life; the result of both which seems to have left him blameless, and unimpeachable, even without any defence of his own. And we say we rather disbelieve the rumour we have felt ourselves called upon to notice, because we do not comprehend how the mere publication of facts (a publicity in which the admiral has no share), can be made a legitimate ground for his supersedure; when the facts themselves, as already taken cognizance of, were not considered as criminal, or as affording sufficient ground for exclusion from employment. For it must be recollected, that subsequent to the former report of the lords of the privy council, Sir Sidney Smith has held a commission as "commander-in-chief upon a particular service", prior to his actual employment as second in command under Sir Edward Pellew. It is possible, after all, that Sir Sidney may be coming home: but we think it right to record our disbelief of the grounds upon which that circumstance is stated and accredited. With respect to the cause itself, we confess ourselves somewhat embarrassed, both by its length and its delicacy, what specific notice to take of it. On the one hand, it is our aim to steer as clear of politics as possible: but we cannot exclude from our minds the conviction, that most of our naval readers must look to the *Naval Chronicle* for information on a case involving the succession to the crown of England, originating with a distinguished officer of the royal marines, and containing by implication charges amounting to no less than high treason, against a flag-officer and a post captain of the royal navy; besides minor imputations, attaching to other naval names high in the estimation of the members of the profession. We think that we shall feel it our duty finally to give these extraordinary proceedings a place in this work; and prior to our next publication shall make up our minds in what form the narrative can be most appropriately and instructively presented to the patrons of the Naval Chronicle.

HMS Captain Burns

On the night of Friday, March 22, the *Captain*, of 74 guns (Lord Nelson's ship when he took the *San Josef*), which had recently been converted into a hulk, at Plymouth, took fire, and was totally destroyed. The *San Josef,* which lay alongside, was with difficulty preserved. No lives were lost.

April–May. ^{XXIX 434}

Some Macedonians Desert to US Navy

It is with concern we hear, that a number of the *Macedonian*'s crew have entered into the American service; yet allowance must be made for the very great difference in the pay which they thus receive. The remainder of the crew of this ship have at length arrived at Bermuda on parole, the American government refusing any further exchange of prisoners, except upon their own principles, which would recognize the validity of their mode of naturalizing the subjects of other governments.

From 'Naval Anecdotes.' ^{XXIX 277-282; 382-386; 449-454; XXX 184}

The Royal Forests Supply Little Lumber

With respect to the royal forests, of which 115,504 acres are withheld from the royal family and the public, for the ostensible purpose of supporting the navy, it appears, from the elaborate report of the commissioners, &c. appointed by parliament in 1788, that for fifty-seven years preceding, the supply of timber to his Majesty's dock-yards from these dignified wastes average only 1,356 loads annually; which, in the proportion of timber then consumed in the construction of ships in the King's dock-yards, is only equal to the building of a ship of 642 tons, being less than the smallest frigate of 32 guns in his Majesty's service, and is little more than half a cubic foot from an acre, which, at the average rent of what the land would have let for, cost the public at the rate of upwards of £68 per load, without the carriage; when the highest price given to individuals at that period was only £4 5s per load. And in 1802, from a greater supply being demanded, the surveyor-general of woods stated to the Navy Board, that "the quantity of improving timber in his Majesty's forests is by far too inconsiderable to afford the smallest expectation of the continuance of even the annual supplies the yards have lately had." Indeed, from the survey made in 1783, it appears, that in four forests the quantity of decayed timber exceed the sound, and that the whole quantity of sound oak timber, fit for naval purposes, then standing in six of the forests out of ten, and containing 83,738 acres, was only 50,456 loads, *being not equal to one year's consumption*, even at that time, as stated by the commissioners appointed by parliament; although, in 1788, the whole tonnage of the navy consisted of only 413,667 tons; which, in 1810, amounted to nearly 800,000 tons, and the consumption of timber was stated at 100,000 loads per annum; and, in 1812, at 110,000 loads for hull timber, without including ordnance, or masts, &c; which, at the average produce on private property of 50 loads of oak timber per acre, in 100 years, would require 220,000 acres, of which 2,200 must be felled and planted every year, to yield a supply equal to such consumption. But it is a melancholy fact, as shewn in an account laid before the House of Commons, dated November 26, 1803, that in the New Forest, of 66,942 acres, "the number of oak trees in an improving state, which may be considered fit for naval purposes, were only 8,012, containing but 8,322 loads of timber;" which, from parliamentary records, appear not be equal to *three months' consumption in the King's dock-yards only*.

Wooden Walls - Marr-Lodge Forest

By a survey lately made, of Marr-Lodge Forest, by order of the Navy Board, it appears that there is an extent of twenty square miles of timber, fit to use as top-masts for ships of the line, and for masts and bowsprits for cutters and schooners. There are thousands of trees fit for building ships of great magnitude; and it is estimated that there is in Marr-Lodge Forest a supply of masts for the whole navy of Great Britain *for sixty years to come*, allowing the expenditure to be 1000 spars per annum; and they are all self planted, so that there will be a constant succession. The forest is situated on the banks of the River Dee, 60 miles from Aberdeen, and is the property of the Earl of Fife.

FNF Aréthuse and HMS Amelia
Comparative Veracity

The Parisian newspapers, of 23d April, 1813, comprise a document which the naval world has been anxious to see - the French narrative of the combat between the frigates *Aréthuse* and *Amelia*, in the form of an extract from the official report of Captain Bouvet to the minister of the marine. It contains that which must "give pause" to every lover of his country; and as the Frenchman, while he fought boldly, tells his tale fairly enough, this document deserves the more serious attention. The only remarkable difference between the two statements, relates to the *Aréthuse's* consort, *Rubis*, which Captain Irby, in his despatch to the Admiralty, mentions as being in sight just before the commencement of the action, whereas, according to Captain Bouvet, that ship had been wrecked the night before, and her crew had saved themselves on board a Portuguese prize in company. So that although Captain Irby seems to have fought under the justifiable impression of his adversary having a reinforcement at hand, yet in point of fact this was only a ship to ship business; in which the relative disproportion of killed and wounded, "all by fair fighting," as Captain Irby says, is not less unaccountable than lamentable.

[It is not possible to reproduce either captain's letters here.]

From the 'Naval History of the Present Year,' 1813
May-June. *XXIX 497*

Armistice Among Russia, Prussia and France

The principal occurrence which has taken place since our last Retrospect (though not strictly naval), we still deem so important as to be noticed under the present head; we mean the Armistice lately concluded between the Emperor of Russia and King of Prussia on one part, and the Emperor of the French on the other. - What effect the present cessation of hostilities between the powers alluded to, may have on the politics of Europe, it is not possible for us to foresee - various are the reports in circulation - the principal one being, that a general Congress is about to take place, for the purpose of putting an end to the present war, and that his Majesty's government have been invited to send a minister to assist at the Convention. If a minister is sent on the part of the British government, we know of no person more fit to fill so high a situation, than the Marquis of Wellesley - that nobleman possessing, in a superior degree, the necessary qualifications for so important a mission. Should a peace be the result of the Congress, we feel confident it would reflect honour on the British government.

June-July 1813. *XXX 69-72*

USS Chesapeake Captured

A prominent feature of the naval intelligence of the past month was, the gallant action of Captain P.B.V. Broke, of H.M.S. *Shannon*, which terminated in 15 minutes, with the capture of the United States frigate *Chesapeake*. The brilliant style in which the business was done, may perhaps be equalled, but we are sure will not be excelled, by any incident that can be quoted from British history. We will not weaken, by any comments, the simple but interesting narrative officially transmitted to government by Captain Broke, and which will appear among the Letters on Service in our present number. We may just mention, however, that so confident were the Americans of victory, that a number of pleasure boats came out with the *Chesapeake* from Boston, to see the *Shannon* compelled to strike; and a grand dinner was actually preparing on shore for the *Chesapeake*'s officers, against their return with the prize! - The private signals of the American navy are said to have been taken on board of the *Chesapeake*.

American Gunnery

The partial victories of the American ships at the commencement of hostilities over the British frigates, are said to be attributable, in a great measure, to an improvement in their shot. The cartridge (instead of being made up in canvas) is ascertained to have been *cased with lead*. This enables them, it seems, to load with greater despatch, and to fire with additional effect; and hence the destructive havoc of their broadsides.

Carden Exonerated

Captain Carden sailed from Bermuda on the 5th of June. Previous, however, to his departure, he, his gallant officers, and crew, had been tried by a court martial, for the loss of the *Macedonian*, and most honourably acquitted. They were highly complimented by the court, on the courage, activity, and firmness, displayed in the action with an enemy of so greatly superior force, as was the American frigate *United States*.

Exchange of Prisoners With America

The *National Intelligenser* of the 16th May says, "We have the pleasure to state, that effectual measures are in progress for the relief of our unfortunate countrymen in captivity. A cartel, by which a system for the proper treatment, release, and exchange of prisoners, has been fixed, and signed some days since, between General Mason, commissary-general of prisoners, on the part of the United States, and Colonel Barclay, general agent for prisoners, on the part of Great Britain. By this, among other things, it is stipulated, the two cartel vessels, of the burthen of 500 tons together, shall be constantly kept by each government, in the service of removing prisoners of the two nations, to be released on account or exchanged. On our part, the two vessels have been already purchased, fitted and despatched, to bring home our prisoners suffering in the West Indies. The United States cartel *Analostan*, Captain Smith, left this place for Jamaica on the 2d instant, to touch in Hampton Roads, and take off British prisioners; and on the 13th instant, the United States cartel ship *Perseverance*, Captain Dill, sailed from Philadelphia for Barbadoes, to touch at New York to take in British prisoners in like manner. Both vessels are to return with American prisoners to Providence, in Rhode Island, one of the stations agreed on for the exchange of prisoners of war.

Toulon Fleet

List of the line of battle ships in Toulon, according to the report of some deserters who escaped with the boat of the *Ville de Marseilles*, on the 25th April:

Commerce de Paris	130	*Magnanime*	74
Majestueux	120	*Sceptre*	80
Austerlitz	120	*Danube*	80
Wagram	130	*Ulm*	80
Impériale [2]	130	*Hannibal*	74
Montebello [3]	130	*Trident*	74
Donawert	80	*Romulus*	74
Genois [4]	74	*Ville de Marseilles*	74
Ajax [5]	74	*Agamemnon*	74
Breslaw	74	*Medée*	44
Suffrein	74	*Amelia*	–
Bordée	74		
On the stocks:			
Hero	74	*Gallus*, or *Gallois*	74
Napoleon	130	*Rancune*	40

2 To receive Massena's flag at the main.
3 Without masts, in the arsenal.
4 In the arsenal.
5 In the arsenal.

1813 - USS Constitution and HMS Java

AT THE END OF DECEMBER 1812, the recently captured French frigate *Renommée* renamed HMS *Java*, taken into British service to carry to India the newly appointed governor to Bombay, Lieutenant-General Hislop, became the latest casualty to the powerful American super-frigates when she put into San Salvador for water. *Java* was so badly manned that she was virtually a training ship, her crew having only been exercised at the guns for the first time the day before she encountered the USS *Constitution* commanded by Commodore Bainbridge. The other ships of the American squadron, *Essex* and *Hornet*, were not in contact. Captain Henry Lambert fought his ship as well as he might, but the outcome was inevitable.

Lieutenant Chads' Reports
Letters on Service
Admiralty Office, April 20, 1813. ^{XXIX 346-349}

Letters, of which the following are Copies and Extracts, have been transmitted to this Office by Rear-Admiral Dixon, addressed to J.W. Croker, Esq. by Lieutenant Chads, late First Lieutenant of H.M.S. Java

United States Frigate Constitution, off St. Salvador, December 31, 1812
Sir, It is with deep regret that I write you, for the information of the Lords Commissioners of the Admiralty, that H.M.S. *Java* is no more, after sustaining an action on the 29th instant, for several hours, with the American frigate, *Constitution*, which resulted in the capture and ultimate destruction of H.M.S. Captain Lambert being dangerously wounded in the height of the action, the melancholy task of writing the detail devolves on me.

On the morning of the 29th instant, at 8 A.M. off St. Salvador (coast of Brazil), the wind at N.E. we perceived a strange sail; made all sail in chase, and soon made her out to be a large frigate; at noon prepared for action, the chase not answering our private signals, and tacking towards us under easy sail: when about four miles distant she made a signal, and immediately tacked and made all sail away upon the wind. We soon found we had the advantage of her in sailing, and came up with her fast, when she hoisted American colours: she then bore about three points on our lee bow. At fifty minutes past one P.M. the enemy shortened sail, upon which we bore down upon her; at ten minutes past two, when about half a mile distant, she opened her fire, giving us her larboard broadside which was not returned till we were close on her weather bow. Both ships now manoeuvred to obtain advantageous positions, our opponent evidently avoiding close action, and firing high to disable our masts, in which he succeeded too well, having shot away the head of our bowsprit, with the jib-boom, and our running rigging so much cut as to prevent our preserving the weather gage.

At five minutes past three, finding the enemy's raking fire extremely heavy, Captain Lambert ordered the ship to be laid on board, in which we should have succeeded, had not our fore-mast been shot away at this moment, the remains of our bowsprit passing over his taffrail; shortly after this the maintop-mast went, leaving the ship totally unmanageable, with most of our starboard guns rendered useless from the wreck lying over them.

At half past three our gallant captain received a dangerous wound in the breast, and was carried below; from this time we could not fire more than two or three guns until a quarter past four, when our mizen-mast was shot away; the ship then fell off a little, and brought many of our starboard guns to bear: the enemy's rigging was so much cut that he could not now avoid shooting ahead, which brought us fairly broadside and broadside. Our main-yard now went in the slings, both ships continued engaged in this manner till thirty-five minutes past four, we frequently on fire in consequence of the wreck lying on the side engaged. Our opponent now made sail ahead out of gun-shot, where he remained an hour repairing his damages, leaving us an unmanageable wreck, with only the main-mast left, and that tottering. Every exertion was made by us during this interval to place the ship in a state to renew the action. We succeeded in clearing the wreck of our masts from our guns, a sail was set on the stumps of the fore-mast and bowsprit, the weather half of the main-yard remaining aloft, the main-tack was got forward in the hope of getting the ship before the wind, our helm being still perfect; the effort unfortunately proved ineffectual, from the main-mast falling over the side, from the heavy rolling of the ship, which nearly covered the whole of our starboard guns. We still waited that attack of the enemy, he now standing towards us for that purpose; on his coming nearly within hail of us, and from his manoeuvre perceiving he intended a position ahead where he could take us without a possibility of our returning a shot; I then consulted the officers, who agreed with myself that our having a great part of our crew killed and wounded, our bowsprit and three masts gone, several guns useless, we should not be justified in wasting the lives of more of those remaining, who I hope their Lordships and the country will think have bravely defended his Majesty's ship; under these circumstances, however, reluctantly, at fifty minutes past five, our colours were lowered from the stump of the mizen-mast, and we were taken possession of, a little after six, by the American frigate *Constitution*, commanded by Commodore Bainbridge, who, immediately after ascertaining the state of the ship, resolved on burning her, which we had the satisfaction of seeing done as soon as the wounded were removed. Annexed I send you a return of the killed and wounded, and it is with pain I perceive it so numerous . . .

I have the honour to be, &c.

Hy. D. CHADS, First Lieutenant,
of His Majesty's Ship *Java*

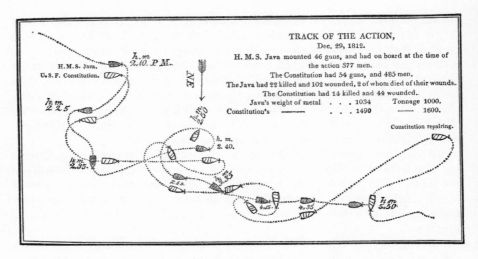

TRACK OF THE ACTION,
Dec. 29, 1812.

H. M. S. Java mounted 46 guns, and had on board at the time of the action 377 men.
The Constitution had 54 guns, and 485 men.
The Java had 22 killed and 102 wounded, 2 of whom died of their wounds.
The Constitution had 14 killed and 44 wounded.

Java's weight of metal . . . 1034   Tonnage 1000.
Constitution's ———   . . . 1490   ——— 1600.

Constitution repairing.

Java's Track. Plate 21

P.S. The *Constitution* has also suffered severely both in her rigging and men, having her fore and mizen-masts, maintop-mast, both maintopsail-yards, spanker-boom, gaff, and trysail-mast badly shot, and the greatest part of the standing rigging very much damaged, with ten men killed, the commodore, fifth lieutenant, and forty-six men wounded, four of whom are since dead.

A Java Lieutenant Writes of the Battle

From 'Naval Anecdotes.' XXIX 452-453

Mercury Cartel, St. Salvador, January 26, 1813

My Dear Friend, I have a most unpleasant commission for you, or rather, it would be better for B. to break it to his father, which is, the death of poor young Keele; he was badly wounded in the action, and was obliged to have his leg amputated, and in consequence died the next day; he was a fine courageous little fellow. The elder Keele also, poor fellow! was very severely wounded in the arm, but is now quite out of danger, and the limb safe. The youngest continued to shew the same undaunted spirit to the last; when the action was over, he inquired if the ship had struck, and seeing a ship's colour spread over him, he grew uneasy, until he was assured it was an English flag. The wound the elder received, must have proceeded from a shot passing between his arm and side: he was particularly noticed by his superior officers, for his great coolness and bravery whilst in action, when he met with the above accident. Both these youths are sons of a Mr. Keele, of Southampton; the younger 16, the other 18, years of age. It is particularly to be remarked, that in no action this war has so great a slaughter happened to that particular class of officers, the midshipmen, as occurred in this, there being no less than five killed, and four wounded. From the manner in which this action was fought, and the unequalled injury the *Java* sustained beyond the *Constitution*, it appears evident that the American had advantages which do not belong to our frigates. It must strike every impartial observer, in noticing how rapidly the *Java*'s masts were carried away, one after the other; but it remains no longer a mystery, when it is known the *Constitution*'s masts are equal to our seventy-four's - and it was noticed by the officers of the *Java*, after the action, that the *Java*'s shot had passed through two of them; but so little did the Americans regard it, that when at St. Salvador, after the action, they did not attempt to fish the masts for security, before going to sea. Most of the crew of the *Constitution* were known to be English, and many of them our prime sailors; some had belonged to the *Iphigenia*, others to the *Guerriere*; and, I am sorry to say, three of the *Java*'s entered when prisoners. The surgeon of the *Constitution* was an Irishman, and lately an assistant-surgeon in our navy.

[*The Naval Chronicle* also published, in a letter from 'I.T.L.', extracts from Lieutenant Chads' court martial, which included a plan showing the action, and a rather technical account of the wounded in the action by *Java*'s surgeon (Vol. XXIX, pp402-408; 414-417).]

1813 – The Capture of USS Chesapeake

THE USS *CHESAPEAKE* was not one of the super-frigates, and she was not fully worked up for service, but her capture in fifteen minutes by HMS *Shannon* was strongly reassuring to the Royal Navy after the shocking losses of *Macedonian* and *Java*. *The Naval Chronicle* published far more about this action than it really deserved. The Consolidated Edition, with the benefit of nearly 200 years' perspective, has given it much less space.

Captain Broke's Dispatch
Letters on Service
Admiralty Office, July 10 1813. ^{XXX 83–84}

Copy of a Letter from the Hon. Captain Capel, of H.M.S. La Hogue, to John Wilson Croker, Esq. dated at Halifax, June 11, 1813
Sir, It is with the greatest pleasure I transmit you a letter I have just received from Captain [Philip Bowes Vere] Broke, of H.M.S. *Shannon*, detailing a most brilliant achievement in the capture of the United States's frigate *Chesapeake*, in fifteen minutes. Captain Broke relates so fully the particulars of this gallant affair, that I feel it unnecessary to add much to his narrative; but I cannot forbear expressing the pleasure I feel . . .
I have the honour to be, &c.

Thos. BLADEN CAPEL
Captain, and Senior Officer at Halifax

H.M.S. Shannon, Halifax, 6 June 1813
I have the honour to inform you, that being close in with Boston Light House, in H.M.S. under my command, on the 1st inst. I had the pleasure of seeing that the United States' frigate *Chesapeake* (whom we had long been watching) was coming out of the harbour to engage the *Shannon*; I took a position between Cape Ann and Cape Cod, and then hove-to for him to join us – the enemy came down in a very handsome manner, having three American ensigns flying; when closing with us he sent down his royal yards. I kept the *Shannon's* up, expecting the breeze would die away. At half-past five P.M. the enemy hauled up within hail of us on the starboard side, and the battle began, both

Portrait of Sir Philip Bowes Vere
Broke. Engraved by Blood, with
permission of the Proprietors of
the *East Anglian Magazine.* Plate 428

ships steering full under the topsails; after exchanging between two and three broadsides, the enemy's ship fell on board of us, her mizen channels locking in with our fore-rigging. I went forward to ascertain her position, and observing that the enemy were flinching from their guns, I gave orders to prepare for boarding. Our gallant bands appointed to that service immediately rushed in, under their respective officers, upon the enemy's decks, driving every thing before them with irresistible fury. The enemy made a desperate, but disorderly resistance.

The firing continued at all the gangways, and between the tops, but in two minutes' time the enemy were driven sword in hand from every post. The American flag was hauled down, and the proud old British Union floated triumphant over it. In another minute they ceased firing from below and called for quarter. The whole of this service was achieved in fifteen minutes from the commencement of the action.

I have to lament the loss of many of my gallant shipmates, but they fell exulting in their conquest. . . .

Having received a severe sabre wound at the first onset, whilst charging a party of the enemy who had rallied on their forecastle, I was only capable of giving command till assured our conquest was complete, and then directing second Lieutenant Wallis to take charge of the *Shannon,* and secure the prisoners. I left the third lieutenant, Mr. Falkiner (who had headed the main-deck boarders), in charge of the prize. . . .

I have the honour to be, &c.

P. B.V. BROKE

To Captain the Hon. T. Bladen Capel, &c. Halifax

Broke's Challenge
From 'Correspondence.' XXX 412-414

Halifax, N.S. 2d October
Mr. Editor, The enclosed animated, yet modest invitation, from the gallant Captain Broke to the late commander of the *Chesapeake,* appeared today, for the first time, in the

Halifax papers. The successful result of the wished for action between those ships, and an acquaintance with Captain Broke's private and public character, renders his letter particularly interesting to every one in this place; and I make no doubt but that it will be equally well received and appreciated by the first, and most to be envied, beings in existence, The People of England! I transmit it for insertion in your valuable work, and am, Sir, your very obedient servant. M.

The public have heard much of the following challenge, sent by Captain Broke, to Captain Lawrence. If the date be correct, it must have been sent on the morning of the day on which the battle was fought. It was first received in Salem, and sent on by mail, and did not reach Boston until after the action, consequently was never seen by Captain Lawrence, and has not before been published:

From Captain Broke to Captain Lawrence
His Britannic Majesty's Ship Shannon off Boston, June 1813
Sir, As the *Chesapeake* appears now ready for sea, I request you will do me the favour to meet the *Shannon* with her, ship to ship, to try the fortune of our respective flags. To an officer of your character, it requires some apology for proceeding to further particulars. Be assured, Sir, that it is not from any doubt I can entertain of your wishing to close with my proposals; but merely to provide an answer to any objection which might be made, and very reasonably, upon the chance of our receiving unfair support.

After the diligent attention we had paid to Commodore Rodgers; the pains I took to detach all force but the *Shannon* and *Tenedos* to such a distance, that they could not possibly join in any action fought in sight of the Capes; and various verbal messages which had been sent into Boston to that effect, we were much disappointed to find the commodore had eluded us by sailing the first chance, after the prevailing easterly winds had obliged us to keep an offing from the coast. He, perhaps, wished for some stronger assurance of a fair meeting. I am, therefore, induced to address you more particularly, and to assure you that what I write I pledge my honour to perform to the utmost of my power.

The *Shannon* mounts 24 guns upon her broadside, and one light boat-gun; 18-pounders on her main deck, and 32-pound carronades on her quarter deck and forecastle; and is manned with a complement of 300 men and boys (a large proportion of the latter), besides 30 seamen, boys, and passengers, who were taken out of recaptured vessels lately. I am thus minute [very detailed], because a report has prevailed in some of the Boston papers, that we had 150 men additional sent us from *La Hogue*, which really never was the case. *La Hogue* is now at Halifax for provisions, and I will send all other ships beyond the power of interfering with us, and meet you wherever it is most agreeable to you, within the limits of the undermentioned rendezvous, viz:

From 6 to 10 leagues east of Cape Cod Lighthouse, from 8 to 10 leagues east of Cape Ann Light, on Cashe's Ledge, in lat. 43. N. at any bearing and distance you please to fix off the South Breakers of Nantucket, or the Shoal in St. George's Bank.

If you will favour me with any plan of signals or telegraph, I will warn you (if sailing under this promise), should any of my friends be too nigh, or anywhere in sight, until I can detach them out of my way; or I would sail with you under a flag of truce to any place you think safest from our cruisers, hauling it down when fair to begin hostilities.

You must, Sir, be aware that my proposals are highly advantageous to you, as you cannot proceed to sea singly in the *Chesapeake*, without imminent risk of being crushed by the superior force of the numerous British squadrons which are now abroad, where all our efforts, in case of a rencontre, would, however gallant, be perfectly hopeless. I entreat you, Sir, not to imagine that I am urged by mere personal vanity to the wish of meeting the *Chesapeake*; or that I depend only upon your personal ambition for your acceding to this invitation: we have both nobler motives. You will feel it as a compliment if I say, that the result of our meeting may be the most grateful service I can render to my country; and I doubt not that you, equally confident of success, will feel convinced that it is only by repeated triumphs in *even combat* that your little navy can now hope to console *your* country for the loss of that trade it cannot protect. Favour me with a speedy reply. We are short of provisions and water, and cannot stay long here. I have the honour to be . . .

Sir, your obedient humble Servant,

P.B.V. BROKE
Captain of H.B.M.'s Ship *Shannon*

N.B. For the general service of watching your coast, it is requisite for me to keep another ship in company, to support with her guns and boats when employed near the land, and particularly to aid each other if either ship in chase should get on shore. You must be aware that I cannot, consistently with my duty, wave so great an advantage for this *general* service, by detaching my consort, without an assurance on your part of meeting me directly; and that you will neither seek nor admit aid from any other of *your* armed vessels, if I detach *mine* expressly for the sake of meeting you. Should any special order restrain you from thus answering a formal challenge, you may yet oblige me by keeping my proposal a secret, and appointing any place you like to meet us (within 300 miles of Boston), in a given number of days after you sail; as, unless you agree to an interview, I may be busied on other service, and perhaps be at a distance from Boston when you go to sea. Choose your terms - but let us meet.

Endorsement on the Envelope

We have thirteen American prisoners on board, which I will give you for as many British sailors if you will send them out; otherwise, being privateers men, they must be detained.

[On 9 July 1813 Admiralty First Secretary J W Croker wrote to Admiral Warren commending Captain Broke, directing that he and his officers should be presented with a medal, and promoting Lieutenants Wallis and Falkner [Falkiner] to the rank of commanders, and Messrs Etough and Smith to that of lieutenants. (Vol. xxx, p486)]

1813 – Naval News Continued

THE NAVAL NEWS DURING THE SUMMER of 1813 was very much a matter of business as usual, marked by several successful small-ship actions ending in the capture of the USS *Argus*, and the French 44-gun frigates *Weser* and *Trave*. At home, the Admiralty Board inspected Portsmouth, and later recommended an expansion of the dockyard. In the Adriatic, it appeared that the Austrian army, supported by the Royal Navy, might soon obtain possession of Trieste and Venice. Better still, the Dutch, taking heart at the catastrophe for the French in Russia, rebelled against the puppet regime and recalled the House of Orange. Everywhere French interests were collapsing. In December it was reported that the French batteries at Cuxhaven controlling the trade of the Elbe had fallen to the Russian army supported by a British squadron.

Across the Atlantic, on the other hand, not all the news was good. A failed attempt to explode a schooner loaded with pyrotechnics alongside HMS *Ramilies* was greeted with anger. Unlike the use of a bomb vessel in Basque Roads by the Channel fleet in 1809, this attack was considered by *The Naval Chronicle* as inhumane. The report of a British defeat on Lake Erie by the squadron under the American commander Commodore Perry was disturbing, although the fact that the British forces engaged were locally raised fencibles, and not Royal Navy, helped to reduce the bitterness.

All that fell into perspective when at the end of the year it began to be apparent that there was a real prospect of the French being forced to seek peace.

From the 'Naval History of the Present Year,' 1813
July–August. XXX *160-162*

Capture of USS Argus

In our last number we had the satisfaction to announce the capture of the American frigate *Chesapeake*, by H.M.S. *Shannon*. We have now to record another event every way honourable to the British arms; we mean, the capture of the American sloop of war

View of Mount Etna, and Sicilian Coast. Engraved by Baily, from a Drawing by Bennet. Plate 332

Argus. She had done much damage to our small shipping in the Atlantic, and had at last ventured into the Irish Channel, where she was taken by the *Pelican* sloop, Captain Maples, after a very severe action. The Americans told us, that we were not to reckon upon our superior valour by sea, till we could boast of more than one instance - that of the *Shannon* and *Chesapeake.* Here, then, is another in point; and we doubt not of giving them yet as many more as they will give us opportunities. The *Pelican* carries sixteen 32-pounder carronades, and a complement of 121 men; the *Argus* 20 guns, of the same description and weight of metal, with a crew of 136 sailors.

Austria Joins Triumphant Coalition

We cannot conclude this article without noticing the important intelligence, that HOSTILITIES HAVE RECOMMENCED IN THE NORTH; and that THE EMPEROR OF GERMANY HAS JOINED THE ALLIES with 150,000 men. The Blessing of Almighty God be on their united endeavours to repress the ambition and destroy the tyranny of him who aspires at the subjugation of the world!

August-September. XXX 232

Admiralty Board Inspect Portsmouth

It is with great pleasure we see that the Board of Admiralty has come to a determination of personally inspecting our principal naval establishments; and we augur from it the best effects. Portsmouth has had the honour of the first visit. On the 20th of September, soon after two o'clock P.M. Lord Viscount Melville, first Lord of the Admiralty, landed at the New Sally Port, from the Hon. Commissioner Grey's yacht, which brought him from Lymington. His Lordship was received by a captain's guard of the royal marines, by Sir George Warrender, Bart. and Lord Henry Paulet, Lords of the Admiralty; Sir Thomas Boulden Thompson, Bart. Comptroller of the Navy; the Hon. George Grey, John Deas Thompson, Esq. and T. Seppings, Esq. Commissioners of the Navy; and the Commissioners of the Transport and Victualling Boards; all of whom had previously arrived in town. Adm. Sir R. Bickerton, Bart., Adm. Foote, Generals Elliot, Winter, and Farmer, and the Captains of H.M. Ships, were also present, and followed in his Lordship's procession to the Crown Inn. - At three o'clock, the flag of the Lord High Admiral of Great Britain was hoisted on board the *Benbow*, 74, Capt. Pearson, and was saluted by each ship at Spithead with 19 guns; the *Benbow* afterwards returned the salute with the same number of guns. The Lords of the Admiralty, soon after, held a levee at the Admiralty House (Sir Richard Bickerton's), which was attended by all the officers and gentlemen stated above; and then proceeded to the Dock-yard, where they were received by the Hon. Commissioner Grey, at whose house they held another levee; when the principal officers of the Dock-yard, and of the Victualling and Transport Services, were introduced. - On the 21st, their Lordships visited the Royal Hospital at Haslar; whence they proceeded to the Royal Naval College, in the Dock-yard, and inspected that establishment. - The Commissioners of the Navy, Victualling, and Transport Boards, inspected the different departments under them. - On the 21st, their Lordships visited the Royal Hospital at Haslar; whence they proceeded to the Royal Naval College, in the Dock-yard, and inspected that establishment. - The Commissioners of the Navy, Victualling, and Transport Boards inspected the different departments under them. - On the 22d, their Lordships, assisted by the Navy Board, visited the Rope-house, in the Dock-yard, and inspected the men, and all the accounts of that branch of the service. - On the 23d, they visited the Builder's, Clerk of the Checque's [sic], Store-keeper's, and other Officers, and spent the day in looking into their accounts, and mustering the artificers and labourers employed in the dock-yard. - On the 24th, their Lordships inspected the Block Machinery, the Copper Re-manufactory, the Mast-house, and various other works departments of the yard; and mustered the warrant officers and men belonging to the ships in a state of ordinary at the port. - On the 25th, their Lordships were engaged in visiting the King's Brewery at Weovil [sic].

It is not known how long their Lordships will remain at Portsmouth. But we understand, that they meant, before they departed, to give audience to the officers on half-pay; to visit the ships at Spithead, inspect the Royal Marine Corps, and dine with the officers in their new mess-room. Their Lordships, it is said, will, previously to leaving Portsmouth, give a dinner at the Crown Inn, to the Admirals and Captains of the navy.

Fir Frigates

From 'Naval Anecdotes.' XXX 184

Two fine fir-built frigates are now ready for the slip, at the Merchants' yard, Limehouse-hole. They have been laid down on the most approved model, and there can be no doubt of their sailing. Fir frigates appear now to meet with the approbation of the Admiralty. The French vessels built of fir have generally out-sailed the British oak, and there can be no question as to the superiority in that respect; there is, however, one inconvenience attached to them - They are more apt to splinter than oak, and consequently more men are generally wounded in action, than on board common built ships. It is well known, that the French fir ships, in contest with the British, have suffered most severely by splinters, and when captured have appeared shattered beyond previous conception. Two frigates of similar construction are nearly ready for launching at Blackwall, and two or three have been recently turned off by other builders.

The Capture of USS Argus

Letters on Service
Admiralty Office, August 24, 1813. XXX 246-247

Extract of a letter from Commander J.F. Maples, of H.M. Sloop Pelican, to Vice-Admiral Thornborough and transmitted by the latter officer to John Wilson Croker, Esq

H.M.Sloop Pelican, St. David's head, East five Leagues, 14 August 1813
I have the honour to inform you, that, in obedience to your orders to me of the 12th instant to cruise in St. George's channel, for the protection of the trade, and to obtain information of an American sloop of war, I had the good fortune to board a brig, the master of which informed me, that he had seen a vessel, apparently a man of war, steering to the N.E.; at four o'clock this morning, I saw a vessel on fire, and a brig standing from her, which I soon made out to be a cruiser, made all sail in chase, and at half past five came alongside of her (she having shortened sail and made herself clear for an obstinate resistance), when, after giving her three cheers, our action commenced, which was kept up with great spirit on both sides forty-three minutes, when we lay her alongside, and were in the act of boarding, when she struck her colours. She proves to be the United States sloop of war *Argus*, of three hundred and sixty tons, eighteen twenty-four pounder carronades, and two long twelve-pounders; had on board when she sailed from America, two months since, a complement of one hundred and forty-nine men, but in the action, one hundred and twenty-seven, commanded by Lieutenant Commander W.H. Allen, who, I regret to say, was wounded early in the action, and has since suffered amputation of his left thigh.

No eulogium I could use would do sufficient justice to the merits of my gallant officers and crew . . .

I have the honour to be, &c.

J.F. MAPLES, Commander

From the 'Naval History of the Present Year,' 1813
September-October. XXX 348-351

Loss of Boxer and Dominica

We have with concern to announce the loss of H.M. brig *Boxer*, Captain Blyth. The *Enterprise*, Lieutenant Burrows, by which she was captured, is, by the American papers, represented as of only equal force with herself. This, however, is incorrect. The *Enterprise* had 16 guns, and 130 men; the *Boxer's* burthen is 180 tons, and was originally designed for a gun-brig; she mounted, when captured, ten 18-pounder carronades, and two 6-pounder guns, and had a complement of 60 men. The American account states, that "the *Boxer* was literally cut to pieces in sails, rigging, spars, hull, &c.; while the *Enterprise* was in a situation to commence another action of the same kind immediately." The stubborn resistance of the officers and crew of the *Boxer* shews, however, that she was not lost for want of heroism. Captain Blyth nailed his colours to the mast, and, happily, did not live to see them struck. The action, which lasted half an hour, appears to have been of the most desperate kind; both the commanders were killed; and they were buried together, with naval honours, at New York, where both vessels had arrived.

To the loss of the *Boxer* brig we are sorry to add that of H.M. schooner *Dominica*, Captain Barrette, captured on the 5th of August by the American privateer *Decatur*, and carried into Charleston on the 20th. The enemy's account says, that the *Dominica* had double the number of guns; but this we know to be likewise incorrect. The engagement was commenced at long shot, and was continued for some time, when the *Decatur* boarded. The action was then maintained for 15 minutes on the *Dominica*'s deck; nor did she strike until all her officers (with the exception of one midshipman named Lindo) and 12 men, were killed, and 44 wounded. Five of the latter have since died. The *Decatur* had 4 killed, and 13 wounded.

Weser Captured by Scylla and Royalist

On the other hand, we have the pleasure of recording the capture of a French frigate of the largest class, called the *Weser*, by H.M. sloops *Scylla* and *Royalist*, after a running fight of about 2 1/2 hours, at the end of which the enemy struck; the *Rippon*, 74, having appeared in sight. The *Weser* lately sailed from the Texel, in company with another frigate or two; of which, also, we hope, a good account will shortly be received. The *Weser* mounted 44 guns, and had 340 men.

American Pyrotechnics

A letter from Sir Thomas Hardy, captain of H.M.S. *Ramilies*, dated off New London, July 14th, 1813, gives an account of the event that was attended with such fatal consequence to Mr. Geddes, second lieutenant of the *Ramilies*, and ten brave seamen; but, we have every reason to believe, a most providential escape for the rest of the officers and ship's company. On Friday, the 25th of June, a master's mate of that ship was sent in a boat to cut off a schooner, which was making for the harbour of New London; which he soon effected, and took possession of her about eleven o'clock, the people having deserted and let go her only anchor and cable. The master's mate brought the schooner near the *Ramilies*, and informed Sir Thomas Hardy that she was loaded with provisions and naval stores. Sir Thomas directed her to be taken alongside a sloop which had been captured a few days before. Mr. Geddes volunteered his services; and to put Sir Thomas's orders into execution, took a fresh boat's crew. While they were in the act of securing her, about half-past two o'clock, horrid to relate, she blew up, with a most tremendous explosion, and poor Geddes and ten valuable seamen lost their lives: three seamen escaped, much scorched, but are doing well. We since learn, that this schooner, the *Eagle*, of New York, was fitted out by two merchants of that place (induced by the American government offering half the value of the British ships of war so destroyed), for the express purpose of blowing up or burning the *Ramilies*; and hearing that the *Ramilies* was short of provisions and stores, placed some on the hatchway, as an inducement for taking her alongside. Under the provisions (it since appears) were deposited several casks of gunpowder, with trains laid to a magazine, which was fitted upon the same mechanical principles as clock-work. When it had run the time given to it by the winder-up, it gave force to a sort of gun-lock, and the explosion of the vessel, and the destruction of all that might be near it, was thereby accomplished! - Most happily, Sir Thomas Hardy's foresight and caution prevented the full accomplishment of their wishes - and they are now held in detestation by every friend of humanity. In Lieutenant Geddes the service has lost a valuable officer; and the country, in whose cause he had spent so many years, and at last lost his life, will no doubt make ample provision for his disconsolate widow. The *Ramilies* is blockading the *United States*, *Macedonian*, and *Hornet* sloop, off New London. Lieutenant Geddes married the fourth daughter of the late Mr. George Rowe, of Portsea, surgeon.

[See Appendix 8 on Gunnery, in Volume IV, p400.]

Mediterranean

Late accounts from Admiral Freemantle have brought the particulars of a successful attack on the town of Fiume; and we confidently anticipate that the Austrian success in Italy will be the means shortly of throwing Trieste into our possession, and eventually Venice, with the naval force and arsenal there.

A most gallant attack has been made by Captain Usher [Ussher], of the *Undaunted*, on the batteries and citadel of Cassis, on the coast of Provence; which terminated in the capture of all the vessels within the Mole, and the destruction of the batteries of the place.

Portsmouth Dockyard to be Improved

It is said to be in contemplation very considerably to extend the Dockyard at Portsmouth. The plan was submitted to Lord Melville, during his recent visit to Portsmouth, and approved of by the Admiralty and Navy Boards. A new mast-house is to be constructed in range with the South store, extending to the low-water mark. On the north part of Common Hard, is to be erected a wall down to low-water mark, inside of which is to be a boat pound. It is also said, that it is in contemplation to take that part of the town of Portsea, called the New Buildings, into the Dock-yard. An intention likewise exists, of forming, on South Sea Common, an extensive establishment for the Royal Marines; their present barracks being much confined, and incapable of affording sufficient accommodation.

Mr. Whitby and Mr. Rennie, appointed by the Navy Board to examine the state of Portsmouth harbour, have been most assiduous in their labours.

Two plans, we are informed, are under consideration to clear the channels of the harbour, which have become choked by a progressive accumulation of mud. One is, to erect a flood-gate at the bridge at Hilsea, where the tide now ebbs and flows, which might be closed at high water to prevent it from ebbing through the channel; this would increase the rapidity of the tide between the Point and Blockhouse fort. The other, to form a large reservoir of water at Titchfield, to communicate with the harbour, which, at low water, might be let off, and would clear the mud from the upper part of the harbour.

From 'Naval Anecdotes.' XXX 397-403

Captain Cathcart, of the Alexandria, and Commodore Rodgers

As the late gallant attempt by Captain Cathcart, to bring to action this successful marauder, has created general admiration, we think a short sketch of her services may be acceptable to our readers.

Captain Cathcart, of the *Alexandria*, represents a most respectable family in Scotland, and entered his Majesty's service when only eleven years old. Since then he has been almost constantly at sea; and was first brought into public notice at the ever-memorable battle of the Nile, serving as 4th lieutenant of the *Bellerophon*; which ship was laid alongside of *L'Orient*, carrying the French admiral's flag, never quitted her til she was in flames, and lost more men than any other on that eventful day. The captain and three senior lieutenants of the *Bellerophon* being killed or wounded, the charge of the ship devolved on Mr. Cathcart, and he was shortly after promoted to the rank of master and commander. He was soon appointed to an armed vessel, and for two years kept actively employed in annoying the small craft, then forming the flotilla on the coast of France. He was promoted to the *Seagull*, which ship he most gallantly fought against a fleet of brigs and gun-boats; and although severely wounded in several places, did not quit the deck, or give her up, till she literally sunk under him. He was next appointed to the *Alexandria*, a fir built frigate, and a very dull sailer. His late exploit, in chasing off her station the *President*, Commodore Rodgers, is already before the public.

When the immense superiority in men and guns is taken into consideration, this will appear one of the most determined and desperate efforts to fulfil the duty of a British officer that is on record.

An American Infernal Machine

The *Atlanta* brig, Captain Hickey, arrived at Halifax on the 10th of August, from the Chesapeake, with the official report from Capt. R. Lloyd, of the *Plantagenet*, of an attempt made by the Americans to destroy that ship, in Lynnhaven Bay, by the explosion of a combustible machine, called a torpedo. - The horrid instrument fortunately went off when it had reached within about half a cable's length of the ship; otherwise, it is apprehended, the effects would have been fatal both to the ship and the whole of the crew! It did not, however, do any injury; it threw up an immense column of flame and water, and excited a temporary alarm, but nothing further.

One of these instruments has been picked up by the *Victorious*, 74, Capt. Talbot, at the same place, and is now on board that ship. It is a case containing about six barrels of gunpowder, to which a lock is affixed; and attached to the lock is a line, reaching to the person or boat that has the execution of the design. It is next suspended to a stage of planks, at each end of which are about 50 fathoms of small line, with a buoy at each end.

The machine thus put together, and let into the water, the combustible case sinking about 12 feet, and being kept at that depth from the surface of the stage, it has many chances of success in close anchorages; the buoys being extended by the line the distance of 100 fathoms, will most probably, one or the other of them, convey the line, by the help of the tide, across the cable of any ship at anchor, which, the moment it touches, will cause the machine to swing round to the side or the bottom of the ship; and the person using it, finding by the line that it has been stopped, judges that it has reached the intended object, pulls the trigger of the lock by the string, and the explosion takes place. Should it, thus situated[,] not blow the ship up, it must start a butt-end of one of her planks; when, from the sudden rush of water, which no efforts of the crew could possibly subdue, she would inevitably founder. One reason, it is considered, why it fortunately did not succeed upon the *Plantagenet*, was, it was the first experiment of its humane projector - a Mr. E. Mix, of the American Navy. Our blockading ships on the coast have kept the most sharp look-out, in their guard-boats, since this infernal attempt was made.

From the 'Naval History of the Present Year,' 1813
October-November. XXX 430-432

Weser's Sister Captured

In our last Retrospect we announced the capture of the *Weser*, a French frigate of the largest class; and expressed a hope that a good account would soon be given of another frigate or two which sailed in her company from the Texel. We have now the satisfaction to record the capture of the *Trave* French frigate of 44 guns, and 340 men, which took place on the 23d of October, off Ushant. She and the *Weser* had both sailed in company from the Texel, and were dismasted in the same gale. The *Trave* was first fallen in with by the *Achates* brig of war, Captain Morrison, who kept dodging and engaging her some time, when, fortunately, the *Andromache*, Captain Tobin, and the *Pyramus*, Captain Dundas, were discovered under a crowd of sail; the former, we understand, was the headmost ship, and to which, it is said, she struck her colours, after a few minutes' action. She is the sister ship, in every respect, to the *Weser*; for their keels were laid down on the same day; they were launched the same day; sailed the same day; were dismasted on the same day; were brought into Plymouth on the same day; and had a similar number of men, and weight of metal. The capture of these two vessels may perhaps be considered as doing Buonaparte a favour, inasmuch as it may spare him hereafter many unpleasant recollections attached to their names. The *Weser* and the *Trave* are German rivers, which, perhaps, he will long and sincerely repent that he ever ventured to approach.

Brest

We hear from Brest, that all naval business was at a stand in that arsenal: and, it being requisite to man two frigates for a particular service, five line-of-battle ships stripped of all their hands were not sufficient for the occasion.

Dutch Revolt

Our old friends and neighbours, the Dutch, have, with a manly fortitude, simultaneously thrown off the yoke of the Corsican despot, and recalled to their government the ancient House of Nassau.

The fleet in the Texel has declared in favour of the glorious cause; and the French fleet in the Scheldt, it is hoped, will be compelled to surrender. Its escape, indeed, seems altogether impossible; for should it even run up the river, and take refuge at Antwerp, its capture or self-destruction must there become inevitable; as the allied armies will speedily have reached that quarter also, where they will be received with joy by the people.

Deserter Hanged

J. Warburton, alias Parker, has been executed on board his Majesty's ship *Prince*, at Spithead; being found guilty by a court-martial, of having, assisted by five others belonging to the *Eolus*, risen against the British prize-master on board an American brig, and carried her into Salem. He was afterwards recognized among the wounded on board the *Chesapeake*, when that frigate was captured.

Trading Voyage to Vancouver Island

The *Columbia*, Robertson, lying at Spithead, will sail under convoy of the *Laurel*, on a trading voyage of discovery to the western shores of North America, to endeavour to open a fur trade with the Indians of the coast lying between Vancouver's Island and Cook's Inlet, on the coast between 120 and 130 W. long. and 60 and 70 N. lat. This trade has been hitherto carried on only by the Americans, who carried the furs to China, and brought teas for the European Continent.

Great Lakes

We must now advert to a miscarriage, of minor importance, affecting our own interests. Nova Scotia and Boston papers have brought intelligence, that our flotilla on Lake Erie has been completely defeated by the American Commodore Perry. It may, however, serve to diminish our vexation at this occurrence, to learn, that the flotilla in question was not any branch of the British navy, but was solely manned, equipped, and managed by the public-spirited exertions of certain Canadians, who had formed themselves into a kind of Lake Fencibles. Yet this conflict, though it left Perry the conqueror of the day, exposes his conduct, and that of his squadron, to the most disgraceful suspicions.

It was on the 10th of September that the Canadian squadron on this lake consisting of *six* vessels, which, as we have already observed, were wholly manned and equipped by the inhabitants of the province, encountered the American squadron commanded by Commodore Perry, consisting of nine vessels. The fire of the Canadians was principally directed against the *Lawrence*, the ship of the American commodore; who quitted her in the midst of the engagement, leaving the command to a lieutenant, who almost immediately *hauled down her flag*. "But," says Mr. Perry, "*the enemy was not able to take possession of her; and circumstances soon permitted her flag to be again hoisted.*" Now, what were those circumstances? Not a recapture by the rest of the American squadron; for that is not asserted: but, as far as appears, merely their approach to support their discomfited comrade. The commodore went on board a vessel which had sustained little injury; and with this, supported by all the rest of his flotilla, he succeeded in breaking the Canadian line. From the general tenor of the letter, it would seem to have been about this time, that the *Lawrence*'s flag was re-hoisted.

Mississippi Floods

In June and July, the Mississippi had risen higher than it had been known for 30 years. The consequences had been dreadful. The water had burst the mounds, and inundated the country on the west side to the distance of 65 miles. The inhabitants fled to the heights, where they and their slaves were encamped; but vast crops, plantations of sugar-canes, with an immense number of horses, cattle, sheep, hogs, and deer, were swept away. The loss of neat cattle alone was estimated at 22,000 head. Every little spot of bare ground was crowded with animals. It was not uncommon to find herds of deer intermixed with wolves, and both, from a sense of common danger, equally domesticated. The total loss of property is variously estimated; the lowest is eight millions of dollars; the highest twenty-two.

November–December. XXX 504

Real Hope for Peace

The close of this eventful year affords us rather a flattering Prospect of Peace; at which, if to be *a bona fide* peace, we anxiously hope the nations of Europe will speedily arrive. All that we at present know is, that Buonaparte, in his Speech to the Legislative Body at Paris on the 19th December, stated, that NEGOTIATIONS HAD BEEN ENTERED INTO WITH THE ALLIED POWERS; AND THAT HE HAD ADHERED TO THE PRELIMINARY BASES WHICH THEY HAD PRESENTED.

Bounties for Enlistment Still to be Paid

An Order in Council, dated 10th November, 1813, has been issued for the continuation, till 31st December, 1814, of the bounties now paid for the encouragement of seamen and landsmen to enter into H.M. navy.

Pay Increase

The pay of captains' clerks in the Royal Navy has been raised – to commence from the 1st of July last. – They have hitherto been paid as Midshipmen. The clerk of a first rate will now receive £445 per ann. and of a third rate, 2s per day.

Whalers Captured

Since our last, we have received the unpleasant information of the capture of eight sail of our South Sea Whalers, off the Gallipagos Islands, by the American frigate *Essex*, Capt. Porter; which continued to cruise, and it was feared would almost annihilate our trade in that Sea.

Mediterranean

Our fleet in the Mediterranean has been at anchor since the 19th of August, off the mouth of the river Rhone, by which the ships avoided the destructive effects of three very severe gales of wind. It was expected Sir Edward Pellew would return to Mahon at the latter end of October for the winter. That gallant and excellent officer, Captain Usher, had commanded in an attack upon the town and batteries of Port Cassis, by 200 seamen and marines from the fleet. Captain Coghlan of the *Caledonia* volunteered his valuable aid. The attack succeeded; the batteries were taken, and 27 vessels brought out, leaving only three in the mould, which were useless. Six were afterwards scuttled; the rest were taken into port by the *Undaunted* and *Redwing*. The gallant band had four men killed and fifteen wounded. Lieutenant Tozen [Tozer?], first of the *Undaunted*, was badly wounded in the hip; Mr. George Sidney Smith, midshipman of the *Redwing* (nephew of Sir Sidney Smith), in the thigh.

Dutch Welcome the Return of the Prince of Orange

From 'Correspondence.' XXX 484-86

Extract of a letter from an officer on board H.M.S. Warrior
North Sea, 4 December 1813
Mr. Editor, On Friday, the 26th of November, his Serene Highness William Frederick

Prince of Orange embarked on board H.M.S. *Warrior*, commanded by Lord Viscount Torrington, to return to his native country, and to assume the station and honours of his forefathers. At two P.M. he entered Vice-admiral Foley's barge, fitted in state, and was preceded by his Lordship, to arrange his public reception on board. His Lordship and all the officers were equipped in full uniform, and mounted the Orange cockade and ribbon in honour of the Prince. A field officer's guard was drawn out on the quarter-deck. At three o'clock, his Highness ascended the quarter-deck, and returned the salute of every officer in the most gracious manner. His courteous and engaging *entrée*, and the placid mildness of his countenance strongly prepossessed all hands in his favour. Every one exclaimed, such a Prince must rule in the hearts of his subjects. His Highness was followed by General Von Phull, Baron Perpoucher, Major Fagel, Mr. Rugay, his suite; and by Lord Clancart, the British ambassador and suite, Messrs. Hoppner and Gunning. The Orange flag was hoisted at the main, and saluted by the *Warrior* (now placed under his direction), and all his Majesty's ships in the Downs, with twenty-one guns, the latter firing after the discharge of the *Warrior*'s second gun. On the 27th, at day-light, the ship weighed, with the wind at S.E. which carried her through the Gulf stream, after which the ship was obliged to work to windward. On Sunday evening, Admiral Young's fleet was seen, and the *Warrior* approached sufficiently near to communicate to him by telegraph, that his Serene Highness was on board, but darkness supervened, and the telegraphic answer of "No news" was deferred till the following morning. The wind continued unfavourable, and the tide made so strong against us, that it was deemed prudent to anchor during the night. On Monday, the 29th, the ship weighed, at day-light, by his serene Highness's order. At eight A.M. perceived a frigate (which proved to the *Nymphen*, Captain Hancock), in-shore, with the Dutch colours flying over the French. Lieutenant Macdonald reported the circumstance to Lord Torrington, while his Highness was seated with him at breakfast, and observed, that the Prince smiled with much evident satisfaction, no doubt from the pleasing idea which the fact excited, of the triumph of the Dutch national spirit of independence over French despotism and military oppression.

The ship was anchored at night; and on Tuesday, the 30th, weighed at day-light, and soon discovered the land, and his Majesty's ships *Cumberland, Princess Caroline*, and the *Raven* brig. The ship worked to windward fast, and brought us in sight of Scheveling, the Hague, and other towns on the coast. At twelve, the *Cumberland* telegraphed "Good news," and shortly afterwards a Dutch pilot exultingly exclaimed, that he saw the Orange flag hoisted on all the steeples and boats, which was the signal established between his Highness and the shore, and denoted security. Captain Baker, of the *Cumberland*, gave information that the Brill was held by the enemy; at which place his Highness was particularly anxious to land, from its being considered the cradle of the liberty the Dutch established in 1572, when they denounced the Spanish dominion. At two o'clock P.M. a boat was sent on shore to announce the Prince's arrival. At 3 P.M. the Prince was ready to disembark, and was received with the same honours on the quarter-deck as at his *entrée*; he saluted every individual most graciously, shook hands with Lord Torrington twice most cordially, as he conveyed to him his most grateful thanks for his attention, accommodation and hospitality; and the various emotions which agitate his mind were evinced by the tear drop of joy, which fell as he went over the side. A royal salute was fired as the Prince and suite pulled from the ship; three cheers were given, and returned from the boat, on which the cheers from the ship were repeated. As the barge steered by Lieutenant Kains, senior lieutenant of the *Warrior*, advanced close to the shore at Scheveling, the Dutch people waded up to their necks to haul the boats to the shore, amidst the hearty huzzas and acclamations of joy of the numbers assembled from all parts to receive him. On landing, his Highness and suite were greeted with the wildest, and most natural and sincere marks of joy and pleasure. All approached without ceremony, to shake hands, and touch their Prince and his suite. . . .

The French Driven Out of Cuxhaven

Letters on Service
December 7, 1813. ᴺᴺᴺ₅₁₂-₅₁₃

Copy of a letter from Captain Farquhar, of H.M.S. Desirée, to John Wilson Croker, Esq. dated off Cuxhaven, the 2d instant
Sir, I have the honour to enclose, for the information of My Lords Commissioners of the Admiralty, a duplicate of a letter I have written to Admiral Young, giving a detail of the capitulation and surrender of the French batteries at Cuxhaven.
I have the honour to be, &c.

ARTHUR FARQUHAR

H.M.S. Desirée, off Cuxhaven, 1 December 1813
I have the honour to acquaint you, that the French batteries of Phare and Napoleon, have yesterday entered into capitulation, and this morning surrendered to a detachment of his Imperial Majesty's Russian troops, commanded by Colonel Alexander Radinger, and his Britannic Majesty's squadron (as per margin),[1] under my command.
On the 28th ultimo, I arrived here (from Bremeriche), where I found Captain Green, of the *Shamrock*, had collected the squadron, to co-operate with the Russian troops. On the same evening, I ordered the gun-boats to take a position above Napoleon, and to cannonade that battery, in concert with the Russian troops, and advanced the squadron ready to attack Phare (or Cuxhaven).
On the 29th, a brisk and well directed fire was kept upon Fort Napoleon by the gun-boats, and from field pieces from the Russian line, with considerable effect; and their tirailleurs annoyed the enemy in both batteries, by a constant fire of musketry, which was returned with vigour, and from the battery of Phare, red-hot shot were fired, which burnt several houses in the town. During this time, we were employed in landing guns from the squadron, and erecting a battery within four hundred yards of the works of Phare. On the morning of the 30th it was completed, and presented to the enemy a formidable appearance, consisting of ten guns, *viz.* six eighteen-pounders, two thirty-two pounders, and two six-pounders. The morning was quite thick, and obscured our works, but as soon as it cleared, and we were ready to commence our attack, the enemy threw out a truce, which has ended in the surrender of these two extremely strong batteries, consisting of twenty-six heavy guns, two thirteen-inch mortars, and a blockhouse, with a garrison of three hundred men and officers, who have been made prisoners of war. . . .
I have very great pleasure in stating to you, Sir, that in the last ten days the small detachment of Russian troops, commanded by Colonel Radinger, assisted by his Majesty's squadron under my command, have been fortunate in reducing four strong batteries, consisting of fifty heavy guns, four mortars, and eight hundred men and officers, all

1 *Desirée, Shamrock, Blazer, Piercer, Redbreast*; gun-boats Nos. 1, 2, 3, 4, 5, 8, 10.

View of the Port of Cuxhaven. Engraved by Baily, from a drawing by W.S.H.
   Mr. Editor, Enclosed I send you a sketch of a port of Cuxhaven, which is partly
formed and defended from the sea by substantial jetties and high banks, extending
from the mouth of the harbour, half a mile up inland, where you enter the village of
Ritzbuttel, which, though small in its district, comprises three parishes, together
with the Port of Cuxhaven, and is subject to the city of Hamburgh. . . .
   Cuxhaven is well known as the general station for packet boats between this
country and the North of Germany, and is also the station of the pilot-captain of the
River Elbe, who is charged with the superintendance of the pilots on the river, and
the care of the navigation. ^{Plate 294}

prisoners of war; and I cannot help expressing the satisfaction which I feel in acquainting
you, that the whole of this service has been carried on with the greatest cordiality between
the co-operating forces, both officers and men; not the smallest misunderstanding on
any occasion.
   I am extremely happy to state, that the loss on this occasion has been very trifling;
on the part of the Russians two killed and three wounded: we have sustained no loss. I
have thought it right to forward this despatch, without delay, by Sir George Keith, in
the *Redbreast*, who takes to England the officers of Port Phare, who are prisoners of war.
   Two days ago I had the pleasure to learn, that Stadt had been taken possession of
by a Russian detachment, under the orders of Count Strogonoffe.
   I have the honour to be, &c.

                                                            ARTHUR FARQUHAR

N.B. These batteries were complete with provisions of all kind for six weeks, and a very
considerable quantity of military stores and ammunition of every description.

To William Young, Esq. Admiral of the White

1813 – Action on the
American Coast

IN DECEMBER 1812 Captain Lawrence of the American sloop of war *Hornet*, sent a challenge to Captain Greene of the *Bonne Citoyenne* sheltering in the harbour of San Salvador. In January 1813 the *Montague*, 74, chased her off, but the *Hornet* fell in with the brig of war *Peacock* on 24 February, which she captured. A report of the challenge and of the action of the *Hornet* is published in Vol. XXIX, pp387-390. From another part of the American theatre, the Delaware, came the news that in March Commodore J P Beresford, commanding HM Squadron in the Delaware, threatened to bombard Lewistown if the governor of Delaware did not supply him with water, which he refused to do (Vol. XXIX, pp386-387).

Pacifying the Chesapeake
Letters on Service
Admiralty Office, July 10, 1813. ^{XXX 162-168}

Copy of a letter from Admiral Sir John Borlase Warren, Bart. and K.E. &c. to John Wilson Croker, Esq. dated at Bermuda, the 23d of May, 1813
Sir, I request you will inform their lordships, that, after the capture of the American privateers on the 3d of April, by the boats of the Squadron, I continued my course up the bay, and being of opinion that a light flotilla of small vessels would be of essential use in cutting off the enemies [sic] supplies, and destroying their foundries, stores, and public works, by penetrating the rivers at the head of the Chesapeake; I directed Rear-admiral Cockburn to take under his orders the *Maidstone, Fantome, Mohawk, Highflyer*, and three of the prize armed schooners; and the rear-admiral having selected a detachment, composed of one hundred and eighty seamen, and two hundred marines, from the naval brigade of the squadron, together with Lieutenant Robertson, of the Royal Artillery, and a small detachment of that corps, which General Horsford, the Lieutenant-Governor of Bermuda, had been so kind, at my request, to permit to serve with me in the squadron, the whole proceeded upon the above-mentioned service.

I herewith enclose a report of the operations of the advanced squadron, from which their lordships will observe, that the enterprise was conducted with distinguished ability

177

and gallantry under Rear-admiral Cockburn, and most zealously and bravely executed by the Captains Burdett, Lawrence, and Byng, their officers and men; and I trust, that when their lordships consider that this service was performed in the interior of the enemy's country, where the detachment was frequently opposed by superior force, and in a difficult and unknown navigation, that the behaviour of the officers and men will entitle them to their lordships' favour and approbation.

I have the honour to be, &c.

JOHN BORLASE WARREN
Admiral of the Blue, and Commander-in-Chief

J.W. Croker, Esq.

His Majesty's Sloop Fantome, in the Elk River, 29th April, 1813

Sir, I have the honour to acquaint you, that having yesterday gained information of the dépôt of flour (alluded to in your note to me of the 23d instant) being with some military and other stores, situated at a place called French Town, a considerable distance up the river Elk, I caused his Majesty's brigs *Fantome* and *Mohawk*, and the *Dolphin*, *Racer*, and *Highflyer* tenders, to be moored, yesterday evening, as far within the entrance of this river as could be prudently effected after dark, and at eleven o'clock last night the detachment of marines now in the advanced squadron, consisting of about one hundred and fifty men, under Captains Wybourn and Carter, of that corps, with five artillerymen, under first Lieutenant Robertson, of the artillery, (who eagerly volunteered his valuable assistance on this occasion), proceeded in the boats of the squadron, the whole being under the immediate direction of Lieutenant G.A. Westphall, First of the *Marlborough*, to take and destroy the aforesaid stores, the *Highflyer* tender; under the command of Lieutenant T. Lewis, being directed to follow, for the support and protection of the boats, as far and as closely as he might find it practicable.

Being ignorant of the way, the boats were unfortunately led up the Bohemian River, instead of keeping in the Elk, and it being daylight before this error was rectified, they therefore did not reach the destined place till between eight and nine o'clock this morning, which occasioned the enemy to have full warning of their approach, and gave him time to collect his force and make his arrangements for the defence of his stores and town, for the security of which a six gun battery had lately been erected, and for whence a heavy fire was opened on our boats the moment they approached within its reach. But the launches, with their carronades, under the orders of Lieutenant Nicholas Alexander, First of the *Dragon*, pulling resolutely up to the work, keeping up at the same time a constant and well directed fire on it, and the marines being in the act of disembarking on the right, the Americans judged it prudent to quit their battery, and to retreat precipitately into the country, abandoning to their fate French Town and its dépôts of stores; the whole of the latter, therefore, consisting of much flour, a large quantity of army clothing, of saddles, bridles, and other equipments for cavalry, &c. &c. together with various articles of merchandise, were immediately set fire to, and entirely consumed, as were five vessels lying near the place; and the guns of the battery, being too heavy to bring away, were disabled as effectually as possible, by Lieutenant Robertson and his artillerymen; after which my orders being completely fulfilled, the boats returned down the river without molestation, and I am happy to add, that one seaman, of the *Maidstone*, wounded in the arm by a grape shot, is the only casualty we have sustained. . . .

I have now anchored the abovementioned brigs and tenders near a farm, on the right bank of this river, where there appears to be a considerable quantity of cattle, which I intend embarking for the use of the fleet under your command, and if I meet with no resistance or impediment in so doing, I shall give the owner bills on the Victualling Office for the fair value of whatsoever is so taken; but should resistance be made, I shall consider them as prize of war, which I trust will meet your approbation; and I propose taking on board a further supply for the fleet tomorrow, on similar terms from Spesutie Island, which lies a little below Havre de Grace, and which I have been informed is also well stocked.

I have the honour to be, &c,

G. COCKBURN, Rear-Admiral

To the Right Honourable Admiral Sir J.B. Warren, Bart. K.B. &c. &c.

His Majesty's Ship Maidstone, Tuesday night
3d May, 1813, at anchor off Turkey Point

Sir, I have the honour to inform you, that whilst anchoring the brigs and tenders off Spesutie Island, agreeable to my intentions notified to you in my official report of the 29th ultimo, No. 10, I observed guns fired and American colours hoisted at a battery lately erected at Havre-de-Grace, at the entrance of the Susquehanna river; this of course immediately gave to the place an importance which I had not before attached to it, and I therefore determined on attacking it after the completion of our operations at the island; consequently having sounded in the direction towards it, and found that the shallowness of the water would only admit of its being approached by boats, I directed their assembling under Lieutenant Westphall (first of the *Marlborough*), last night at twelve o'clock, alongside the *Fantome*, when our detachments of marines, consisting of about one hundred and fifty men (as before), under Captains Wybourn and Carter, with a small party of artillerymen, under Lieutenant Robertson, of the artillery, embarked in them, and the whole being under the immediate direction of Captain Lawrence, of the *Fantome* (who with much zeal and readiness took upon himself at my request, the conducting of this service), proceeded towards Havre, to take up under cover of the night, the necessary positions for commencing the attack at dawn of day. The *Dolphine* and *Highflyer* tenders, commanded by Lieutenants Hutchinson and Lewis, followed for the support of the boats, but the shoalness of the water prevented their getting within six miles of the place. Captain Lawrence, however, having got up with the boats, and having very ably and judiciously placed them during the dark, a warm fire was opened on the place at daylight from our launches and rocket-boats, which was smartly returned from the battery for a short time, but the launches constantly closing with it, and their fire rather increasing than decreasing, that from the battery soon began to slacken, and Captain Lawrence observing this, very judiciously directed the landing of the marines on the left, which movement, added to the hot fire they were under, induced the Americans to commence withdrawing from the battery, to take shelter in the town; Lieutenant G.A. Westphall, who had taken his station in the rocket-boat close to the battery, therefore now judging the moment to be favourable, pulled directly up under the work, and landing with his boat's crew, got immediate possession of it, turning their own guns on them, and thereby soon obliged them to retreat with their whole force to the furthest extremity of the town, whither (the marines having by this time landed) they were closely pursued, and no longer feeling themselves equal to a manly and open resistance, they commenced a teazing and irritating fire from behind the houses, walls, trees, &c, from which I am sorry to say my gallant first lieutenant received a shot through his hand whilst leading the pursuing party; he, however, continued to head the advance, with which he soon succeeded in dislodging the whole of the enemy from their lurking places, and driving them from shelter to the neighbouring woods, and whilst performing which service, he had the satisfaction to overtake, and with his remaining hand to make prisoner, and bring in a captain of their militia. We also took an ensign and some armed individuals, but the rest of the force which had been opposed to us, having penetrated into the woods, I did not judge it prudent to allow of their being further followed with our small numbers, therefore after setting fire to some of the houses, to cause the proprietors (who had deserted them, and formed part of the militia who had fled to the woods,) to understand and feel what they were liable to bring upon themselves, by building batteries and acting towards us with so much useless rancour, I embarked in the boats the guns from the battery, and having also taken and destroyed about one hundred and thirty stand of small arms, I detached a small division of boats up the Susquehanna, to take and destroy whatever they might meet with in it, and proceeded myself with the remaining boats under Captain Lawrence, in search of a cannon foundry, which I had gained intelligence of, whilst on shore in Havre, as being situated about three or four miles to the northward, where we found it accordingly, and getting possession of it without difficulty, commenced instantly its destruction, and that of the guns and other materials we found there, to complete which, occupied us during the remainder of the day, as there were several buildings and much complicated heavy machinery attached to it. It was known by the names of the Cecil or Principio Foundry, and was one of the most valuable works of the kind in America; the destruction of it, therefore, at this moment, will, I trust, prove of much national importance. . . .

I have the honour to be, &c.

G. COCKBURN, Rear Admiral

To the Right Honourable Admiral Sir J.B. Warren, Bart. and K.B. &c.

H.M.S. Maidstone, off the Sasafras River, May 6, 1813

Sir, I have the honour to acquaint you, that, understanding Georgetown and Frederickstown, situated up the Sasafras River, were places of some trade and importance, and the Sasafras being the only river or place of shelter for vessels at this upper extremity of the Chesapeake, which I had not examined and cleared, I directed last night the assembling of the boats alongside the *Mohawk*, from whence with the marines, as before, under Captain Wybourn and Carter, with my friend Lieutenant Robertson, of the artillery, and his small party, they proceeded up this river, being placed by me for this operation, under the immediate directions of Captain Byng, of the *Mohawk*.

I intended that they should arrive before the above-mentioned towns by dawn of day, but in this I was frustrated by the intricacy of the river, our total want of local knowledge in it, the darkness of the night, and the great distance the towns lay up it; it, therefore, unavoidably became late in the morning before we approached them, when, having intercepted a small boat with two of the inhabitants, I directed Captain Byng to halt our boats about two miles below the town, and sent forward the two Americans in their boat to warn their countrymen against acting in the same rash manner the people of Havre de Grace had done; assuring them, if they did , that their towns would inevitably meet with a similar fate, but, on the contrary, if they did not attempt resistance, no injury should be done to them or their towns, that vessels and public property only would be seized, that the strictest discipline would be maintained, and that whatever provisions or other property of individuals I might require for the use of the squadron, should be instantly paid for in its fullest value; after having allowed sufficient time for this message to be digested, and their resolution taken thereon, I directed the boats to advance, and I am sorry to say I soon found the more unwise alternative was adopted, for on our reaching within about a mile of the town, between two projecting elevated points of the river, a most heavy fire of musketry was opened on us from about four hundred men, divided and entrenched on the two opposite banks, aided by one long gun: the launches and rocket boat smartly returned this fire with good effect, and with the other boats and the marines I pushed ashore immediately above the enemy's position, thereby ensuring the capture of his towns, or the bringing him to a decided action; he determined, however, not to risk the latter, for the moment he discerned we had gained the shore, and that the marines had fixed bayonets, he fled with his whole force to the woods, and was neither seen nor heard of afterwards, though several parties were sent out to ascertain whether he had taken up any new position, or what had become of him; I gave him, however, the mortification of seeing, from wherever he had hid himself, that I was keeping my word, with respect to the towns, which (excepting the houses of those who had continued peaceably in them, and had taken no part in the attack made on us) were forthwith destroyed, as were four vessels laying in the river, and some stores of sugar, of lumber, of leather, and other merchandise; I then directed the re-embarkation of our small force, and we proceeded down the river again, to a town I had observed, situated in a branch of it, about half way up, and here I had the satisfaction to find, that what had passed at Havre, Georgetown, and Frederickstown, had its effect, and led these people to understand, that they had more to hope for from our generosity, than from erecting batteries, and opposing us by means within their power; the inhabitants of this place having met me at landing, to say that they had not permitted either guns or militia to be stationed there, and that whilst there I should not meet with any opposition whatever; I therefore landed with the officers and a small guard only, and having ascertained that there was no public property of any kind, or warlike stores, and having allowed of such articles as we stood in need of being embarked in the boats, on payment to the owners of their full value, I again re-embarked, leaving the people of this place well pleased with the wisdom of their determination on their mode of receiving us; I also had a deputation from Charlestown, in the north-east river, to assure me that that place is considered by them at your mercy, and that neither guns nor militia-men shall be suffered there, and as I am assured that all the places in the upper part of the Chesapeake have adopted similar resolutions, and as there is now neither property, vessels, nor warlike stores remaining in this neighbourhood, I propose returning to you with the light squadron to-morrow morning. . . .

I have the honour to be, &c.

G. COCKBURN, Rear-Admiral

To the Right Hon. Admiral Sir J. B. Warren, Bart. K.B. &c.

Attack on Craney Island

From 'Naval Anecdotes.' XXX 182-183

The following interesting account of the attack upon Craney Island, [Virginia] together with some of the subsequent proceedings on the American coast, has been received from an officer on board the fleet at the time:

Halifax, Nova Scotia, July 7, 1813

On the 22d of June in the morning, the marines were landed at Pig's point, in Virginia, about two miles below Craney Island, which is fortified, and commands the passage to Norfolk: it was afterwards found necessary to storm the island, on which were 800 picked men, and thirty 24-pounders, flanked on its eastern end by 16 large American gun-boats, and the American frigate *Constellation* lying behind them; 500 men, and the boats of the fleet, were put under the command of Captain Pechell, of H.M.S. *San Domingo.* Captain Hanchett, of the *Diadem,* was ordered in his boat to lead the men to the attack: it was about eleven o'clock in the forenoon; he advanced about sixty yards ahead of the rest; and after being about two hours under the fire of the enemy's very heavy batteries and gun-boats, his boat took the ground about 100 yards from the muzzles of their guns: there was too much water and mud for the men to wade on shore, and three boats which were astern were very soon sunk by some shot which passed through the sails of the first boat: the fire of grape and canister at this time was tremendous; and while Captain Hanchett was endeavouring to save the crews of the boats which were sunk, and cheering them up, he received a canister-shot in his left thigh. He kept on his legs as long as possible, but sunk at last from the loss of blood. The boats immediately gave up the attack, and retreated. The wounded captain ordered himself to be put into a small boat, and was carried twelve miles to the *Diadem,* the ship he commanded, having frequently fainted from the loss of blood. An attack of this kind is a desperate thing to do at night, but in the middle of the day it requires some strong nerves: we are said to have lost 90 men that day.

On the 25th we attacked the American camp at Hampton, took and destroyed it, and killed about 300 Americans: we lost 49 men. We embarked again on the 27th; the fleet were then lying in Hampton-roads; some part had gone up James's river to water. The next attack it was supposed would be Baltimore. I forgot to tell you, that when our boats were sunk, the Americans came down and shot the men swimming in the water; but the brutes got punished for it at Hampton.

Admiralty Office, August 10, 1813. [XXX 245]

San Domingo, Hampton Roads, Chesapeake, June 27, 1813
Sir, I request you will inform their lordships, that the enemy having a post at Hampton, defended by a considerable corps, commanding the communication between the upper part of the country and Norfolk, I considered it advisable, and with a view to cut off their resources, to direct it to be attacked by the troops composing the flying corps attached to this squadron; and having instructed Rear-Admiral Cockburn to conduct the naval part of the expedition, and placed Captain Pechell with the *Mohawk* sloop and launches, as a covering force, under his orders, the troops were disembarked with the greatest zeal and alacrity.

Sir Sydney Beckwith, commanding the troops, having most ably attacked and defeated the enemy's force, and took their guns, colours, and camp, I refer their lordships to the quarter-master-general's report, (which is enclosed) and that will explain the gallantry and behaviour of the several officers and men employed upon this occasion, and I trust will entitle them to the favour of his Royal Highness the Prince Regent, and the approbation of the Lords Commissioners of the Admiralty.

Sir Sydney Beckwith having reported to me that the defences of the town were entirely destroyed, and the enemy completely dispersed in the neighbourhood, I ordered the troops to be re-embarked, which was performed with the utmost good order by the several officers of the squadron, under the orders of Rear-Admiral Cockburn.

Mr. Editor, The accompanying sketch of the City of New York was taken from the Anchoring Ground near Governor's Island; a pilot boat is introduced in the foreground, and a ship in the distance, sailing towards the passage of Hell Gates, formed by York and Long Islands.

Your humble Servant,   G.T.

August 27, 1805   Plate 189

I have the honour to be, &c.

JOHN BORLASE WARREN

John Wilson Croker, Esq,

H.M.S. San Domingo, Hampton Roads, June 28, 1813
Sir, I have the honour to report to you, that, in compliance with your orders to attack the enemy in town and camp at Hampton, the troops under my command, were put into light sailing vessels and boats, during the night of the 25th instant, and by the excellent arrangements of Rear-Admiral Cockburn, who was pleased in person to superintend the advance under Lieutenant Colonel Napier, consisting of the 102nd regiment, two companies of Canadian Chasseurs, three companies of marines from the squadron, with two six-pounders from the royal marine artillery, were landed half an hour before daylight the next morning, about two miles to the westward of the town, and the royal marine battalions, under Lieutenant-Colonel Williams, were brought on shore so expeditiously, that the column was speedily enabled to move forward.

With a view to turn the enemy's position, our march was directed towards the great road, leading from the country into the rear of the town; whilst the troops moved off in this direction, Rear-Admiral Cockburn, to engage the enemy's attention, ordered the armed launches and rocket boats to commence a fire upon their batteries; this succeeded so completely, that the head of our advanced guard had cleared a wood, and

View of Roseau, or Charlotte Town, in the island of Dominica. Engraved by
Bennet, from a drawing by Pocock. Plate 272

were already on the enemy's flank before our approach was perceived: they then moved
from their camp to their position in rear of the town, and here they were vigorously
attacked by Lieutenant-Colonel Napier, and the advance; unable to stand which, they
continued their march to the rear of the town, when a detachment, under Lieutenant-
Colonel Williams, conducted by Captain Powell, assistant-quarter-master-general,
pushed through the town, and forced their way across a bridge of planks into the enemy's
encampment, of which, and the batteries, immediate possession was gained. In the
mean time, some artillerymen stormed and took the enemy's remaining field-piece. . . .

From the woody country, and the strength of their position, our troops have sustained
some loss; that of the enemy was very considerable; every exertion was made to collect
the wounded Americans, who were attended by a surgeon of their own, and by the
British surgeons, who performed amputations on such as required it, and afforded every
assistance in their power; the dead bodies of such as could be collected were also carefully
buried. . . .

I have the honour to be, &c.

SYDNEY BECKWITH, Q.M. General

Right Hon. Admiral Sir J.B. Warren, K.B. &c

1813 – The Mediterranean and Iberian Theatres

IT IS IMPOSSIBLE TO DO MORE than include a sample of the small actions which continued to keep the Royal Navy very active during this period in the Mediterranean and Iberian theatres in support of allies ashore. In February the Tyrrhenian Sea island of Ponza was taken by storm by troops under Colonel Coffin, who were transported there by Captain Charles Napier commanding the *Thames* and *Furieuse*; in April Captains the Hon George Granville Waldegrave and Usher raided the French coast near Marseilles and destroyed batteries which were protecting the coastal trade, and Captain Sir Charles Adam commanding the *Invincible* co-operated with Baron de Eroles of the Spanish royal army in attacks on Ampolla and Perello which interrupted enemy communica-tions along the shore road. At the end of the month Captain James Black attacked an enemy convoy near Spalatro but was forced to retire under heavy fire, and in June Adam was again in action, this time on the Spanish coast where he landed soldiers to besiege and take a small fort which commanded the road to Tarragona. Forces commanded by Captain George Collier laid siege to, and in September captured, San Sebastian in the northwest corner of Spain. And at the end of the year a squadron commanded by Captain Thomas Fremantle stormed the defences of Fiume, and supported an army under General Nugent which succeeded in clearing the enemy from the head of the Adriatic.

Letters on Service
Admiralty Office, June 15, 1813. [XXX 71-85]

The Capture of Ponza

H.M.S. Thames, Ponza Harbour, February 27, 1813
Sir, Agreeable to your directions, I embarked Lieutenant-colonel Coffin, and the 2d battalion of the 10th regiment, on the 16th inst. and arrived off Ponza on the 23d, the harbour of which is about a quarter of a mile wide, with a mole at the extreme end of it, defended by four batteries, mounting ten twenty-four and eighteen-pounders, and two nine-inch mortars.

View of Cagliari-Sardinia. Engraved by Baily, from a drawing by Richard S. 1813.
Plate 416

Colonel Coffin and myself agreed, that the shortest, and surest road to success was by running both ships into the mole, and carrying the place by assault; but the weather was unfavourable for such an attack, until the morning of the 26th, when the ships bore up in close order with a fine breeze.

The enemy were prepared for our reception, and opened their fire nearly half an hour before our guns could bear: the batteries were, however, passed with little injury, the ships engaging on both sides, and the *Thames* was anchored across the mole-head, the *Furieuse* bringing up a little astern of her.

Colonel Coffin and the troops landed the same instant, and pushed for the height of a strong tower, into which the enemy had retreated, and their appearance, together with the severe fire from the ships, induced the governor to hoist a flag of truce, and agree to the enclosed capitulation.

I have much pleasure in informing you, that this service has been performed without the loss of a man in either profession: our being hulled three times, and *Furieuse* twice, sails and rigging a good deal cut, is the only damage suffered. . . .

I have the honour to be, &c.

CHARLES NAPIER, Captain

Sir Robert Laurie, Bart., Captain of H.M.S. Ajax

Raid on Morgeon

Copy of another letter from Vice-admiral Sir Edward Pellew, to John Wilson Croker, Esq. dated on board the Caledonia, Port Mahon, April 7, 1813

Sir, I have the honour to enclose copies of letters from Captains Waldegrave and Usher, detailing the particulars of the destruction of two batteries, and the capture of several small vessels near Marseilles, which reflected very great credit on the officers and men engaged on those services, who, I trust, will receive their lordships' favourable notice.

I have the honour to be, &c.

EDWARD PELLEW

H.M.S. Volontaire, Cape Croisette, 31 March, 1813

Sir, Yesterday we perceived fourteen merchant vessels at Morgeon. This added to the importance of the destruction of the two batteries, erected there last year, which affords so much protection to the coast.

The night favoured for embracing Lieutenant Shaw's offer of attacking the place. The marines, under Lieutenants Barton and Hunt, royal marines, and boats of the ships, *Undaunted*, and *Redwing*, were placed under his orders for that purpose, and this morning justified my high confidence in him. He landed at Sormion, and marching over the hills at day-light, carried the batteries in the rear, after a partial resistance of forty troops there. Five 36-pounders in one, and two 24-pounders in the other battery, were thrown into the sea; one mortar well spiked, and all their ammunition destroyed. The boats under Lieutenant Syer, though elsewhere opposed by two field pieces, brought eleven vessels out laded with oil, and destroyed one other loaded, and two empty, which were aground. While completing the destruction of the works, many troops arrived from Marseilles, and the enemy's fleet in motion prevented further operations. . . .

The captures are hardly worthy of consideration, compared to the destruction of this strong post, which was doubly re-enforced within these two days. . . .

I have, &c.

Captain G.G. WALDEGRAVE

Vice-Admiral Sir Edward Pellew, Bart. &c.

July 6

Co-operation with Spanish Forces at Ampolla and Perello

Copy of a letter from Captain Adam, of H.M.S. Invincible, addressed to Vice-Admiral Sir Edward Pellew, and transmitted by the latter to John Wilson Croker, Esq.
H.M.S. Invincible, Salon Bay, April 4, 1813

Sir, The Baron de Eroles having requested I would co-operate in an attack on the enemy's posts at Ampolla and Perello, near to Ebro, two boats of H.M.S. under my command, armed with carronades, under the directions of Lieutenant Corbyn, the first lieutenant, and a Spanish felucca, in which a party of troops were embarked, left this bay on the afternoon of the 1st inst. with orders to attack the post at Ampolla.

The troops were landed within two miles of it, about one o'clock in the morning, and the battery of two 18-pounders was completely surprised, the sentry having been shot. The guns were then turned on the fortified house, in which the greater part of the guard were posted, who evacuated it immediately, and most of them escaped, but some of them were afterwards taken at Perello.

That place, which is two leagues inland from Ampolla, was invested by a detachment of the Baron de Eroles's troops on the morning of the 2d inst. and upon the enemy refusing to receive a flag of truce, the walls of the town, which were filled with loop holes, were scaled, and a large square tower in the middle of the town, into which the French troops retreated, was immediately surrounded.

Owing to light winds and calms, I was not able to anchor the *Invincible* in Ampolla bay until the afternoon of the 2d. Two field-pieces were immediately landed, and sent to Perello, under the direction of Lieutenant Corbyn, assisted by Lieutenant Pidgley [Pidgely?], and the midshipmen and men attached to the guns. They were placed in a house near the tower, and at daylight the next morning opened upon it.

After a very resolute defence, two breaches having been made in the tower, it surrendered, and a lieutenant and thirty-three soldiers were made prisoners. The enemy had one killed, and three wounded. They kept up a very heavy fire of musketry the whole time, but I have the satisfaction to say, that only one man belonging to this ship was wounded. The Spanish troops had two killed and six wounded.

At Ampolla two small privateers fell into our hands, which had been employed in communicating with Tarragona, and intercepting the trade passing the mouth of the Ebro. The post appears to have been established chiefly for the protection of this description of vessels and their prizes.

By the taking of Perello, the enemy's communications with the Col de Balageur is very much straitened, as it is on the high road from that place to Tortosa. . . .

I have the honour to be, &c,

C. ADAM, Captain

Vice-Admiral Sir Edward Pellew, &c.

July 10, 1813. XXX 168-170

Action Near Spalatro

Copy of a letter from Rear-Admiral Fremantle, to John Wilson Croker, Esq., dated on board H.M.S. Milford, at Lissa, May 1, 1813

Sir, In having the honour of forwarding, for the information of the Lords Commissioners of the Admiralty, Captain Black's report of his attack on an enemy's convoy near Spalatro, it is my duty to represent what his modesty has not allowed him to make of official report of, namely, that he is himself badly wounded by a musket-ball, which passed through his right hand, and now confines him.

Having made it my business to inquire and examine into all the particulars, I can have no hesitation in saying, that many would have undertaken the enterprise, but few vessels under such circumstances could have been extricated from such a force, and such difficulties as were opposed to them.

Much credit is due to Captain Black, his officers and ship's company, for their gallantry, as well as for their perseverance and steadiness, on this occasion.

I have the honour to be, &c.

THOS. FRAS FREMANTLE

H.M.S. Weazle, Lissa, April 26, 1813

Sir, I beg leave to report to you, that while cruising in H.M.'s sloop under my command, in pursuance of your orders of the 10th instant, at day-light of the 22d, the island of Zirona bearing W.S.W. distant about four miles, we discovered a convoy close to the main land, making for the port of Tran and Spalatro, to which we immediately gave chase; as we came up they separated in different directions, the greater part, with ten gunboats, bore up for the Bay of Boscaline; these we continued chasing under all sail; at half-past five A.M. they anchored in a line about a mile from the shore, hoisted their French colours, and commenced firing at us; the wind blowing strong at S.E. directly into the bay, our sails and rigging were considerably damaged before we could close with them; and seeing the enemy erecting batteries on shore, I was at first unwilling to go close to the enemy, when the action immediately commenced on our part; they stood our fire for about twenty minutes, when the whole cut their cables, ran closer in, and again opened their fire; their increased distance was now too great for our carronades to have their proper effect, we cut the cable, ran within half-pistol shot, and recommenced the action; the enemy now opened their fire upon us from three large guns, at the distance of thirty yards from each other, and two or three hundred musketry on the heights immediately over us; we continued closely engaged in this manner; at ten three of them struck their colours, two were driven on shore, and one sunk. They were now reinforced by four gun-boats from the eastward, who at first anchored outside, and commenced firing at us, which obliged us to engage on both sides; but they shortly after ran in and joined the others, who placed themselves behind a point of land, where we could only see their masts from the deck, when they commenced a most destructive fire, their grape-shot striking us over the land in every part; at this time our number was so reduced, that we could with difficulty man four guns, the marines and a few seamen firing musketry, our grape all expended. We continued in close action until three P.M. when the enemy discontinued their fire. After forty minutes the action again commenced, and continued, without intermission, till half-past six in the evening, when the firing entirely ceased on both sides. The enemy during the day had received considerable supplies of troops on shore, who had kept up an incessant fire upon us. We were now in a very critical situation, being but a very few yards from a lee-shore, almost a complete wreck, the whole of our running and greater part of the standing rigging gone, most of the sails shot from yards, the masts shot through in several places, and many shot in the hull, five between wind and water, both our pumps also shot away between the decks, with difficulty we could keep her free by constantly bailing at both hatches. In the action of this day, I found we had lost five killed, and wounded. At dark, the boats succeeded in burning and destroying besides the gun-boats, eight sail of the convoy, bringing away their anchors, all ours being shot to pieces, and rendered entirely unserviceable; indeed it is to this I am to attribute the being enabled to warp his Majesty's sloop out. At daylight on the 23d, having warped about a mile from the land, the remaining gunboats again attacked us, and musketry from the shore; this was most annoying, they having us in a raking position, our last cable half shot through, the wind blowing strong in, we could not venture to bring our broadside to bear upon them; all this day and night we were warping out from the shore, but very slowly, the people being reduced in number, and exhausted with fatigue.

On the 24th, the enemy had erected a battery of three guns on a point of the bay, close to which we must pass; this they opened upon us about noon, when we got within their range; the gun-boats pulling out in a line astern, commenced their fire about one P.M. during all the time we were warping out under their fire, and that of musketry from the shore. Wind now moderate, and shortly after quite calm. At four, nearly out of the bay, the gun-boats following and firing at us. At five, they got within the range of our guns, when we opened our larboard broadside, and drove them off, but it continuing calm, we were unable to follow them.

The conduct of the whole of my officers and ship's company, during these three days of most arduous service, merits my warmest praise; indeed, I am at a loss which most to admire, their determined bravery in action, or their steady perseverance in warping the brig out. . . .

I have the honour to be, &c.

JAMES BLACK

Rear-Admiral Fremantle, &c.

Admiralty Office, July 13, 1813. ^XXX 233-234^

Securing the Road to Tarragona

Copy of a letter from Captain Adam, of H.M.S. the Invincible, addressed to Rear-Admiral Hallowell, and transmitted by the latter to John Wilson Croker, Esq

H.M.S. Invincible, off the Coll de Balageur, June 8, 1813

Sir, In pursuance of your directions to take the ships and vessels, named in the margin,[1] under my orders, and co-operated with Lieutenant-colonel Prevost in the siege of the fort of the Coll de Balageur, I have the honour to inform you, that the troops were landed about noon of the 3d instant, and the Lieutenant-colonel immediately invested the fort, the riflemen of De Roll's regiment, and other light troops, being pushed close up to the walls.

The fort is situated in a most difficult pass, through which the high road from Tortosa to Tarragona winds, and it is absolutely the key of the only road for cannon into this province, from the westward, without going round by Lerida. It is armed with twelve pieces of ordnance, including two ten-inch mortars, and two howitzers, and the surrounding heights are so difficult of access, that it has been a work of the greatest labour to establish the necessary batteries before it.

Two six-pounder field-pieces, and a howitzer, were landed on the evening of the 3d instant, dragged up, and placed on the ridge of a steep and rugged mountain, to the S.E. of the fort: two twelve-pounders were added to the former by noon of the next day. The whole remained under the command of Lieutenant Corbyn, first of the *Invincible*, having under his orders a detachment of midshipmen and seamen from this ship, and a most excellent fire was kept up from them, which considerably damaged the defences of the fort, and checked its fire upon our working parties.

In the mean time, three Spanish twenty-four-pounders were landed, and two more guns, of the same calibre, from this ship, to be got up by the high road to the foot of a very steep height, on the crest of which the breaching battery was to be constructed, at about three hundred yards from the eastern face of the fort.

In the afternoon of the 4th instant the fort was summoned to surrender; and the commandant answered, that he should defend the place committed to his charge.

During the night of the 4th, every exertion was used to bring the guns up to the hill, and to complete the breaching-battery; but, as it could not be completed by daylight, the men were withdrawn.

The seamen and marines were landed early in the afternoon of the 5th, and carried up the stores for the battery, under a brisk fire of shot and shells from the fort.

The three Spanish twenty-four-pounders, notwithstanding their immense size and weight, were conveyed up the side of the hill, over the most difficult and rugged ground, by the united exertions of the soldiers, seamen, and marines, under the immediate direction of Captain Carroll, of the *Volcano*. Two eight-inch mortars were brought as far along the road as was practicable before dark; and the iron twenty-four-pounders were conveyed to the foot of the hill as soon as it was dark.

The work of the battery advanced rapidly, although it was necessary to fill all the sand-bags at the bottom of the hill; and I was in confident expectation that the battery

1 *Thames, Volcano, Strombolo, Brune*, and eight gun-boats.

would open soon after daylight; but by ten o'clock the rain fell in torrents, attended by the most violent thunder and lightning I almost ever witnessed.

The quantity of ammunition which had been brought up for the battery, laying in exposed situations, made it the more awful, and the enemy kept up an incessant fire of shells and grape shot.

In defiance of all these obstacles, two of the guns were got high enough up to mount on the platforms, but all our exertion was unequal to place them there, owing to the violence of the rain, and the excessive difficulty of working in the extreme darkness of the night. From the same reason, too, the mortars could not be be brought forward, and after a night of the most excessive labour, we had the mortification of being again obliged to retire; the officers and men being quite worn out.

The weather continued very bad until the afternoon of the 6th instant, when a party was landed, and the mortars were got forward; before daylight, the seamen and marines were on the pile, and all the guns were placed on the battery ready for mounting. The two mortars opened soon after daylight, and the shells were thrown with great precision, by Lieutenant James, of the Royal Marine artillery, landed from the *Strombolo*, who worked the mortars with his party; and the fire from Lieutenant Corbyn's battery was resumed with excellent effect. This united force made very considerable impression on the fort: an expense magazine was blown up, and the enemy's fire was very much slackened.

At seven o'clock, just before the breaching battery was ready to open, a white flag was shewn from the fort, Captain Stoddart, of the *Strombolo*, and Captain Zehnpfenning, were immediately sent to the fort, and the latter returned in a few minutes with an offer from the commandant, to surrender the fort and garrison upon conditions of marching out with the honours of war, the officers and men preserving their private property.

This was immediately acceded to by Lieutenant-colonel Prevost and myself: the fort was taken possession of by the advance of the troops. The garrison marched out, grounded their arms on the glacis, and were immediately embarked. . . .

I have the honour to be, &c.

CHARLES ADAM, Captain

To Rear-admiral Hallowell, &c.

Admiralty Office, September 14, 1813. [XXX 258]

Action Against Trade on the Italian Coast

H.M.S. Bacchante, at anchor off Guila Nova, 12 June 1813
Sir, At daylight this morning, an enemy's convoy were discovered under the town of Gala Nova, on the coast of Abruzza; as I was six or seven miles to leeward of them, with a light breeze and a current against me, I thought it best to detach the boats, with discretionary orders, to the First Lieutenant, Hood, either to attack them, or wait till I arrived. He found the enemy much stronger than was expected, consisting of seven large gun-boats each, mounting one eighteen-pounder in the bow, three smaller gun-vessels with a four-pounder in the bow, and fourteen sail of merchant-vessels under their convoy, four of which had guns in the bow also. The shore astern of the vessels was lined with troops, entrenched on the beach, with two field pieces with them. This was the force opposed to a frigate's boats; but no disparity of numbers could check the spirit of the brave officers and men employed on this service. The attack was determined

on instantly, and executed with all the gallantry and spirit which men accustomed to danger and to despise it have so frequently shewn; and never was there a finer display of it than on this occasion. The boats as they advanced were exposed to a heavy fire of grape and musketry; and it was not till they were fairly alongside that the enemy slackened their fire, and were driven from their vessels with great loss.

The troops on the beach, which the French officers mention as amounting to upwards of one hundred men, fled on the first fire, and the field-pieces were destroyed by our marines. Our boats were now in possession of the convoy, many of which were aground, and our men were exposed to a scattering fire of musketry, whilst employed in getting them afloat. . . .

I have the honour to be, &c.

Captain W. HOSTE

F. Fremantle, Esq. Rear-Admiral of the White

Admiralty Office, September 19, 1813. ^{XXX 351-352}

Copy of a letter from Admiral Lord Keith, K.B. to John Wilson Croker, Esq. dated on board the Royal Sovereign, in Hamoaze, 18th September, 1813, with copies of its enclosures
Sir, I have the highest satisfaction in transmitting to their Lordships the accompanying despatches (which I have just received by Captain Bloye, from Captain Sir G.R. Collier), giving an account of the fall of St. Sebastian, and the surrender of the French garrison; and the professional skill and perseverance of the officers and men who have been employed in the co-operation with the army before that place, has been so eminently conspicuous, and particularly that of Sir George R. Collier himself, that I beg to recommend him, and the several officers and petty officers whom he names, to their Lordships' notice.

I have the honour to be, &c.

KEITH, Admiral

P.S. Captain Bloye landed at Falmouth, and as he may be able to give their Lordships much useful information, I have directed him to deliver this despatch.

Surveillante off St. Sebastian, 9 September 1813
My Lord, It is with sincere pleasure that I do myself the honour to report to your Lordship the fall of St. Sebastian, the northern Gibraltar of Spain. Yesterday, at 10 A.M. the breaching and mortar batteries opened a most ruinous fire against the Castle of La Motte (situated on the crown of the hill), and the adjoining works. In a very short time General Rey, the governor, sent out a flag of truce to propose terms of capitulation, which were concluded at five in the evening, when the Battery du Gouverneur and the Mirador were immediately taken possession of by our troops. The garrison, still upwards of seventeen hundred, became prisoners of war, and are to be conveyed to England from Passages. At this season of the year the possession of St. Sebastian becomes doubly valuable; it may be considered the western key of the Pyrennees [sic], and its importance as to the future operations of the allied army is incalculable. The town and works have suffered considerably, and it must be a long time before the former can recover its original splendour; I cannot, however, avoid congratulating your Lordship on its fall on any terms, as the gales now blow home, and the sea is prodigious; all the squadrons were yesterday forced to sea, with the exception of the *Surveillante* and *President*. The

former good conduct and gallantry of the seamen landed from the squadron, under Lieutenant O'Reilly, of the *Surveillante*, and serving in the breaching batteries, have been most conspicuously maintained. . . .

I have, &c.

GEORGE R. COLLIER, Captain

To the Right Hon. Lord Keith, K.B.,
Admiral of the Red, Commander-in-Chief, &c.

Admiralty Office, October 12, 1813. XXX 433-434

Operations in the Adriatic

The letters, of which the following are copies and extracts, have been transmitted to John Wilson Croker, Esq. by Vice-admiral Sir Edward Pellew, commander-in-chief of his Majesty's ships and vessels in the Mediterranean

H.M.S. Milford off Porto Ré, 6 July 1813

Sir, I have the honour to acquaint you, that on the 28th ult. I left Melada, and on the 30th, assembled the *Elizabeth* and *Eagle*, off Promontorio. On the 1st inst. the squadron entered the Quarnier Channel, and on the 2d, in the evening, anchored about four miles from Fiume, which was defended by four batteries, mounting fifteen heavy guns. On the 3d, in the morning, the ships named in the margin weighed,[2] and with a light breeze from the S.W. with the intention of attacking the sea line of batteries (for which the arrangement had been previously made and communicated), leaving a detachment of boats and marines with the *Haughty*, to storm the battery at the Mole Head, as soon as the guns were silenced; but the wind very light, shifting to the S.E. with current from the river, broke the ships off, and the *Eagle* could only fetch the second battery, opposite to which she anchored. The enemy could not stand the well-directed fire of that ship. This being communicated by telegraph, I made the signal to storm, when Captain Rowley, leading in his gig the first detachment of marines, took possession of the fort, and hoisted the King's colours, whilst Captain Hoste, with the marines of the Milford, took and spiked the guns of the first battery, which was under the fire of the *Milford* and *Bacchante*, and early evacuated. Captain Rowley leaving a party of seamen to turn the guns of the second battery against the others, without losing time, boldly dashed on through the town, although annoyed by the enemy's musketry from the windows of the houses, and a field-piece placed in the centre of the great street; but the marines, headed by Lieutenants Lloyd and Nepean, and the seamen of the boats, proceeded with such firmness, that the enemy retreated before them, drawing the field piece until they came to the square, where they made a stand, taking post in a large house. At this time, the boats with their carronades, under Captain Markland, opened against the gable end of it with such effect, that the enemy gave way at all points, and I was gratified at seeing them forsake the town in every direction. Captain Hoste, with his division, followed close to Captain Rowley, and on their junction, the two batteries, with the field-piece, stores, and shipping were taken possession of, the governor and every officer and man of the garrison having run away. Considering the number of troops in the town, above three hundred and fifty, besides natives, our loss has been trifling; one marine of the *Eagle*, killed; Lieutenant Lloyd, and five seamen and marines, wounded. Nothing could

2 *Milford, Elizabeth, Eagle, Bacchante* and *Haughty*.

View of San Sebastian. Engraved by Baily, from a drawing by W.P. ^{Plate 402}

A. Great breach.
B. Little breach.
C. Houses set on fire by the enemy on
   the 24th July.
D. Ditch.
E. Hornwork.
F. English sap.
G. Advances of the storming parties
   25th July, at 3 A.M.
H. Small river, shallow at low water.

I. Castle.
J. Battery connected with the castle.
K. Breaching battery.
L. Battery of four 68-pounders.
M. Battery of 4 24-pounders.
N. Mortar batteries.
O. Light-house where the British
   have two guns.
P. Broken wooden bridge.
X. Sea-weeds, gravel, flat rocks, &c.

exceed the spirit and disposition manifested by every captain, officer, seaman, and marine, in the squadron.

Although the town was stormed in every part, by the prudent management of Captains Rowley and Hoste, not an individual has been plundered, nor has any thing been taken away, except what was afloat, and in the government stores.

I herewith send a return of the property and vessels captured, and have the honour to be, &c.

THOMAS FRANCIS FREMANTLE

Vice-Admiral Sir Edward Pellew, Bart. &c.

Admiralty Office, November 23, 1813. ^{XXX 508-510}

The following are extracts and copies of despatches received by Vice-admiral Sir Edward Pellew, Bart. from Rear-admiral Fremantle, and transmitted by the former to John Wilson Croker, Esq.

(Extract)

On the 6th of September arrived at Fiume, and found his Majesty's ships *Milford* and *Wizard* at anchor off the town, and the Imperial flag flying, the whole of Istria and Croatia (nearly) up in arms against the French, and are driving them out in all directions. Signi, Porto Re, and Fiume, are under the Austrian flag. General Nugent has his head-quarters at Lippa, about 22 miles from Fiume; his force consists of two thousand Austrians, and some Croats; the French garrison of Pola, of six hundred men, with about fifteen hundred Croats, were marching to relieve Fiume, but the Croats, on hearing that their countrymen were in arms against the French, surrounded, disarmed, and took the six hundred Frenchmen prisoners, and sent them to General Nugent into Fiume. . . .

December 11. XXX514-515

Copy of a letter from Rear-Admiral Fremantle, John Wilson Croker, Esq., dated on board the Milford, off Trieste, 31 October 1813

Sir, I have the honour to acquaint you, for the information of the Lords Commissioners of the Admiralty, that I left Pola on the 19th ultimo, and arrived at Capo D'Istria on the 21st, when General Count Nugent met me on the same day. Much credit is due to Captain Gower, of the *Elizabeth*, for having opened a communication with the army, and for assisting materially in putting the place in a good state of defence.

On the 27th September, the army under General Nugent moved; the *Elizabeth* was ordered off Mugia, whilst the *Bacchante*, with a company of Austrian troops, proceeded to Dwino.

I remained at Capo D'Istria in constant correspondence with General Nugent, who was harassing the army of the Viceroy on his retreat, until the morning of the 5th instant, when I sailed for Trieste, and advanced the *Elizabeth* to Dwino. General Nugent, who continued to follow the enemy, left some troops near Trieste, and the port was completely blockaded by sea. About noon, on the 10th, the enemy surprised us by opening a masked battery, with a field-piece and a howitzer, upon the *Milford*, whose stern was towards the shore, and began firing. Captain Markland in a few minutes got a spring upon the cable, and opened a steady well-directed fire upon the battery; in a quarter of an hour both guns were completely disabled, two men killed and seven wounded, whilst not a person was touched on board the ship, although one shell exploded on the poop deck. On the 10th I landed the marines and two field pieces under Captain Markland: on the 11th the General returned from Gorizia, having obliged the Viceroy to pass the Isonzo. It was then determined to lay siege to the castle. By the 16th, in the morning, we had twelve guns in two batteries, which opened their fire and continued nearly the whole day; towards the evening the enemy was driven from the Windmill, which was taken possession of by the Austrian troops, and two howitzers advanced there. The firing was continued occasionally until noon on the 23rd, by which time Captain Rowley had got a thirty-two-pounder within two hundred yards of the Shanza, where there was a strong building with one gun and loop holes in it, standing upon a hill, with a wall round it nearly fourteen feet high, an officer and sixty men.

We had had some communication with the castle in the morning, and the truce was broken off at a very short notice by the enemy, who opened on all sides. The thirty-two-pounder was fired upon the Shanza. The first shot the gun recoiled, and the ground giving way, it fell backward off the platform, which was six feet above the level. It was fine to see Captain Rowley and his people immediately get a triangle above the work, and the thirty-two pounder with its carriage, run up to its place again, under a shower of grape and musketry, which occasioned a severe loss. Towards evening, the enemy in the Shanza held out the white flag, and surrendered to Captain Rowley. Having now possession of the Shanza, which commanded the castle and the Windmill hill, we set to work upon some advanced batteries within four hundred yards of the castle, but the weather was so wet, and the labour was so great, that it was not until the morning of the 29th that they were complete, when the enemy acceded to our altered propositions for surrendering the castle. We were prepared to have opened with eleven thirty-two-pounders, twelve eighteen-pounders, four mortars, and four howitzers. . . .

The consequences of taking this place will be felt throughout this country, and General Nugent has deservedly all the merit of having liberated these provinces in the space of two months, with so small a force. . . .

I have the honour to be, &c

THOMAS FREMANTLE

1813 – Defence of the Canadas

THE DEFENCE OF THE CANADAS was entrusted to British and Canadian professional soldiers, reinforced with volunteers 'embodied' from the militia, not all of whom could be relied upon to be loyal. Against the greater numbers the Americans could muster, the British had to use professionalism. In 1812 this had served to bring the capture of Michilimackinac at the bottom of Lake Michigan, which convinced the western tribes to lend their support, and invasion across Niagara had been beaten off in the battle of Queenstown heights, in which Major-General Isaac Brock had lost his life.

American forces were too weak to risk a direct attack on Montreal, but in 1813 their fortunes began to improve. The key to control of Upper Canada (Ontario) lay in naval control of lakes Erie and Ontario. An American raid on York (Toronto) succeeded in burning the public buildings, and the heights of Niagara were occupied. The low point in the fortunes of Canadians came with the American naval victory on Lake Erie in the autumn over Canadian naval levies who were almost entirely inexperienced in the horrors and discipline of naval war. The army, and its Indian allies, were defeated at Moraviantown. However, the Burlington heights were successfully held, and by the end of the year American forces had withdrawn from Canada.

East of York, the American thrusts had been defeated. Colonel Charles de Salaberry, a Canadian officer in the regular army, at Chateauguay, and Colonel J W Morrison at Crystler's Farm, defeated an attempted invasion of Lower Canada (Quebec). From the provincial dockyard at Kingston, local naval forces, stiffened with a few regulars under Captain James Yeo, were able to deny the Americans command of Lake Ontario. With the winding down of the war in Europe, more regular soldiers and sailors, and shipwrights, could be spared for the Canadas.

This selection of papers from *The Naval Chronicle*'s account of the war in the Canadas contains Captain Yeo's accounts of efforts to defeat the American flotilla on Lake Ontario, Lieutenant Barclay's report to him of his defeat on Lake Erie, and ends with an horrific account of the march

of naval reinforcements from Saint John, New Brunswick, up the St John
River in the depths of the early winter of 1814.

Commodore Yeo's Dispatches From Lake Ontario

Letters on Service
Admiralty Office, October 23, 1813. XXX 440

Copy of a letter from Commodore James Lucas Yeo, to John Wilson Croker, Esq.
dated on board H.M.S. Wolfe at Kingston, Upper Canada, 29 June 1813
Sir, I have the honour to inform you, for the information of the Lords Commissioners
of the Admiralty, that on the 3d instant, I sailed, with his Majesty's squadron under my
command, from this port, to co-operate with our army at the head of the lake, and
annoy the enemy, by intercepting all supplies going to the army, and thereby oblige his
squadron to come out for its protection.

At day-light, on the 8th, the enemy's camp was discovered close to us at Forty Mile
Creek; it being calm, the large vessels could not get in: but the *Beresford*, Captain
Spilsbury, the *Sir Sidney Smith*, Lieutenant Majoribanks, and the gun-boats, under the
orders of Lieutenant Anthony (first of this ship), succeeded in getting close under the
enemy's batteries, and by a sharp and well-directed fire, soon obliged him to make a
precipitate retreat, leaving all his camp equipage, provisions, stores, &c. behind, which
fell into our hands; the *Beresford* also captured all his bateaux, laden with stores, &c.
Our troops immediately occupied the post. I then proceeded along shore to the westward
of the enemy's camp, leaving our army in his front. On the 13th we captured two
schooners and some boats, going to the enemy with supplies; by them I received
information, that there was a dépôt of provisions at Genessee [sic] River; I accordingly
proceeded off that river, landed some seamen and marines of the squadron, and brought
off all the provisions found in the government stores, as also a sloop laden with grain,
for the army; on the 19th I anchored off the Great Sodas, landed a party of the 1st
regiment of Royal Scots, and took off six hundred barrels of flour and port, which had
arrived there for their army.

I have, &c.

JAMES LUCAS YEO, Commodore

Copy of a letter from Commodore James Lucas Yeo, addressed to Admiral Sir John
Borlase Warren, Bart. and K.B., and a duplicate of which has been transmitted by the
former to John Wilson Croker, Esq
H.M.S. Wolfe on Lake Ontario, 10 August 1813
Sir, I have the honour to inform you, that the enemy's squadron was discovered at
anchor off Fort Niagara, on the morning of the 8th inst. consisting of thirteen sail; that
of his Majesty at six. They immediately weighed, and stood out in a line of battle; but
on our approaching nearly within gun shot, they fired their broadsides, wore, and stood
under their batteries: light airs and calms prevented me closing with them again until
this night, when having a fine breeze we stood for them.

At eleven we came within gun-shot of their line of schooners, who opened a heavy
fire, their ships keeping off the wind to prevent our closing; at half-past twelve, this
ship came within gun-shot of the *Pike* and *Madison*, when they immediately bore up,
fired their stern chase guns, and made sail for Niagara, leaving two of their schooners

Portrait of Captain Sir James
Lucas Yeo, Knt. Captain R.N.
Engraved by Simpkin, from
Captain Shortland's sketch. Plate 321

astern, which we captured, the *Growler* and *Julia*, each mounting one long thirty-two, and one long twelve, and 40 men.

From information obtained from the prisoners, I hear that their new ship, the *General Pike*, mounts 28 long 24-pounders, and 400 men; and that all their schooners mount from two to four long 32-pounders.

The enemy have disappeared, I, therefore, suppose they are gone to Sacket's harbour to refit.

I am happy to add, that (except in the sails and rigging) his Majesty's squadron have not sustained any injury; and have the honour to be, . .

Admiralty Office, November 6, 1813. XXX 507

Extract of a letter from Commodore Sir James Yeo, to Admiral Sir John Borlase Warren, Bart. and K.B. &c. and transmitted to John Wilson Croker, Esq.
H.M.S. Wolfe, off the False Duck Islands on Lake Ontario, 12 September 1813
Sir, I have the honour to acquaint you, that his Majesty's squadron under my command, being becalmed off Genesee River, on the 11th instant, the enemy's fleet of eleven sail, having a partial wind, succeeded in getting within range of their long twenty-four, and 32-pounders; and from their having the wind of us, and the dull sailing of some of our squadron, I found it impossible to bring them to close action. We remained in this mortifying situation five hours, having only six guns in all the squadron that would reach the enemy (not a carronade being fired); at sunset a breeze sprang up from the westward, when I steered for the False Duck Islands, under which the enemy could not keep the weather gage, but be obliged to meet us on equal terms; this, however, he carefully avoided.

Although I have to regret the loss of Mr. William Ellerey, midshipman, and three seamen killed, and seven wounded, I cannot but conceive it fortunate that none of the squadron have received any material damage, which must have been considerable had the enemy acted with the least spirit, and taken advantage of the superiority of position they possessed. Enclosed is a list of killed and wounded.

Sacketts Harbour. Plate 519

General Prevost's Despatches From Montreal

Colonial Department
Downing-Street, February 8, 1814. XXXI 249-253

Despatches, of which the following are copies, have been this day received from Lieutenant-general Sir G. Prevost, Bart. addressed to Earl Bathurst, one of his Majesty's principal Secretaries of State.

Head-Quarters, Montreal, December 12, 1813

My Lord, Having had the honour to report to your Lordship, on the 30th of October and the 15th November last, the affairs which took place between his Majesty's forces and the American armies, led on by Major-general Hampton and Major-general Wilkinson, I have now the satisfaction to inform your Lordship, that the signal defeats experienced by the enemy on the Chateauguay River, in Lower Canada, and near Chrystler's Farm, in Upper Canada, have relieved both provinces from the pressure of the armies invading them, and have obliged the divisions of General Hampton and General Wilkinson to retire to their own territory, and seek for winter quarters, under circumstances so highly disadvantageous as to have produced in both of them discontent, desertion, and disease.

The well-timed appearance of a small regular force in General Wilkinson's front, which I had pushed forward from the Coteau de Lac to support and give confidence to the Glengarry and Stormont militia, very shortly after the severe lesson his vanity had received from the corps of observation, operating so powerfully as to induce him to commence a precipitate retreat from our shore to St. Regis, and up the Salmon River, and to abandon his avowed project, of passing his winter in Montreal.

It appears the American army, upon arriving at the French Mills, which are situated on the Salmon River, about six miles from its mouth, proceeded to dismantle their river craft and gun-boats, and to arrange on shore, round their block-house, a most cumbersome train of artillery, for the preservation of which the whole of Major-general Wilkinson's infantry is retained in tents and huts, at this most inclement season of the year, until the winter roads should be sufficiently established to enable him to retire his guns to Platsburg.

A rapid succession of severe frost, light snow, and sudden thaw, to which the American army has been so long so much exposed, has made it impossible for me to execute any enterprize against it, without risking more than my means could justify.

A division of gun-boats, with a detachment of troops, which I had ordered on the 1st of this month to advance into Lake Champlain, for the purpose of molesting General Hampton's division, succeeded in burning an extensive building lately erected near Platsburg, as a dépôt magazine; some batteaux, together with the ammunition, provisions, and stores found in it, were either brought away or destroyed.

The severity of the weather obliged Captain Pring, of the Royal Navy, under whose command I had placed the expedition, to return to the Isle aux Noix on the 5th; in effecting which, he was obliged to cut a channel for his boats through several miles of ice. The enemy's troops were in considerable number in the vicinity of Platsburg, but no attempt was made to annoy our force employed on this occasion.

In Upper Canada a conjoint attack on Burlington Heights, planned by Major-general Harrison and Commodore Chauncey, has been frustrated by the lateness of the season and severity of the weather.

Defeat on Lake Erie

Captain R.H. Barclay, Commander, and late Senior Officer, to Commodore Sir James Yeo
His Majesty's late Ship Detroit, Put-in Bay, Lake Erie, September 12, 1813
Sir, The last letter I had the honour of writing to you, dated the 6th instant, I informed you, that unless certain intimation was received of more seamen being on their way to Amherstburg, I should be obliged to sail with the squadron, deplorably manned as it was, to fight the enemy (who blockaded the port) to enable us to get supplies of provisions and stores of every description; so perfectly destitute of provisions as the post, that there was not a day's flour in store, and the crews of the squadron under my command were on half allowance of many things, and when that was done there was no more. Such were the motives which induced Major-general Proctor (whom by your instructions I was directed to consult, and whose wishes I was enjoined to execute, as far as related to the good of the country) to concur in the necessity of a battle being risked, under the many disadvantages which I laboured, and it now remains for me the most melancholy task to relate to you the unfortunate issue of that battle, as well as the many untoward circumstances that led to that event.

No intelligence of seamen having arrived, I sailed, on the 9th instant, fully expecting to meet the enemy next morning, as they had been seen among the islands; nor was I mistaken: soon after daylight they were seen in motion in Put-in-Bay, the wind then at south-west, and light giving us the weather gage. I bore up for them, in hopes of bringing them to action among the islands, but that intention was soon frustrated, by the wind suddenly shifting to the south-east, which brought the enemy directly to windward.

The line was formed according to a given plan, so that each ship might be supported against the superior force of the two brigs opposed to them. About ten the enemy had cleared the islands, and immediately bore up, under easy sail, in a line abreast, each brig being also supported by the small vessels. At a quarter before twelve I commenced the action, by firing a few long guns; about a quarter past the American commodore, also supported by two schooners, one carrying four long twelve-pounders, the other a long thirty-two and twenty-four-pounder, came to close action with the *Detroit*: the other brig of the enemy, apparently destined to engage the *Queen Charlotte*, supported in like manner by two schooners, kept so far to windward as to render the *Queen Charlotte*'s twenty-pounder carronades useless, while she was, with the *Lady Prevost*, exposed to the heavy and destructive fire of the *Caledonia* and four other schooners, armed with long and heavy guns, like those I have already described.

Too soon, alas! was I deprived of the services of the noble and intrepid Captain Finnis, who soon after the commencement of the action fell, and with him fell my greatest support; soon after Lieutenant Stokes, of the *Queen Charlotte*, was struck senseless by a splinter, which deprived the country of his services at this very critical period.

As I perceived the *Detroit* had enough to contend with, without the prospect of a fresh brig, Provincial Lieutenant Irvine, who then had charge of the *Queen Charlotte*, behaved with great courage, but his experience was much too limited to supply the place of such an officer as Captain Finnis, hence she proved of far less assistance than I expected.

The action continued with great fury until half-past two, when I perceived my opponent drop astern, and a boat passing from him to the *Niagara* (which vessel was at this time perfectly fresh), the American commodore seeing that as yet the day was against him (his vessel having struck soon after he left her), and also the very defenceless state of the *Detroit*, which ship was now a perfect wreck, principally from the raking fire of the gun-boats, and also that the *Queen Charlotte* was in such a situation, that I could receive very little assistance from her, and the *Lady Prevost* being at this time too far to leeward, from her rudder being injured, made a noble, and, alas! too successful an effort to regain it, for he bore up, and, supported by his small vessels, passed within pistol-shot, and took a raking position on our bow; nor could I prevent it, as the unfortunate situation of the *Queen Charlotte* prevented us from wearing; in attempting it we fell on board her; my gallant first lieutenant, Garland, was now mortally wounded, and myself so severely, that I was obliged to quit the deck. Manned as the squadron was, with not more than fifty British seamen, the rest a mixed crew of Canadians and solders, and who were totally unacquainted with such service, rendered the loss of officers more sensibly felt, and never in any action was the loss more severe; every officer commanding vessels, and their seconds, was either killed, or wounded so severely, as to be unable to keep the deck. . . .

The weather gage gave the enemy a prodigious advantage, as it enabled them not only to choose their position, but their distance also, which they did in such a manner as to prevent the carronades of the *Queen Charlotte* and *Lady Prevost* from having much effect; while their long guns did great execution, particularly against the *Queen Charlotte*. . . .

I have the honour to be, &c.

R.H. BARCLAY

Commander, and late Senior Officer

Lieutenant George Inglis to Captain Barclay
His Majesty's late Ship Detroit, September 10, 1813
Sir, I have the honour to transmit you an account of the termination of the late unfortunate battle with the enemy's squadron.

On coming on the quarter-deck, after your being wounded, the enemy's second brig, at that time on our weather beam, shortly afterwards took a position on our weather bow, to rake us, to prevent which, in attempting to wear, to get our starboard broadside to bear upon her, a number of the guns of the larboard broadside being at this time disabled, fell on board the *Queen Charlotte*, at this time running up to leeward of us; in this situation the two ships remained for some time. As soon as we got clear of her, I ordered the *Queen Charlotte* to shoot ahead of us if possible, and attempted to back our fore-top-sail to get astern, but the ship laying completely unmanageable, every brace cut away, the mizzen-top-mast and gaff down, all the other masts badly wounded, not a stay left forward, hull shattered very much, a number of the guns disabled, and the enemy's squadron raking both ships ahead and astern, none of our own in a situation to support us, I was under the painful necessity of answering the enemy, to say we had struck, the *Queen Charlotte* having previously done so.

I have the honour to be,

GEORGE INGLIS

To Captain Barclay, &c.

Naval Reinforcements for Canada Make Winter March from Saint John to Montreal and Kingston
From 'Correspondence.' XXXIII 123-127

John Kent to the Editor, Royal Hospital, Plymouth, 22d October, 1814
Mr. Editor, I do myself the honour of transmitting to you, an account of the march of my youngest son, Lieutenant Henry Kent, which if you think likely to prove interesting to the readers of the *Naval Chronicle*, the insertion of it will oblige, Sir, your humble servant,

JOHN KENT

Extraordinary March of Lieutenant Henry Kent, from St. John's [sic], New Brunswick, to Kingston, in Upper Canada, being a distance of 900 miles, in the depth of winter
Kingston, on Lake Ontario, June 20th, 1814
We left Halifax in the *Fantome*, on the 22d of January last, and arrived at St. John's (New Brunswick), on the 26th, making a passage of four days, the weather extremely bad: the brig appeared a complete mass of ice, it freezing as fast as the sea broke over us. The inhabitants of St. John's came forward in the most handsome manner in a subscription to forward us in sleighs to Fredericston [sic], the seat of government, a distance of 80 miles. The seamen were divided into three divisions, each of 70 men, the first under Captain Collier, of the *Manly*, the second under Lieutenant Russel, and the third under myself. On the 29th of January, the first division proceeded about nine in the morning, and in the afternoon the second followed; the next morning I disembarked, the rigging of all the ships being manned, and the crews cheering us. On landing, we were received by the band of the 8th regiment, and a large concourse of people, who

escorted us to the sleighs, when we set off at full speed. In eight hours we went fifty miles, and then halted for the night at a small house on the banks of the river; started again in the morning, and in the afternoon reached Frederickston [Fredericton], and found both divisions had halted there. - The seamen were lodged in a barrack, which was walled in, but they soon scaled the walls, and were running about the town; you may therefore judge what trouble we had to collect them again. The seamen were now divided into two divisions, the first under Captain Collier's command, the second under mine, as being the senior officer.

On the 2d of February, Captain Collier proceeded with his division in sleighs, furnished by the inhabitants at their own expense, and the day following I left it with mine: I was obliged to leave one of my best seamen sick at the hospital, frost bitten, and I have since learnt he has lost two of his toes. From Frederickston we continued on the ice of the river St. John, except in places where, from shoals, the ice is thrown up in heaps. The country, after leaving Frederickston, is but thinly inhabited; a settlement you may see occasionally, but never more than three houses together. I kept always in the wake of the first division, halting where they had the day before. On the third evening, at the house where I halted, I found the master of the *Thistle* a corpse, having died with intense cold. Captain Collier having made every arrangement for burying him, I put his body into a sleigh, and sent it to a village a few miles distant. On the 7th reached Presque Isle, where there is a barrack and dépôt for provisions, but no houses near it; this place is 82 miles from Frederickston. Discharged the sleighs, and began making preparations for our march, each of us being furnished with a pair of snow shoes, two pair of moccasins, a toboggan between every four men, a camp kettle to every twelve, with axes and tinder-box. As you may not know the use of those articles by their Indian names, I will endeavour to describe them: Snow shoes are of a singular shape, something like a pear, formed by a hoop, and the bottom of them netted across with the hides of some animal; they are fixed on by a strap round the heel, and tied across the instep, as you do a pair of skates; they are about two feet in length, and one in breadth. Moccasins are made of buffalo's hide, sole and tops in one, roughly sewed up with twine, a stripe of hide run through notches, cut round the quarters, to haul it tight on your foot. Toboggans are hand sleighs, about four feet in length, and one in breadth, made of such light wood that they do not weigh above four pounds. On these you lash your provisions and clothes, and with the bight of a rope over your shoulder, drag it with great ease on the snow. I provided myself at Halifax with a jacket, trousers, and waistcoat, lined with fine flannel, so that with those, three flannel shirts, and a linen one on, three pair of stockings, and a square piece of blanket wrapped on my feet, with moccasins over all, I felt pretty warm.

At day-break, commenced lashing our provisions on the toboggans, and at eight o'clock commenced our march. The clothes I had with me being four shirts, the same of stockings, a coat and trousers, with a great coat, and a cap to sleep in. We marched daily from fifteen to twenty-two miles, and though that appears but a little distance, yet, with the snow up to our knees, was as much as any man could do. The first night we reached two small huts, the next the same accommodation, and the third slept in the woods. On the fourth, reached the Grand Falls,[1] which are about forty feet in height; none of us saw them, as they were a mile distant, and all of us too fatigued to go that distance: next day reached a small French settlement on Grande Riviere. The march

1 Although this place is denominated the Grand Falls, the cataract is a mile distant.

from here to Madawaska (another French settlement), was beyond any thing you can conceive; it blew a gale of wind from the northward, and the drift of snow was so great, it was almost impossible to discern a man a hundred yards distant: before I got half way, the men lay down, saying they could not possibly go further; I endeavoured by every persuasion to cheer them, and succeeded in getting about one half to accompany me. We reached it about nine o'clock at night, almost fainting, a distance of 21 miles. The following morning, having sent all the midshipmen in search of the men, got them all collected, but out of 110, only 10 able to proceed on the march; I was therefore obliged to halt for a day to recruit them. The next morning, being the 15th of February, renewed our march, leaving a midshipman and 12 men behind sick, chiefly frost bitten. The three following nights slept in the woods, after going each day about 15 miles on the river Madawaska, where, finding the ice in many places broken through, I made the men take the banks of the river, but continued on the ice all the way myself. On the 18th, crossing the Lake Tamasquata: it was here we were apprehensive of being cut off by the enemy, being in the territory of the United States; however, we did not fall in with them. On the 19th, commenced our march across the Grande Portage, or neck of land between the above Lake and the river St. Lawrence; this was dreadfully fatiguing, continually marching up and down hill, and the show upwards of five feet deep. The other division being ahead, was very serviceable to us by their treading the snow down, which made a small path just sufficient for one man to walk on, but frequently, in slipping our feet off the path, we went up to our shoulders in show; got half way through this night, and again slept in the woods: the distance through is 38 miles. On the afternoon of the 20th reached the St. Lawrence, and found thirty carioles waiting to convey us to Riviere de Caps, a French village about three miles distant. The next day procured carioles for all the men to Kamaraska, another village 15 miles distant. On the 22d reached Riviere Oneille, a neat little village, distant from Kamaraska about 12 miles. I should mention, that from Kamaraska to Kingston is 478 miles, which we were obliged to march, as on our arrival at Quebec we had not sufficient interest to procure more sleighs than sufficient to carry our provisions, baggage, and sick. On the 24th reached St. Rocques, another village, distant 13 miles; the 25th, La Forte, 15 miles; the 26th, St. Thomas, 18 miles; the 27th, Berthier, 10 miles; and on the 28th, Point Levy, opposite Quebec, a distance of 20 miles. On the following morning launched the canoes through the broken ice, and crossed over to the city. You would have been much diverted to see the Canadians in the canoes, watching a favourable opportunity to get through the ice, and perhaps each taking a different route; some got entangled, and were not able to extricate themselves for hours; at the same time drifting up and down as the current set them. In attempting to launch one over the ice, I fell through it up to my neck, and was two hours before I could get my clothes shifted. Marched the people on board the *Aeolus* and *Indian*, lying in Wolf's Cove, and then gave them leave to go on shore. The following morning the first division again proceeded on the march, and the next morning myself, with the second, followed. I forgot mentioning to you an unfortunate accident which happened to me on the second day of our march from Presque Isle: by a severe fall on the ice, I broke the bone of the fore finger of my right hand, between the knuckle and the wrist, so that for five weeks I had my hand in splints, and suspended in a sling, which I found not a little inconvenience from, and not until my arrival here did the bone unite, and then so awkwardly as to leave a very considerable lump on my hand; I have lost the use of my knuckle, but can use the finger, as you may see by my writing.

The first day of our march from Quebec, stopped for the night at St. Augustine, 15 miles distant from that city. On the 3d, at Cape Sante, 15 miles. On the 4th, at Grondines, 18 miles. On the 5th, at Baptisca, 16 miles. On the 6th, arrived at Trois Rivieres, 21 miles; this is considered the third river in Canada. - I did not halt here, but marched three miles beyond it, to avoid the trouble of collecting the people, as I knew they were too tired to walk back that distance. On the 7th, stopped at Machiche, 15 miles. On the 8th, at Masquinonge, 16 miles. On the 9th, at Berthier, 17 miles. On the 10th, at La Valtre, 15 miles. On the 11th, at Pegerrigue, 15 miles; and the next morning marched through Montreal to La Chiene, 12 miles beyond it. On passing the monument erected to the memory of the immortal Lord Nelson, halted, and gave three cheers, which much pleased the inhabitants.

From Montreal to this place we were eleven days performing a journey of 190 miles; the places where we stopped I have not noted, as we seldom found a village, but mostly scattered houses, inhabited by all nations; *viz.* English, Scotch, Dutch, American, and a few French. We passed several tremendous Rapids; the Long Son [ie Sault] in particular, which was most awfully grand to look at. We likewise passed Chrystian's [Chrystler's] Farm, where Colonel Morrison defeated General Wilkin's army, with a mere handful of men. On the 22d of March we reached this place: the officers and seamen of the squadron were drawn out to receive us with three cheers; we were lodged in a block-house, and allowed four days to recruit. I was then appointed to the gun-boat service (as was Lieutenant Russel), under Captain Owen. In a few days I joined the *Princess Charlotte*, of 42 guns, commanded by Captain William Howe Mulcaster, as first lieutenant. The *Regent* and her were on the stocks, planked up, and their decks laying. The *Regent* is about eight feet longer than our 38-gun frigates, having fifteen ports on each side of her main-deck, and guns on her gangways, so that she carries twenty-eight long 24-pounders on her main-deck; eight 68-pound carronades, two long 18, and eighteen 32-pound carronades on her upper deck, with a complement of 550 men. The *Princess Charlotte* is about the length of a 32-gun frigate, but eighteen inches more beam, pierced for thirteen ports on each side of her main-deck, and carrying twenty-four long 24-pounders on that deck, with two 68-pound carronades, and sixteen 32-pound carronades on her upper deck, and a complement of 330 men. The other ships are the *Wolfe* (now the *Montreal*), a ship corvette, of 20 guns, chiefly 32-pounder carronades, and 120 men. Two brigs, the *Star* and *Charwell*, the former of 14, the latter of 16 guns; the largest 100, the other 90 men. Two schooners, the *Magnet* and *Netley*, of 10 guns each, and 75 men. Ten or twelve gun-boats (none of them covered over), one carrying a long 18-pounder and a 32-pound carronade; the others a 32-pound carronade each. The establishment is for three lieutenants to be on the gunboat service, each to have a division of four boats, commanded by midshipmen.

From the time of my joining the *Princess Charlotte* I never quitted the ship or barracks. The interval between her launching, till we went to sea, was but eleven days, three of which were occupied in heaving down the ship, to get the cleats off her bottom. The result of our attack upon the enemy's Fort Oswego you already know.

1814 – Naval News

THIS SECTION ON THE EARLY MONTHS of 1814 starts with an account of the state of French naval forces in the Scheldt. In a March reconnaissance British naval forces became heavily engaged with the shore batteries. However, the danger of the French squadron being employed was minimal. The important news included the decision of the Danish government to break with the French empire, Wellington's invasion of France, and the entry of the British army into Bordeaux. The end of the war in Europe became an imminent reality.

This made an increased effort in North American waters possible. Admiral Sir Alexander Cochrane was sent out in command of the North American station, with instructions which took him on the offensive. The American coast was closely blockaded, with the exception of that of New England which was spared because of the New Englanders' known aversion to the war. Offensive operations were carried out in the Chesapeake, eventually leading to the raid on Washington, and an unsuccessful attempt against Baltimore. Seamen and shipwrights continued to be hurried out to Canada where they were to secure the control of Lake Ontario, which had been held in 1813 by a very narrow margin. At Kingston, a first rate ship, HMS *St Lawrence*, was set up on the ways. She was never completed, but nonetheless was to be the dominant force in the area.

The State of French Naval Forces in the Scheldt
From 'Nautical Anecdotes.' XXXI 28

3 ships of 80 guns disarming, having still two or three hundred men on board.
4 in ordinary.
6 ships of 74 guns, entirely fitted out with guns in, but having only two or three hundred men on board.
2 of 74, fitted out without guns, with only three hundred men on board.
5 of 74 in ordinary.
2 frigates in ordinary.
10 or 12 gun-brigs fitted out and manned.

```
             20  ships of the line.
              2  frigates
             12  gun-brigs
Total        34  vessels
```

Off Flushing, in the Basin:
1 80 gun-ship, without guns, having only 80 men on board.
3 frigates, idem, only 20 men; several gun-brigs and gun-boats.

In the Road at Flushing:
4 frigates of 44 guns ready for sea.

Hague, December 4th, 1813

From the 'Naval History of the Present Year,' 1813-1814 December-January. *XXXI 63-66*

Renewed French Port Closures

In order to restrain that *shopkeeping* turn for commerce, which the English are apt to indulge in too freely, Buonaparte had very obligingly ordered all the ports under his dominion to be shut, and extended his civility even to many foreign ones. Our Prince Regent has now, in return for his politeness, given orders that the *French ports* shall be opened for English trade, merely for the sake of accommodating the inhabitants of France; an instance of urbanity that could scarcely have been expected from "*a nation of shopkeepers!*"

[A late Gazette contained an Order of Council, releasing from the restriction of blockade 'all such ports and places in France as now are, or may be, placed in the military occupation, or under the protection, of his Majesty, in consequence of the success of his Majesty's arms, or by the voluntary submission of the inhabitants; and opening the same to the free trade of this country, and the subjects of friendly and neutral powers.']

Petty Officer's Juries Revived

An old naval practice has been lately revived, by order of the Lords Commissioners of the Admiralty; *viz*, the forming the warrant and petty officers of the navy into juries, to sit on the bodies of such persons as unfortunately meet with accidental death. The first of these juries sat, at the beginning of the month, on board the *Gladiator* at Portsmouth, on the body of a seaman, who fell from the main-yard of the *Illustrious* at Spithead.

Broke Honoured

We have been informed, that Sir Philip Broke is to be honoured with a gold medal, to be worn with his full uniform, for the capture of the *Chesapeake* frigate.

Cochrane for North American Station

Admiral Sir Alexander Cochrane is going out to America, with a considerable force, to relieve Sir J.B. Warren, on that station; and the newspapers have stated, that his nephew, Lord Cochrane, was appointed to act under him, with a squadron of five frigates and three sloops of war, and a large flotilla of flat-bottomed boats. But, says *the Morning*

Chronicle, "there is no foundation for the report of Lord Cochrane's being to have the command of a squadron of frigates. That would look like energy in the Admiralty Board."

Denmark, the Last of Napoleon's Allies, Joins his Enemies

We have not an enemy now left in Europe, except one, with whom it is our proud and glorious distinction to be at war. DENMARK has at last joined the COMMON CAUSE! Definitive treaties of peace and alliance have been concluded by Denmark with our government, and that of Sweden; signed by Mr. Thornton on our part, and by Baron Weterstedt for Sweden. The following is an official summary of the conditions:

> All conquests are to be restored, except Heligoland.
> Prisoners of war on both sides to be released.
> Denmark to join the Allies with 10,000 men, if England will give a subsidy of £400,000 in the year 1814.
> Pomerania to be ceded by Sweden to Denmark in lieu of Norway.
> Stralsund still to continue a dépôt for English produce.
> Denmark to do all in her power to abolish the slave trade.
> England to mediate between Denmark and the other allies.

Peace is most evidently at hand! The black clouds with which our political horizon has been so long surcharged, have separated, and all the symptoms of a serene and undisturbed futurity are visible.

[The Treaty of Peace, dated 14 January 1814, was published in Vol. XXXI, pp462-646.]

New Port of Refuge on Minorca

The harbour of Fournelles, on the north side of Minorca, immediately opposite to Toulon, has been surveyed by the master of the *Hibernia*, with a view to consider the eligibility of the Mediterranean fleet making that their port of refuge in future.

January–February. XXXI 165-168

Duckworth and Broke Honoured

H.R.H. the Prince Regent has been pleased to reward the meritorious services of Admiral Sir John Thomas Duckworth, K.B. and Captain P.B.V. Broke, R.N. with the dignity of Baronets of the United Kingdom. . . .

Convoy 'Runner' Imprisoned

Caution to Masters of Merchantmen. - Mr. Newlands, master of the *Coquette*, of Glasgow, sailed from St. Thomas's on the 12th February, 1813, under convoy of H.M.S. *Kangaroo*, and ran away from the fleet. The Lords Commissioners of the Admiralty instituted a prosecution against him for the offence; and he has been sentenced to a month's imprisonment in the Marshalsea, where he is now confined.

Shipwrights Sent to Canada

In consequence of an invitation from the Admiralty, 150 shipwrights (unmarried) from

Plymouth yard have volunteered to go to the Lakes in Canada, to construct vessels. They are, we are told, to have 10s a day; 15s for Sunday; 2s subsistence; 1s for lodging; and 1s for every extra hour; and those who conduct themselves properly will be entitled to an apprentice on their return.

From 'Naval Ancedotes.' XXXI 114. 191–194

Extraordinary Voyage;
Russian Establishment in North America to be Completed

The Russian ship *General Suwarroff*, now at Portsmouth, is about to proceed on what may appear a most extraordinary voyage, being none other than the completion of two military and commercial establishments on the West Coast of North America. The Russian government have, for nearly ten years past, had a fort, with a few pieces of ordnance, mounted on the island of Rodiak, in lat. 55°N. and long. 160°W. [Kodiak, at 57.3°N 153.3°W ?] being the nearest point of the American continent to their establishment at Kamtschatka. Within these four years they have begun to form another establishment, on the neck of land called California, and this ship takes out ordnance and ordnance stores of every description, to give to it an appearance of military strength. – The trade the Russians carry on thither, which is very great, is wholly in furs; for which article they find a lucrative market in China, from whence they bring to Europe the produce and manufactures of that country, and are enabled, from their competition with each other, to afford it to the European continent at a cheaper rate than this country. The *General Suwarroff* will also endeavour, in the height of next summer, to discover a passage through Bhering's Straits, and, in a north westerly direction, to Archangel. A gentleman who is on board her, declares, that on a former voyage of discovery, he was more than half way through the Northern Seas of Cape North to Archangel, when the ship was stopped by the ice: this adventure left only about 400 miles unexplored, to complete the circuit of the world.

Neptune, Cupid and Hymen

Dundee, February 25
Two faithful lovers were united in the hymeneal bands on Monday, after a courtship and separation of more than ordinary length. The happy husband had just returned, with honourable scars and spoils, from the sea, where, in his country's service, he had spent the last five-and-twenty years of his life, without having once seen or written to, or received a letter from, his love. The disconsolate lady, now the blithesome bride, in the mean time supported herself with the wages of honest industry. About the middle of last week, she was astonished and delighted at the re-appearance of her long-lost sailor, whose first care, on returning to this his native place, was to discover the mistress of his youthful affections. We need not say with what raptures she listened to the renewal of his suit. – The bans of marriage were proclaimed on Sunday, the nuptials were celebrated on the day following, and the parties are now solacing themselves with a matrimonial pleasure jaunt. Their ages are alike; and, united, amount to 106.

Forcing the West Scheldt

Shortly after the *Forth* and *Nymphen* frigates had penetrated into the West Scheldt, and passed the batteries of Flushing and Cadsand without loss, certain movements of the enemy, both at Antwerp and Flushing, rendered it necessary to send a reinforcement into that branch of the river, to support our frigates, in the event of an unequal contest. - About the 11th of February, the *Antelope*, of 50 guns, the *Sweabourg* Russian frigate, and *Resolution* cutter to lead, were despatched from the Roompot, to lie at the entrance of the Wieland channel, and be ready to make a dash into the West Scheldt, as soon as circumstances proved favourable. It so happened, however, that a series of easterly winds set in, and completely precluded any attempt till the 1st of March. About mid-day (March 1) the wind veered from S. to S.S.W. and cleared; and the ships prepared to weigh anchor. The enemy seemed aware of our intention, and tried the range of their shot between Flushing and Cadsand. On the latter island a strong battery (Buonaparte) has been erected since our last expedition, mounting the heaviest ordnance; in fact, it is now ascertained that nearly 200 pieces of cannon, including mortars, can play upon the passage into the West Scheldt, which is precisely three miles from shore to shore. At 40 minutes past three the ships weighed, and in 18 minutes the Wulpia battery opened a heavy fire upon us. At 4:10 we were abreast of the point of Breskins, when forts Buonaparte and Imperial opened on one side and at the same instant the batteries of Flushing and the other. The *Antelope* and *Sweabourg* now commenced a well-directed cannonade on the Cadsand batteries, along which they ran pretty close, in consequence of the wind being so scant, that they were obliged to haul their bowlines on the starboard tack. This running fight continued about half an hour, without any material injury to our ships. The *Antelope*, however, received many shot; and one, from the Imperial battery on Cadsand, which penetrated through the hammocks on the starboard side of the poop, and went out through the bulwark on the other side, was very destructive; it carried off both legs of a Dutch pilot, who was standing on the poop, and waiting to take charge of the ship, as soon as she should get past the Hoog-plat; two other men (a sailor and a marine) each lost a leg by the same ball, which also wounded several others, but not severely. The frigate lost no men, nor had any wounded; and the *Resolution* cutter had only her gaff top-sail shot away by a shell from off Flushing, which occasioned her to fall astern of the ships, instead of leading ahead, and directing their course by her soundings.

A little before five o'clock, it being thick and hazy, the *Antelope* unfortunately grounded on the hook of the Hoog-plat, and nearly at the same time the frigate also took the ground astern of the *Antelope*. In ten minutes the wind shifted, all at once, round to W.N.W. and blew fresh, with a strong flood-tide right upon the shoal. The stream anchor was got out, but the wind and tide counteracted all attempts to heave off the ship. At high tide the ship was shored up, and yards and top-masts struck. Next day, March 2, the *Cretan* and *Banterer* came to our assistance; and at high water all sail was made in order to force her over the shoal, but without success. The *Sweabourg*, however, got off, and anchored in deep water. All this day, while the crew were using every exertion to lighten the ship, the shells from a battery to the westward of Rammekins were falling in every direction round the ship, the officers and men exhibiting the most undaunted courage and firmness in this trying scene, and never for an instant interrupting their labours. Meanwhile the *Nymphen* frigate, Captain Hancock, anchored close ahead of the *Antelope*, and within range of shot from Walcheren: and the end of her bower cable was got on board the *Antelope*, for the purpose of heaving her off, if possible, next high water. The enemy now redoubled his fire, and shot and shells were incessantly poured at the *Nymphen* and *Antelope*; but, strange to say, without producing any material effect. One shell burst in the centre of a cluster of boats, without injuring a single person! The undaunted boats' crews only returned three huzzas, and coolly went on with their work.

All efforts were this day also ineffectual, even in the night the enemy kept up their fire from the mortar batteries. On the 3d of March, at ten in the forenoon, the ship was fortunately hove off, amid showers of shot and shells, without much injury, and to the utter mortification of the enemy, who considered her as lost. Too much praise cannot be bestowed on Captain Butcher, his officers and men, for their steady courage and unwearied exertions; while Commodore Owen and Mr. Douglas (master of the fleet, who went in the *Antelope*) most ably and judiciously united their efforts in the common cause. Captain Hancock displayed his usual zeal and ability in placing the *Nymphen* in an admirable though dangerous situation, for heaving the *Antelope* off the shoal. Admiral Scott, from South Beveland, arrived on board at the instant of her starting from her position. Thus this boasted and narrow channel, bristled on each side with cannon of the widest calibre, was forced in the open day; and when misfortune threw our ships into a situation (the most galling of all others) where they could not return their adversary's fire, it only proved the touchstone of Anglo-Russian bravery, and taught our enemies what they may expect when, in future wars, new Nelsons shall rise to perpetuate the invincibility of the British navy.

From the 'Naval History of the Present Year,' 1814
February-March. XXXI 242-245

Bordeaux Falls to Wellington

We have much satisfaction in announcing to our readers, that since our last retrospective address, the army under the command of Field Marshal the Marquis of Wellington has got possession of the important port and city of Bordeaux; and we hope, before another month elapses, to be enabled to place on record the further successes of our gallant countrymen in the capture of other ports belonging to the French.

On the entry of our army into Bordeaux, the French inhabitants displayed the white flag and cockade, and declared in favour of the Bourbons, issuing at the same time a well-written and spirited address (signed by the Mayor), inviting their countrymen to follow their example.

What effect this address and example of the Bordelaise may have, a few weeks, nay days, may probably decide; - should success attend their endeavours, a *general peace* must be the result; but, on the contrary, should Buonaparte's army prove victorious, and re-possess themselves of Bourdeaux, we tremble for the fate of its inhabitants. . . .

Reinforcements Nearly Ready to Sail to Quebec

The means which have been some time in preparation, for a more vigorous and powerful prosecution of the war in America, are nearly completed, and on the point of proceeding to Quebec. The *Spencer*, 74, Captain Raggett, has the convoy in charge. Four post-captains, eight lieutenants, and 14 midshipmen, are going out to command, under Sir James Yeo. The frigates going out in frame are to be called the *Psyche* and *Prompte*; the brigs, *Calibre* and *Goshawk*. The *Vittoria*, and another frigate, are ready for launching on the Lakes. Sir G. Collier has also sailed for the American station, in the *Leander*, a new ship, of the same tonnage and force, in every respect as the large American frigates. . . .

View of the Port of Bordeaux. The harbour of Bordeaux is capacious, and well secured. From its form it is called *La Port de la Lune*, being like a crescent. The tide flows into it to a great height, by which means ships of the largest tonnage are brought up to the quay. The city is of a triangular form, and is well built. The newest as well as the finest part of the town is the square facing the harbour, which is adorned by two very noble buildings: the merchants' warehouse and the Exchange. . . . The town and harbour are defended by three forts, which were constructed by the famous Vauban. The citadel, called *Chateau Trompette*, partly serves to cover the harbour, and partly to keep the town in awe. It is magnificently built of entire pieces of square free stone; and, as the ramparts are not made of earth, but arched over, one may walk quite round them. The arsenal contains upwards of 6,ooo stand of arms. The other two forts *Le Chateau de Kau* and *St. Cruix*, are not considerable. Plate 85

Light for the Wolf Rock

On the 14th February, H.M.S. *Orestes*, Captain Smith, sailed from Plymouth Sound, with Mr. Stevenson, the engineer, employed in the erection of a light-house on the Bellrock, off the coast of Scotland. Mr. Stevenson is to make a survey of the Wolf Rock, which is a dangerous sunken reef, situated between the Land's End, and the Scilly Islands, and has long formed a great bar to the navigation of the British channel; on which, it is hoped, that it may be found practicable to erect some permanent land-mark, for the safety and protection of the innumerable ships which navigate the Strait. . . .

French Move Prisoners of War

The progress of the Allies in France has caused a very general removal of the prisoners of war; but, we believe, no statement has yet been published, of the precise situation to which they have been transferred.

The following is a list of British prisoners in France:

At Arras	1,800
Longwy, removed to Amiens	1,400
Besançon, removing to ditto	1,600
Bitche, removing to Sedan	200
Briançon, removing to Maubeuge	1,900
Givet, removing to Poitiers	2,600
Montly, removing to Autun	1,050
Sarrelouis and Sarreliou, removing to Bauchain and Baupsaume	2,380
Sisteron, removing to Guise; depot of punishment for sailors and soldiers	300
Cambray	1,670
Valenciennes	1,600
Verdun	230
	16,890

Anti-Slaving Success

The *Favourite*, of 20 guns, Captain John Maxwell, arrived at Portsmouth, from the coast of Africa, has been absent nine months; in the course of which time, she visited all the British settlements on that coast, burnt and destroyed several slave factories on the Rio Pongus, and captured four Portuguese ships, which were found employed in that cruel traffic.

1814 – The Invasion of France and the Re-establishment of Royal Government

WELLINGTON'S MARCH INTO FRANCE was facilitated by the boats of a Royal Navy squadron which, after shooting the dangerous bar of the Adour river, carried the soldiers from the lower Pyrenees to Bayonne, and thence into the lowlands of western France and the approach to Bordeaux. The navy was also employed in carrying to France the royal government of Louis XVIII who was proclaimed in Calais on 10 April, and on 4 June the Prince Regent and visiting sovereigns attended a fleet review at Spithead. Somehow, *The Naval Chronicle* failed to give formal notice of the banishment of Buonaparte to the small island of Elba off the Tuscan coast, but it did include an account of its absorption into the French state in 1801 (Vol. XXXI, p285), and it published a verse contrasting Buonaparte's new kingdom with the empire his unfettered ambition had lost for him.

Naturally the problems of demobilisation interested the readers of *The Naval Chronicle*, which urged the Government to make adequate provision for the officers and men soon to be out of work. The return of prisoners of war was of course a matter of interest, and *The Naval Chronicle* also printed a letter from a correspondent giving an account of life in Verdun, which had improved greatly after the retirement of General Wirion, and his successor Courcelles in 1811.

While the events in France were highly satisfactory, *The Naval Chronicle* was concerned for the future. The attempt by the Norwegians to secure their independence from Sweden was earnestly followed, and the Government was urged to support it, and also to ensure that the Netherlands was re-established as a genuinely independent state. At the same time, *The Naval Chronicle* began to urge in the strongest terms the importance of reaching a settlement with the United States.

Crossing the Adour

Letters on Service
Admiralty Office, March 22 1814. XXXI 347-348

Admiral Lord Keith has transmitted to John Wilson Croker, Esq. a letter from Rear-admiral Penrose, dated on board H.M.S. *Porcupine*, off the Bar of the Adour, the 25th of February, stating, that the boats and small vessels destined to assist the operations of the army under the Marquess of Wellington, succeeded in crossing the Bar of the above river on the preceding day.

A breeze, which sprung up in the night of the 23d, was the first that had offered itself since the necessary preparations had been in forwardness, to enable the vessels to reach the mouth of the Adour; and early on the following morning the Rear-admiral was off the bar with the vessels and boats collected for the service.

The boats of the vessels of war, with two flat boats, were sent directly to the bar to endeavour to find a passage through the surf, the British troops being at that time seen from the ships crossing over to the north side of the river, but greatly in want of the boats intended for their assistance.

Captain O'Reilly, in a Spanish-built boat, selected as the most safe for the service, and having with him the principal pilot, was overset in his attempt to enter, but escaped on shore. Lieutenant Debenham, in a six-oared cutter, succeeded in reaching the beach; the other boats returned to wait the result of the next tide, it being scarcely possible that one in fifty could then have crossed.

A pilot was sent to land to the south-west of the river, and walk from thence to the Adour, in order to make a concerted signal from within the Bar, to guide the vessels through the safest parts. Without the bar there appeared no interval; a long and heavy line of surf alone presenting itself. Rewards were offered to the leading vessel, the second, third, &c.

Lieutenant Collins, flag-lieutenant to Rear-admiral Penrose, was despatched also to endeavour to land, and walk to the army; and the Rear-admiral was informed, about that time, by Sir John Hope, of the progress made by the troops, and the great utility of which the boats would prove, if they could join.

The tide being at length at a proper height, and all the vessels well up for the attempt, several drew near the bar, but hauled off again, till at last Lieutenant Cheyne (of the *Woodlark* sloop), in a Spanish boat with five British seamen, crossed the surf and ran up the river. The next was a prize boat, manned from a transport, closely followed by a gun-boat, commanded by Lieutenant Chesshyre, who was the first that has hoisted the British colours in the Adour.

The rest of the boats and vessels followed in rapid succession, and with extraordinary success: the zeal and science of the officers triumphing over all the difficulties of the navigation.

The Rear-admiral was not yet enabled to transmit a return of the casualties: it was hoped from the nearness of the shore that they would fall mostly on the vessels.

Admiral Lord Keith has transmitted to John Wilson Croker, Esq. the following return of the casualties in the passage of the Bar of the Adour, an account of which was inserted in the Gazette of the 15th instant.

A Return of Casualties in the Passage of the Bar of Bayonne, on the 24th Day of February, 1814

His Majesty's brig *Martial*. - Captain Elliott, drowned; Surgeon (Mr. Norman), killed; four seamen, drowned.

His Majesty's brig *Lyra*. - Mr. Henry Bloye, master's mate, leading the passage of the Bar, drowned; five seamen drowned.

His Majesty's ship *Porcupine*. - Two seamen drowned.

Three transport boats lost, number of men unknown.

Gun-boat, No. 20. - One seaman and one artilleryman badly wounded.

One Spanish chasse marée, the whole of whose crew perished in an instant.

D. O'REILLY, Commander of the Naval Detachment on the Adour.

From 'Naval Anecdotes.' XXXI 283-287

Events at Calais –
The Proclamation of Louis XVIII

On Easter-day, the 10th of April, 1814, His Majesty Louis the XVIIIth was Proclaimed with general joy.

At twelve in the morning, the English navy brig *Cadmus*, Captain Evans, cruising before the harbour, and perceiving the white flag on the tower, gallantly sent an officer in a boat with a letter to the Mayor, expressing the wish to come, if possible, on shore, and share the general joy. The officer, Mr. Stevenson, came at the moment the Mayor and principal authorities were marching out to make the proclamation. He was received with the greatest joy, and placed close to the Mayor, and went with him about the town during the whole ceremony.

In the mean time, Chevalier Tomsonville, of the navy, was despatched in the English boat to bring on shore the captain of the *Cadmus*, Mr. Evans, and such of his officers as could conveniently come on shore with him. They were received by the principal authorities on the quay, and complimented by Mr. Pigault Maubaillareg, banker to the English ambassadors, as were his father and grandfather, and who, when all placemen were obliged to vote for Buonaparte as French Emperor, by placing on a public register yes or no, was the only one in Calais who boldly dared write *no*, and experienced ever since the severity of Buonaparte's police, and was often in danger of being taken up. They marched into town with a band playing alternatively *God save the King*, and the French national tune of the favourite royal song *Vive Henre Quatre*, amidst shouts and huzzas for the Prince Regent and for Louis XVIII. They were thus conducted, amidst an innumerable crowd of the whole population, to the Hotel d'Angleterre, where an elegant dinner was prepared. . . .

[On 14 May officers of the British squadron at anchor in Basque Roads were invited to attend celebrations in Rochefort. (Vol. XXXI, p445)]

Nautical Illuminations

The *Thisbe*. This frigate, lying off Greenwich, Rear-admiral Legg's flag-ship, was most splendidly illuminated on Monday night (11th April). Within a few minutes of the time appointed, some very powerful rockets were let off from the main deck, and afterwards from the main-top-mast head; on the explosion of which, at their utmost height, the air was illuminated by a mass of brilliant lights. After near a dozen had ascended in grand style, the *Thisbe*, from yard-arm to yard-arm, and from the deck to the main-top-mast head, became instantaneously a most beautiful illumination of what are called blue lights, whose chastened lustre produced an effect the most pleasing and beautiful. This was done twice, and with the same celerity as with gas lights. The sight was very novel, and highly gratifying to a great number of spectators.

Jenner Secures Millman's Release

Captain Millman, son of Sir Francis Millman, Bart. just arrived from Verdun, where he was some time a prisoner of war, owed his liberation to the influence of Doctor Jenner, now in Paris, who was in such high esteem with Buonaparte on account of the success of his vaccination in that capital, that he was informed the French Emperor would readily grant him any favour he might request. The Doctor, in consequence, solicited the exchange of Captain Millman, which was immediately granted.

From 'Correspondence.' XXXI 308-310

Prisoners of War

"Zeno" to the Editor
Peele's Coffee-House, 5th of April, 1814
Mr. Editor, Having very recently returned from Verdun where I had been resident on parole upwards of seven years, it struck me that it might not be uninteresting to your general readers, and that it would be interesting to naval ones, were I to attempt a character of the different commandants who have governed at that grand dépôt since the commencement of the present eventful war, now apparently about to close in a manner so decisively glorious, as two years since it was improbable.

Of the multifarious instances of knavery and extortion, fraud, insolence, and despotism, practised by the ever execrable Wirion and his vulgar spouse, I have the less occasion to treat because the Chevalier Lawrence, in his picture of Verdun, has given a correct and animated description of those *distinguished* characters and most disgraceful scenes. During the reign of that contemptible tyrant there was nothing odious in power abused by vulgar hands, - nothing base and disgusting in meanness or rapacity, but what was exercised with impunity against the feelings, property, and persons of the *detenus* and prisoners of war. If our reformers wanted a finished picture of insolence, fraud, and despotism, combined, Verdun, under the sway of General Wirion, was, of all others, the place best calculated to gratify his wish. - Having accumulated a large fortune by the open exercise of every dishonourable artifice, he was displaced and succeeded by *Courcelles*, a creature who trod in the vile footsteps of his predecessor. This officer, as well as I can recollect, succeeded Wirion, about 1808, and kept in power till 1811. During the reign of those two miscreants, it was in vain, or it was dangerous, in any individual to attempt to convey a statement of his wrongs, however grievous, to the ear of the ministers. It was intercepted by the agents of the petty despots of Verdun, or passed over without attention; and not few were the instances wherein the complaints were made to feel the dark and cowardly revenge of which their base and contaminated minds were so eminently susceptible.

The Baron de Beauchesne succeeded the infamous Courcelles; of the latter it is difficult to speak too highly. It was an angel presiding where a fiend had ruled before. Full of generosity, honour, and dignity, this worthy nobleman, in every respect, was the reverse of his base predecessors. When he died, which was early in 1813, his death was deeply and generally deplored by the *detenus* and officers, who raised six thousand francs to rear a monument to his memory in token of their love and gratitude.

It was an arduous duty for an officer to succeed this worthy man, without suffering greatly by comparison. It was however, the happy lot of our countrymen at Verdun to have Major de Meulan appointed to succeed Baron de Beauchesne. I cannot recollect the place of the Major's nativity, but his father was an *Intendant de Provins*. His family was wrecked and his fortune destroyed, by the early storms of the revolution; and at the age of 14 he emigrated to Cayenne. There he remained till the tempest was a little wasted, when he returned to his native country. Here he found himself rich only in honour, for of his patrimony nothing could be gleaned. Being liable to the conscription he was soon called into the field; and not having wealth to hire a substitute, he was forced to serve in person. He had thus his military career to begin *de novo*. He served as a private in the ranks, but his courage, activity, and soldier-like conduct, soon recommended him to notice, and before he was twenty-eight, he had by dint of merit alone, attained the rank of *Major*, which assimilates with that of Lieutenant-colonel in the British service. He distinguished himself in Italy, Germany, and Spain; he received many medals and other flattering marks of distinction. In different actions he received seven musket balls in his body, of which some of the wounds are yet open, besides sabre cuts, and contusions. Such is Major de Meulan, and I dare with confidence anticipate the general voice of my countrymen, when they shall read this unsought tribute of respect, will unanimously admit its justice. Accessible to the meanest individual: dignified, yet unassuming, he was distinguished more by the urbanity of his manners and integrity of his mind, than by the glare of official pomp.

When our officers broke their parole, which from the fear of a gaol was sometime the case, and were retaken, this generous man never failed to mitigate if not totally remit their punishment, and not infrequently procured their re-admission to the comforts of parole, by becoming personally responsible for their future conduct. He kept within proper bounds the Gens d'armes, whose insolence and rapacity had been so severely felt under the infamous patronage of Wirion and Courcelles. Endowed by nature with a heart filled with the noblest qualities, no unfortunate person ever appealed to him in vain. The few whom he honoured with his friendship know what an inexhaustible fund of sensibility was covered by the stern front of a warrior. Towards many a friendless officer has he acted the part of an affectionate brother, - towards many an unguarded youth, exposed in a peculiar manner at Verdun, to the most dangerous seductions, has the brave and good De Meulan displayed the tenderness and solicitude of a parent, and snatched them from impending ruin and indelible disgrace.

Distinguished no less by valour, science, and military enterprize, than by the most active benevolence, he was a formidable enemy to whomsoever he was opposed. But his was the warfare of a Sidney or Bayard! The Spaniards too often felt his prowess in the field, but happy, in comparison with others, was the captive who fell into his merciful hands. By his bravery he rendered himself respected, - and dreaded by his activity and enterprise; - but it was dread unmixed with hatred. Ask the gallant Mina, or D'Eroles, what was the character of Major de Meulan, and they will tell it was that of a brave and generous foe. And farther, that whenever they captured any soldiers serving under his command, they treated them with peculiar respect in return for the honourable manner in which he conducted the warfare in which he was engaged.

Far from availing himself of the opportunities afforded by the situation he occupied, his very manner repelled the idea of *a present*, and as to *a bribe*, no one, in all probability, ever harboured the idea of insulting him by an allusion of that base kind. He was much more likely to divide his purse with some poor lieutenant or friendless midshipman; and most certainly, when the sudden route came to remove the dépôt from Verdun, he left that city richer only in honour; and happy it was for our countrymen he was continued in his command.

It is impossible *to know* such a man without loving him. How often, have we regretted the just war we wage should oblige us to call him *an enemy*! Let whatever be the part he may take in the terrible tragedy now drawing to its catastrophe in France, he will act honourably. May he survive the storms which now distract his unhappy country. May he live long and happy in the land of his forefathers; and should he ever visit this happy and envied island, I am sure there is not a *detenu* or an officer, naval or military, who would not vie with each other in demonstrations of the warmest regard and sincerest attachment.

[See account of conditions at Verdun, Volume III, pp311-17.]

From the 'Naval History of the Present Year,' 1814 March–April. *XXXI 345-347*

Europe Transformed - Editorial

We feel it a duty to curtail the naval history of the present month, to make room for a few observations on the astonishing change which has just taken place in the political state of Europe. The passing hour teems with moral and political prodigies. It is crowded with events of a size truly stupendous, and of a nature and tendency immeasurably important.

The first subject that now occupies the public mind is the conditions of that peace, which exists in spirit, as it will soon in all its formalities, between Great Britain and France. It should be considered by those who calculate upon dictating our own terms, that, although the Bourbon princes are restored in France, that the old monarchy is not; that the power of the king is more limited, and the spirit of the government less monarchial than our own; thence we think it probable that Louis will find it extremely difficult to infuse any considerable portion of that spirit of amity towards Great Britain into the great public functionaries of his government, which may be supposed to fill his own bosom. The arm that executes will be a Bourbon; the mind that plans, the will that ordains - decidedly revolutionary and Anti-Britannic. But, whatever may be the feelings or the politics of the new government of France, the fall of Buonaparté, and the establishment of a limited and constitutional monarchy, on the foundation of his former greatness, are events of a truly refreshing and exhilarating kind; for, had not Buonaparté's gigantic designs been frustrated, and his power annihilated, the world would have been but one vast prison, and no spot sufficiently remote or obscure to have shielded the exiled patriot from the iron hand of the oppressor.

How will the new government act respecting our maritime rights? Will they

Embarkation of Napoleon Buonaparte from St. Raphael for the Island of Elba.
Engraved by Baily, from a drawing by Lieutenant G.S. Smith, R.N.

The unremitted attention paid to Buonaparte in every movement of his career in
Europe, has produced such a connected series of particulars respecting him, and of
which the public are already so generally in possession, that it can only be necessary
to refer our readers to their recollection of the various and rapid gradations of his
fall, for this memorable epoch in his extraordinary fortunes.

The annexed engraving is from a sketch of the scene by moonlight of Buonaparte's
embarkation to quit France after the treaty of Fontainbleau, by Lieutenant George
Sidney Smith, of H.M.S. *Undaunted*, the officer commanding the boat in which
Napoleon embarked at St. Raphael in the Gulph of Frejus, at 9 in the night of the
28th April, 1814, to proceed in that ship to Elba.

The coach in which he came to the beach was within three sides of a square of
Austrian cavalry which escorted and guarded him thither. Three british marines
were on each side [of] the approach to the boat; previous to stopping, he with an
affability of manner desired the officer of the boat to be presented to him, which was
accordingly done by Captain Usher; but on hearing the name he repeated it, and
remained silent the whole way off to the ship. ^{Plate 462}

endeavour to include America in the negotiation? Will they abandon the principles
invariably contended for by France, as defined in the treaty of Utrecht? May we hope
to see established a commercial treaty, grounded on the broad basis of reciprocal interests?
Are ministers prepared to abandon the absurd policy of prohibiting the light, cheap,
and wholesome wines of Bourdeaux [sic], which for centuries were in common use in
England, to promote the consumption of the harsh liquid yielded by the Portugal grape?
Would our ministers procure admission for British cottons, hardware, or cutlery, into
France, they must permit French wines, brandies, cambrics, and cloths, to circulate in
England; we might then drink good Medoc wine at a shilling the bottle, and the revenue

be increased, instead of paying a crown for a bottle of home-manufactured port. Reciprocity forms a wisest basis for commercial treaties, without which peace itself is but a barren gift, and affords the surest prospect of duration.

A Truly Free Netherlands Needed

The next great feature of the altered relation in which we stand in regard to the governments of Europe, is, the restoration of the ancient and illustrious house of Orange and the independence of Holland. For the alliance to be valuable it is essentially necessary that we abandon all narrow and selfish calculations about *British objects*, and restore with a liberal hand, to the government of Holland, the colonies they have lost. If the establishment of the house of Orange is expected to be durable, we must put the Dutch in full possession of all their former sources of strength and prosperity. In our future numbers we shall, probably, devote a moderate space to the naval history, biography, and commerce of Holland.

What Fate for Norway?

Amidst the smiling prospect which gilds the political horizon of Europe, there is one dark and lowering cloud, and one alone, from the contemplation of which we turn with the heaviest grief. It hangs portentously over devoted Norway! Are there no means to be found to rescue the honour of the allies from the indelible stain of brutally transferring a gallant race of freemen to the dominion of a stranger? From whose dominions was Finland torn; and under what circumstances? How god-like would it make Alexander appear, were he to restore that province to Sweden, and spare this impending effusion of blood, and the violation of moral and political justice.

Peace Needed With America

A more determined spirit of hostility seems to develop itself between this country and America. Wisdom and humanity require that the sword may be speedily sheathed, and peace restored. America cannot be conquered, but she may be half destroyed; whereby we should ultimately suffer. The subject in debate between the two countries turns chiefly upon disputed points of public law. Those might be best arranged by a general congress; where the law of nations should be revised, defined, and condensed into one general code, sanctioned by every state, and held binding on them all.

Demobilisation - Editorial

In the reduction of our navy, thousands of veteran seamen will be discharged, with, perhaps, very slender resources, and no prospect of immediate employ. To those men (under which head we comprise our petty officers) are we principally indebted for our naval triumphs; and many, grown old in the service of their country, will find but little encouragement in the merchant service. After the treaty of Amiens, thousands of those valuable men, abandoned by an ungrateful country, were driven by want to seek their bread in America; and, it is to be feared, they pointed the guns that caused the flag of the United States to float above that of Britain. If the Lords of the Admiralty were to order that *the seaman's duty* on board *all* the ships in ordinary should be performed by *able seamen*, it would afford an excellent asylum for a very great proportion of those gallant fellows, who may otherwise be left to perish of want and misery. On former occasions the *ordinary service* has been filled by *landsmen* and *watermen*, who disappeared when war took place. We respectfully recommend this important subject to the *immediate* attention of the Board of Admiralty and the commissioners of the dock-yards.

A Commander of Old Standing
From 'Naval Anecdotes.' *XXXI 363*

There is now standing, within *five* of the top of the list of commanders, one who was made under the following circumstances. He was a lieutenant of thirty years' standing, and was first of the *Anson*, 64, in 1782, and was deservedly esteemed a good seaman and respectable officer. He had been *twenty years* a *first* lieutenant, when Admiral Rodney appointed his son as captain of that ship. The appointment of that young gentleman as a post captain, induced the Duke of Clarence to complain to the King his father, that "*Jack Rodney* and *Kit Parker*" were both post captains, and he only a midshipman: the King replied, "*your* friends can make you one at any time, theirs did it *when they could*." When the young post captain took the command, he did not like the grave, sedate, and parent-like carriage of the first lieutenant. He did not feel in his presence to be the captain of the *Anson*, and complained of this to his father, who promised a speedy remedy, which was effected, by purchasing a small vessel on the government account, and making the officer in question a commander. In this manner was his promotion procured. In a short time afterwards, the admiral superseded him, and Captain — returned to England, where he appears to have remained ever since, without employ or promotion. This officer had served thirty years as a lieutenant, before the caprice of a youthful post captain led to his elevation - and he has remained a second term of thirty years a commander; that is to say, he was a captain in the navy some years before many of our juvenile post captains were born. We could never hear of any reproach attaching to this officer; and had Admiral Rodney finished what he begun, and procured him to have been made post, this gentleman had now been vice-admiral of the red! but had not the son of Admiral Rodney wished to have had for his first lieutenant a young person, he would most likely now have been a lieutenant of sixty years' standing! - Such things are!

From 'Correspondence.' *XXXI 385-386*

Cruiser Warfare

"Albion" to the Editor, 8th April, 1814
Having on former occasions adverted in pretty strong terms on the conduct of the American war, so far as the navy was concerned, I cannot suffer the late brilliant successes of our cruisers, in capturing *ten* out of *thirteen* French frigates which were at sea, to pass without notice; it would be equally unjust to the officers who have, by their judicious and gallant conduct, brought them in triumph into British ports, after some of the hardest fought actions in our naval annals; and to the prompt and vigilant measures of the Board of Admiralty, which provided so well for cutting off their return to their own ports: in this instance, our success and good management have been most conspicuous, and cannot fail to raise the character of the officers concerned (and many of them before stood high) to the highest pitch of fame and estimation; and whilst the country beholds with admiration the recent brilliant achievements of the navy (for in some instances the enemy's capture was attended with circumstances which displayed talents, courage,

and seamanship of no common kind), I allude to the *Eurotas* and *Hebrus*, both newly fitted out, and manned but indifferently; and it will rely on the same good fortune attending their efforts against our American foes on the ocean, who have, it is true, escaped us hitherto most wonderfully; but I will not despair of seeing them ere long finding their way also into our ports, with the British Union proudly waving over them: the contest, however, will be severe; but we have now so many fine 44 and 50-gun frigates, or ships [of the line] cruising on the American coast, or fitting for that station, that I think they must be at least encountered and taken. From the last accounts we have from America, it would appear both sides were desirous to try their prowess again, as the *Shannon* and *Chesapeake* did; and although the *Endymion* was a much smaller ship than the *United States*, yet I firmly believe, seconded by the *Statira*, the American ships would have found them determined never to strike the British flag: the contest was, however, prevented, by the interference of the English admiral; and that gallant, enterprising, and judicious officer, Sir Thomas Hardy, the friend of Nelson, was again left to blockade them; and what vigilance, and the strongest desire of serving his king and country can effect, may certainly be expected from him. The great and powerful reinforcements now ready to sail for the Lakes, will, I trust, regain and preserve our ascendancy in that quarter; and the command of the admiral lately appointed will be commenced under the most favourable circumstances; hitherto the efforts of those excellent officers, Sir George Provost, and Sir James Yeo (who I had hoped to find would have been honoured with a vote of thanks), have been of necessity confined to the defensive from want of means; how properly they employed what was committed to them, is well known: and any thing from my pen cannot, I am sensible, add to the characters they have already attained for military naval enterprise. Hoping their efforts during the present campaign will be attended with glory to the British arms,

   I am, &c.

ALBION

[The Prince Regent's proclamation of a cessation of arms with France, dated 6 May 1814, and the Treaty of Peace dated 30 May, was published in Vol. XXXI, pp414-415; 464-474.]

From the 'Naval History of the Present Year,' 1814
April–May. XXXI 416-420

Genoa Captured

The principal naval exploit for the present month, is the share that the British fleet had in the reduction of Genoa, under the command of Sir Joshua [sic] Rowley; for the particulars of which we refer to the Extraordinary Gazette.

[In Vol. XXXIV, pp404-488 and 489-494 was published: 'An account of the expedition against the Italian coast, by the squadron commanded by Commodore Sir Josias Rowley, Bart. and a detachment of 1009 men of the 1st and 3d Regiments of Italian troops, commanded by Lieutenant colonel Cattinelli, attached to the Sicilian staff of Lieutenant general Lord William Bentinck, with a particular detail of the Attacks on the Town of Leghorn or Livorno; by a Naval Officer employed with the Troops.' In Vol. XXXV, pp54-56; 398-401 and 474-477 appears an account of the Genoese Campaign.]

Cessation of Hostilities, Demobilisation

On the 17th May, the Lords of the Admiralty issued a proclamation addressed to the fleet, highly commendatory to our gallant naval defenders, announcing the cessation of hostilities, and the mode in which the navy will be paid off.

Antwerp Occupied

Antwerp has been taken possession of by the British troops; and the Helder fleet has been given up by Admiral Verheul.

Louis XVIII

Amongst a crowd of strange occurrences, may be enumerated, the arrival of the French line of battle ship the *Polonais* at Spithead from Cherbourg; which it has been reported came to receive Louis the 18th and suite, and convey him over to take possession of his throne. The captain was received with every mark of cordial respect by those, who, but a few days before, were watching his movements at Cherbourg, and very ambitious of *escorting* the *Polonais* to Spithead, or of *sending her to the bottom.*

A most splendid naval spectacle, on a small scale, was exhibited in the recent embarkation of Louis the XVIIIth at Dover, on board of the *Royal Sovereign* yacht, and his passage to Calais, under convoy of the *Jason* frigate, on board of which was his Royal Highness the Duke of Clarence. In our next we expect we shall have to give a description of the embarkation of the Emperor of Russia, and the King of Prussia, and their arrival in this country. What rich subjects for historians, bards, and artists!

Norway

We are much concerned that the prospects of the brave and injured Norwegians are no less gloomy than when we last touched on that melancholy subject. In compliance with political engagements, our fleets are now employed in blockading the Norwegian coasts; and a powerful army is said to be advancing to force obedience, should famine and negotiation fail. We are convinced that our ministers would have escaped inflicting the horrors of famine on that inoffensive nation, had it been in their power: what the issue will be, we know not - but we think, should Bernadotte succeed, and bend by force a race of freemen to his sway, *the union will not be desirable.*

America - The Need for Peace is Apparent

Too much inflated by the torrent of success that has latterly rushed upon this country, the public mind at the present moment is filled with vindictive feelings against America. Were ministers inclined, the voice *of the multitude* would applaud a general invasion of America, with a view to its final reduction! But, happily, that mania is confined to the thoughtless and the vulgar. Ministers are too wise, and too cautious, to lose sight of the strange vicissitudes of war! They will not risk upon the American continent, *in a war of subjugation*, that army which saved Portugal and Spain, and planted our Standard on the Towers of Toulouse! They would not incur the responsibility of so hazardous an experiment! The intelligence from Europe that had been received in America when the last accounts came away, gave a very gloomy picture of the state of the Emperor Napoleon's prospects: the Americans knew of the defection of the Danes, and the actual invasion of France. A proposition had been received for an armistice in Canada, from General Sir George Prevost, which was readily listened to. The government had recommended the repeal of the embargo and the non-importation laws; and hopes were held out of a speedy armistice by sea and land: and the most confident reports were circulated of an immediate peace! Meanwhile, the whole of the coasts of America, from Black point to the N.E. boundary, were declared in a state of blockade, by Admiral Sir Alexander Cochrane, and will probably be followed by some important blow aimed at the vitals of the United States.

[Notification of the proclamation of blockade, dated 25 April 1814, was made to the states of Europe on 31 May, and published in Vol. XXXI, p475.]

Such was the aspect of affairs *then* - but what must be the state of the public mind now that the news of Napoleon's abdication has been received, and that our conquering army is about to embark at Bordeaux - for the invasion of their shores! - The *merchants* will press strongly for immediate peace: *in them*, we shall find our best auxiliaries. But we should be cautious not to push our pretension too far. The great mass of the American population are deeply imbued with an Anti-Britannic spirit. If we aim at the conquest of the United States, we may create an inextinguishable spirit of hatred and revenge. We may capture her cities, and lay waste her coasts; but in doing so, we shall waste and consume our armies, and too probably - wither the laurels gathered in Europe. Let us rather secure the respect of America, by our justice and moderation - and accept of her proffered amity, whenever we can do it on terms compatible with our honour and our safety.

Keith and Pellew Honoured

In the honours distributed to the chiefs of our triumphant army, the navy has not been forgotten. Lord Keith has been made a Viscount; and Sir Edward Pellew a Baron, by the title of Baron Exmouth.

Parliament may Reward Inventor

Of the parliamentary debates in which the navy was peculiarly interested, we must mention the proposal for a pension, we believe of £500 per annum, to Captain Manby, for his *invention* to save persons from shipwreck: some one mentioned the *cork jackets* introduced by Mr. Mallison; and proposed that he should also be remunerated, which was objected to, because, however valuable the jacket, it was only - an *improvement*! Such is the case with Captain Manby. We are advocates for the liberal reward of all useful *inventions* or *improvements*, having for their object the saving the lives of our seamen: and we know that Sergeant (afterwards Lieutenant) Bell, of the artillery, tried and succeeded in the same experiment upwards of 20 years since, in the presence of the Duke of Richmond. He has been dead some years - his widow soon followed him to the grave; he left a daughter, who is said to be in indigent circumstances. We mention this, not at all to diminish the merit due to Captain Manby. We are solely actuated by a spirit of equal justice.

[See Appendix 7 on Life Saving in Volume III.]

Naval Promotion

We have just been favoured with the following communication. It is certainly time that such a measure as that announced in it should take place:

"A naval promotion on an extensive scale, to adjust the claims of those officers, whose pretensions and periods of service appear most distinguished, is said to be about to take place, and also an arrangement of the Naval List, founded on the system, and calculated to embrace all the advantages of the army brevet, a measure which must give general satisfaction, and reflect infinite credit on the respectable quarter whence it has originated."

Naval Review

Not less than fifty sail of the line, it is said, are ordered to rendezvous at Spithead by the 4th of June, in order to form a naval spectacle worthy of the maritime power that so pre-eminently distinguishes the British Isles. It is to be composed of two distinct lines of battle, each accompanied with various vessels of inferior force, fire-ships, &c. in order that the scene may convey to the Royal foreigners who will be present, a more correct idea of a naval action, which will be represented with all its tactical manoeuvres as nearly as can possibly be effected. We shall of course take care that our readers shall be furnished with the best description of this grand spectacle, if it takes place.

[The May-June Naval History was devoted entirely to the visit of the Prince Regent and visiting sovereigns to Portsmouth, and the review of the fleet at Spithead. There was not, however, a mock battle (Vol. XXXI, pp491-494).]

POWs

We have not inserted the names of the military officers confined at Verdun, as announced, on account of the certainty of peace, and their immediate return home.

Death of Lord Bridport

By the death of Lord Bridport, Sir Chaloner Ogle, of Worthy, becomes the Senior Admiral of Great Britain, and Father of the Fleet.

Telegraphs to be Abandoned

The Telegraphs communicating between the Admiralty and Yarmouth are to be immediately broken up; as are the several signal stations on the coasts of this country and Ireland.

June-July. *XXXII 82-83*

American War News

The war between this country and America still rages; and we anticipate in our next we shall have to communicate events of greater interest than have yet occurred in that quarter of the globe. We have at present only to notice events of comparative insignificance and varied result. In the first, the American frigate *Essex* has been captured by the *Phoebe* and the *Cherub*, after a most obstinate defence, attended by the destruction of more than half her crew. In this event, owing to our superiority of force, we have nothing to boast, any farther than the smallness of our own loss, and the diminution of the enemy's naval resources. The manner in which Captain Hillyar has mentioned the gallant and ardent conduct of Mr. George O'Brien, does him honour; and we hope it may be the means of restoring that gentleman to a rank he appears to have lost from some act of youthful indiscretion.

[Captain Hillyar's service letter, dated 30 March 1814, was published in Vol. XXXII, pp168-170.]

In the Connecticut river, a considerable quantity of American shipping was attacked and destroyed on the 8th of April last, by a boat party belonging to H.M. Ships *La Hogue, Maidstone, Endymion,* and the *Borer,* who passed the enemy's batteries, and returned in triumph to their ships, with the loss of only two men killed, and two wounded. The success of this enterprise was complete, and the destruction of the enemy's property very considerable.

On Lake Ontario we have been unfortunate. A boat expedition was undertaken against a flotilla of the enemy's craft, laden with naval stores, which had got into Sandy Creek. Captains Popham and Spilsbury of the Royal Navy conducted this enterprise, which, unfortunately, terminated in the capture or destruction of the whole party, amounting to about 200. We regret having to state that Captain Popham died soon after his captivity, of the wounds he had received in the gallant resistance made by his small party against a greatly superior force.

[News of Stephen Popham's death was premature, as he lived on to 1842.]

Norway

The fate of Norway still remains in suspense! - We are decidedly of opinion, that the union of Norway with Sweden will not be of long duration, although it should take place by compromise instead of slaughter. From the hour that Sweden was deprived of Finland, the possessor of the crown of Sweden became a tenant at will of the court of St. Petersburg; and in the very first war that occurs between those powers, in all human probability Sweden will be over-run, and became herself a province to Russia! Norway of course must follow the fate of Sweden; and the people of Great Britain will be able to appreciate the wisdom of our statesmen guaranteeing this cession, when the grand Russian fleet is removed from Kronstadt to North Bergen - This act probably arose from some petty feelings of personal pique indulged against the king of Denmark; the integrity of whose dominions it was our interest to have insisted upon; instead of being the foremost to lay violent hands upon that monarchy.

To Elba XXXI 490

Elba! when Jason stole the golden fleece,
And was returning to his native Greece,
By chroniclers, in days of yore, 'tis said,
He stopped, and there a friendly visit paid.
But now a guest of quite a different cast,
To pitch his tent on thy contracted strand,
And change an *empire* for a *speck* of land;
Glad to escape from just resentment's storm,
And hide behind thy rocks his hated form.
O guard him well! for Tuscany ne'er sent
A guiltier culprit into banishment.

From 'Naval Anecdotes.' XXXII 55-56; 110-111

Launch of the Nelson

On the 4th July, 1814, the *Nelson,* the largest line-of-battle ship ever built in England,

ELBA.

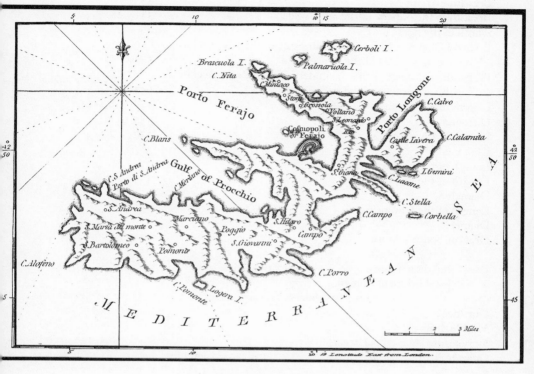

Chart of the Island of Elba. ^{Plate 419}

was launched at the King's Yard, Woolwich. The royal marines were drawn up in the street, in front of the entrance gate, the royal artillery was ranged in extended files in every direction, without the Dock-yard, for the purpose of preserving order, and the Fermanagh militia were stationed around. Stages for the accommodation of the spectators were erected contiguous to the vessel ready to be launched. They were lined inside with the colours of the shipping, which had a grand and striking effect. One on the larboard side, with the royal standard, was appropriated to the Lords of the Admiralty, and another on the opposite side to correspond, to the Commissioners. The St. George's red and the blue ensigns were displayed at the fore, main, and mizen-masts. A red ensign was also hanging over her stern, and the union jack forward. She appeared a beautiful ship, and is the finest of the class ever built in British docks, constructed purposely to commemorate the numerous and glorious victories achieved by the hero from whom she derives her name, and as a tribute of national gratitude to the memory of departed bravery and merit.

The following are her dimensions:

Length on the range of the lower gun-deck from the rabbit of
    the stem to the rabbit of the stern-post   205 ft. 1/4 in.

Length from the aft part of the fife-rail to the fore part of
    the figure head   244   0

Length of the keel for tonnage   170   10

Breadth moulded	52	11
Breadth extreme	53	8
Breadth to the outside of the main walls	54	6
Depth in the hold	28	
Perpendicular height from the underside of the false keel to the upper part of the figure-head	552	
Perpendicular height from the underside of the false keel to the upper part of the taff-rail	652	
Length of the foremast	118	0 1/2
Diameter	3	2
Length of the mainmast	127	1 1/4
Diameter	3	5
Length of the maintop-mast	77	0 1/4
Length of the main-yard	109	3
Diameter	2	2
Length of the bowsprit	75	1
Diameter	3	1
Draft of Water - Afore	24	
- Abaft	25	

Burthen in tons,   2617 4/94 tons
Establishment of men,   875

	Guns	pounders	Carronades	
Gun-deck	32	32		
Middle ditto	34	24		
Upper ditto	34	18		
Quarter ditto	6	12	10	23 pounders
Forecastle	2	12	2	32

    The head exemplifies the whole art, ingenuity, and workmanship of our professed artists; it is ornamented with the bust of our brave and ever-to-be-lamented hero, "Nelson," supported by Fame and Britannia, with the motto, "England expects every Man to do his Duty." - The stern is one of the most magnificent ever seen.

    At ten minutes past one Count Platoff arrived in a private carriage, accompanied by some of his aides-de-camps. As soon as he was recognized, the shouts of the multitude rent the air; he was accompanied by Commissioner Cunningham to his stage or box, on the starboard side. The band struck up "God save the King." Marshal Blucher joined him about ten minutes previous to the launch. Lord Melville, accompanied by several officers, ladies, and gentlemen, arrived in the Admiralty barge about twenty minutes past one, and went on board the Nelson, where they were shewn the state cabins; they afterwards returned and took their seats in the box prepared for them.

    The dock-yard men soon after began to remove the shores which supported the ship on slips. By two o'clock the tide had flowed nearly high enough, and at 32 minutes past two the usual signal was given, the remaining shores were taken away, and the Nelson began to move. She went off the slips and glided into the river, amidst the shouts of at least 20,000 spectators. Having been named with the usual ceremony of throwing a bottle of wine against her bows, she drifted to the middle of the river, and dropped anchor. The spectators on board the ships and on shore greeted her with three cheers. The bands again played martial music, and the launch ended: and we are happy to state the pleasure of the day was not damped by the smallest accident.

An Affecting Meeting Between a Sailor and his Wife

At the beginning of the late war with France, a sailor named C...l, who lived in Shoreditch parish, was so reduced by sickness and poverty that he could not maintain his wife and children. He entered on board the tender, – and left his wife half his pay. She was, however, driven by distress to the workhouse, where she lay-in of the child with which she was pregnant, which was reared in that poor-house. At the close of the fourth year, her pay was stopped, – and her husband supposed to be dead.

Left thus destitute, she struggled on for three years more, – when she married a carpenter, who died a short time since, and left her again plunged in greater distress than ever. She used to carry the child she had by him at her back, – and with a basket of matches and ballads, sought a precarious livelihood, – she had no home but a two-penny lodging-house, – and if she had no pence, the sky was her canopy, and the earth her bed.

It happened one night about the beginning of this month (August, 1814) that chance directed her wandering steps to a public house where her first husband used to frequent; and as she begged the humble guests who were drinking in the tap-room, to lay out a halfpenny with a poor widow, a sailor, just discharged from a man of war, sprung up, and almost over-turning both table and guests, seized the poor ragged supplicant in his arms, calling her his long-lost wife! – She was so much overpowered at thus meeting alive with one whom she had long reckoned amongst the dead, that she was near fainting. Mutual explanations were soon made, amidst the tearful eyes of the spectators – "I deserted you in the midst of want and misery," said the penitent, "but I have sought you since for years, without being able to hear of you. We must forget and forgive. I am now well to do, and will henceforth be a good husband to you." After regaling her with the best the house afforded, he took his astonished wife under his arm, and completely new rigged her. His boy – still in the workhouse – he went to see, to reclaim, and provide for. He purchased some decent household furniture, – and is now looking out for a coal-shed, whereby to support himself and family.

From the 'Naval History of the Present Year,' 1814
July–August. XXXII 152-153

No News from America

Contrary to our expectations, no news of importance has as yet arrived from America, – the ministers of the belligerent states have met at Ghent, but nothing has transpired to enable the public to form any idea as the result to be expected: nor have we any naval events of moment to record, farther than the ravages committed upon our commerce by American privateers, a misfortune, that, however it may be regretted, is the inevitable result of the great extent of coast and maritime resources possessed by the foe, and not of supineness in the British Navy.

Peace with America must be Negotiated – Editorial

Greatly as our manufacturers suffer, – and repulsive to our feelings as is this unnatural war, – it is regarded by too many with indifference, whilst others look forward to the *final subjugation* of the United States, from the greatly increased disposable quantum of military force that ministers are said to be on the point of dispatching to those shores. – This is exactly the spirit and conduct that distinguished the first American war. Each new armament was to complete the reduction of the Americans, and failure only stimulated to new attempts, until the aggregate of loss, and the force of popular feeling, put an end to the sanguinary conflict.

Had we any influence, without neglecting the field, it would be to the *cabinet* we should look for an honourable and speedy termination of the war. It is true, that we are become much more powerful than we were, and are able to send far mightier armies against America; – but we seem to have forgotten, that the strength of America has far outgrown the progress of our own; – and that they are better able to repel the utmost force we can *now* send against them, than they were the small armies of 1780. We are not for the sacrifice of an iota of our just maritime rights, – nor for any concession that could cast a shadow on our honour; but we should wish to see distinctly stated to America and Europe, what it is for which we are fighting; – and if it should prove that we contend for that to which a free and independent people ought not to submit, – we had better withdraw our pretensions, to avoid the possibility of being a second time foiled and disgraced; – and if, on the other hand, we claim nothing but what is founded in justice, – a plain and manly avowal of our pretensions, free from subtleties and reservations – would, in a representative government, go farther to overthrow the *men in power*, than fifty thousand British bayonets landed on their soil. – The Americans *invaded* Canada, and hitherto they have met with little else than defeat and disgrace; – let us beware – lest – *becoming the invaders*, we should suffer the fate which, on moral principles, ought always to await an invader. The GREAT EXPEDITION under the command of Lord Hill *has not yet* sailed. We confess our hopes are not sanguine, that the result will answer the expectation of its projectors. To have secured the sovereignty of the Lakes, and have completely defeated the American forces despatched for the conquest of Canada, – to have kept the whole sea coast in a constant state of alarm during summer, by floating armies, – and partial descents directed against the principal rendezvous of their shipping, – experience would have proved to be the wisest plan of warfare ministers could have adopted. Except by *superior force* upon the ocean – not a trophy would the war-party have to boast, – and stripped of their commerce, and kept in a state of wearisome anxiety, – the clamours of the enemies to Mr. Madison's politics, might have greatly embarrassed him. But it is to be feared, – as soon as the Americans find that we are sending over armies too powerful to be regarded as intended merely to vex and alarm them, – they will to a man rally round the executive, and say as Admiral Blake did to our forefathers – "*Disturb not one another with domestic disputes – remember that we are Americans, and our enemies are foreigners! Enemies! which, let what party soever prevail, – it is equally the interest of our country to humble and restrain.*"

From 'Correspondence.' *XXXII 207-208; XXXIII 221-222*

On the Inadequacy of British Ship Design

C.H. to the Editor, Glasgow, 16th July, 1814
Mr. Editor, When I last addressed you upon the successes of our trans-atlantic foe, I fondly flattered myself the victory I then alluded to would terminate their naval triumphs, and be the lst which we should have cause to lament. Events, however, have turned out far otherwise; and we have now to regret the destruction of one, and the accession to the American navy of another, beautiful sloop of war [HMS *Boxer*]. The loss of these vessels has taught us, now too late, that our ships of that description are altogether as

unfit to cope with the American sloops, as our frigates were with theirs of a like name; and the great difference in weight of metal, tonnage, and height, will, I fear, still secure to them the victory. It was hinted at by a correspondent in a former part of the *Naval Chronicle*, that the Americans were about to try their strength with us in line-of-battle ships, and he also mentioned the unequal manner in which ours of that description were manned. This, however, is the only time I recollect that the building of such vessels has been mentioned in your publication; permit me, then, to lay before your readers, an extract of a private letter from Halifax, which may tend to give some information not altogether useless.

The writer says - "Many people in England are no doubt informed that several seventy-four gun ships are building in the United States; but the extraordinary size of these vessels, in reference to their rates, may not be generally known: the opportunity I had lately of seeing the *Monmouth*, seventy-four, enables me to give you the length of her keel, which I found to be 173 feet 6 inches; her lower-deck guns are to be 42-pounders, and the whole number of the guns which she is to carry is *ninety-six*."

Should the gentleman who wrote the above be correct, and of which I entertain no doubt, a 74, with her 32-pounders, would be in a similar situation to our frigates formerly captured, and would have even less chance of overcoming her enemy. It will behove us then, in order to match these ships, to fit out our first and second rates with 42-pounders, and despatch them to the American station; for unless this is done, it is not impossible that we may hear of a 74 or two being taken by these Americans, in the same way as our three frigates.

I am of opinion, that a peace with America would at this time be hurtful to us: how often would our disasters be thrown in our teeth, and the loss of our ships be a subject for their triumph? - Besides - in order to keep up that character and consequence which it is so necessary for us to possess, we should make them feel the weight of our arm - *they have shewn to other nations that the British navy is not invincible* - these nations will not inquire the difference of force, but believe the Americans, and we cannot deny it, that THEIR FRIGATES *have* CAPTURED OURS. Already, indeed, the French have profited by their example; for of all the late captures, none of their vessels, with any thing like an equal force, made an inglorious defence, but fought with an obstinacy which nothing but the knowledge of the American victories could have inspired.

Let the latter nation now feel the power of Britannia, the sword to them has all along remained sheathed, but since we now begin to draw it, let it be wielded with double energy - and since

"Our country cries *Vengeance*, her cause we'll make good,
We swear by our swords, and we'll write it in blood."

On the Remarkable Success of the Young American Navy

"Albion" to the Editor, February 6th, *1815*
Mr. Editor, The events of the war with America, now, perhaps, about to close, afford *much* cause for *reflection, none* for *exultation*, to those who are interested in the success and prosperity of their country. Only three years ago, we despised this new enemy *so much*, as to content ourselves with sending out *two* frigates as a reinforcement (the *Spartan* and *Shannon*), and even when war was declared, two line of battle ships were deemed amply sufficient, in addition to the very slender force then on the station. How

very differently we estimate their strength now, sufficiently appears, from our having, during the last twelve months, employed on their shores a force of from fifteen to twenty sail of the line, double that number of large frigates, perhaps altogether one hundred sail of men of war, and with all this truly formidable force, commanded by able and experienced officers, it cannot be pretended we have made any great impression on the enemy, taken any of their men of war, or destroyed them in their own ports: with the exception of one frigate building at Washington, and one destroyed at Penobscot, we have done nothing of this kind; it is true, their ships have been blockaded in port; but they have waited their opportunity, and have obtained it; one of their squadrons being at the time I write, known to be cruising in the chops of the English channel, and information having been received by government, that *all* their men of war, including one or two line of battle ships of 96 guns were ready for sea, and *a second* squadron actually *at sea*; for this, I believe our board of Admiralty were not prepared; when, I would ask, have they been prepared? But fortunately there were several sail of the line, and frigates, preparing for sea, as convoys to outward bound fleets, and they have been sent out in quest of this bold and successful enemy with as little delay as possible: two squadrons of this kind are gone down Channel already; and two more are fitting with all expedition to follow. I sincerely hope one of these, or Sir George Collier's, of similar force to the Americans, will have the good fortune to fall in with them, and the glory of conducting them into a British port; we want something of this kind to reconcile the minds of the people and of the navy to the many reverses we have sustained during this American war, and to a termination of it, *without* our having been able to assert our wonted naval superiority. It is true, our enemy has possessed many great and decided advantages; but putting these aside, it must be allowed, the Americans have fought us bravely at sea, they have, almost in every instance, been successful; and there cannot be a doubt, they will speedily become a respectable, and, ere long, a truly formidable naval power. We have, I fear, been lulled asleep by our former glorious victories over the fleets of France, Spain, and Holland; and have, until too late, despised this new, but rapidly rising rival of our maritime greatness. The American navy is *already* respectable, from the ability and valour which its officers and seamen have displayed: it is the hope, the cherished favourite of the States; and during the period of peace (can a long one be reasonably expected? I think not), every nerve will be strained to increase its force, and its claim to the respect of foreign powers.

I shall not be surprised to hear of an American ambassador landing at Portsmouth or Brest from a 98 gun ship, and a Decatur or a Bainbridge, perhaps a Rodgers, receiving admirals' salutes from an English or French flag in those harbours, this is likely soon to happen. Let us then profit by *dear-bought experience*; let us build ships of adequate force; let our line of battle ships, frigates, and sloops, be no longer incapable of meeting and contending with this rising enemy. I would strongly recommend, that during peace, not less than *five* very large line of battle ships; *six* frigates of the *Leander*'s class; and eight or ten twenty-gun ships be *annually* built, to be in readiness for coming events. Let us look before us *now*, and again bend beneath the stroke of an enemy whom, had we not despised, we might have easily conquered.

N.B. I have often already borne testimony to the bravery of our naval officers; they have supported the honour of the British flag, and lost their lives in many instances, in defending it; but enquiry is wanted into the management of the navy, and if it is to take place, it will I hope be temperate, but serious, and shew clearly where is the blame, and how our misfortunes are to be remedied, and our naval means better applied.

Debarkation of Napoleon Buonaparte at Porto Ferraio, in the Island of Elba.
Engraved by Baily, from a drawing by Lieutenant G.S. Smith, R.N.

It will be obvious to the reader, that we have adopted this plate as a companion to
the former: it is engraven from a sketch made by an officer present at the
debarkation of Napoleon Buonaparté at Porto Ferraio, the capital of the Island of
Elba, from H.M.S. *Undaunted*, the 8th of May, 1814, under a salute fired by that
ship with yards manned. The new sovereign (he being such by treaty,) was received
by the Clergy (who brought down a canopy to the end of the wharf) and by the
garrison under arms.

The new standard which he designed and had made on board the *Undaunted*,
being, "*Argent*, a bend *sinister* gules charged with three Bees *proper*," was hoisted on
the fort, and displayed in the boat which conveyed him. Plate 463

1814 – United States the Only Enemy

THE CAPTURE OF HMS *AVON* and the unprecedented success of American commerce raiders set a sombre note in *The Naval Chronicle*'s account of the American war, which it had always considered parricidal. The news from the Canadian front was not inspiring, although the worst of it, the defeat on Lake Champlain, was not yet known. However, the period ended with the startling news of the raid on the American capital in Washington, and the burning of its public buildings. In this war there could only be losers, and the Americans were beginning to suffer themselves. The vague reports that peace negotiations were being carried on at Ghent did not as yet hold much promise.

From the 'Naval History of the Present Year,' 1814
August–September. *XXXII 243-251*

USS Wasp Captures Avon

An action that has proved fatal to another of our sloops of war, took place on the 1st inst. about 1/2 past 8 in the evening, in lat. 47° 35′ long. 10° 37′ between Kinsale and Cape Clear, between H.M. late sloop the *Avon*, Honourable Captain Arbuthnot, and the United States sloop of war, the *Wasp*.

The battle, sustained at close quarters, lasted two hours and twenty minutes. On board the *Avon* there were forty-one persons killed and wounded; the main-mast was shot away; and she received so many shot in her hull, that she was actually sinking, and some accounts state that she had struck, when providentially the *Castilian* hove in sight, and after giving the *Wasp* a broadside, hastened to the relief of the gallant crew of the sinking vessel. The captain was wounded in both his legs, but not dangerously. The first lieutenant, Mr. Prendergast, who was dangerously wounded, died the next day. Lieutenant Harvey, the last person that quitted the *Avon*, was also wounded. Mr. John Travers, midshipman, severely. The gallant survivors were landed at Cork, and it was reported and believed, that the *Wasp* had gone down.

A neutral vessel has since landed at the Downs the masters of three of our merchantmen, that were prisoners on board the *Wasp*, during the engagement, who

236

have reported that she had only two men killed and three wounded during this long and desperate battle: to us this assertion appears incredible, and shews the necessity of *immediately* building vessels capable of carrying more men, and heavier metal, as the present disparity is truly discouraging to both sailor and officer. The *Avon* was a very fine brig sloop, and had a large complement of men. The *Wasp* is rated in the *American Navy List,* of the same force, though undoubtedly greatly superior in tonnage, and weight of metal, and number of hands. Nothing could exceed the bravery of Captain Arbuthnot and his bold shipmates.

Success of American Trade War Unprecedented

The depredations committed on our commerce by American ships of war, and privateers, has attained an extent beyond all former precedent.

It will be seen in our correspondence, that A.D. affirms they have literally swept our seas, blockaded our ports, and cut up our Irish and coasting trade. Another of our able epistolary friends, resident at Greenock, expresses his fears lest some enterprising American should enter the Clyde and destroy the shipping in that estuary. We refer our readers to the respective letters. The insurance between Bristol and Waterford or Cork, is now *three times higher* than it was when we were at war with all Europe! The admiralty lords have been overwhelmed with letters of complaint or remonstrance; public meetings have been held at Liverpool and Bristol, by the merchants and ship–owners, and many several strictures passed upon the public conduct of those at the head of the naval department. The answers returned by the lords of the Admiralty to the *remonstrances* of the merchants of Liverpool and Bristol, state that three or four frigates, and fourteen sloops, were cruising at the time of the captures of which they complained, off the Irish station.

But the truth is, that our navy contains scarcely a single sloop that is fairly a match for the weakest *American built* vessel of that class of ships of war. And most of them are so obviously deficient, that their commanders, whatever be their character for valour and skill, run the risk of compromising their reputations in the event of a battle with an American, almost without a chance of victory.

The system of maritime warfare adopted by the United States consists in burning, scuttling, and destroying every thing they capture. The eagerness with which they seize on the papers of the ships they take, points out the proofs they must exhibit in America to attain their remuneration. By this system America loses the amount of the premium, and also the duties she would otherwise derive from the sale of the prizes, and the service of such warlike stores as they may chance to capture; but, on the other hand, *they make destruction sure*; cut off the chance of recaptures by our cruisers, whilst their own remain longer at sea, and by retaining all their force, commit more extended devastation.

The *Saucy Jack*, that recently sailed from Charlestown upon her *sixth cruise*, is stated to have destroyed property on the sea to the amount of *a million of dollars*! It is conjectured that a hundred stout privateers well armed and manned are forwarding this ruinous occupation in different parts of the globe.

American Coast Dwellers Pay War's Price

Whilst the fears of our merchants have been thus excited, and their property destroyed, – according to the American papers, their own shores were in a state of unparalleled dismay, their bays and rivers occupied by our triumphal fleets, their capital in imminent danger. Our accounts state that Sir Alexander Cochrane had penetrated far into the Chesapeake and had landed four thousand troops menacing either Washington or Baltimore. The Plymouth paper of Tuesday announced that Baltimore has been taken with "*lots of ships.*" The news from Canada is chequered. Commodore Chauncey is said to be blockading Sir James Yeo in Kingston Harbour. A catalogue of the present naval force upon the Lakes, may be seen in the following.

British and American Force on Lake Champlain, August 1814

BRITISH

Confiance	28 guns, ship, to be launched August 31.
Linnet	brig, 16 guns, 80 men.
Chub (late *Shannon*)	sloop, 13 guns, 50 men.
Finch (late *Broke*)	sloop, 11 guns, 40 men.
Icicle	sloop, 4 guns, 7 men.

The last four are ready for service.

Gun-boats ready for service:

			swivels	
Sir James Yeo	lugger,	40	1 long 24,	1 32?-pdr cannon.
Sir George Provost	"	46	"	"
Lord Wellington	"	38	1 long 18,	1 18-pdr cannon.
General Simcoe	"	36	"	1 32-pdr cannon.
Marshal Beresford	"	26	-	"
Sir Home Popham	"	22	-	"
General Brock	"	22	-	"
Tecumsch	"	26	1 long 6	-
Lord Cochrane	latine	14	-	1 12-pdr cannon.
Canada	sloop	10	3 long 6	-
Blucher	lugger	34	1 long 18,	1 18-pdr cannon.
Sir Sydney Beckwith	"	32	1 long 18	-

AMERICAN

Saratoga	ship	28 guns	240 men
Ticonderoga	brig	22 guns	160 men
Commodore Preble	sloop	11 guns	80 men
Six new gun-boats		36 guns	800 men
Four old ditto		16 guns	/

Brig (building) 26 guns, to be launched Aug 11th, 1814

British Force on Lake Ontario, July 20, 1814

Regent, 56 guns, Commodore Sir James Yeo, Captain Hicky, main deck 28 long 24-pounders, upper-deck 28 carronades, 68 and 32-pound.

Princess Charlotte, Captain Dounil, main-deck, 24 long 24-pounders, upper deck 2 68 and 16 32-pounder carronades.

Montreal corvette,	22 32-pounder carronades
Niagara ditto,	22 32-pounder "
Star brig, Captain Dotts,	16 32-pounder "

Charwell brig	14 24-pounder "
Schooner	12 12-pounder "
Schooner	5 12-pounder "

With twelve gun-boats, some of 2 and some of 1 gun each.

The English three-deck ship [*St. Lawrence*], which it is expected was launched about the latter end of August last, will mount 108 guns, is much longer and broader than the *Caledonia*, her main-deck flush, and no poop.

[The *St Lawrence*, although never completed, dominated the strategic situation on Lake Ontario at the close of 1814 and for several years following the peace treaty.]

American Force In Sackett's Harbour, Lake Ontario, July 20, 1814

Superior	64 long 32 and 24-pounders
New frigate	52 long 24 and 32-pdr carronades.
General Pike frigate	28 long 32 "
Madison corvette	22 " "
Oneida brig	16 " "
Sylph brig	12 long 24 "
New brig	22 long 32 "
New brig	22 " "
Governor Tompkins schooner	4 " 12 "
Fair American schooner	2 " "
Conquest schooner	2 " "
Asp schooner	2 " "
Inbi schooner	2 " "
Lady of the Lake schooner	2 " "

Besides 12 gun-boats, of 2 and 1 gun each, making the American force superior to ours by eighty pieces of cannon.

The fort of Michelimackainac, situated on St. Mary's straits, is said to have been captured by the Americans: it is most essential to the maintenance of our trade in the N.W. districts. The ships of the enemy are also said to have passed through the straits of Lake Huron, and that the entire command of that part of the country is thus acquired by the Americans.

There have been several murderous conflicts in Canada. Our army under General Drummond repulsed a furious attack made by the Americans upon our lines at Chippawa, occasioning the assailants a loss amounting to *fifteen hundred men*, our own being upwards of eight hundred in killed, wounded and missing. The enemy was pursued to Fort Erie, where he fortified himself, and received reinforcements. Anxious to follow up the successes of our brave troops, General Drummond despatched a force that he deemed competent to carry that position; which enterprise, in its turn, failed, owing to a magazine blowing up, that destroyed a great number of our troops. The American accounts carry our total loss as high as from eight hundred to a thousand men.

Peace Talks Resume

The negotiations at Ghent were reported to have broken off, as we have stated in the structures on the American question; but they are now *said to be resumed with more activity than ever*. On this head every thing is wrapped in obscurity.

First News of the Raid on Washington

After the preceding part of our retrospect had been composed, intelligence arrived at the Admiralty that our gallant navy and army, penetrating to the very core of the United States, had made the most brilliant and fortunate dash on record against the CAPITAL OF AMERICA, and been completely successful, with a loss so trivial, compared with the magnitude of the enterprise, as to excite equal admiration with the suddenness and temerity of the blow! As the whole of the extraordinary gazette will be given in its proper place, we shall now merely insert the following official bulletin.

Admiralty-Office, September 27, 1814

Captain Wainwright of his Majesty's ship *Tonnant*, arrived early this morning, at this office, with despatches from Vice-Admiral Sir A. Cochrane, commander-in-chief on the American station, with an account of the capture and destruction, by his Majesty's forces, of the city of Washington, on the 24th ult. after a severe, but brilliant action, in which the enemy was defeated with great loss.

On the 19th, the army under Major-general Ross, with the marine battalion, a detachment of seamen, and the rocket corps, were landed at Benedict, on the right bank of the Patuxent.

On the 21st, the army advanced to Nottingham, higher up the river, on the same bank; the armed boats and tenders of the fleet, under Rear-admiral Cockburn, making a corresponding movement in communication with the troops ashore, and in pursuit of Commodore Barney, who, with his flotilla of 17 gun-vessels, retired before them.

On the 22d, the army moved to Marlborough, while the boats pursued the flotilla; and, on their near approach, the sloop which bore Commodore Barney's broad pendant was observed to be on fire, and the whole flotilla was blown up in succession, except the last gun-boat, which, with about 17 merchant vessels, and a considerable quantity of property, were captured, and such as were worth transporting have been brought away.

In consequence of this success, the right flank of the army was secured and Major-general Ross, in concert with Rear-admiral Cockburn, determined to advance upon the city of Washington.

In the course of the 23d, all necessary preparations were made for the advance, and in the afternoon, the troops (an additional number of seamen and marines being landed from the fleet) proceeded six miles toward Washington, where they bivouacked for that night.

On the morning of the 24th, the whole, with the major-general and the Rear-admiral, accompanied by Captain Wainwright, of the *Tonnant*, Captain Palmer, of the *Hubris*, and Captain Money, of the *Trave*, advanced to Bladensburgh, a village and strong position about five miles from Washington, where the enemy's army, estimated at 8,000 men, with Commodore Barney, and the remainder of the crew of his flotilla, were posted on very strong ground, defended by two batteries. Notwithstanding the great fatigue which the state of the weather, and their previous march and labours had occasioned, his Majesty's forces evinced the greatest alacrity, and while a part only of the army was come up, the major-general seeing a favourable opportunity of attack, resolved not to defer it; and a column of about 1,500 men advanced upon the enemy, stormed his position, and totally routed him, taking all their cannon, killing great numbers, and making many prisoners. Among the latter was Commodore Barney, who was also wounded.

Mr. Madison, the president, the secretary at war, and the secretaries of state and of the navy, are stated to have been present, at the beginning at least, of the action.

The British loss in this decisive affair, was about 43 men killed, and 193 wounded. Colonel Thornton, of the 85th: Lieutenant-colonel Wood, and Major Brown, of the same regiment; Lieutenant John Stavely, and Ensign James Buchanan, of the 4th regiment, were wounded; as was Mr. M'Daniel, midshipman of the *Tonnant*.

Immediately after the action, the remains of the American army retreated through Washington, and across the Potomac into Virginia, and the British army advanced; and, after a slight resistance by a few shot from the first houses of the town, took possession of the city of Washington.

All that evening and night, the time was employed in destroying all the public buildings and property, to a great amount, were totally destroyed in the course of the 25th; in the evening of which day the army began to return to its embarkation, in which movement it was totally unmolested by the enemy. On the 26th, the troops again reached Marlborough; on the 27th, they were at Nottingham, where they remained till the 28th; and on the 29th proceeded to Benedict, where the army embarked the following morning; having accomplished all the objects of the expedition with the utmost celerity and success, and with a very disproportionate loss.

While this main attack was in progress, Vice-admiral Sir Alexander Cochrane had directed two diversions to be made, the one towards Baltimore, by the *Menelaus*, Captain Sir Peter Parker; the other up the Potomac, against Fort Washington, under Captain Gordon, of the *Seahorse*, both of which had the desired effect, though, in the course of his operations Captain Sir Peter Parker was mortally wounded in a most gallant attack on a camp of the enemy's on shore, for which he had disembarked the seamen and marines of his ship.

The details of the operations in the Potomac had not been received, but the country people reported that the squadron had completely succeeded in destroying Fort Washington.

By the preceding document, it will be seen, that the victory, and the work of devastation have been equally complete! Not only has the whole naval defence of the Potomac been annihilated; the arsenal, dock-yard, the States' rope walk, with a frigate of the first class ready to launch, and a sloop of war afloat, been destroyed, together with an immense and costly assemblage of naval stores of all kinds; but the vast and splendid public edifices that so lately adorned that maiden capital; the PALACE of the PRESIDENT, the SENATE HOUSE, the HOUSE of REPRESENTATIVES, the TREASURY, the WAR-OFFICE, and the GREAT BRIDGE across the Potomac, have been devoured by the flames, blown up from their foundations, or otherwise destroyed!

This vast destruction of edifices, not devoted to the purposes of war, would tarnish the glory of our victory, and fix an indelible stain on our national honour, if the American military commanders, during their invasion of Canada, had not set the frightful example, in wantonly burning, plundering, and destroying the defenceless farms and villages that lay in the way; which violations of the laws of war, and the dictates of humanity, have never been disowned by the executive government, nor the commanding officers punished. Admitting our allegations to be well grounded, RETALIATION became a public duty, and most impressively has it been inflicted; not by clapping the torch to the lowly thatch of cottages; not by burning the naked towns and villages which clothe the shores of the majestic Potomac, but by seizing upon the AMERICAN METROPOLIS, and leveling with the dust the splendid palaces and sumptuous edifices by which the city of WASHINGTON was so liberally embellished. Yet, however justifiable this savage mode of warfare may be made to appear, humanity will for ever deplore the occurrence, and most painful will be the sensations excited in the bosoms of those who have not become callous by upwards of twenty years of warfare, in contemplating such awful visitations inflicted upon a race of freemen, sprung from ourselves - using our language, laws, and religion, and whom the voice of nature owns as kindred and brethren!

Its effects in America cannot be otherwise than powerful and decisive. It will appall the government, and destroy its power - or strengthen its arm, by calling into action every thing fierce and vindictive in their nature, and give birth to irreconcilable hatred and interminable war. It has also supplied a test that will decide the character of the present race of Americans. If the executive government be indeed, held in that deep contempt so vehemently expressed in some of their journals; and which its apparent imbecility seems in some measure to confirm - the union of the States will speedily be dissolved, and the sun of America has set, never to rise again! She will quickly exhibit the wretched condition so finely described by our Bard -

> "Her rulers sunk;
> Her high-built honour moulder'd to the dust;
> Unnerv'd her force; her spirits vanish'd quite;
> With rapid wing her riches fled away;
> Her unfrequented ports alone the sign
> Of what she was; her merchants scatter'd wide;
> Her hollow shops shut up; and in her streets
> Her fields, woods, markets, villages, and roads,
> The cheerful voice of labour heard no more."

When our officers entered Washington city, they found the tables laid at Mr. Madison's palace for a *grand supper*; the champaign was in coolers - a fine dessert on the side-boards - little did they dream who would be their guests! The unexpected visitants took the liberty of ordering the supper to be served up - and the health of his Majesty was drank at the head of the President's table!

The American papers state the stores destroyed at Washington cost the United States *seven* millions of dollars! *The loss is irreparable*, at least, during the present war; the last, perhaps, that ever will be waged by the *United States.*

In addition to the devastation of public property already enumerated, our troops, it appears, demolished the *National Intelligencer*-office, and the *cannon foundry* at George Town. 500 pieces of cannon are said to have been spiked.

Alexandria has surrendered to a couple of our frigates! Baltimore was said to be preparing to capitulate! At Boston - New York - Philadelphia - all was dismay and confusion! The President and suite were said to have arrived at Baltimore.

Commodore Barney took an active part in the Revolutionary War. He was the person whom the beautiful and unfortunate Marie Antoinette, the Queen of Louis XVI, *honoured with a salute*, at the commencement of the last American war, to shew that our good friends the Bourbons countenanced them in their struggle for independence! The flotilla he commanded is stated to have been superior in force to ours, but he did not wait an attack, *but as soon as our boats appeared*, set the whole on fire; all of which, except one that we captured, were destroyed.

The island of Nantucket, in the state of Massachusetts, in consequence of an application from the Magistrate to Sir Alexander Cochrane, has been declared *neutral*. All the government property had previously been given up to the British. A communication is thus opened with the continent, and vessels, provided with British licenses, admitted to trade. A wedge is thus inserted that may lead to a schism in the United States! It remains, however, to be seen whether the government accede or not to the conditions of this singular treaty.

Baltic Storm

It is reported – we sincerely hope it may prove unfounded – that in a recent and destructive storm in the Baltic, a number of transports, having on board the Russian Imperial Guard returning from France, have been wrecked, and that all on board perished.

Norwegians Betrayed and Defeated

We are no longer at war with Norway: the sacrifice has been made! The lowering tempest, which we noticed in April last, has exploded. The hardy Norwegians fought bravely; and if the foulest treachery had not undermined them, the fate of war might not have been adverse to justice. It was chiefly by the means we have depicted that the invader triumphed, and a gallant nation been delivered over to an abhorred foreign yoke – the patriot and philanthropist avert their eyes from laurels that drip with the blood of freemen! Surely better means might have been found of gratifying Sweden. In 1808 the shores of the Baltic resounded with the shrieks of the Swedes massacred at Wasa! How loud were her complaints of violence and treachery! In 1814 she perpetrates upon the peaceful Norwegians all the evils by which she had so recently been oppressed and mutilated: and heaven knows how soon a stronger arm may interpose and gather up the victor and his prey!

St Domingo Braces for French Attack

The accounts from the important colony of St. Domingo state, that the existing authorities, aware of the impending storm, have made preparations – on the landing taking place of a French army – to devote the cities and towns to the flames, and retire to the mountains! From France the intelligence seems to indicate that an army is to be sent to reduce the blacks to obedience. If so, the result will probably be, the destruction of the invaders. This is not the only instance in which it appears how difficult it is for kings to learn wisdom from experience.

September–October. XXXII 335-336

Disaster at Fort Erie

We are compelled to be brief indeed in the retrospective view of the occurrences of this month. – On the 1st, intelligence arrived stating, that Captain Dobbs, R.N. with a party of seamen and marines, attacked, and carried, by boarding, two armed American schooners, anchored close to Fort Erie. The fort being thus deprived of part of its defence, General Drummond was induced to follow up this success by an attack on the fort itself, which nearly succeeded, when the explosion of a mine blew up multitudes of our troops: the consequence was, an immediate retreat; we are truly concerned to state our loss at upwards of nine hundred men, and officers in proportion. On this melancholy occasion Captain Dobbs was wounded.

Successful Attack on the Penobscot

On the 8th, intelligence was received at the Admiralty from Admiral Griffiths, announcing the success of an expedition, directed against the possessions of the United States, on the river and bay of Penobscot. The *John Adams*, United States frigate, was set on fire by the enemy and destroyed; the district of Penobscot was taken possession of, and a proclamation issued by General Sir John Sherbrooke, K.B.; and it has been affirmed, that this territory is to be permanently retained: if so, we think the prospect of peace with America is remote indeed!

Reverse at Baltimore and Plattsburg

The next important event was, the unsuccessful attack made upon Baltimore; the army succeeded in defeating the Americans, and approached close to the city, but so efficient were the naval means of defence, that our ships of war could not co-operate, and all the brilliant achievements of our soldiers proved useless. General Ross was killed at the commencement of the action. The same gazette contained the particulars of the capture of Alexandria by the naval force under the command of that distinguished officer, Captain James Alexander Gordon, who has verified our predictions much earlier than we expected, and added a new wreath to the laurels he had previously gained. The accounts of these important advantages were, however, accompanied by rumours of a most unfavourable kind; namely, of the total destruction of our fleet on Lake Champlain, and the retreat of Sir George Prevost, with considerable loss, from before Plattsburg: these disastrous reports are unhappily confirmed, although the official accounts have not yet appeared. The effects of the failure of our attack on Baltimore, and the events in Canada, have already produced consequences in America very different from those calculated on by the advocates for this unnatural and dangerous war; whilst at home the public feelings are vehemently and variously agitated. Some our of our leading journals are for crushing all the United States at once, by sending the Duke of Wellington and fifty thousand troops there! We fear other work may too soon be cut out for that Hero and his army much nearer home, and that this ruinous contest will continue till we become again involved in a new war, with a power we need not name.

Are American Editors in British Pay?

The American government disavow the atrocities said to have been committed by their army in Canada. The President reprobates our conduct, in burning the public edifices at Washington, in pointed terms of indignation. If the American journals were worthy of credit, a general revolt was to have been expected before this, if the *imbecile* President should not resign! So far from these predictions being verified, the leading men, of all parties, seem to rally round the executive power. It is surely a strange mode, adopted by those trans-atlantic editors, of proving *their patriotism* by degrading their own national character, and praising the invaders of their shores! We fear that those philippics are derived from a source nearer to our Treasury than is generally suspected. They operate much more powerfully in England than America, and are admirably calculated to render the war popular, by holding out delusive hopes of disunion and revolt amongst the United States; thus blinding the credulous and unwary to the ruinous results with which this unnatural war is teeming.

What Role for Russian Mediation?

It has been stated by some of our journals that the Emperor of Russia has *notified* to the American plenipotentiaries, that he *will not* interfere in the questions at issue between the United States and Great Britain at the ensuing Congress! After having proffered his mediation, which the Americans accepted, and Great Britain declined; the truth of this asserted notification appears. On the other hand, the ministerial journals affirm, that the Emperor Alexander has been opposed by Great Britain in his views upon Poland, and in consequence thereof has relinquished them. This interference, if true, must, of course, have a powerful tendency to induce him to support our maritime pretensions.

Captain Manners, and the Brave Crew of the Reindeer
From 'Naval Anecdotes.' XXXII 297

The late Captain Manners, of the *Reindeer*, received no fewer than 17 wounds, in the action between that brig and the *Wasp* (American sloop of war). The calves of his legs were carried away early in the action, yet he kept the deck, cheering up his brave crew, and animating the few officers which were on board by his example. Again a shot passed through both thighs, and he fell on his knees, but recovered, stood up, and though bleeding profusely, resolutely refused to quit his deck. Perceiving, however, the great superiority of the enemy in point of guns, and the dreadful havoc which the musketry in the tops was causing on the decks of the *Reindeer*, he called out to his men, "*Follow me, my boys, we must board them.*" He was in the act of getting on board the enemy, when balls from the *Wasp*'s top entered his head, which they completely perforated: he put his hand for a moment to his head, exclaimed, "*Oh God,*" and dropped breathless. Numerous are the instances of individual bravery which have been related to us; suffice it to say, that a braver crew than that of the *Reindeer* never sustained the lustre of the British flag. In the mean time, we are happy to assure our readers, that the intrepid seaman who was sent to the hospital in consequence of having a ramrod shot through his head, is fast recovering. After receiving his desperate wound, he, like his commander, refused to quit the deck, saying to those who begged him to leave his gun, "*If all the wounded of the Reindeer were as able to fight as I am, we should soon make the Americans strike.*"

Captain Manners, soon after the action, was sewed up in his cot and committed to the deep. He was the son of Lord Robert Manners, and inherited all the hereditary bravery of his family. Never was a man more esteemed by all who knew him – he was the idol, the delight of his ship's company, and well did they support him in the trying hour of battle; for long after he had fallen, his brave crew fought the brig till the decks were a sheet of blood, *and no officer remained to commend them but the captain's clerk*!!

1814 – Canadian Campaign

IN THE CAMPAIGN OF 1814 in the Canadas, American offensive operations were again turned, but the polish of military discipline which the American army had acquired defeated all attempts to dislodge it from the Indian territories in the upper Great Lakes, and also defeated a British counter-offensive into Lake Champlain. The only military success for the British cause was the retention of control of Lake Ontario, and British occupation of Maine. Employing two new vessels built over the winter at Kingston, the American dockyard at Oswego was raided in May. The sequel, an engagement with the American flotilla in Sandy Creek, was a signal reverse, but by then the reinforcements which had crossed New Brunswick in the dead of winter had arrived in Kingston to more than replace the losses. The flotilla on Lake Champlain was lost to the Americans during an abortive attack on Plattsburg in September.

The poor relationship between General Prevost and Commodore Yeo, who had had a brilliant war record before he went to Canada, was exacerbated by reverse. This situation is commented on editorially below, pages 263-64 and 266. A letter from 'Iron Gun' suggests that the main reason for the reverse on Lake Champlain was the failure of the flotilla commander to understand the best tactical use of his long guns.

In the end, events on the Virginia coast, and in Louisiana, were to determine the outcome of the war in the north. Maine, the only British conquest, was to be lost when the peace commissioners met at Ghent. The border of 1783 was renewed, with the exception of the Passamaquoddy Islands. Having failed to persuade the Americans to recognise a neutral Indian territory in Michigan and Wisconsin, the Indians of the west were finally left to their fate. Canada was largely restricted to the rocky pre-cambrian shield which did not appear to be of much value at the time.

Letters on Service

Despatches from General Prevost and Commodore Yeo:
Two Points of View

Colonial Department
Downing Street, July 3 1814. XXXII 155-168

Despatches, of which the following are a copy and extract, have been this day received by Earl Bathurst, from Lieutenant-general Sir G. Prevost, Bart.

Head-quarters, L'Acadie, March 31
My Lord, I had scarcely closed the session of the Provisional Legislature, when information arrived, of the enemy having concentrated a considerable force at Plattsburg, for the invasion of Lower Canada.

Major-general Wilkinson advanced on the 19th instant to Chazy, and detached Brigadier-general M'Comb, with a corps of riflemen, and a brigade of infantry in sleighs, across the ice to Isle La Motte, and from thence to Swanton, in the State of Vermont.

On the 22d this corps crossed the line of separation between the United States and Lower Canada, and took possession of Philipsburg, in the seigniority of St. Armand, and on the 23d several guns followed, and a judicious position was selected and occupied, with demonstrations of an intention to establish themselves there in force.

Having previously assembled, at St. John's and in its vicinity, the 13th and 49th regiments, and the Canadian voltigeurs, with a sufficient field train, and one troop of the 19th light dragoons, I placed the whole under the command of Colonel Sir S. Beckwith, and ordered him to advance to dislodge the enemy, should circumstances not disclose this movement to be a feint made to cover other operations. On this I left Quebec. On my route I received a report from Major-general De Rottenburg, of the enemy having retired precipitately from Philipsburg on the 26th, and again crossed Lake Champlain, for the purpose of joining the main body of the American army, near Champlain Town.

On the 30th the enemy's light troops entered Odell Town, followed by three brigades of infantry, commanded by Brigadier-generals Smith, Bissett, and M'Comb, and composed of the 4th, 6th, 10th, 13th, 14th, 20th, 23d, 25th, 29th, 30th, and 34th regiments, a squadron of cavalry, and one eighteen, three twelve, and four six-pounders, drove in our piquets on the road leading from Odell Town to Burton Ville, and commenced an attack on the latter position, but were so well received by the light troops supported by the grenadiers of the Canadian fencibles, that it was not persevered in, and the brigades in advance were directed upon the post at La Cole, entrusted to Major Handcock, of the 13th regiment, whose able conduct on this occasion your Lordship will find detailed in the accompanying report from Lieutenant-colonel Williams, of the 13th, who had the charge of the advanced posts on the Richelieu.

In consequence of the sudden rise of water in every direction, from the melting of the snow and ice, it was with extreme difficulty the enemy withdrew their cannon, and it is now almost impossible for either party to make a movement.

The troops brought forward to support those at Burton Ville and the mill at La Cole, were obliged to wade through mud and water up to their waists, for many miles, before they could attain the points they were directed to occupy. The Indian warriors alone were able to hang on the enemy's rear, whilst retreating to Champlain Town.

I have ascertained the loss of the American army to have exceeded three hundred men in killed and wounded: it is also stated, many of their officers suffered on this occasion.

I have the honour to be,

GEORGE PREVOST

Earl Bathurst, &c.

Head-quarters, Montreal, May 18 1814

My Lord, Since the report which I had the honour to make to your Lordship from L'Acadie, on the 31st March, the enemy have gradually withdrawn their force from the frontiers of Lower Canada, and after having placed garrisons in Plattsburg, Burlington, and Vergennes, have marched the residue of it either to reinforce Sackett's Harbour, or to add to the army forming at Batavia. The two new ships which I had caused to be constructed during the winter at Kingston, having been launched on the 14th of April, and subsequently completely equipped, armed, and manned, I determined to preserve the naval ascendancy which by this accession of strength had been acquired, by employing the squadron with a division of troops in capturing and destroying the dépôts of provisions, naval stores, and ordnance, formed by the enemy at Oswego, for the facility of transport from thence to Sackett's Harbour. I have now the high satisfaction of transmitting to your Lordship a copy of Lieutenant-general Drummond's report to me of the successful termination of that expedition, in which your Lordship will be gratified to observe the spirit of union and cordiality prevailing in both services, and an emulation in the discharge of duty equally honourable to themselves, and advantageous to their country. The principal object in the attack on Oswego being to cripple the resources of the enemy in fitting out their squadron, and particularly their new ships at Sackett's Harbour (their guns and stores of every description being drawn from the former port), and thus to delay, if not altogether to prevent, the sailing of their fleet; I determined to pursue the same policy on Lake Champlain, and therefore directed Captain Pring to proceed with his squadron, on board of which I had placed a strong detachment of the first battalion of marines, towards Vergennes, for the purpose, if practicable, of destroying the new vessels lately launched there, and of intercepting the stores and supplies for their armament and equipment.

Captain Pring accordingly sailed on the 9th instant, having been prevented by contrary winds from reaching his destination until the 14th instant. He found, on arriving off Otter Creek, the enemy so fully prepared to receive him, and their vessels so strongly defended by batteries, and a considerable body of troops, that, after a cannonading with some effect from his gun-boats, he judged it most advisable to abandon his intended plan of attacking them, and to return to Isle Aux Noix. The appearance of our squadron on the Lake has been productive of great confusion and alarm at Burlington, and other places along its shores; and the whole of the population appeared to be turned out for their defence.

GEORGE PREVOST

[It has not been possible to include Lieutenant-General Drummond's account of the attack on Oswego.]

Admiralty Office, July 5, 1814

Copy of a Letter from Commodore Sir J.L. Yeo, Commander-in-chief of his Majesty's Ships and Vessels on the Lakes of Canada, to J.W. Croker, Esq. dated on board H.M.S. Prince Regent, 9th May, 1814

H.M.S. Prince Regent, 9th May, 1814
Sir, My letter of the 15th April last, will have informed their Lordships, that his Majesty's ships *Prince Regent* and *Princess Charlotte* were launched on the preceding day. I now have the satisfaction to acquaint you, for their Lordships' information, that the squadron, by the unremitting exertions of the officers and men under my command, were ready on the 3d instant, when it was determined by Lieutenant-general Drummond and myself that an immediate attack should be made on the forts and town of Oswego, which, in point of position, is the most formidable I have seen in Upper Canada, and where the enemy had, by river navigation, collected from the interior several heavy guns, and naval stores for the ships, and large dépôts of provisions for their army.

At noon, on the 5th, we got off the port, and were on the point of landing, when a heavy gale from the N.W. obliged me to gain an offing. On the morning of the 6th, every thing being ready, 140 troops, 200 seamen, armed with pikes, under Captain Mulcaster, and 400 marines, were put into the boats; the *Montreal* and *Niagara* took their stations abreast, and within a quarter of a mile of the fort, the *Magnet* opposite the town, and the *Star* and *Charwell* to cover the landing, which was effected under a most heavy fire of round, grape, and musketry, kept up with great spirit. Our men having to ascend a very steep and long hill, were consequently exposed to a destructive fire; their gallantry overcoming every difficulty, they soon gained the summit of the hill, and throwing themselves into the foss, mounted the ramparts on all sides, vying with each other who should be foremost. Lieutenant Laurie, my secretary, was the first who gained the ramparts, and Lieutenant Hewett climbed the flag-staff under a heavy fire, and in the most gallant style struck the American colours, which had been nailed to the mast.

My gallant and much esteemed friend, Captain Mulcaster, led the seamen to the assault with his accustomed bravery, but I lament to say, he received a dangerous wound in the act of entering the fort, which I apprehend will, for a considerable time, deprive me of his valuable services; Mr. Scott, my first lieutenant, who was next in command, nobly led them on, and soon gained the ramparts. . . . [etc.]

I have the honour to be, &c.

JAMES LUCAS YEO
Commodore, and Commander in Chief
J.W. Croker, Esq. &c.

Colonial Department
Downing Street, July 19 1814

A despatch, of which the following is an extract, was this day received by Earl Bathurst from Lieutenant-general Sir G. Prevost, dated headquarters, Montreal, June 8 1814
It is with regret I have to report to your Lordship, the unfortunate result of an enterprise made by the boats of the squadron on Lake Ontario, under the commands of Captains Popham and Spilsbury, of the Royal Navy, with nearly 200 seamen and marines, against a flotilla of the enemy's craft laden with naval stores, from Oswego, at Sandy Creek, from whence the stores were to have been conveyed by land to Sackett's Harbour. A large boat, with two long 24-pounders, and a 19 and a half inch cable for the enemy's new ship, having been taken by our squadron then blockading Sackett's Harbour, the information obtained from the prisoners of the sailing from Oswego, of 15 other boats

with stores, led to the attempt which has terminated so disastrously, and for the particulars of which, I beg leave to refer your Lordship to the copy of Captain Popham's letter to Commodore Sir J. Yeo, herewith transmitted.

It is some consolation, under this severe loss, to know, that after this time it will have been supplied by the arrival at Kingston of the first division of the officers and seamen lately landed here from England: the second and third divisions have also passed this place, on their route to Lake Ontario.

By accounts from Major-general Riall, all was quiet on the Niagara frontier on the 27th ult.; and as I have not had any accounts from Michillimackinac since Lieutenant-colonel M'Doual proceeded for that place on the 20th of April, I have every reason to think he must have reached that post in safety, and be fully prepared to defend it against any attempt of the enemy.

[It is not possible to include Captain Stephen Popham's account of this action.]

Defeat on Lake Champlain

Admiralty Office, November 26, 1814. XXXIII 254-257

Copy of a letter from Commodore Sir James Lucas Yeo, Commander-in-chief of his Majesty's Ships and Vessels on the Lakes of Canada, to John Wilson Croker, Esq. dated on board H.M.S. St. Lawrence, at Kingston, 24th September, 1814
Sir, I have the honour to transmit, for the information of the Lords Commissioners of the Admiralty, a copy of a letter from Captain Pring, late commander of his Majesty's brig *Linnet*.

It appears to me, and I have good reason to believe, that Captain Downie was urged, and his ship hurried into action, before she was in a fit state to meet the enemy.

I am also of opinion that there was not the least necessity for our squadron giving the enemy such decided advantages, by going into their bay to engage them; even had they been successful, it would not in the least have assisted the troops in storming the batteries; whereas, had our troops taken their batteries first, it would have obliged the enemy's squadron to quit the bay, and given ours a fair chance.

I have the honour to be, &c.

JAMES LUCAS YEO
Commodore and Commander-in-Chief

United States Ship Saratoga, Plattsburg-bay, lake Champlain, September 12 1814
Sir, The painful task of making you acquainted with the circumstances attending the capture of his Majesty's squadron, yesterday, by that of the Americans, under Commodore M'Donough, it grieves me to state, becomes my duty to perform, from the ever-to-be-lamented loss of that worthy and gallant officer, Captain Downie, who unfortunately fell early in the action.

In consequence of the earnest solicitation of his Excellency, Sir G. Prevost, for the co-operation of the naval force on this Lake to attack that of the enemy, who were placed for the support of their works at Plattsburg, which it was proposed should be stormed by the troops, at the same moment the naval action should commence in the bay; every possible exertion was used to accelerate the armament of the new ship, that the military movements might not be postponed at such an advanced season of the year, longer than was absolutely necessary.

On the 3d instant, I was directed to proceed in command of the flotilla of gun-boats, to protect the left flank of our army advancing towards Plattsburg, and, on the following day, after taking possession, and patrolling the Isle La Motte, I caused a battery of three long 18-pounder guns to be constructed for the support of our position abreast of Little Chazey, where the supplies for the army were ordered to be landed.

The fleet came up on the 8th instant, but for want of stores for the equipment of the guns, could not move forward until the 11th; at day-light we weighed, and at seven were in full view of the enemy's fleet; consisting of a ship, brig, schooner, and one sloop, moored in line, abreast of their encampment, with a division of five gun-boats on each flank; at forty minutes past seven, after the officers commanding vessels and the flotilla had received their final instructions as to the plan of attack, we made sail in order of battle. Captain Downie had determined on laying his ship athwart-hawse of the enemy's, directing Lieutenant M'Ghee, of the *Chubb*, to support me in the *Linnet*, in engaging the brig to the right, and Lieutenant Hicks, of the *Finch*, with the flotilla of gun-boats, to attack the schooner and sloop on the left of the enemy's line.

At eight the enemy's gun-boats and smaller vessels commenced a heavy and galling fire on our line; at ten minutes after eight, the *Confiance* having two anchors shot away from her larboard bow, and the wind baffling, was obliged to anchor (though not in the situation proposed), within two cables' length of her adversary; the *Linnet* and *Chubb* soon afterwards took their allotted stations, something short of that distance, when the crews on both sides cheered, and commenced a spirited and close action; a short time, however, deprived me of the valuable services of Lieutenant M'Ghee, who, from having his cables, bowsprit, and main-boom shot away, drifted within the enemy's line, and was obliged to surrender.

From the light airs and smoothness of the water, the fire on each side proved very destructive from the commencement of the engagement, and with the exception of the brig, that of the enemy appeared united against the *Confiance*. After two hours' severe conflict with our opponent, she cut her cable, run down, and took shelter between the ship and schooner, which enabled us to direct our fire against the division of the enemy's gunboats and ship which had so long annoyed us during our close engagement with the brig, without any return on our part; at this time the fire of the enemy's ship slackened considerably, having several of her guns dismounted, when she cut her cable, and winded her larboard broadside to bear on the *Confiance*, who in vain endeavoured to effect the same operation; at thirty-three minutes after ten, I was much distressed to observe the *Confiance* had struck her colours. The whole attention of the enemy's force then became directed towards the *Linnet*; the shattered and disabled state of the masts, sails, rigging, and yards, precluded the most distant hope of being able to effect an escape by cutting the cable; the result of doing so must, in a few minutes, have been her drifting alongside the enemy's vessels, close under our lee; but in the hope that the flotilla of gun-boats, who had abandoned the object assigned them, would perceive our wants, and come to our assistance, which would afford a reasonable prospect of being towed clear, I determined to resist the then destructive cannonading of the whole of the enemy's fleet, and at the same time despatched Lieutenant H. Drew to ascertain the state of the *Confiance*. At forty-five minutes after ten, I was apprised of the irreparable loss she had sustained by the death of her brave commander (whose merits it would be presumption in me to extol), as well as the great slaughter which had taken place on board, and observing, from the manoeuvres of the flotilla, that I could enjoy no further expectation of relief, the situation of my gallant comrades who had so nobly fought, and even now fast falling by my side, demanded the surrender of his Majesty's brig entrusted to my command, to prevent a useless waste of valuable lives, and, at the request of the surviving officers and men, I gave the painful orders for the colours to be struck.

Lieutenant Hicks, of the *Finch*, had the mortification to strike on a reef of rocks, to the eastward of Crab Island, about the middle of the engagement, which prevented his rendering that assistance to the squadron, that might, from an officer of such ability, have been expected.

The misfortune which this day befell us by capture, will, Sir, I trust, apologize for the lengthy detail, which, in justice to the sufferers, I have deemed necessary to give of the particulars which led to it; and when it is taken into consideration that the *Confiance* was sixteen days before on the stocks, with an unorganized crew, composed of several drafts of men who had recently arrived from different ships at Quebec, many of whom only joined the day before, and were totally unknown either to the officers or to each other, with the want of gun-locks, as well as other necessary appointments not to be procured in this country, I trust you will feel satisfied of the decided advantage the enemy possessed, exclusive of their great superiority in point of force, a comparative statement of which I have the honour to annex. . . .

I have the honour to be, &c.

DAN PRING
Captain, late of H.M. Sloop, *Linnet*

[See lists of the forces of Britain and the United States in the Lakes, pp238-239.]

Correspondence on Tactics and Gunnery: What Went Wrong on Lake Champlain XXXIII 129-132

"Iron Gun" to the Editor, Bristol, 19th December, 1814
Mr. Editor, It is with deep regret that I beg to draw your attention to the late naval engagement on Lake Champlain. Agreeably to Captain Pring's statement, as set forth in the Gazette, he attributes the defeat we have sustained - firstly, to the unorganised state of the crew of the *Confiance*, which was composed of several drafts of men, who had recently arrived from different ships at Quebec, and were totally unknown, either to their officers, or to each other. - Secondly, to the want of gun-locks, as well as other necessary appointments, not attainable in that part of the country; and finally trusts that Sir James Yeo will feel satisfied of the decided advantage the enemy possessed; exclusive of their great superiority in point of force. To investigate and point out a remedy for some of these defects, is the object of this letter.

It is to be lamented, that the crew of the *Confiance* were found to be in that unorganised state as they are reported to have been. This, as well as the unfortunate circumstance of Captain Downie falling so early in the action, must be admitted to have been very disadvantageous; but even under these unfavourable circumstances, the determined and spirited resistance of the crew for two hours and a half, under a constant and severe heavy fire, redounds to their honour and credit. This unorganised state of a crew, might in future be easily obviated, by paying off in England the crews of ships of equal force to those building in Canada, and transmitting thither *both officers and men*; so as to arrive there by the time the vessels are launched they are intended to man: by this simple method the crews would be known to their officers, and they to each other; and would prevent the pretext of their inefficaciousness from ever being again adduced as a cause of defeat.

With respect to the want of gun-locks, as well as other necessary appointments, not procurable in that country, which is asserted as being another cause that led to defeat - it is very hard that such an important expedition should fail, and totally miscarry, through the neglect of those to whom the charge of forwarding them were entrusted. It is to be hoped, that not only a strict inquiry be had, but that a severe example should be made for their delinquency, be their station ever so exalted. This circumstance does of itself speak volumes in support of a measure I suggested the adoption of some time ago, of having committees of naval officers at every dépôt, to survey, inspect, and report on all manner of naval stores previous to their being received into, and issued from every dépôt. If the stores that were intended for the *Confiance*, had been surveyed at Quebec previous to their being sent, the want of gun-locks, &c. would have been immediately discovered, and measures might have been adopted to meet this exigency, by being supplied from any of his Majesty's ships at Quebec, or otherwise.

As to the decided advantage the enemy possessed, exclusive of their great superiority in point of force, Captain P. not having particularised those advantages, nothing can be said on this head; nor from what has been officially published can any judgment be formed of the enemy's great superiority, although a comparative statement is said to be annexed. The American force only is published, whether the omission of the British force proceeded from inadvertence or not, is immaterial; as the Americans have published a statement of the force on both sides, and as the statement of their force nearly corresponds with the statement published in the Gazette, it may be presumed that their account of the English force is also nearly correct. . . .

The number of vessels are equal; the Americans have three galleys less in number than the English, also in the aggregate three guns less than what the English had; but they have a superiority of 137 lbs. in the weight of shot. If the superior force of the Americans should be ascribed to this trifling difference in the weight of their shot, I trust there are but few other British commanders who would deem it of sufficient importance, even to mention it; much less to state it as one of the causes that led to defeat.

From the gallant manner in which Captain Downie led his ship into action, and closing with his opponent at the short distance of only 300 yards, agreeably to the American account, but, as we are officially informed, (it was his intention to lay his ship athwart hawse of the enemy's, which it seems light baffling winds prevented), came to an anchor within two cables' length (nearly 480 yards) little doubt need be entertained, that in adopting this measure, he was confident of success (admitting that his crew was not in the best possible state, and that there was a deficiency of gun-locks).[1] The equipment of the *Confiance* and *Linnet*, agreeable to the above statement, undoubtedly bred this confidence, by their having ordnance of a larger calibre, consequently of superior force than were ever before carried by British vessels of these classes; and considering the comparatively small squadron of the enemy, whereas the British commander that would not have been animated with the same motive, and that would have hesitated in attacking the Americans.

Unfortunately Captain D. did not duly appreciate the weapons he was provided

---

1 Without this article, many a successful action has been fought; nor does it appear that the enemy used them. It is doubtful whether they would have contributed to make the fire of the *Confiance* more destructive than it actually was, and which is attributed to the light airs and smoothness of the water. The utility of a gun-lock is not so manifest in such a state of the elements, as when the winds and water happen to be the reverse of this.

with: if, instead of closing with the enemy, he had brought up at the distance of 10 or 1100 yards, he would have had a decided superiority, from having the greatest number of long guns (and the calm state of the elements at the time), with which he could have annoyed the enemy with equal, if not with better, effect, than at the distance he actually engaged at; but the great point he would have gained, would have been the little service the enemy could have derived from the great superiority they possessed in the number of carronades; for the elevation necessary to be given to a carronade to carry this distance, would have been so great, that none but chance shot would have taken effect; whereby, in closing, he gave up this advantage, and the enemy's 42 and 32-pounder carronades told, not only from greater weight of shot, but from their being quicker loaded; and the facility of running them up, produced every effect over the long guns the enemy could have wished for.

The inducement he had for closing, must have proceeded, not only from the confidence he had in being successful, but to terminate the action speedily; to have accomplished this desirable purpose, he should have directed his guns to have been loaded with two shot each round, which, at the distance he engaged at, would have ranged with effect together; but as there is no account of his having adopted this mode of firing, it may be presumed it was not acted on. I have said thus much, without having the least intention of detracting from his professional ability or judgment as a naval officer, but from the probability of his not being aware of the advantage it was in his power to have possessed. This shews how indispensably necessary it is for a naval officer to acquire a perfect knowledge in the practice of artillery. It has now become equally as imperative on him, to perfect himself on this subject, as any other part of his professional duties. It will almost be impossible for him to attain this desirable object, if government does not afford the means; and this can only be done by having a small establishment, for carrying on a series of artillery experimental practice *afloat*, at one or more of our naval stations, where there is a sufficiency of room in its vicinity for such purposes, such as Portsmouth, Plymouth, or Milford; the adopting of which would be the means of disseminating a practical knowledge, from which the service would derive an inestimable benefit.

[This letter might perhaps have been included in Appendix 8 on Gunnery, Volume IV. Other letters from 'Iron Gun' can be found there.]

1814 – Raids on Washington and Baltimore

THE NAVAL CHRONICLE'S RECORD of the raids on Washington and Baltimore is too extensive for all the letters to be reprinted here. Vice-Admiral Cochrane's dispatch of 2 September was used by the editor to write the account inserted directly into the 'Naval History' section, see above pp240–243. The following service letters from subordinate commanders are placed in chronological order.

Letters on Service
Admiralty Office, September 27, 1814. XXXII 341-348

Captain Wainright [Wainwright], of His majesty's ship *Tonnant*, arrived this morning at this office with despatches from Vice-Admiral the Honourable Sir Alexander Cockrane, K.B. to John Wilson Croker, Esq. of which the following are copies. . .

On board the Resolution Tender, off Mount Calvert,
Monday night, 22d August 1814
I have the honour to inform you, that, after parting from you at Benedict on the evening of the 20th instant, I proceeded up the Patuxent with the boats and tenders, the marines of the ships being embarked in them, under the command of Captain Robyns (the senior officer of that corps in the fleet), and the marine artillery, under Captain Harrison, in their two tenders; the *Severn* and *Hubris* frigates, and the *Manly* sloop, being directed to follow us up the river, as far as might prove practicable.

The boats and tenders I placed in three divisions: the first under the immediate command of Captain Sullivan (the senior commander employed on the occasion) and Badcock; the second, under Captains Money and Somerville; the third, under Captain Ramsay; – the whole under the superintendence and immediate management of Captain Wainwright of the *Tonnant*, Lieutenant James Scott, (1st of the *Albion*) attending as my aide-de-camp.

I endeavoured to keep with the boats and tenders as nearly as possible abreast of the army under Major-general Ross, that I might communicate with him as occasion offered, according to the plan previously arranged; and about mid-day yesterday I accordingly anchored at the ferry-house opposite Lower Marlborough, where I met the General, and where the army halted from some hours, after which he marched for

Nottingham, and I proceeded on for some place with the boats. On our approaching that town a few shot were exchanged between the leading boats and some of the enemy's cavalry; but the appearance of our army advancing caused them to retire with precipitation. Captains Nourse and Palmer, of the *Severn* and *Hubris*, joined me this day with their boats, having found it impracticable to get their ships higher than Benedict.

The Major-General remained with the army at Nottingham, and the boats and tenders continued anchored off it during the night; and soon after day-light this morning the whole moved again forward but the wind blowing during the morning down the river, and the channel being excessively narrow, and the advance of our tenders consequently slow, I judged it advisable to push on with the boats, only leaving the tenders to follow as they could.

On approaching Pig Point (where the enemy's flotilla was said to be), I landed the marines under Captain Robyns on the left bank of the river, and directed him to march round and attack, on the land side, the town situated on the point, to draw from us the attention of such troops as might be there for its defence, and the defence of the flotilla: I then proceeded on with the boats, and, as we opened the reach above Pig Point, I plainly discovered Commodore Barney's broad pendant in the headmost vessel, a large sloop, and the remainder of the flotilla extending in a long line astern of her. Our boats now advanced towards them as rapidly as possible; but, on nearing them, we observed the sloop bearing the broad pendant to be on fire, and she very soon afterwards blew up. I now saw clearly that they were all abandoned, and on fire, with trains to their magazines; and out of the 17 vessels which composed this formidable, and so much vaunted flotilla, 16 were in quick succession blown to atoms, and the seventeenth (in which the fire had not taken) we captured. The commodore's sloop was a large armed vessel; the others were gun-boats, all having a long gun in the bow, and a carronade in the stern; the calibre of the guns and number of the crew of each differed in proportion to the size of the boat, varying from 32-pounders and 60 men to 18-pounders and 40 men. I found here lying above the flotilla, under its protection 18 merchant schooners, some of which not being worth bringing away I caused to be burnt; such as were in good condition I directed to be moved to Pig Point. Whilst employed taking these vessels a few shot were fired at us by some of the men of the flotilla from the bushes on the shore near us; but Lieutenant Scott, whom I had landed for that purpose, soon got hold of them, and made them prisoners. Some horsemen likewise showed themselves on the neighbouring heights, but a rocket or two dispersed them; and Captain Robyns, who had got possession of Pig Point without resistance, now spreading his men through the country, the enemy retreated to a distance, and left us in quiet possession of the town, the neighbourhood, and our prizes.

A large quantity of tobacco having been found in the town at Pig Point, I have left Captain Robyns, with the marines, and Captain Nourse, with two divisions of the boats, to hold the place, and ship the tobacco into the prizes, and I have moved back with the third division to this point, to enable me to confer on our future operations, with the Major-General, who has been good enough to send his Aid-de-camp to inform me of his safe arrival, with the army under his command, at Upper Marlborough. . . .

I have the honour to be, &c.

G. COCKBURN
Rear-Admiral

Vice-Admiral the Hon. Cochrane, K.B. &c.

Colonial Department
Downing Street, September 27, 1814

Captain Smith, Assistant-adjutant-general to the troops under the command of Major-general Ross, arrived this morning with a despatch from that officer, addressed to Earl Bathurst, one of his Majesty's principal secretaries of state, of which the following is a copy:

Tonnant, in the Patuxent, 30th August, 1814
My Lord, I have the honour to communicate to your Lordship, that on the night of the 24th instant, after defeating the army of the United States on that day, the troops under my command entered and took possession of the city of Washington.

It was determined between Sir A. Cochrane and myself, to disembark the army at the village of Benedict, on the right bank of the Patuxent, with the intention of co-operating with Rear-admiral Cockburn, in an attack upon a flotilla of the enemy's gun-boats, under the command of Commodore Barney. On the 20th instant, the army commenced its march, having landed the previous day without opposition: on the 21st it reached Nottingham, and on the 22d moved on to Upper Marlborough, a few miles distant from Pig Point, on the Patuxent, where Admiral Cockburn fell in with and defeated the flotilla, taking and destroying the whole. Having advanced to within sixteen miles of Washington, and ascertaining the force of the enemy to be such as might authorize an attempt at carrying his capital, I determined to make it, and accordingly put the troops in movement on the evening of the 23d. A corps of about 1200 men appeared to oppose us, but retired after firing a few shots. On the 24th, the troops resumed their march, and reached Baldensburg, a village situated on the left bank of the eastern branch of the Potomac, about five miles from Washington.

On the opposite side of that river the enemy was discovered strongly posted on very commanding heights, formed in two lines, his advance occupying a fortified house, which, with artillery, covered the bridge over the eastern branch, across which the British troops had to pass. A broad and straight road leading from the bridge to Washington, ran through the enemy's position, which was carefully defended by artillery and riflemen.

The disposition for the attack being made, it was commenced with so much impetuosity by the light brigade, consisting of the 85th light infantry and the light infantry companies of the army, under the command of Colonel Thornton, that the fortified house was shortly carried, the enemy retiring to the higher grounds.

In support of the light brigade, I ordered up a brigade under the command of Colonel Brooke, who, with the 44th regiment, attacked the enemy's left, the 4th regiment pressing his right with such effect as to cause him to abandon his guns. His first line giving way, was driven on the second, which, yielding to the irresistible attack of the bayonet, and the well-directed discharge of rockets, got into confusion and fled, leaving the British masters of the field. The rapid flight of the enemy, and his knowledge of the country, precluded the possibility of many prisoners being taken, more particularly as the troops had, during the day, undergone considerable fatigue.

The enemy's army, amounting to eight or nine thousand men, with three or four hundred cavalry, was under the command of General Winder, being formed of troops drawn from Baltimore and Pennsylvania. His artillery, ten pieces of which fell into our hands, was commanded by Commodore Barney, who was wounded and taken prisoner. The artillery I directed to be destroyed.

Having halted the army for a short time, I determined to march upon Washington, and reached that city at eight o'clock that night. Judging it of consequence to complete the destruction of the public buildings with the least possible delay, so that the army might retire without loss of time, the following buildings were set fire to and consumed – the Capital, including the Senate-house and House of Representation, the arsenal, the dock-yard, treasury, war-office, President's palace, rope-walk, and the great bridge across the Potomac: in the dockyard a frigate nearly ready to be launched, and a sloop of war, were consumed. The two bridges leading to Washington over the eastern branch had been destroyed by the enemy, who apprehended an attack from that quarter. The object of the expedition being accomplished, I determined, before any greater force of the enemy could be assembled, to withdraw the troops, and accordingly commenced retiring on the night of the 25th. On the evening of the 29th we reached Benedict, and reembarked the following day. In the performance of the operation I have detailed, it is with the utmost satisfaction I observe to your Lordship, that cheerfulness in undergoing fatigue, and anxiety for the accomplishment of the object were conspicuous in all ranks. . . .

I have, &c.

ROB. ROSS
Major-General

Admiralty Office, October 17, 1814. ^{XXXIII 160-172}

Captain Crofton, acting Captain of H.M.S. the *Royal Oak*, arrived this morning at this office, with dispatches from Vice-admiral the Honourable Sir Alexander Cochrane, K.B. addressed to J.W. Croker, Esq. of which the following are copies:

H.M.S. Tonnant, Chesapeake, September 17 1814
Sir, I request that you will be pleased to inform my Lords Commissioners of the Admiralty, that the approaching equinoctial new moon rendering it unsafe to proceed immediately out of the Chesapeake with the combined expedition, to act upon the plans which had been concerted previous to the departure of the *Iphigenia*: Major-general Ross and myself resolved to occupy the intermediate time to advantage, by making a demonstration upon the city of Baltimore, which might be converted into a real attack, should circumstances appear to justify it; and as our arrangements were soon made, I proceeded up this river, and anchored off the mouth of the Patapsco, on the 11th instant, where the frigates and smaller vessels entered at a convenient distance for landing the troops.

At an early hour next morning, the disembarkation of the army was effected without opposition, having attached to it a brigade of six hundred seamen, under Captain Edward Crofton (late of the *Leopard*); the second battalion of marines; the marines of the squadron, and the colonial black marines. Rear-admiral Cockburn accompanied the General, to advise and arrange as might be deemed necessary for our combined efforts.

As soon as the army moved forward, I hoisted my flag in the *Surprise*, and with the remainder of the frigates, bombs, sloops, and the rocket ship, passed further up the river, to render what co-operation could be found practicable.

While the bomb-vessels were working up, in order that we might open our fire upon the enemy's fort at day-break next morning, an account was brought to me, that Major-general Ross, when reconnoitring the enemy, had received a mortal wound by a musket ball, which closed his glorious career before he could be brought off to the ship. It is a tribute due to the memory of this gallant and respected officer, to pause in my relation, while I lament the loss that His Majesty's service, and the army, of which he was one of the brightest ornaments, have sustained by his death. The unanimity, the zeal which he manifested on every occasion, while I had the honour of serving with him, gave life and ease to the most arduous undertakings. Too heedless of his personal security when in the field, his devotion to the care and honour of his army, has caused the termination of his valuable life. The Major-general has left a wife and family, for whom I am confident his grateful country will provide.

The skirmish which had deprived the army of its brave general was a prelude to a most decisive victory over the flower of the enemy's troops. Colonel Brooke, on whom the command devolved, having pushed forward our force to within five miles of Baltimore, where the enemy, about six or seven thousand, had taken up an advanced position, strengthened by field-pieces, and where he had disposed himself, apparently with the intention of making a determined resistance, fell upon the enemy, with such impetuosity, that he was obliged soon to give way, and fly in every direction, leaving on the field of battle a considerable number of killed and wounded, and two pieces of cannon.

For the particulars of this brilliant affair, I beg leave to refer their Lordships to Rear-admiral Cockburn's despatch, transmitted herewith.

[Unfortunately it has not been possible to reproduce it in the Consolidated Edition.]

At day-break the next morning, the bombs having taken their stations within shell range, supported by the *Surprise*, with the other frigates and sloops, opened fire upon the fort that protected the entrance of the harbour, and I had now an opportunity of observing the strength and the preparations of the enemy.

The approach to the town on the land-side was defended by commanding heights, upon which was constructed a chain of redoubts, connected by a breast-work, with a ditch in front, an extensive train of artillery, and a shew of force that was reported to be from fifteen to twenty thousand men.

The entrance by sea, within which the town is retired nearly three miles, was entirely obstructed by a barrier of vessels sunk at the mouth of the harbour, defended inside by gun-boats, flanked on the right by a strong and regular fortification, and on the left by a battery of several heavy guns.

These preparations rendering it impracticable to afford any essential co-operation by sea, I considered that an attack on the enemy's strong position by the army only, with such disparity of force, though confident of success, might risk a greater loss than the possession of the town would compensate for, while holding in view the ulterior operations of this force in the contemplation of His Majesty's Government; and, therefore, as the primary object of our movement had been already fully accomplished, I communicated my observations to Colonel Brooke, who coinciding with me in opinion, it was mutually agreed that we should withdraw.

The following morning the army began leisurely to retire: and so salutary was the effect produced on the enemy by the defeat he had experienced, that notwithstanding every opportunity was offered for his repeating the conflict, with an infinite superiority, our troops re-embarked without molestation; the ships of war dropped down as the army retired.

The result of this demonstration has been the defeat of the army of the enemy, the destruction, by themselves, of a quantity of shipping, the burning of an extensive rope-walk, and other public erections, the causing of them to remove their property from the city, and above all, the collecting and harassing of his armed inhabitants from the surrounding country; producing a total stagnation of their commerce; and heaping upon them considerable expenses, at the same time effectually drawing off their attention and support from other important quarters. . . .

I have the honour to be, &c.

ALEXANDER COCHRANE
Vice Admiral and Commander in Chief

To. J.W. Croker, Esq. &c.

Captain James A. Gordon to Sir Alexander Cochrane, Commander in Chief, &c.
Seahorse, Chesapeake, September 9 1814

Sir, In obedience to your orders, I proceeded into the river Potomac, with the ships named in the margin,[1] on the 17th of last month; but, from being without pilots to assist us through that difficult part of the river called the Kettle-Bottoms, and from contrary winds, we were unable to reach Fort Washington, until the evening of the 27th. Nor was this effected but by the severest labour. I believe each of the ships was not less than twenty different times aground, and each time we were obliged to haul off by main strength; and we were employed warping for five whole successive days, with the exception of a few hours, a distance of more than fifty miles.

The bomb-ships were placed on the evening of the 17th, and immediately began the bombardment of the fort, it being my intention to attack it with the frigates at day-light the following morning. On the bursting of the first shell, the garrison were observed to retreat; but supposing some concealed design, I directed the fire to be continued. At eight o'clock, however, my doubts were removed by the explosion of the powder magazine, which destroyed the inner-buildings, and at day-light on the 28th we took possession. Besides the principal fort, which contained two 52-pounders, two 32 pounders, and eight 24-pounders, there was a battery on the beach of five 18-pounders, a martello tower, with two 12-pounders, and loop-holes for musquetry, and a battery in the rear of two 12 and six 6-pound field-pieces. The whole of these guns were already spiked by the enemy, and their complete destruction, with their carriages also, was effected by the seamen and marines sent on that service in less than two hours. The populous city of Alexandria thus lost its only defence; and, having buoyed the channel, I deemed it better to postpone giving any answer to a proposal made to me for its capitulation until the following morning, when I was enabled to place the shipping in such a position, as would ensure assent to the terms I had decided to enforce.

To this measure I attributed their ready acquiescence, as it removed that doubt of my determination to proceed, which had been raised in the minds of the inhabitants of our army having retired from Washington: this part of our proceedings will be farther explained by the accompanying documents. [Not reproduced here.]

The Honourable Lieutenant Gordon, of this ship, was sent on the evening of the 28th to prevent the escape of any of the vessels comprised in the capitulation, and the whole of those which were sea-worthy, amounting to seventy-one in number, were fitted and loaded by the 31st.

Captain Baker, of the *Fairy*, bringing your orders of the 27th, having fought his way up the river past a battery of five guns, and a large military force, confirmed the rumours, which had already reached me, of strong measures having been taken to oppose our return; and I therefore quitted Alexandria without waiting to destroy those remaining stores which we had not the means of bringing away.

1 *Seahorse, Euryalus, Devastation, Aetna, Meteor, Erebus, Anna-Maria* despatch-boat.

Contrary winds again occasioned us the laborious task of warping the ships down the river, in which a day's delay took place, owing to the *Devastation* grounding. The enemy took advantage of this circumstance to attempt her destruction by three fire vessels, attended by five row-boats; but their object was defeated by the promptitude and gallantry of Captain Alexander, who pushed off with his own boats, and being followed by those of the other ships, chased the boats of the enemy up to the town of Alexandria. The cool and steady conduct of Mr. John Moore, midshipman of the *Seahorse*, in towing the nearest fire-vessel on shore, while the others were removed from the power of doing mischief by the smaller boats of the *Devastation*, entitles him to my highest commendation.

The *Meteor* and the *Fairy*, assisted by the *Anna-Maria* despatch-boat, a prize gun-boat, and a boat belonging to the *Euryalus*, with a howitzer, had greatly impeded the progress of the enemy in their works, notwithstanding which they were enabled to increase their battery to eleven guns, with a furnace for heating shot. On the 3d, the wind coming to the N.W. the *Etna* [*Aetna*] and *Erebus* succeeded in getting down to their assistance, and the whole of us, with the prizes, were assembled there on the 4th, except the *Devastation*, which, in spite of our utmost exertion in warping her, still remained five miles higher up the river. This was the moment when the enemy made his greatest efforts to effect our destruction.

The *Erebus* being judiciously placed by Captain Bartholomew in an admirable position for harassing the workmen employed in the trenches, was attacked by three field-pieces, which did her considerable damage before they were beaten off. And, another attempt being made to destroy the *Devastation* with fire-vessels, I sent the boats, under Captain Baker, to her assistance; nothing could exceed the alacrity with which Captain Baker went on this service, to which I attribute the immediate retreat of the boats and fire-vessels. His loss, however, was considerable, owing to their having sought refuge under some guns in a narrow creek thickly wooded, from which it was impossible for him to dislodge them.

On the 5th at noon, the wind coming fair, and all my arrangements being made, the *Seahorse* and *Euryalus* anchored within short musket-shot of the batteries, while the whole of the prizes passed betwixt us and the shoal; the bombs, the *Fairy* and *Erebus*, firing as they passed, and afterwards anchoring in a favourable position for facilitating by means of their force, the further removal of the frigates. At 3 p.m. having completely silenced the enemy's fire, the *Seahorse* and *Euryalus* cut their cables, and the whole of us proceeded to the next position taken up by the troops, where they had two batteries, mounting from 14 to 18 guns, on a range of cliffs of about a mile extent, under which we were of necessity obliged to pass very close. I did not intend to make the attack that evening, but the *Erebus* grounding within range, we were necessarily called into action. On this occasion the fire of the *Fairy* had the most decisive effect, as well as that of the *Erebus*, while the bombs threw their shells with excellent precision, and the guns of the batteries were thereby completely silenced by about eight o'clock.

At day light on the 6th, I made signal to weigh, and so satisfied were the whole of the parties opposed to us of their opposition being ineffectual, that they allowed us to pass without further molestation. . . .

1814 – The End of the War With America

THE DISAPPOINTING OUTCOME of the campaign in the Canadas was very demoralising for *The Naval Chronicle*'s correspondents. The editors had long ago concluded that no good could come of the war, and reported that the raid on Washington appeared to be strengthening, rather than weakening, the American resolve. Suddenly at the end of the year, however, it was learnt that terms of peace had been negotiated at Ghent, and that USS *President*, one of the super-frigates, had been defeated by HMS *Endymion*. The expedition to carry the war to Louisiana had already sailed, but the news of that disaster was yet to arrive.

From the 'Naval History of the Present Year,' 1814
October–November. XXXII 431-433

The War with America Britain Cannot Win

Just as our last was published, the Speech of the American President Mr. Madison arrived in this metropolis. It betrays no symptoms of fear or despondency; but on the contrary, pronounces with confidence a prophecy we fear will prove too true; i.e. that the longer we continue our hostile efforts, the more certain and decisive will be our final discomfiture.

The President affirms that no compensation can atone for the loss of character with the world occasioned by the destruction of the public edifices at Washington.

Mr. Madison laid before Congress the proposals made by our ministers at Ghent, and those, joined to the recent conflagration of the capital, seems to have concentrated all the energies of America decisively in favour of war. All parties seem united, and the general cry is for vengeance against Great Britain!

Were Blacks Betrayed?

The most flagitious charge adduced against this country, is that of having sold in the West Indies the slaves whom we decoyed to our ships, under the promise of freedom! - We dare not affirm that no individuals belonging to our civil or military department

262

have been guilty of this infamous practice, although we earnestly hope it will prove so; but sure we are, that the most signal punishment in the power of the government to inflict awaits the miscreants who have so dishonoured themselves and country. We think it scarcely necessary to say, that ministers disowned the imputation in the most indignant terms. It is a charge admirably calculated to increase the dislike of our national character, which is too predominant on the continent of Europe.

Defeat on Lake Champlain

The rumoured defeat of our naval squadron on Lake Champlain turned out but too well founded - it has been taken or dispersed, and its gallant commander slain! - On the heels of this disastrous intelligence came the news of the retreat of our army from before Plattsburg, attended with circumstances peculiarly galling to the feelings of the nation.

These defeats and disasters in America excited the most rapturous applause from the friends of that people in Paris. In the theatres, coffee-houses, and places of public resort were heard the loudest acclamations and prognostics of our fall!

Desertion to the Enemy a Growing Problem

But the worst, the most alarming feature, is the desertion of our forces, particularly from the army, to the Americans. Our officers invited the American negroes to desert their masters; what those masters say we did with them, we have already noticed. What the United States have done by way of retaliation, it is to be feared we shall shortly feel, if the ruinous and destructive contest is not speedily closed.

In addition to other temptations, such as money, and protection offered on the spot, it has been proposed in Congress, and scarcely a doubt remains but it will pass into a law, to bestow one hundred acres of fertile land upon every military person who would desert from our army. This measure will of course extend to our seamen: with such inducements, it may be found impossible to prevent desertions growing to an extend truly alarming; nor have our Government the means of gaining the seamen or soldiers of the United States by bribes equally attractive. The *principle* of this mode of warfare is loudly decried; but alas! we have ourselves made too free with *principles* to expect much pity, suffer what we may. Our disreputable mode of predatory war, the proclamations calling on the negroes to desert, and the destruction of Washington, are events that constantly stare us in the face, and furnish an apology for every mode of retaliation adopted by the enemy.

Prevost and Yeo Openly at Odds

In the *Gazette* of Saturday evening last (26th inst.), appeared the despatches of General Sir George Prevost, and Commodore Sir James Lucas Yeo. They oppose the most flat contradictions to each other, and prove that those two officers can no longer act in conjunction. The public feeling is decidedly against the commander of our army; but it should not be forgotten, that Captain Sir James Yeo was distant from the scene of action, and his judgment, of course, more liable to err than that of a commander-in-chief upon the spot.

To counterbalance the gloomy narrations of discomfiture and disgrace, the public mind has been flattered for a week past with the hope of our fleet and army having taken Sackett's Harbour, and destroyed Commodore Chauncey's squadron: no official intelligence had arrived when these sheets went to press.

In our article relative to the American Question, will be found some observations on the negotiations and negotiators at Ghent that are yet proceeding.

Want of room obliges us to pass over many interesting points connected with the American naval war.

Congress at Vienna

As to the proceedings of Congress at Vienna, it seems to be animated by a spirit we hoped not to have seen appear. The general sentiment appears to be, that the great powers have abandoned that moderation and self-denial which gave them so strong a claim to the gratitude and confidence of mankind; and if so, the speedy downfall of the fabric they are rearing will inevitably ensue.

Plymouth Breakwater

The total expence of the erection of the breakwater at Plymouth, will, it is understood, fall considerably under the estimate. It will not be finished in a rough state under five years more. When all the massive stones, &c. have formed a solid and imperishable base, an elegant pier, with a light-house, will be erected; and when completed, it will be a lasting memorial worthy of the nation and the age.

Correspondence: The Poverty of British Naval Leadership XXXII 487-488

"Alfred" to the Editor
December 16, 1814
Mr. Editor, The almost complete want of success which has attended the operation of the British fleet and armies during the last campaign, which may be now said to be entirely terminated, has produced, as was to be expected, the greatest sensation throughout the kingdom; the force, of both descriptions [ie naval and military], sent to the American coast, was certainly ample, and of the best description; and, had it been *properly directed*, must infallibly have produced such an impression, as to have effected the strongest hopes of our being able, in the course of *another* campaign, to have brought our arrogant enemy to terms, commensurate with the heavy expenses incurred in carrying on the war, and securing the naval rights of our country. But the spell is *now* broke; - the Americans believe, and experience nearly justifies the belief, that their men of war are an equal match, if not *superior*, to ours; the fatal action on Lake Champlain confirms *them*, no doubt, in such hopes, and must make every man, at all interested in the glory and honour of his country, truly anxious to see the boasted superiority of the British navy re-established on the firmest foundation. Nor have we been unfortunate at sea only; it is with no small degree of mortification, that, when we turn our eyes to the victorious hands of a Wellington; when, placed under another commander in chief, we no longer hear the pleasure of victory. No: we hear the bursting exclamations of disappointed valour on every hand, demanding a leader who will lead them to victory, or glorious death! During the last campaign in Canada, without gaining a single trophy except in the hard-fought action at Chippawa, we have lost a *very great number of men*, and *many* of our best officers. The names of Colonels Drummond, Scott, and Gordon,

will long be remembered with enthusiasm and admiration in the regiments they commanded (now complete skeletons), and by the whole British army. Will it be believed that, with an army of twenty thousand men, we have not *gained*, but *lost*, *ground*, in Canada; when the Americans, opposed to us, never amounted to the same number, and were composed partly of militia. It is not for me, at present, to blame our commander-in-chief in that country; they will, no doubt, have an opportunity of *shewing*, whether they obeyed their instructions, whether they did all they *might* have done, and whether the blame rests with the general at home, or with them. At the same time I must declare my satisfaction, that an early investigation is to take place in both Houses of Parliament, relative to the management of the navy: that this is necessary, few will be hardy enough to deny; for the whole country are sensible, that the glory of the British arms, both by sea and land, have been tarnished: that our want of success cannot be owing to want of means, and that the blame must lay with the ministry or commanders; and it is fit the country should know who *were* in fault. I have no doubt the subject will receive all the consideration it deserves; and I hope it will be recollected, that it is the possession of the trident, the dominion of the seas, the interest of Britain's best bulwarks that is at stake, and that if these are lost, the greatness of the country is endangered, the pillars of her prosperity undermined, and the downfall of her empire at hand. I would therefore entreat of the members of both Houses, to go into the consideration of this momentous question, with the firmest determination of doing their duty to their country. The power of Britain is great indeed; her naval power and resources what country in Europe, or the world, nay, what combination of hostile fleets, can withstand? Shall then the small, but rapidly increasing, and active squadron of American men of war, be able to set us at defiance? This is strange, 'tis passing strange; and were it not a fact, could scarcely be credited.

Would it have been believed, when the war commenced, that three years afterwards they would have had a single man of war to send to sea; scarcely, I think: yet, during that long period, we have taken *only two* of their frigates at *sea*, and destroyed *two* in harbour. With the powerful force we sent, or might have sent, to the coast of America, certainly their whole navy ought to have been destroyed in port; this was the easiest way to get at them; for when once at sea, they have uniformly (with the exception of the *Essex* and *Argus*) eluded our search. After pointing out what *might* have been done *some time ago*, it would be some consolation if I could shew what might *now* be done to restore the lustre of our arms. On the coast of America, I greatly fear, the enemy will, ere the commencement of another campaign, be well, too well, prepared for us; and that any attempts to destroy their men of war by coup de main, will be too late; and in Canada we have ground to recover, and disasters by sea and land to repair; that this may be effectually done, if the war continues, is my earnest wish, as it must be of every true Briton.

I would only beg to recommend, in the most earnest manner, that, if we *do* continue the war, as it must be a most expensive one, and if unsuccessful, most ruinous to the *greatness* of the British empire, that we put forth *all* our strength, and effectually rescue Canada, by a formidable army, and an entire superiority on the lakes; which, I hope, the brave Owen will accomplish. If the American coast is still vulnerable, a considerable force ought to be kept afloat to annoy them in every possible way; but let us not fritter away our means, as has been hitherto done in America; let us play a great game, and teach our arrogant enemy, that the British Lion, when he shakes his mane in earnest, fears not the power of any foe - let our naval force be kept full and effective on the Lakes and coast, and let it be carefully borne in mind, that *one* more unsuccessful campaign, if war goes on, will entirely ruin our cause, and blast our maritime greatness.

N.B. It would be great injustice to Captain Gordon of the *Seahorse*, not to mention the very complete success which attended his expedition, as well as our brilliant coup de main, at Washington - these, however, comprise our successful efforts: at Penobscot there was no resistance.

From the 'Naval History of the Present Year,' 1814
November-December. ^{XXXII 502-503}

Why is America so Powerful at Sea?

The latest accounts from America announced that their line-of-battle ships were launched, fitted out, manned with a thousand prime seamen each, and were soon expected to sail: the *Guerriere* frigate, of 64 guns, was also ready for sea, as were several strong ships - their navy thus growing into importance under the pressure of a war with the greatest naval power that ever existed! There is something inexplicably strange in this phenomena - the country may perhaps demand the solution at the hands of those who have had the absolute disposal of our thousand ships of war!

Yeo vs Prevost

In the last Retrospect, the Editor remotely hinted at the possibility of Commodore Sir James Yeo having given too hasty an opinion respecting the late unfortunate battle of Lake Champlain. He has authority on which he has every right to place reliance, for stating, that General Sir George Prevost *did not* act in the way that has been so generally stated, nor perhaps deserve the very severe ex-parte censures that have been pronounced against him.

Three thousand seamen, according to the latest accounts, were stated to be wanting to complete the complements of our ships of war on the American station. Without alluding to our loss by desertions to the Americans, we need but state that the merchants of Quebec gave £6 or £8 per month for able seamen, whilst the pay in the King's ships was less than a fourth part of that sum.

Peace with America

The last accounts from America were warlike in the extreme: they held out the prospect of a long and bloody war, in which one of the two countries must succumb: the public mind was in daily expectance of hearing of the rupture of the negotiations at Ghent - when, lo and behold! - on the 26th of December, news arrived that a Treaty of Peace was signed at Ghent on the 24th - which was officially announced to the Lord Mayor; and on the 27th the Treaty was ratified by the Prince Regent!

The Editor closed his last essay on the American Question, with the following lines: - "The best that now remains for us to *hope is*, that a speedy peace may arrest the progress of an hopeless war." His Majesty's ministers seem to have become converts to his opinion!

December-January. ^{XXXIII 70-72}

The Terms of Peace

The following is, in substance, stated to be the terms of peace with the United States:

1. All discussions of our maritime rights to be waived on both sides.

2. Mr. Madison does not insist on our giving up the prizes captured in retaliation of the Berlin and Milan Decrees.

3 We leave our Indian allies as we found them in 1812.

4 We give up our conquests, and particularly the Province of Maine, of which our commandants took permanent possession by a solemn proclamation, and required from the inhabitants an oath of allegiance to his Majesty. We are, however, permitted to retain the islands in Passamaquoddy Bay, which were ours by the treaty of 1783.

5 Commissioners are to be appointed on both sides, to determine whether there shall be any, and what safe and practicable communication between Quebec and Upper Canada, together with all other disputed questions of territory.

6 We are to be allowed the exclusive enjoyment of the right of fishing on our own coast of Newfoundland, and of trading to our own settlements in the East Indies.

[The Peace Treaty, Gazetted 14 March 1815, was printed in Vol. XXXIII, pp242-248; and President Madison's speech to Congress, 18 February 1815, recommending the treaty, was printed on pp389-390.]

Earl St Vincent's Birthday
From 'Naval Anecdotes.' *XXXIII 112*

Earl St. Vincent attained the 80th year of his age on Friday, the 20th of January, on which occasion his Lordship gave an elegant entertainment at Rochets-hall, in Essex, at which the Noble Admiral presided in perfect health and spirits.

From the 'Naval History of the Present Year,' 1815
January–February. *XXXIII 156-158*

USS President Captured

Our hopes have been most honourably realized in the capture of the United States ship *President*, Commodore Decatur commander, by the British frigate *Endymion*; and we most cordially congratulate Captain Hope, his officers and men, on the merited success of their gallantry and skill, in so bravely maintaining the reputation of their country - accustomed to capture and destroy, in a few hours, whole fleets of powerful and superior magnitude. We say, *maintaining* the reputation of this country; for, surely, it can never have been seriously considered as lost by *two* or *three* instances of advantage obtained by a morally-insuperable superiority of force. It was, however, necessary to check the conceited sauciness of the enemy, thus assumed; - and to Captain Hope, his officers and men, the country is indebted for having contributed so honourably and effectually to that desirable end; - Nor are the vigilance and exertions of the whole of that small squadron of observation, of which the *Endymion* was a part, to be overlooked, in contemplating the brilliant achievement resulting from them.

It appears that the *Majestic*, Captain Hayes; the *Tenedos*, Captain Hyde Parker; *Endymion*, Captain Hope; and *Pomone*, Captain Lumley, were stationed off Sandy Hook, to prevent the escape of the *President*, and other vessels ready for sea at Staten Island. They had been repeatedly blown off from their station, and had as often, under the direction of Captain Hayes, been judiciously placed on that point of bearing that was conceived likely would be the enemy's track in his egress. They were ultimately blown off in a snow storm, when, still adhering to their plan of getting in to the supposed track of the enemy in the event of his sailing, they, an hour before day-light saw a ship and a brig standing south and east, about two miles on the *Majestic*'s weather-bow; - the signal for chase was made, and it is hardly necessary to say, was promptly obeyed. In the course of the day, we are told, the chase became extremely interesting, by the endeavours of the enemy to escape, and the exertions of all the captains to bring their ships alongside of him. At half past five in the evening the exertions of Captain Hope effected his purpose, and the action commenced on both sides, and was continued during two hours and a half with the utmost gallantry and spirit; the *Endymion*'s sails being then cut from the yards, the enemy got ahead; - the action ceased, and the *Endymion* bent new sails to enable her to renew it. In the meanwhile at half past eleven at night, the *Pomone* got up with the *President*, and firing a few shots, the enemy hailed to say she had already surrendered.

The vessel in company was the *Macedonian* brig, but by her superior sailing she effected her escape.

The following comparative statement of force will prove it an *honourable* victory on the part of Captain Hope and his brave companions.

President	Endymion
34 24-pounder guns	26 24-pounder guns
20 42-pounder carronades	22 32-pounder carronades
4 6-pounder guns \ in the	
2 4-pounder guns / tops	
60 guns of all sizes	48 guns of all sizes
Full complement 490	Full complement 240 men

The weight of shot fired at one round:
1688 lb.   1324 lb.

Tonnage, about 1600 tons   1277 tons

The killed and wounded:
said to have been 100 men   25 men

The *President* was bound to the Island of Pulo Aor, to cruise against our trade between Barbary and China, with several masters of American East India ships, bound as pilots and volunteers.

We look for (and we hope, not in vain) the capture of the remaining principals, at least, of the American navy. . . .

1814 – USS President and HMS Endymion

THE CAPTURE OF ONE OF the American super-frigates was, for the Royal Navy, a satisfactory conclusion of the naval war against the United States. It was *Endymion* which fought her, and suffered in return. *The Naval Chronicle* calculated that the *President* could deliver 1688 pounds of shot in a single discharge, both broadsides simultaneously, while the *Endymion*, an exceptionally strong frigate by Royal Navy standards, could deliver only 1324 pounds. *Endymion*, however, was part of a strong squadron which considerably outnumbered the American. It was Sir Henry Hotham's management of the problem of blockading New York harbour which ensured the triumphant outcome.

Despatches Reporting the Battle
Letters on Service
Admiralty Office, February 18 1815. XXXIII 259-262

Copy of a letter from Rear-Admiral the Hon. Sir H. Hotham, K.C.B. to John Wilson Croker, Esq. dated on board H.M.S. Superb, at anchor before New London, January 23
Sir, I have the honour to request you will be pleased to lay the enclosed copy of a letter and its enclosures, which I have this day addressed to Vice-Admiral Sir Alexander Cochrane, the commander-in-chief, detailing the capture of the United States' ship *President*, on the 15th instant, under the circumstances therein mentioned, before the Lords Commissioners of the Admiralty, with which, in his absence, I have directed Lieutenant Hare, commanding his Majesty's schooner, *Picton*, to proceed forthwith to England for their Lordships' information.

I have the honour to be, &c.

HENRY HOTHAM, Rear Admiral

[John Hayes to Rear-Admiral the Honourable Sir H. Hotham]
Majestic, at Sea, January 17, 1815, lat. 39 min, 43 deg. N. long. 7 minutes 53 deg. W.
Sir, I have the honour to acquaint you, that notwithstanding my utmost endeavours to

269

keep the squadron committed to my charge close in with Sandy Hook, agreeably to your directions, for the purpose of preventing the escape of the United States' ship *President*, and other vessels ready for sea at Staten Island, we were repeatedly blown off by frequent gales; but the very great attention paid to my orders and instructions by the respective captains, in situations difficult to keep company, prevented separation; and whenever the wind did force us from the coast, I invariably, on the gale moderating, placed the squadron on that point of bearing from the Hook I judged it likely, from existing circumstances, would be the enemy's track; and it is with great pleasure I have now to inform you of the success of the squadron, in the capture of the United States' ship *President*, Commodore Decatur, on Sunday night, after an anxious chase of 18 hours.

On Friday, the *Tenedos* joined me, with your order to take Captain Parker in that ship under my command; we were then in company with the *Endymion* and *Pomone*, off the Hook, and in sight of the enemy's ships; but that night the squadron was blown off again in a severe snow-storm. On Saturday, the wind and weather became favourable for the enemy, and I had no doubt but he would attempt his escape that night; it was impossible, from the direction of the wind, to get in with the Hook, and, as before stated (in preference to closing the land to the southward), we stood away to the northward and eastward, till the squadron reached the supposed track of the enemy; and what is a little singular, at the very instant of arriving at that point, an hour before day-light, Sandy Hook bearing W.N.W. fifteen leagues, we were made happy by the sight of a ship and brig standing to the southward and eastward, and not more than two miles on the *Majestic*'s weather bow; the night signal for a general chase was made, and promptly obeyed by all the ships.

In the course of the day, the chase became extremely interesting by the endeavours of the enemy to escape, and the exertions of the captains to get their respective ships alongside of him; the former by cutting away his anchors, and throwing overboard every movable article, with a great quantity of provisions, and the latter by trimming their ships in every way possible to effect their purpose. As the day advanced, the wind declined, giving the *Endymion* an evident advantage in sailing; and Captain Hope's exertions enabled him to get his ship alongside of the enemy, and commence close action, at half an hour past five o'clock in the evening, which was continued with great gallantry and spirit on both sides, for two hours and a half, when the *Endymion*'s sails being cut from the yards, the enemy got ahead; Captain Hope taking this opportunity to bend new sails to enable him to get his ship alongside again, the action ceased, till the *Pomone* getting up at half past eleven at night, and firing a few shots, the enemy hailed to say, she had already surrendered.

The ship on being taken possession of, proved to be the *President*, as above stated, commended by Commodore Decatur. ...

I have the honour to be, &c.

JOHN HAYES
Captain

Rear-Admiral the Honourable Sir H. Hotham

[In Vol. xxxv, pp34-35 were published 'Minutes of the Action between H.M.S. *Endymion*, and the United States Ship *President*, on the 15th January, 1815, extracted from the *Endymion*'s Log-book.']

Commodore Decatur's Account of the Capture of the President
XXXIII 215-217

Commodore Decatur to the Honourable Benjamin Crowninshield, Secretary of the Navy.

His Britannic Majesty's ship Endymion, at sea, January 18, 1815
Sir, The painful duty of detailing to you the particular causes which preceded and led to the capture of the late United States frigate *President*, by a squadron of His Britannic Majesty's ships (as per margin) has devolved upon me. In my communication of the 14th, I made known to you my intention to sail on that evening; owing to some mistake of the pilots, the ship in proceeding to sea grounded on the bar, where she continued to strike heavily for an hour and a half. Although she had broken several of her rudder braces, and had received such other material injury as to render her return into port desirable, I was unable to do so from the strong westerly wind which was then blowing; it being now high water, it became necessary to force her over the bar before the tide fell; in this we succeeded by ten o'clock, when we shaped our course along the shore of Long Island for 50 miles, and then steered S.E. by E.; at five o'clock three ships were discovered ahead, we hauled the ship up immediately, and passed two miles to the northward of them; at day-light we discovered four ships in chase, one on each quarter, and two astern, the leading ship of the enemy a razee, and about three miles distant: at meridian, the wind became light and baffling; we had increased our distance from the razee, but the next ship astern, which was also a large ship, had gained and continued to gain upon us considerably; we immediately occupied all hands to lighten ship, by starting water, cutting away the anchors, throwing overboard provisions, cables, spare spars, boats, and every article that could be got at, keeping the sails wet from the royal down. At three, we had the wind quite light; the enemy, who had now been joined by a brig had a strong breeze, and were coming up with us rapidly; the *Endymion* (mounting 50 guns, 24-pounders on her main-deck), had now approached us within gun shot, and had commenced a fire with her bow-guns, which we returned from our stern; at five o'clock she had obtained a position on our starboard quarter, within half point blank shot, on which neither our stern nor our quarter guns would bear; we were now steering E. by N. the wind N.W. I remained with her in this position for half an hour, in the hope that she would close with us on our broadside, in which case I had prepared my crews to board; but from his continuing to yaw his ship to maintain his position, it became evident that to close was not his intention; every fire now cut some of our sails or rigging; to have continued our course under these circumstances would have been placing it in his power to cripple us without being subject to injury himself; and to have hauled up more to the northward to bring our stern-guns to bear, would have exposed us to his raking fire.

It was now dusk, when I determined to alter my course south, for the purpose of bringing the enemy abeam; and although their ships astern were drawing up fast, I felt satisfied I should be enabled to throw him out of the combat before they could come up, and was not without hopes, if the night proved dark (of which there was every appearance) that I might still be enabled to effect my escape. Our opponent kept off at the same instant that we did, and our fire commenced at the same time; we continued engaged steering south, with steering sails set, two hours and a half, when we completely succeeded in dismantling her. - Previously to her dropping entirely out of the action, there were intervals of minutes when the ships were broadside and broadside, in which she did not fire a gun.

At this period (half-past eight o'clock) although dark, the other ships of the squadron were in sight and nearly within gun-shot, we were, of course, compelled to abandon her; in assuming our former course for the purpose of avoiding the squadron, we were compelled to present our stern to our antagonist; but such was his state, although we were thus exposed and within range of his guns, that he did not avail himself of this favourable opportunity of raking us; we continued this course until 11 o'clock, when two fresh ships of the enemy (the *Pomone* and *Tenedos*) had come up; the *Pomone* had opened her fire on the larboard bow, within musket-shot, the other about two cables' length astern, taking a raking position on one quarter, and the rest (with the exception of the *Endymion*, which ship was not in sight) within gun-shot.

Thus situated, with about one-fifth of my crew killed or wounded, my ship crippled, and a more than fourfold force opposed to me, without a chance of escape left, I deemed it my duty to surrender. ...

For twenty-four hours after the action it was nearly calm, and the squadron were occupied in repairing the crippled ships; such of the crew of the *President* as were not badly wounded were distributed on board the different ships: myself, and a part of my crew, were put on board this ship.

On the 17th we had a gale from the eastward, when this ship lost her bowsprit, fore and main-masts, and mizen top-mast, all of which were badly wounded, and was, in consequence of her shattered condition, obliged to throw overboard all her upper-deck guns. Her loss in killed and wounded must have been very great: they appear extremely anxious to conceal it. The number thrown overboard during the action, and the day following, I have not been able to ascertain: ten were buried after I came on board (36 hours after the action); the badly wounded, such as are compelled to keep their cots, occupy the gun-deck from the cabin bulk-head to the main-mast.

[According to Captain Hope's return, *Endymion* lost 11 killed and 14 wounded.]

From the crippled state of the *President*'s spars, I feel satisfied she could not have saved her masts; and I feel serious apprehensions for the safety of our wounded left on board.

It is due to Captain Hope to state, that every attention has been paid by him to myself and Officers that have been placed on board his ship, that delicacy and humanity could dictate.

I have the honour to be, with much respect, Sir, your obedient servant,

S. DECATUR

The Hon. Benjamin Crowninshield, Secretary of the Navy

The British squadron referred to in above letter: *Majestic* (razee), *Endymion*, *Pomone*, *Tenedos*, and *Dispatch* brig.

1815 – Defeat at New Orleans

THE RAID ON NEW ORLEANS was the last act of the American war, and a British defeat. The operation failed largely because poor intelligence led to dangerous deployment. As not infrequently happened in the centuries before electronic communication systems, the attack took place subsequent to the terms of peace being agreed at Ghent on 14 December 1814. The Americans, although triumphant, had little reason to wish to renew the struggle, which had not led to the conquest of Canada and had never been popular amongst the mercantile community, which had been badly hurt by the naval blockade.

Overleaf - Sketch of the position of the British and American Forces during the operations against New Orleans, from 23d December, 1814, to 18th January, 1815. Engraved by Rowe, from a drawing by J.E. XXXIII 484-488.

The peace with America enables us to view with calmness the operations of that unfortunate contest to which it has happily succeeded - *esto perpetua* - May we henceforth consider ourselves as we really are, two nations from one stock - one family separated for the greater extension of mutual benefit - and whatever privileges may have been assumed by the elder branch, the parent stock, let it be also considered that they have never been exercised beyond the necessity imposed by adventitious and unavoidable circumstances. The annexed plate is a view of the respective positions, &c. of the adverse forces in the late expedition to New Orleans, and will be found useful as an illustration of the received statements respecting its progress and result.

The combined land and sea forces employed in this expedition, were commanded by Major-general Sir E.M. Pakenham, K.B., and Vice-admiral the Honourable Sir A. Cochrane, K.B., and arrived at the entrance of Chandeleur islands, on the 8th December, 1814. Captain Gordon in the *Seahorse*, with the *Armide* and *Sophie*, had been sent by Sir A. Cochrane from off Pensacola to the anchorage within Isle au Vaisseau, and reported the *Armide* to have been fired at by two gun-vessels of the enemy from within a chain of small islands that run parallel to the coast from Mobile towards Lac Borgne, which had been afterwards joined by three others.

The necessity of destroying these vessels was immediately evident as the Bayou Catalan, at the head of Lac Borgne, was the destined place of disembarkation, and between sixty and seventy miles from the inner anchorage of the frigates and troop ships. On the 12th, Sir A. Cochrane ordered Captain Lockyer of the *Sophie*, with Captain Montresor of the *Manly*, and Captain Roberts of the *Meteor*, and the launches, barges, and pinnaces of the squadron under his command to proceed for that purpose.

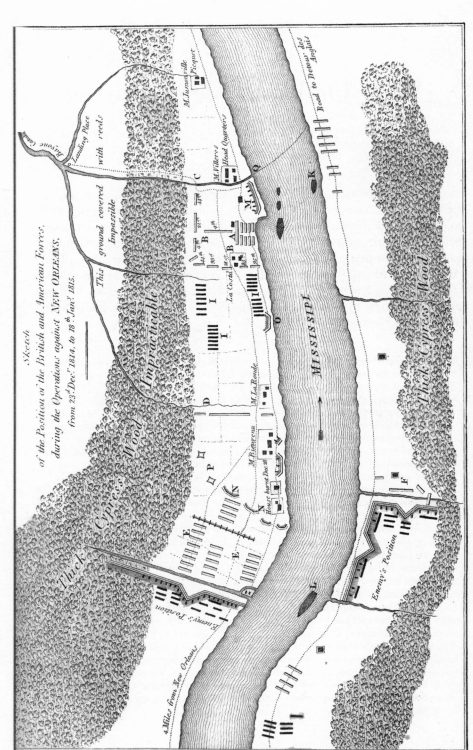

Sketch
of the Position of the British and American Forces,
during the Operations against NEW ORLEANS,
from 23ᵈ Decʳ 1814, to 18 ᵗʰ Janʸ 1815.

Bayou Coast

Landing Place

This ground covered
with reeds
Impassible

Thick Cypress Wood

Impracticable

Cypress Wood

Thick Cypress Wood

M. Jumonville

Picquet

M. Villere's

Head Quarters

C

M

B

44ᵗʰ
93ᵈ
4ᵗʰ
7ᵗʰ

B

La Coste

I

I

I

I

M. La Ronde

D

P

P

N

M. Bienvenu

House burnt Dec 28

E

E

E

Enemy's Position

MISSISSIPI

Road to Detours des

K

O

O

L

F

Enemy's Position

4 Miles from New Orleans

Published June 30 1815, by J.Gold, Naval Chronicle Office, 103, Shoe Lane, London.

Accordingly Captain Lockyer formed the boats into three divisions, the first being headed by himself, the second by Captain Montresor, and the third by Captain Roberts. After a thirty-six hours' row in pursuit of the enemy, who endeavoured to escape, the boats, on the morning of the 14th discovered his force, consisting of five gun-vessels, of the largest dimensions, moored in a line abreast, with springs on their cables, and boarding nettings triced up, off St. Joseph's island. On approaching the flotilla, an armed sloop was observed endeavouring to join it, which Captain Roberts, having volunteered the service, cut off and captured. About ten o'clock the boats were within long gun shot of the enemy, and were ordered to come to a grapnel while the crews were refreshed, when they again took to their oars, and pulling up against a strong current, and exposed to a destructive fire of round and grape shot, about noon Captain Lockyer closed with the commodore in the *Seahorse*'s barge. After a desperate resistance, Captain Lockyer being severely wounded, and the greater part of his officers and crew killed or wounded, the enemy's vessel was boarded, and shortly after captured; her guns were successfully turned upon the remaining four, and by the combined exertions of Captains Montresor and Roberts, in the course of five minutes the whole was in our possession.

By the capture of these vessels we got the command of Lac Borgne, and some addition to our means of transport, but which being still inadequate to the conveyance of more than half the army, exclusive of the supplies, it was determined, in order to have support for the division that would first land, to assemble the whole at some intermediate position, from whence the second division could be re-embarked in vessels brought light into the lakes, as near the Bayou as might be practicable, and remain there until the boats could land the first division and return.

On the 16th the advance, commanded by Colonel Thornton, of the 83d Regiment, was put into the gun-vessels and boats, and Captain Gordon, of the *Seahorse*, proceeded with them, and took post upon the Isle aux Poix, a small swampy spot at the mouth of the Pearl river, about mid-way, between the anchorage and Bayou. On the following day they were joined by Major-general Keene [or Keane], Sir A. Cochrane, and Rear-admiral Codrington, the boats and gun-vessels having returned to the shipping for troops, stores, &c.

The Bayou Catalan having been reconnoitred by the Honourable Captain Spencer of the Carron, and Lieutenant Piddy of the quarter-master-general's department, and reported perfectly eligible as a place of dis-embarkation; after repeated passages to and from the shipping, in which the boats had been greatly retarded by the weather, on the 21st the embarkation of the second division commenced in the gun-vessels, such of the hired craft as could be brought into the lakes, and the *Anaconda*.

In these vessels about two thousand four hundred men were embarked on the 22d. The advance, consisting of about sixteen hundred men, got into the boats, and at 11 o'clock the whole sailed with a fair wind to cross Lac Borgne. They had not, however, proceeded above two miles when the *Anaconda* grounded, and the hired craft and gun-vessels, before they had got within ten miles of the Bayou, having also grounded in succession; the advance pushed on, and at about midnight reached the entrance of the Bayou, where a picquet, placed there by the enemy, was surprised and cut off, and at day-break made good their landing.

"The place we landed in" (says a correspondent in the N.C. [p386]) "the *Americans* say was never before explored but by alligators, and wild ducks; it was up a creek, so narrow, and so completely hid by the canes, that I believe it had never before been discovered by the Americans: it was pointed out by some Spanish fishermen, who had appropriated one part of it for the purpose of smuggling. The head of this creek was distant from Mississippi about three miles; from the high-road to New Orleans a mile and a half; from the city six or eight."

About two o'clock, the army having advanced, took up a position on the banks of the Mississippi, having the river on their left, a wood on their right, and the main road before them (A). About eight o'clock in the evening of the 23d, while the boats were despatched for the second division, and the men, fatigued with the length of time they had been in them, were asleep in their bivouac, (B), a schooner of fourteen guns and an armed ship of sixteen, [Major-General Keane's report says a large schooner and two gun-vessels] sent down by the enemy, commenced a heavy flanking fire of round and grape, which was followed by a vigorous attack (I) on the advanced front and right flank picquets, the former of the 95th under Captain Hallan, the latter of the 85th under Captain Schaw. The attack was maintained with great firmness, and ultimately checked, but being renewed with increased force, the remainder of both corps was brought up by Colonel Thornton. On the approach of the 85th, under Brevet major Gubbins, to the point of attack, the enemy, favoured by the darkness of the night, concealed themselves behind a fence which separated the fields, hailed them as part of their own force, and offered to assist them in getting over, which they no sooner did than they found themselves in the midst of the enemy, greatly superior in numbers, and who called on them instantly to surrender; the answer to this summons was a general and instantaneous attack, and the enemy was repulsed with the loss of thirty prisoners. A like attempt was made on the 95th regiment with the same success. At half-past ten a large column of the enemy was brought against the centre of the British force, when Major-general Keane ordered 30 men of the 193d regiment just arrived, to attack it with the bayonet, retaining the 4th regiment in line as a last reserve. The endeavours of Colonel Dale for the execution of this order were frustrated by the retreat of the enemy after a heavy fire. Colonel Brooke now arrived with four companies of the 21st regiment on their right flank, and the enemy, determined on making a last effort, collected his whole force, and formed in an extensive line, moved directly against the light brigade. By this formidable force, the advanced posts were driven in, when Colonel Thornton having rallied his brave comrades, moved forward again with a determination to charge, and the enemy finally retired (C).

On the arrival of Major-general Sir E. Pakenham, and Major-general Gibbs, on the 25th, the former assumed the command. On the 27th, some batteries (M) having been raised against the schooner, (K) which had continued its annoyance of the troops, it was burnt and blown up, by hot shot from the artillery; and the armed ship (L) having warped further up the river, on the following day the general moved to within gun shot of an entrenchment thrown up by the enemy across the cultivated ground from the Mississippi, to an impassable swampy wood on his left, in extent about one thousand yards (D). Guns were brought up from the shipping, and on the 1st of January batteries (N) were opened, but owing to the swampiness of the ground they were rendered ineffective; and it was resolved to wait the arrival of the troops under Major-general Lambert, who on the same day reached the outer anchorage in the *Vengeur* with a convoy of transports, having on board the 7th and 43d regiments, and on the 6th joined the main body under Sir E. Pakenham.

The position of the army was then in a flat country, the Mississippi on its left, a thick extensive wood on its right, and open in front to the enemy. On the 8th the army was formed for a general attack (E) on the enemy's line extending as we have before observed, about one thousand yards on the left bank of the river - the right of the line resting on the river, and the left on a wood rendered impervious to any body of troops - it was strengthened by flank works (O), and had a canal of about four feet deep, but not in every part of an equal width; it was supposed to narrow towards the left: eight heavy guns were in position on this line. The river is here about 800 yards across, and on the right bank was a heavy battery of 12 guns (P), which enfiladed the whole front of the position on the left bank.

At the suggestion of Sir Alexander Cochrane, a canal (Q) was cleared out and widened, with considerable labour, which communicated with a stream, by which the boats had passed up to the place of disembarkation, to open it into the Mississippi, and thus obtain a passage for troops to the right bank of the river, and the co-operation of armed boats.

The plan of attack was - A corps consisting of the 85th regiment, 200 seamen, 400 marines, the 5th West Indian regiment, and four pieces of artillery, under the command of Colonel Thornton, of the 85th, to pass over during the night and move along the right bank towards New Orleans, clearing its front until it reached the flanking battery of the enemy on that side, which it was to carry. The front of the enemy's line was to be attacked by the 4th, 21st, and 44th regiments, with three companies of the 95th, under Major-general Gibbs, and by the 3d brigade consisting of the 93d, two companies of the 95th, and two companies of the fusiliers, and 43d, under Major-general Keane; some black troops were to skirmish in the wood on the night: the principal attack to be made by Major-general Gibbs: the fusiliers and 43d to form the reserve: the attacking columns to be provided with fascines, scaling ladders, and rafts: the whole to be at their stations before day-light, and the attack to be made at the earliest hour. An advanced battery in front, of six 18-pounders was thrown up during the night, about 800 yards from the enemy's line.

Such was the plan and preparation, and a general confidence of success prevailed. But the plan appears to have been most negligently executed, independently of those unforeseen difficulties which are so often found to impede the execution of the best-concerted projects. The movement assigned to Colonel Thornton was obstructed by physical difficulties, the particulars of which are thus stated by our correspondent at page 387.

"The engineers, or, more properly speaking, the staff corps, had declared the canal sufficiently deep for the boats to pass, and to appearance it was so: but we calculated rather more on the gush of water from the river than was quite right - we had dragged the boats up as far as the village, with guns, stores, every thing which could be necessary, and remained within about two hundred yards of the river until dark; but on our advancing about fifty yards, the boat stuck, the labour then became extreme, and after a night of most severe hardship for the men, we succeeded in getting through the whole of the boats, but only four with guns, among which I was fortunate enough to be. We still dreaded the approach of day-light; therefore, fearing by waiting for all, we might not get over sufficiently early, we started with nine boats, our four, and five others, which contained the 85th, and a few marines and seamen, the whole not, I am sure, exceeding four hundred; but, unfortunately, they seemed altogether to have forgotten us on the left side, and before we could be of sufficient use to create a diversion, everything had failed in that quarter; while every thing had quite the contrary result on our side. The 85th advanced, and we at first rather headed them. The Americans were not aware of their advance, but when they were, endeavoured to form, and I believed intended to make a stand. - The advance did not discover them quite so soon as the boats, owing to, to use a sea phrase, 'their being under the *lee of a house*', but we gave them a shot or two (F) which apprized the advance (I really think not exceeding twenty) of the enemy's situation; but, Jonathan, the moment he received their fire and cheers, with a shot or two from the boats started for his works, and was driven from them almost as soon as he entered, leaving a redoubt with 15 pieces of cannon and a stand of colours."

Thus in the language of the Gazette "the *ensemble* of the general movement was lost," and the attack delayed until the enemy had sufficient time to prepare our reception. The exertions of the brave Sir E. Pakenham in the onset were great, but, alas! of short duration - while encouraging the troops on the crest of the glacis he received two wounds, one in his knee and another almost instantly fatal in his body: he fell in the arms of Major M'Dougall, at the same time that Major-general Gibbs and Major-general Keane, with several other commanding officers were borne off wounded. These events, together with the fascines, scaling ladders and rafts for crossing the ditch not being in readiness, caused a wavering in the column, and on the approach of Major-general Sir John Lambert with the reserve, he met the whole falling back on him in confusion. Thus circumstanced, Sir John having placed the reserve in position, went to meet Sir Alexander Cochrane, whom he informed of the failure, and that he did not think it prudent to renew the attack that day. At about ten o'clock, Sir John Lambert was informed of Colonel Thornton's success on the right bank, and of his being in possession of the enemy's redoubt, and he immediately sent Colonel Dickson, commanding officers of the artillery to examine the situation of the battery, and report his opinion on the means of holding it. But being informed that it could not be secured with a force less than 2,000 men; Lieutenant-Colonel Gubbins, who had succeeded to the command (Colonel Thornton being wounded) was ordered to retire. The army remained in position till night, when the 18-pounder battery being destroyed, the troops returned to the ground they occupied previous to the attack. On the 9th of January it was determined to withdraw the army, and on the night of the 18th it was effected. On the morning of the 19th the troops occupied the ground on both sides of the Bayou, or creek, where they had disembarked, 14 miles from their position before the enemy's line, and one mile from the entrance into lac Borgne, and on the 27th the whole was re-embarked.

References to the Plate

A Bivouac of the troops 23 Dec.	K American schooner blown up 27th Dec.
B Position on the night "	L An American 24-gun ship.
C " " " " 24 Dec.	M Batteries against the schooner.
D " after the advance on 28th Dec.	N Batteries thrown up by English.
E The attack on the 8th Jan.	O " to protect the flank of the army.
F Colonel Thornton's attack.	P Redoubts.
I The enemy's attack on the 33d Dec.	Q Canal cut to pass boats.

   The Mississippi is a considerable river of North America, which is the great channel of the waters of the Ohio, the Illinois, and their numerous branches from the East and of the Missouri and other rivers from the West. Its source is unknown, but its length (in a southerly direction) is supposed to be upwards of 3,000 miles. In all its windings, to its entrance into the gulf of Mexico, between the 89th and 90th degrees of West longitude. In this river, in latitude 44° 30' N. are the Falls of St. Anthony, where the whole river, which is more than 250 yards wide, falls perpendicularly about 30 feet. New Orleans, a city of North America, capital of Louisiana, was built in the time of the regency of the Duke of Orleans. In 1788, seven-eighths of it were destroyed by fire; but great progress has been since made in rebuilding it. Here are two convents, a parish church, magazines, forges, and some public buildings. The houses are chiefly of wood, on foundations of brick. It never contained above 1500 inhabitants, and is seated in a rich, fertile soil, and with an excellent climate, on the East side of the Mississippi, 54 miles from its mouth. Lat. 30° 2' N. Long. 89° 53' W. ^{Plate 439}

Cochrane's Dispatches

Letters on Service
Admiralty Office, March 9, 1815. ^{XXXIII 337-348}

Despatches, of which the following are copies, addressed by Vice-admiral the Honourable Sir Alexander Cochrane, G.C.B. &c to John Wilson Croker, Esq. were yesterday brought to this office by the Honourable Captain William Henry Percy, late of H.M.S. Hermes

Armide, off Isle au Chat, January 18, 1815

Sir, An unsuccessful attempt to gain possession of the enemy's lines near New Orleans on the 8th instant, having left me to deplore the fall of Major-general the Honourable Sir Edward Pakenham, and Major-general Gibbs; and deprived the service of the present assistance of Major-general Keane, who is severely wounded, I send the *Plantagenet* to England to convey a despatch from Major-general Lambert, upon whom the command of the army has devolved, and to inform my Lords Commissioners of the Admiralty of the operations of the combined forces since my arrival upon this coast.

The accompanying letters, Nos. 163 and 169, of the 7th and 16th ult. will acquaint their Lordships of the proceeding of the squadron to the 15th December.

[These letters cannot be included in this edition.]

The great distance from the anchorage of the frigates and troop-ships to the Bayou Catalan, which from the best information we could gain appeared to offer the most secure, and was indeed the only unprotected, spot whereat to effect a disembarkation, and our means, even with the addition of the captured enemy's gun-vessels, only affording us transport for half the army, exclusive of the supplies that were required, it became necessary, in order to have support for the division that would first land, to assemble the whole at some intermediate position, from whence the second division could be re-embarked in vessels brought light into the Lake, as near the bayou as might be practicable, and remain there until the boats could land the first division and return.

Upon the 16th therefore the advance, commanded by Colonel Thornton, of the 85th regiment, was put into the gun-vessels and boats, and Captain Gordon, of the *Seahorse*, proceeded with them, and took post upon the Isle aux Poix, a small swampy spot at the mouth of the Pearl river, about thirty miles from the anchorage, and nearly the same distance from the bayou, where Major-general Keane, Rear-admiral Codrington, and myself joined them on the following day; meeting the gun-vessels, and boats returning to the shipping for troops, and supplies of stores and provisions.

The Honourable Captain Spencer, of the *Carron*, and Lieutenant Peddy, of the quarter-master-general's department, who were sent to reconnoitre the Bayou Catalan, now returned with a favourable report of its position for disembarking the army; having, with their guide, pulled up in a canoe to the head of the bayou, a distance of eight miles, and landed within a mile and a half of the high road to, and about six miles below New Orleans, where they crossed the road without meeting with any interruption, or perceiving the least preparation on the part of the enemy.

The severe changes of the weather, from rain to fresh gales and hard frost, retarding the boats in their repeated passages to and from the shipping, it was not until the 21st that (leaving on board the greater part of the two black regiments and the dragoons), we could assemble troops and supplies sufficient to admit of our proceeding; and on that day we commenced the embarkation of the second division in the gun-vessels, such of the hired craft as could be brought into the Lakes, and the *Anaconda*, which by the greatest exertions had been got over the shoal passages.

On the 22d these vessels being filled with about two thousand four hundred men, the advance, consisting of about sixteen hundred, got into the boats, and at eleven o'clock the whole started, with a fair wind, to cross Lac Borgne. We had not, however, proceeded above two miles, when the *Anaconda* grounded, and the hired craft and gun-vessels taking the ground in succession before they had got within ten miles of the bayou; the advance pushed on, and at about midnight reached the entrance.

A picquet, which the enemy had taken the precaution to place there, being surprised and cut off, Major-general Keane, with Rear-admiral Malcolm and the advance, moved up the bayou, and having effected a landing at daybreak, in the course of the day was enabled to take up a position across the main road to New Orleans, between the river Mississippi and the bayou.

In this situation, about an hour after sun-set, and before the boats could return with the second division, an enemy's schooner of fourteen guns, and an armed ship of sixteen guns, having dropped down the Mississippi, the former commenced a brisk cannonading, which was followed up by an attack of the whole of the American army. Their troops were, however, beaten back, and obliged to retire with considerable loss, and Major-general Keane advanced somewhat beyond his former position. As soon as the second division was brought up, the gun-vessels and boats returned for the remainder of the troops, the small-armed seamen and marines of the squadron, and such supplies as were required.

On the 25th, Major-general Sir E. Packenham and Major-general Gibbs arrived at head-quarters, when the former took command of the army.

The schooner which had continued at intervals to annoy the troops having been burnt on the 27th by hot shot from our artillery, and the ship having warped farther up the river, the following day the general moved forward to within gun-shot of an entrenchment which the enemy had newly thrown up, extending across the cultivated ground from the Mississippi to an impassable swampy wood on his left, a distance of about one thousand yards.

It being thought necessary to bring heavy artillery against this work, and also against the ship which had cannonaded the army when advancing, guns were brought up from the shipping, and on the 1st instant batteries were opened; but our fire not having the desired effect, the attack was deferred until the arrival of the troops under Major-general Lambert, which were daily expected.

Major-general Lambert, in the *Vengeur*, with a convoy to transports, having on board the 7th and 43d regiments, reached the outer anchorage on the 1st; and this reinforcement was all brought up to the advance on the 6th instant, while preparations were making for a second attack, in the proposed plan for which, it was decided to throw a body of men across the river to gain possession of the enemy's guns on the right bank. For this purpose, the canal by which we were enabled to conduct provisions and stores toward the camp, was widened and extended to the river, and about fifty barges, pinnaces, and cutters, having, in the day-time of the [2]7th, been traced under cover and unperceived, close up to the bank, at night the whole were dragged into the Mississippi, and placed under the command of Captain Roberts, of the *Meteor*.

The boats having grounded in the canal, a distance of three hundred and fifty yards from the river, and the bank being composed of wet clay thrown out of the canal, it was not until nearly day-light that with the utmost possible exertions this service was completed.

The 35th regiment, with a division of seamen under Captain Money, and a division of marines under Major Adair, the whole amounting to about six hundred men, commanded by Colonel Thornton, of the 85th regiment, were embarked and landed on the right bank of the river without opposition, just after day-light; and the armed boats moving up the river as the troops advanced, this part of the operations succeeded perfectly; the enemy having been driven from every position, leaving behind him seventeen pieces of cannon.

The great loss, however, sustained by the principle attack, having induced General Lambert to send orders to Colonel Thornton to retire, after spiking the guns and destroying the carriages, the whole were reembarked and brought back, and the boats, by a similar process of hard labour, were again dragged into the canal, and from thence to the bayou, conveying at the same time such of the wounded as it was thought requisite to send off to the ships.

Major-general Lambert having determined to withdraw the army, measures were taken to re-embark the whole of the sick and wounded, that it was possible to move, and the stores, ammunition, ordnance, &c. with such detachments of the army, seamen, and marines, as were not immediately wanted; in order that the remainder of the army may retire unencumbered, and the last division be furnished with sufficient means of transport.

This arrangement being in a forward state of execution, I quitted headquarters on the 14th instant, leaving Rear-admiral Malcolm to conduct the naval part of the operations in that quarter, and I arrived at this anchorage on the 16th, where I am arranging for the reception of the army, and preparing the fleet for further operations. ...

From 'Correspondence.' XXXIII 295-296; 385-388

'Albion' Blames God for the Defeat

"Albion" to the Editor, March 12th, 1815
Mr. Editor, The satisfaction and pleasure which every well-wisher to his country naturally derived from the recent brilliant achievement of Captain Hope, in the *Endymion*, I fondly, but vainly, hoped would be unalloyed by any future reverse of fortune, before the war with America was brought to a final close. I fear, Mr. Editor, in common with other sanguine minds, I anticipated that it would be closed by the conquest, at least of New Orleans, if not by the capture of more of the American men of war; but, alas! how uncertain is the success of the best arranged schemes of man, and how fickle is fortune; surely the many sad and blood-stained reverses, which our arms (every where victorious in Portugal, Spain, and France) have lately sustained in America, is to the British nation a most melancholy proof of this uncertainty. The intelligence just arrived from the brave, but unsuccessful bands of heroes lately commanded by *the gallant and lamented Pakenham*, who can read, without admitting that victory is awarded *from on high*, and that the battle is not *always* to the strong. In this instance, if valour, discipline, science, and ample experience in the art of war, could have availed, it was on our side; a general of first-rate abilities, accustomed to conquer, was sent to command our gallant but *disjointed* troops; he was seconded by excellent officers, and the perseverance and devoted heroism of soldiers never was more conspicuous, than on the late attack on New Orleans: it is clear, therefore, the fault was not with the army; and it appears to me easily demonstrable, that the expedition, or expeditions, for there were several, were undertaken *without* our possessing a proper knowledge of the country, or of the force and obstacles to be overcome. Our general began the attempt, and two superior officers landed soon after, directly from England, and in time only to head the attack, and gallantly leading on their brave followers to perish nobly in their country's battles. It is, therefore, evident that there must be combination and proper information as to the force and obstacles to be overcome before victory can be seized from a determined enemy; and such, in most instances, we have found the Americans. Thus clouded and obscured, thus drooping and withered, are the laurels of Wellington's brave associates, and thus has fallen, unconsoled *by the smile of Victory*, one of his noblest, bravest, and most highly respected generals; a man from whom, had he survived, England might have expected the most valuable services; but Victory or Westminster-Abbey was the leading principle of this gallant soldier's life, and he has sunk into the heroes' grave, beloved and lamented; he went out to conquer or to die.

Thus has ended in defeat all our attempts on the American coast, and thus have the measures and inadequate force provided by our government brought disgrace - no never

- our troops are Englishmen, and have performed prodigies of valour; but ministers have, by their weak, irresolute, and contemptible conduct, thrown victory into the lap of America; and, having uselessly devoted brave men to destruction, have at last concluded a peace far from glorious to Britain; certainly it must be allowed we have *not* conquered a better one; an inglorious, unsuccessful, war must naturally end in such a peace as America chose to give; for assuredly we have now done our worst against this infant enemy, which has already shewn a *giant's* power. Soon will the rising greatness of this distant empire (and its distance is, perhaps, fortunate for Europe) astonish the nations who have looked on with wonder, and seen the mightiest efforts of Britain, at the era of her greatest power, so easily parried, so completely foiled.

Lamenting the fallen fortunes of my country, and the unavailing loss of so many brave men, I now take my leave of the American contest; it is to all appearance over, but history *will* record our defeats, and posterity will see and appreciate their consequences. *Sic transit gloria mundi.*

A Junior Officer's Observations from the Field of Battle

D.L. to the Editor

Mr. Editor, I transmit to you the enclosed copy of a letter, written by a young but intelligent naval officer, giving some new and interesting details of the late unfortunate enterprise of the American war, and explaining causes of the failure, yet imperfectly known.

His Majesty's ship —, *off the coast of New Orleons, January 30, 1815.* [It is only possible to publish an excerpt here, because of the extensive quotations used in *The Naval Chronicle*'s account of the battle.]

"A short time previous to day-light, General Pakenham rode down to see if all was prepared as he wished, and meeting .... of the ...., asked where he had left the fascines and ladders, he was answered, 'In the battery.' Now this battery was so far in the rear as to require some time before the fascines could be got up from it. But before this could be done, the rocket was fired, according to previous arrangement, for the attack. The regiments advanced: there were no fascines - no ladders - the ditch was too deep to wade - and our unfortunate men were cut to pieces: the regiment in advance gave way, and broke through the lines of the 93d and 4th. Some officers of the 93d declared in my hearing publicly that General Keane, before receiving his wounds, called to the regiment in advance, on their retiring, "*Remember Egypt*"; but finding that useless, called to the 93d to "*Bayonet the rascals.*" ...... ran away; the scaling-ladders were dropped; the regiments were in confusion; poor Sir Edward Pakenham rode up to endeavour to restore some order, was wounded in the knee; his horse soon after fell; and Major M'Dougall was assisting him to mount another, when a shot entered his breast, and lodged in the spine. Thus fell as brave a fellow, probably, as ever existed. Previous to his death, he declared, should he survive, that if possible he would hang .....; and General Gibbs, who was soon after mortally wounded, said, that whoever should find the ...., of the ...., ought to hang him to the first tree for cowardice.

The fire was tremendous. I had an opportunity of seeing a good deal without being at all exposed, Jonathan having been too busily employed, so much so, that we had passed the American head-quarters with the boats before they deigned to give us a shot, and almost as soon the general order for retreat was given. The position defended by the Americans is, I am told, one of those which Moreau pointed out when there; at the same time observing, "Give me five thousand men, and I will defend it against any ten thousand you can bring against me." "

1815 – The Hundred Days
to Waterloo

THE NAVAL CHRONICLE was dismayed by Napoleon Buonaparte's return to France, but the 'Hundred Days' from his landing until his defeat at Waterloo involved the navy only to the extent that demobilisation had to be suspended. Of more immediate naval interest were the after-shocks from the American war, in which there continued to be encounters between ships which had not been informed of the conclusion of the conflict. American plans for its postwar navy, and the discovery of the descendants of the *Bounty* mutineers, were also matters of great interest. The capture of the fleeing Buonaparte in July, and his transportation to St Helena as a prisoner of state, however, was a most gratifying conclusion to the twenty-two years of naval conflict.

From the 'Naval History of the Present Year,' 1815
February–March. XXXIII 249-252

Buonaparte Returns to Power in France

The events of the past month constitute an enigma that must baffle all human judgment to solve – events which confound all human calculations as the sum of good or evil they are pregnant with.

No sooner had the ratification of Peace, on the part of the government of the United States, been received, and Commerce was expected once more to have spread her sails for the mutual benefit of both nations, and the Congress at Vienna had nearly completed the arrangement that was to render permanent the Peace of Europe, than forth steps the Daemon of Mischief [ie Buonaparte] to subvert the hopeful fabric, and new again the scenes of blood and rapine.

It would be almost impious to suppose, that an almighty, all-wise, and good Being should, but a year ago, have hurled from his throne the greatest tyrant that modern ages have produced, and broken his power, only to reinstate him now, to recommence his career of havoc and spoliation. Is it that the demoralized state of France requires further purgation? – or is it but the natural result of the ill-judged clemency of his conquerors . . . . "Buonaparte took his departure from Porto Ferrajo on the 26th February, at nine

283

o'clock in the evening, when the weather was extremely calm, which continued to the 1st March. He got on board a brig, and was followed by four other vessels, such as pinks and feluccas, carrying from 1,000 to 1,100 men at most, consisting of a small number of Frenchmen, the rest Poles, Corsicans, Neapolitans, and natives of the island of Elba. - These vessels anchored in the roads of the Gulf of Juan, near Cannes, on the 1st of March; the men were landed. Fifty men went the same day to Cannes, where they urged the Mayor to go and take orders from him, whom they named the General in Chief in the Gulf of Juan, but the Mayor absolutely refused; he received immediately orders to provide three thousand rations that same evening. - The same day, fifteen men of the expedition presented themselves before Antibes, demanding to enter it as deserters from the island of Elba. General Baron Corsin, a distinguished soldier, covered with honourable wounds, who was in the command of that place, received them, and disarmed them. A short time afterwards, an officer came to summon the place in the name of Buonaparte; he was arrested and thrown into prison. At last, a third emissary presented himself to the Commandant, to reclaim the fifteen men detained, and to invite him, in the name of General Drouet, to repair to the Gulf of Juan, with the civil authorities; the only answer this embassy received was, being arrested."

It was our intention to have given a continued diary of the progress of Buonaparte from Elba to Paris; but henceforth it exhibits to *our* eyes (with some few exceptions of honourable conduct) such a course of farcical treachery, that we turn from it with disgust. We see Buonaparte at Grenoble, telling the soldiers *opposed* to him, that it had been said he was afraid of death - and immediately exposing his breast to place his life in their hands; - but death then had laid aside his terrors - had covered his bare bones with good firm flesh; and in the shape of a soldier, multiplied in a thousand distinct forms, had *previously* shaken hands and signed his reprieve, *sine die.* He was not quite so bold when, quitting France, he shunned death, in the disguise of a servant behind his own carriage - such *then* was the courage of this mighty man.

The contrivance of the scheme was intended to impose on the world an idea that, by his mere presence, he subdued and overcame all before him. We heard of 10,000 on this side of him, 20,000 on that - one army behind him, and another before him - but as he approached, they were awed into submission - some indeed seem to have been overcome by the mere *effluvia* of his presence in a distant part - we shall, therefore, bring him into the neighbourhood of Fontainebleau, as quietly as his army did, where the last act of the Farce was performed - to be succeeded by, we fear, a most deep and bloody Tragedy!

"Early on the morning of the 21st, preparations were made on both sides for the encounter which was expected to take place. The French army was drawn up *en etages* on three lines, the intervals and the flanks armed with batteries. The centre occupied the Paris road. The ground from Fontainebleau to Melun is a continual declivity, so that on emerging from the forest you have a clear view of the country before you, whilst, on the other hand, those below can easily descry whatever appears on the eminence. An awful silence, broken only at times by peals of martial music, intended to confirm the loyalty of the troops by repeating the Royal airs of *Vive Henry Quatre, et la Belle Gabrielle*, or by the voice of the Commanders and the march of divisions to their appointed ground, pervaded the King's army. All was anxious expectation; the Chiefs, conscious that a moment would decide the fate of the Bourbon dynasty, and the troops, perhaps, secretly awed at the thought of meeting in hostility the man whom they had been accustomed to obey. On the side of Fontainebleau no sound, as of an army rushing to battle, was heard. If the enemy was advancing, his troops evidently moved in silence. Perhaps his heart had failed him, and he had retreated during the night. If so, France was saved and Europe free. At length a light trampling of horses became audible. It approached: an open carriage, attended by a few hussars and dragoons, appeared on the skirts of the forest. It drove down the hills with the rapidity of lightning: it reached the advanced posts – "*Long live the Emperor*" burst from the astonished soldiery! "*Napoleon! Napoleon the Great!*" spread from rank to rank; for, bareheaded Bertrand seated at his right, and Drouet at his left, Napoleon continued his course, now waving his hand, now opening his arms to the soldiers, whom he called his friends, his companions in arms, whose honour, whose glories, whose country, (the Tyrant said) he now came to restore. All discipline was forgotten, disobeyed, and insulted; the Commanders-in-Chief took flight; thousands rushed on his passage; acclamations rent the sky. At that moment his own guard descended the hill – the Imperial March was played – the eagles were once more displayed, and those whose deadly weapons were to have aimed at each other's life, embraced as brothers, and joined the universal shouts. In the midst of these greetings did Napoleon pass through the whole of the Royal army, and placing himself at its head, pursued his course to Paris. The population of the villages flocked round him; the inhabitants of Paris, informed of his approach, came out to meet him, and at the head of two hundred thousand persons, (to the eternal disgrace of Frenchmen be it said) in the midst of enthusiastic acclamations, did he re-enter the capital, and seat himself in the Palace of Kings.

The Royal army, at least 100,000 in number, were in the mean time collected at Melun, to oppose his march, and the best spirit seemed to prevail amongst them. A powerful artillery strengthened their positions; and the Court and Officers, confident in the superiority of numbers, and in their good inclinations, had no apprehension of the event."

[Buonaparte's account of his voyage from Elba was printed in Vol. XXXIII, pp288-290.]

Demobilisation Suspended

The following circular from the Admiralty, dated March 21, has been read to the crews of all his Majesty's ships at Portsmouth:

"The Lords Commissioners of the Admiralty had hoped that the ratification of the Treaty of Peace with the United States of America would have enabled them to execute without any delay, the intention intimated in their Lordships' general memorandum of the 30th April last, of paying off, whenever that event should take place, the whole fleet, and recommissioning and remanning, by volunteers, the ships which should be thought necessary for a peace establishment: but the critical state in which the affairs of France have been so unexpectedly placed, renders it an indispensable duty on the British Government not suddenly to disarm and leave the most important interests of this country exposed to danger. Their Lordships are, therefore, with great reluctance obliged to keep for some time longer the fleet in commission; and they confidently expect that the seamen and marines will cheerfully acquiesce in a delay, which their Lordships sincerely hope, may be short; but which at all events, the safety and honour of the country, imperiously demand. Their Lordships, however, feel great satisfaction in thinking, that they may proceed in the present system of discharging all seamen who have been in the service previous to the 1st January, 1814, and have since remained in it, unless any petty officers and seamen should volunteer to continue their services at this critical period of affairs; which, considering the great advantages held

out to long service by the Order in Council relative to pensions, their Lordships cannot
but expect that many will be inclined to do. Whenever the state of affairs will permit,
their Lordships will take measures for paying off the fleet with as little delay as may be
practicable, and for discharging every petty officer and seaman now serving on board
his Majesty's ships."

Exmouth to Command in the Mediterranean

The greatest activity prevails at Portsmouth and Plymouth, in fitting out his Majesty's
ships for foreign service. Rear admiral Sir Israel Pellew, goes out with Lord Exmouth
to the Mediterranean as his first captain of the fleet, and will sail from Portsmouth in
a few days.

From 'Correspondence.' XXXIII 295-296

A Letter on the Power of Influence

"One of the Gun-room Mess" to the Editor
March 15th, 1815
Mr. Editor, Through the medium of your valuable publication, I wish the following
circumstance to be made known. In August 1812, a court martial took place in Madras
Roads, on the captain of H.M.S. *Malacca*; one of the members of the said court,
consisting of only five, dined on board H.M. frigate, *Hussar*, in the gun-room, some
days previous to the above-named court-martial; and, in presence of the whole mess,
asserted he was to get the ship on the dismissal of the said captain; a clear proof he was
condemned before trial: the said captain of the *Malacca* was dismissed, and this member
of the court did get the ship and was confirmed by the Admiralty.

As this statement will be read by many clever naval characters, I wish, as a young
man seeking information, to inquire whether this was a strictly fair dismissal, or to
make room for *honourables*, of which there are at present too many in our service.

[For another letter discussing the problem of social status see Appendix 6 on Naval
Discipline, Volume III, pp338-357.]

Nelson Estate
From 'Nautical Anecdotes.' XXXIII 285

It appears from "the Report of the Proceedings of Earl Nelson's Trustees," dated the
18th inst. that they have at length, by their agent, Mr. Litchfield, entered into an
agreement for the purchase of an estate, mansion-house, and park, at Standlynch, in
the country of Wilts, the property of the late Henry Dawkins, Esq. which is situated
near the road leading from Portsmouth to Bath and Bristol, on the banks of the Avon,
about four miles south of Salisbury. This estate comprises the manor of Standlynch,
the whole of the extra-parochial hamlet of the same name, a large and respectable
mansion-house and offices, nearly 1,900 acres of land, of which about 1,290 acres are
freehold, 515 copyhold of inheritance, subject to certain small fines, and 93 acres
copyhold, for lives, with a fishery in the river Avon, and a water corn-mill, and the right
of appointing the curate of Standlynch. The whole of the land-tax, with a very small
exception, is redeemed.

The price which the trustees have agreed to give for this estate, including the timber, which is considerable, is £93,450 and it has been reported to them by their architect, who surveyed the buildings, that about £3,000 will be wanted for repairs. The trustees, being aware that they could not be warranted in entering into an agreement for the payment of any purchase money beyond the amount of the grant of £90,000 thought it necessary, before they authorised their agent to enter into the negotiation, to require from Earl Nelson, with whose approbation and concurrence the negotiation was entered upon, an undertaking that he would, in the hope that Parliament might think proper to make good the same, pay the excess of price beyond the sum of £87,000; a portion of the estate equivalent in value being, in case no such grant shall be made, conveyed to his Lordship as his private property; by which arrangement, £3,000 would be set apart for the repairs, according to the estimate.

From the 'Naval History of the Present Year,' 1815 March-April. *XXXIII 332-336*

No Naval News is Good News

Nothing naval, of importance, has occurred during the last month. The dying embers of enmity in America appear in the attack of Fort Mobile, and long may it be ere the breath of faction shall again blow them into flame. Rear-admiral Sir Edward Codrington, in the *Havannah*, Captain Hamilton, brought home the despatches, from which we learn that intelligence of peace between the two countries was received, soon after the reduction of the fort, and that in consequence the British forces were withdrawn, and sailed for the *Havannah*, where they were preparing to return to England. Sir A. Cochrane had sailed in the *Tonnant* for Bermuda, leaving Rear-admiral Sir Pultney Malcolm, to make the arrangements for the return home of the fleet with the troops. The *Havannah* arrived at Bermuda on the 22d ult, and sailed again for England on the next day. . . .

The Nations Unite

The following is a brief abstract of the substance of the Treaty concluded on the 25th of March, between Russia, Austria, Prussia, and Great Britain, in consequence of the entrance of Napoleon Buonaparte into France.

It states, that the resolutions of the High Contracting Parties are, in consideration of the consequences which Napoleon Buonaparte's invasion of France may produce on the safety of Europe, and to carry into effect the principles consecrated by the Treaty of Chaumont, they therefore resolve, by a solemn treaty, to preserve against every attack the order of things so happily established in Europe, and to determine upon the most effectual means of fulfilling that engagement. Accordingly they engage by Art. 1, to maintain entire the conditions of the Treaty of Peace concluded at Paris, 30th May, 1814, as also the stipulations determined upon and signed at the Congress of Vienna, with the view to complete the dispositions of that treaty - to preserve them against all infringement, and particularly against the designs of Napoleon Buonaparte. And they engage in the spirit of the declaration of the 13th March last, to direct in common, and with one accord, should the case require it, all their efforts to force him to desist from his projects, and to render him unable to disturb in future the tranquillity of Europe, and the general peace, under the protection of which, the rights, the liberties, and independence of nations had been recently placed and secured. - By Art. 2 The High

Contracting Parties engage definitively to keep constantly in the field, each a force of 150,000 men, of which, at least one tenth to be cavalry, and a just proportion of artillery, not reckoning garrisons. - By Art. 3 They reciprocally engage not to lay down their arms but by common consent, nor before the object of the war designated in the first article shall have been attained, nor until Buonaparte shall have been rendered unable to create disturbance, and to renew his attempts for possessing himself of the supreme power in France. Art. 4 Engages that the stipulations of the treaty of Chaumont shall be again in force, as soon as the object actually in view shall have been attained. By Art. 5 Whatever relates to the command of the combined armies, to supplies, &c shall be regulated by a particular convention. By Art. 6 The High Contracting Parties are allowed respectively to accredit to the generals commanding their armies, officers, who shall have the liberty of corresponding with their armies, officers, who shall have the liberty of corresponding with their governments for the purpose of giving information of military events &c. Art. 7 Invites all the powers of Europe to accede to the present treaty. Art. 8 Invites especially his Most Christian Majesty to accede to it.

By a separate Article, his Britannic Majesty is to have the option either of furnishing his contingent in men, or of paying at the rate of £30 per annum for each cavalry soldier, or £20 per annum for each infantry soldier that may be deficient of the stipulated number. - And by an explanatory declaration, the Prince Regent on the part of his Britannic Majesty is not to be understood (however solicitous to see his Most Christian Majesty restored to the throne) as bound to prosecute the war, with the view of imposing on France any particular government.

Authority and instructions have also been given to the Earl of Clancarty, to sign a subsidiary engagement, consequent upon the said treaty.

April-May. XXXIII 430-433

Squadrons Return from American Waters

The present aspect of naval affairs presents us with nothing of greater interest than the return of our brave countrymen from the shores of America, and from a contest nobly maintained, though not always with its merited success. The causes of failure have, however, been so clearly ascertained without the limits of their responsibility, and pointed out to those with whom it lies, that we trust the like failures will in future have a more inevitable origin. . . .

A Last Frigate Action

It is with considerable mortification and regret, that we state the capture of the *Levant*, 24, Honourable Captain G. Douglas, and the *Cyane*, 24, Captain Falcon, by the American frigate *Constitution*. They were captured together early in February, on the coast of Africa, after a very sharp action. It will, however, afford some gratification to hear, that Sir George Collier had at length obtained information of the course which the *Constitution* was taking, and that he was so close in pursuit, that the *Newcastle*, Lord George Stuart, arrived off one of the ports on the coast, the morning following the evening in which the *Constitution* had left it; which she did by slipping her cables, on hearing that our ships were near to her. - The *Newcastle* re-captured the *Levant*, and, we are informed, might also have retaken the *Cyane*, but she unfortunately, in the ardour of pursuit, supposed that she was a Brazilman. The *Levant* had arrived at Bermuda, and Sir Alexander Cochrane had commissioned her: Captain Sheridan, of the *Terror* bomb, was promoted to the rank of post captain, and appointed to command her; and Captain Moorsom (son of Admiral Sir Robert Moorsom) of the *Gorée*, was appointed to the *Terror*. . . .

American Postwar Naval Plans

The determination of the government of the United States to have a navy, is sufficiently evident from the following intimation of its naval secretary:

The secretary of the American navy, in a letter to the Commissioners of Ways and Means, recommends that to secure success in the operations to be made against the Barbary powers, the squadron do consist of two seventy-fours, six frigates, three sloops, and six or eight small armed vessels; the flotilla, he says, may be discharged, and the gun-boats (with the above exception) may be generally laid up or sold; the ships and vessels on the Lakes of Canada, or on the stocks for the Lake service, may also be laid up or sold, as the President shall direct: but he thinks that no greater reduction ought, at this time, to be made; and, as the destinies of the nation appear to be intimately connected with her maritime superiority, and the erection of a navy is not a work to be quickly performed, he recommends the annual construction of at least one seventy-four and two frigates. . . .

Mediterranean Fleet

The *Caledonia*, of 120 guns, is fitting for the flag of Admiral Lord Exmouth. There are no fewer than four first rates and one 74 fitting in the port of Plymouth to receive the flags of admirals. It is said that these ships are to carry 24-pounders on the forecastle, for the purpose of throwing Congreve's Rockets. The gun-brigs are also to be fitted with a furnace to heat red-hot shot, and one 24-pounder to throw rockets.

Other Fleets

A fleet of observation is rapidly forming in Plymouth-Sound and Cawsand-Bay. Admiral Lord Keith is expected there to hoist his flag. The port of Plymouth is to be the rendezvous of the Channel fleet. . . .

Russian World Cruise

The Russian government has ordered another expedition to be fitted out for a voyage round the world; it is to be commanded by Captain Krusenstern, an officer of great skill and enterprise. Several Russian officers, and others who are to make part of the expedition, have lately been in this country for the purpose of completing their scientific apparatus. It is intended again to explore Behring's Straits and the Frozen Ocean, and to find a passage from the north-west of America to Archangel, either by the Continent of America or of Asia.

May-June. XXXIII 500-501

Victory at Waterloo!

Active hostilities have been commenced by Buonaparte, and his formidable attack repelled with the most gratifying and glorious success [at Waterloo]. The repulse, and

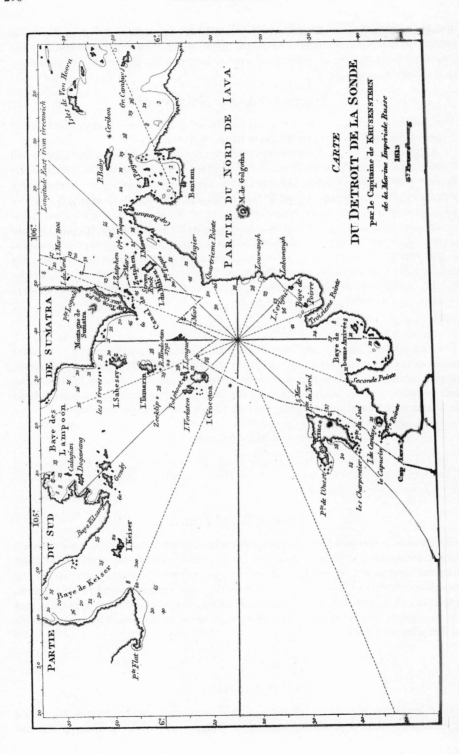

CARTE
DU DÉTROIT DE LA SONDE
par le Capitaine de KRUSENSTERN
de la Marine Impériale Russe
1813

subsequent rout, have conferred, on every individual engaged, from the marshal to the private, all the characteristic honour that real bravery can bestow; while the anxiety of all Europe is cheered by the most confident hopes of an early and happy termination of its struggles for a lasting peace.

Amusing Narrative, or the Hopes and Fears of Jonathan
XXXIV 377-380

From the 'National Intelligencer.'

Narrative of the Escape of the Hornet from a British Seventy-four, after a Chase of 42 Hours; extracted from a private Journal of one of the Officers on board the Hornet

United States Ship Hornet, off the Cape of Good Hope, Saturday, May 9, 1815
Thursday, April 27th, 1815

At 7 P.M. the *Peacock* made a signal for a strange sail bearing S.E. by S. We immediately made all sail in chase. Friday, 28th, commenced with light breezes and pleasant weather; all sails set in chase; at sun-down we neared the stranger considerably, when it fell perfectly calm, and remained so during the whole of the night; the stranger ahead, and could just discern his topsails out of the water. At day-light the sail not to be seen from the deck; at 5 A.M. a breeze sprung up from the N.W. we immediately crowded all sail, in order, if possible, to get sight of the chase again; soon after descried him standing to the northward and eastward on a wind.

Saturday, the 29th, at three quarters past two P.M. the *Peacock* was about ten miles ahead of the *Hornet*, we observed Captain Warrington approaching the stranger with much precaution: we therefore took in all our larboard steering-sails, set the stay-sails, and hauled up for the *Peacock*, still under the impression the sail in sight was an English Indiaman, and from the apparent conduct of the commander of the *Peacock*, we were under an impression, as the ship looked very large, that Captain W. was waiting until we came up with him, in order to make a joint attack. At half-past 3 P.M. the *Peacock* made the signal, that the chase was a line-of-battle ship, and an enemy. Our astonishment may easily be conceived; we took in all steering-sails, and hauled upon the wind, bringing the enemy upon our lee quarter, about 3 leagues distance; the *Peacock* on his weather-bow, and apparently not more than 3 miles from the enemy; at sun down the enemy bore E 1/2 S. the *Peacock* E. by N. We soon perceived the enemy sailed remarkably fast, but the *Peacock* left him, running off to the eastward. The enemy continued by the wind, and evidently in chase of us; at six loosed the wedges of the lower masts; at eight we discovered the enemy weathered upon us fast, and that there was every appearance he would, if not come up with us, continue in sight all night. It was thought necessary to lighten the ship; at nine we cut away the sheet anchor, and hove overboard the cable, a quantity of rigging, spars, &c. At half-past nine scuttled the ward-room deck to get at the kentledge; hove overboard about 90 pieces, weighing about 50 tons. At two A.M. tacked ship to the southward and westward, which the enemy no sooner discovered than he tacked also. At day-light he was within shot distance, on our lee quarter; at

Carte Du Detroit de la Sonde, from a Survey by Captain Krusenstern, of the Imperial Russian Navy, in 1813. Engraved by Rowe.
The annexed Chart of the Strait of Sunda, is properly, a companion to the memoir by Captain Krusenstern, given in our last volume [XXXII], pages 419-489, which particular circumstances at that time prevented our annexing to the text. [Plate 435]

seven A.M. he hoisted English colours, and a rear-admiral's flag at his mizzen-top-gallant-mast head, and commenced firing from his bow guns, his shot over reaching us about one mile. We therefore commenced again to lighten the ship, by cutting away our remaining anchors, and throwing overboard the cables, cut up the launch and hove it overboard, a quantity of provisions, with more kentledge, shot, capstan, spars, all rigging, sails, guns, and, in fact, every heavy article that could possibly tend to impede the ship's sailing. The enemy continued to fire very heavy, and in quick succession, but his British thunder could neither terrify the Yankee spirit, nor diminish Yankee skill, nor compel us to shew him the Yankee stripes, which must have irritated him excessively. None of his shot as yet had taken effect, although he had been firing for near four hours incessantly, his shot generally passing between our masts. We thought at this period we discovered we were dropping him, as his shot began to fall short; this stimulated our gallant crew to fresh exertion. At 11 A.M. his firing ceased, and the breeze began to freshen, we discovered the enemy was again coming up with us fast, which induced a general belief that he had made some alteration to the trim of his ship. At meridian, squally and fresh breezes; wind from the westward. Sunday, 30th, fresh breezes and squally; the enemy still gaining on the *Hornet*. At 1 P.M. being within gun-shot distance, he commenced a very spirited and heavy fire with round and grape, the former passing between our masts, and the latter falling all round us. The enemy fired shells, but were so ill-directed as to be perfectly harmless.

From two to three P.M. threw overboard all the muskets, cutlasses, forge, &c. and broke up the bell; also cut up the top-gallant forecastle. It was now our capture appeared inevitable; the enemy three-fourths of a mile on the lee quarter, pouring his shot and shells in great number all around us – continued to lighten the ship by heaving every thing overboard that could either be of service to the enemy, or an impediment to the *Hornet*'s sailing. The men were ordered to lie down on the quarter-deck, in order to trim ship, and to facilitate the ship's sailing. At 4, one of the shot from the enemy struck the jib-boom, another struck the starboard bulwark, just forward of the gangway, and a third struck on the deck forward of the main hatch, on the larboard side, glanced off, and passed through the foresail.

At half-past 4, we again began to leave the enemy, and to appearance, by magic – set the larboard lower steering sail, the wind drawing more aft. At 5, the enemy's shot fell short. At 6, fresh breezes – the enemy hull-down in our wake. At 7, could just see his lower steering-sail above the horizon; from 8 to 12, descried him at intervals, with the night glasses. At day-light, discovered the enemy astern of us, distance five leagues. At 9 A.M. the enemy shortened sail, reefed his top-sails, and hauled upon a wind to the eastward, after a chase of forty-two hours. During this tedious and anxious chase, the wind was variable, so as to oblige us to make a perfect circle round the enemy. Between two and three o'clock yesterday, not a person on board had the most distant idea that there was a possibility of escape. We all packed up our things, and waited until the enemy's shot would compel us to heave to and surrender, which appeared certain.

Never has there been so evident an interposition of the goodness of a Divine Father – my heart with gratitude acknowledges his supreme power and goodness. On the morning of the 28th, it was very calm, and nothing but murmurs were heard throughout the ship, as it was feared we should lose our anticipated prize – many plans had been formed by us for the disposal of our plunder. The seamen declared they would have the birth-deck carpeted with East India silk, supposing her an Indiaman, from India, while the officers, under the impression she was from England, were making arrangements how we should dispose of the money, porter, cheese, &c &c Nothing perplexed us more than the idea, that we should not be able to take out all the good things before we should be obliged to destroy her. We were regretting our ship did not sail faster, as the *Peacock* would certainly capture her first, and would take out many of the best and most valuable articles before we should get up - (this very circumstance of our not sailing so fast as the *Peacock*, saved us, in the first instance, from inevitable capture; for when Captain W. made the signal for the sail to be an enemy of superior force, we were four leagues to windward.) We all calculated our fortunes were made, but, alas! we "caught a Tartar."

During the latter part of the chase, when the shot and shells were whistling about our ears, it was an interesting sight to behold the varied countenances of our crew. They had kept the deck during all the preceding night, employed continually in lightening the ship, were excessively fatigued, and under momentary expectation of falling into the hands of an enraged enemy. The shot that fell on the main deck (as before related) struck immediately over the head of one of our gallant fellows, who had been wounded in our glorious action with the *Penguin*, where he was lying in his cot very ill with his wounds; the shot was near coming through the deck, and it threw innumerable splinters around this poor fellow, and struck down a small paper American ensign, which he had hoisted over his head - destruction apparently stared us in the face, if we did not soon surrender, yet no officer, no man in the ship, shewed any disposition to let the enemy have the poor little *Hornet*. Many of our men had been impressed and imprisoned for years in that horrible service, and hated them and their nation with the most deadly animosity; while the rest of the crew, horror-struck by the relation of the sufferings of their shipmates, who had been in the power of the English, and now equally flushed with rage, joined heartily in execrating the present authors of our misfortune. Captain Biddle mustered the crew, and told them he was pleased with their conduct during the chase, and hoped still to perceive the propriety of conduct which had always marked their character, and that of the American tar generally, that we might soon expect to be captured, &c. Not a dry eye was to be seen at the mention of capture; the rugged hearts of the sailors, like ice before the sun, warmed by the divine power of sympathy, wept with their brave commander. About two o'clock, the wind, which had crossed us, and put to the test all our nautical skill to steer clear of the enemy, now veered in our favour (as before stated), and we left him. This was truly a glorious victory over the horrors of banishment, and the terrors of a British floating dungeon. Quick as thought, every face was changed from the gloom of despair to the highest smile of delight, and we began, once more, to breathe the sweets of liberty - the bitter sighs of regret were now changed, and I put forth my expression of everlasting gratitude to him, the supreme Author of our being - who had thus signally delivered us from the power of a cruel and vindictive enemy.

The Disappointment XXXIII 499

A Turtle, floating on the swelling deep,
Calm, gliding with the current, fast asleep,
Soon from the busy deck, near dusk, was spied,
And, by each epicure, was eager ey'd.
I thought I saw the Doctor's anxious look,
Which seem'd to say, "Run, Cressy, call the cook;
Quick, lower a boat to pick that turtle up;

And of the sav'ry produce let me sup!"
The officer with zeal each effort tries;
Soon comes the boat, but not the wished-for-prize:
The noise and bustle which the crew did make,
Soon caused the sleeping luxury to wake,
Which to the bottom div'd, as I'm a sinner,
And baulk'd the ward-room of a turtle dinner!

1815 – Mutineers of the Bounty[1]

XXXV 17-25; see also XXXIII 217-218; 377

The following particulars respecting the descendants of the survivors of these men cannot fail to be perused with great interest by all our readers:

"It is well known that, in the year 1789, his Majesty's armed ship the *Bounty*, while employed in conveying the bread-fruit tree from Otaheite to the West Indies, was run away with by her men, and the captain and some of his officers put on board a boat, which, after a passage of 1200 leagues, providentially arrived at a Dutch settlement on the island of Timor. The mutineers, 25 in number, were supposed, from some expressions which escaped them, to have made sail towards Otaheite. As soon as this circumstance was made known to the Admiralty, Captain Edwards was ordered to proceed in the *Pandora* to that island, and endeavour to discover and bring to England the *Bounty*, with such of the crew as he might be able to secure. On his arrival, March 1791, at Matavai-bay, in Otaheite, four of the mutineers came voluntarily on board the *Pandora* to surrender themselves; and from information given by them, ten others (the whole number alive upon the island) were in the course of a few days taken; and, with the exception of four, who perished in the wreck of the *Pandora*, near Endeavour Straight, conveyed to England for trial before a court-martial, which adjudged six of them to suffer death, and acquitted the other four.

From the accounts given by these men, as well as from some documents that were preserved, it appeared, that as soon as Lieutenant Bligh had been driven from the ship, the 25 mutineers proceeded with her to Toobouai, where they proposed to settle; but the place being found to hold out little encouragement, they returned to Otaheite, and having there laid in a large supply of stock, they once more took their departure for Toobouai, carrying with them eight men, nine women, and seven boys, natives of Otaheite.

They commenced on their second arrival the building of a fort; but by divisions among themselves, and quarrels with the natives, the design was abandoned. Christian, the leader, also very soon discovered that his authority over his accomplices was at an

---

1 We have great pleasure in stating to the public, who have been so much interested in the fate of the recently discovered demi-British colony in Pitcairn's island, the descendants of the mutineers of the *Bounty*, that it is the laudable purpose of government to render them every possible assistance; they will be amply supplied with implements of husbandry and of useful handicrafts, and with all those utensils of European manufacture, which can contribute to their comfort or increase their happiness.

end; he therefore proposed that they should return to Otaheite; that as many as chose it should be put on shore at that island, and that the rest should proceed in the ship to any other place they might think proper. Accordingly they once more put to sea, and reached Matavai, 20th September 1789.

Here 16 of the 25 desired to be landed, 14 of whom, as already mentioned, were taken on board the *Pandora*; of the other two, as reported by Coleman (the first who surrendered himself to Captain Edwards), one had been made a Chief, killed his companion, and was shortly afterwards murdered himself by the natives.

Christian, with the remaining eight of the mutineers, having taken on board several of the natives of Otaheite, the greater part women, put to sea 21st September 1789; in the morning the ship was discovered from Point Venus, steering in a north-westerly direction; and here terminated the accounts given by the mutineers who were either taken or surrendered themselves at Matavai-bay. They stated, however, that Christian, on the night of his departure, was heard to declare, that he should seek for some uninhabited island, and, having established his party, break up the ship; but all endeavours of Captain Edwards to gain intelligence either of the ship or her crew, at any of the numerous islands visited by the *Pandora*, failed.

From this period, no information respecting Christian or his companions reached England for 20 years;[2] when, about the beginning of 1809, Sir Sidney Smith, then commander-in-chief on the Brazil station, transmitted to the Admiralty a paper, which he had received from Lieutenant Fitzmaurice, purporting to be an "Extract from the log-book of Captain Folger, of the American ship *Topaz*," and dated "Valparaiso, 10th October, 1808."

About the commencement of the present year, Rear-admiral Hotham, when cruising off New London, received a letter, addressed to the Lords of the Admiralty, of which the following is a copy, together with the azimuth compass, to which it refers:

Nantucket, March 1, 1813
My Lords, The remarkable circumstance which took place on my last voyage to the Pacific Ocean, will, I trust, plead my apology for addressing your Lordships at this time. In February, 1808, I touched at Pitcairn's Island, in latitude 25° 2'S. long 1° 30'W. from Greenwich. My principal object was, to procure seal-skins for the China market; and, from the account given to the island in Captain Carteret's voyage, I supposed it was uninhabited; but, on approaching the shore in my boat, I was met by three young men in a double canoe, with a present, consisting of some fruit and a hog. They spoke to me in the English language, and informed me that they were born on the island, and their father was an Englishman, who had sailed with Captain Bligh.

After discoursing with them a short time, I landed with them, and found an Englishman, of the name of Alexander Smith, who informed me that he was one of the *Bounty*'s crew, and that after putting Captain Bligh in the boat, with half the ship's company, they returned to Otaheite, where part of their crew chose to tarry; but Mr. Christian, with eight others, including himself, preferred going to a more remote place; and, after making a short stay at Otaheite, where they took wives and six men servants, they proceeded to Pitcairn's island, where they destroyed the ship, after taking every thing out of her which they thought would be useful to them. About six years after they landed at this place, their servants attacked and killed all the English, excepting the

2 *Vide N.C.* Vol. xxi page 454.

informant, and he was severely wounded. The same night, the Otaheitean widows arose and murdered all their countrymen, leaving Smith with the widows and children, where he had resided ever since without being resisted.

I remained but a short time on this island, and on leaving it, Smith presented me a time-piece, and an azimuth compass, which he told me belonged to the *Bounty*. The time-keeper was taken from me by the governor of the island of Juan Fernandez, after I had it in my possession about six weeks. The compass I put in repair on board my ship, and made use of it on my homeward passage, since which a new card has been put to it by an instrument-maker in Boston. I now forward it to your Lordships, thinking there will be a kind of satisfaction in receiving it, merely from the extraordinary circumstances attending it.

MAYHEW FOLGER"

Nearly about the same time, a further account of these interesting people was received from Vice-admiral Dixon, in a letter addressed to him by Sir Thomas Staines, of his Majesty's ship *Briton*, of which the following is a copy:

Briton, Valparaiso, October 18, 1814
Sir, I have the honour to inform you, that on my passage from the Marquesas Islands to this port, on the morning of the 17th September, I fell in with an Island where none is laid down either in the Admiralty or other Charts, according to the several Chronometers of *Briton* and *Tagus*; I therefore hove-to until day-light, and then closed to ascertain whether it was inhabited, which I soon discovered it to be, and to my great astonishment found that every individual on the island (40 in number) spoke very good English. They proved to be the descendants of the deluded crew of the *Bounty*, which from Otaheite proceeded to the above mentioned island, where the ship was burnt.

Christian appeared to have been the leader and sole cause of the mutiny in that ship. A venerable old man, named John Adams,[3] is the only surviving Englishman of those who last quitted Otaheite in her, and whose exemplary conduct and fatherly care of the whole of the little colony could not but command admiration. The pious manner in which all those born on the island have been reared, the correct sense of religion which has been instilled into their young minds by this old man, has given him the preeminence over the whole of them, to whom they look up as the father of the whole and one family.

A son of Christian was the first born on the island, now about 25 years of age, named Thursday October Christian; the elder Christian fell a sacrifice to the jealousy of an Otaheitean man within three or four years after their arrival on the island. They were accompanied thither by six Otaheitean men and twelve women; the former were all swept away by desperate contentions between them and the Englishmen, and five of the latter have died at different periods, leaving at present only one man and seven women of the original settlers.

The island must undoubtedly be that called Pitcairn's, although erroneously laid down in the charts. We had the meridian sun close to it, which gave us $25° 4'$ S. for its latitude; and longitude per chronometers of *Briton* and *Tagus*, $130° 25'$ W.

It is abundant in yams, plantains, hogs, goats, and fowls, but affords no shelter for a ship or vessel of any description; neither could a ship water there without great difficulty.

---

3 There was no such name in the *Bounty*'s crew; he must have assumed it in lieu of his real name, Alexander Smith.

I cannot, however, refrain from offering my opinion, that it is well worthy the attention of our laudable religious Societies, particularly that for propagating the Christian Religion, the whole of the inhabitants speaking the Otaheitean tongue as well as the English.

During the whole of the time that they have been on the island, only one ship has ever communicated with them, which took place about six years since by an American ship, called the *Topaz* of Boston, Mayhew Folger master.

The island is completely ironbound, with rocky shores, and landing in boats at all times difficult, although safe to approach within a short distance in a ship.

J. STAINES

We have been favoured with some further particulars of this singular society, which, we doubt not, will interest our readers as much as they have ourselves. As the real position of the island was ascertained to be so far distant from that in which it is usually laid down in the charts, and as the captains of the *Briton* and *Tagus* seem to have still considered it as uninhabited, they were not a little surprised, on approaching its shores, to behold plantations regularly laid out, and huts or houses more neatly constructed than those on the Marquesas islands. When about two miles from the shore, some natives were observed bringing down their canoes on their shoulders, dashing through a heavy surf, and paddling off to the ships; but their astonishment was unbounded, on hearing one of them, on approaching the ship, call out in the English language, "Won't you heave us a rope, now?"

The first man who got on board the *Briton* soon proved who they were. His name, he said, was Thursday-October-Christian, the first-born on the island. He was then about 25 years of age, and is described as being a fine young man, about six feet high, his hair deep black, his countenance open and interesting, of a brownish cast, but free from that mixture of a reddish tint, which prevails on the Pacific Islands; his only dress was a piece of cloth round his loins, and a straw hat, ornamented with the black feathers of the domestic fowl. - "With a great share of good humour," says Captain Pipon, "we were glad to trace in his benevolent countenance all the features of an honest English face; and I must confess, I could not survey this interesting person without feelings of tenderness and compassion." His companion was named George Young, a fine youth, about 18.

If the astonishment of the captain was great on hearing their first salutations in English, their surprise and interest were not a little increased on Sir Thomas Staines taking the youths below, and setting before them something to eat; when one of them rose up, and placing his hands together in a posture of devotion, distinctly repeated, and in a pleasing tone and manner "For what we are going to receive, the Lord make us truly thankful." They expressed great surprise on seeing a cow on board the *Briton*, and were in doubt whether she was a great goat or a horned sow.

The two captains of his Majesty's ships accompanied these young men on shore. With some difficulty, and a good wetting, and with the assistance of their conductors, they accomplished a landing through the surf, and were soon after met by John Adams, a man between 50 and 60, who conducted them to his house. His wife accompanied him, a very old lady, blind with age. He was at first alarmed, lest the visit was to apprehend him. But on being told that they were perfectly ignorant of his existence, he was relieved from his anxiety. Being once assured that this visit was of a peaceable nature, it is impossible to describe the joy these poor people manifested, on seeing those whom they were pleased to consider as their countrymen. Yams, cocoa-nuts, and other fruits, with fine fresh eggs, were laid before them; and the old man would have killed and dressed a hog for his visitors, but time would not allow them to partake of his intended feast.

The interesting new colony, it seemed, now consisted of about 46 persons, mostly grown up young people, besides a number of infants. The young men, all born on the island, were very athletic, and of the finest forms - their countenances open and pleasing, indicating much benevolence and goodness of heart; but the young women were objects of particular admiration, tall, robust, and beautifully formed, their faces beaming with smiles and ruffled good humour, but wearing a degree of modesty and bashfulness that would do honour to the most virtuous nation on earth; their teeth, like ivory, were regular and beautiful, without a single exception; and all of them, both male and female, had the most marked English features.

The clothing of the young females consisted of a piece of linen reaching from the waist to the knees, and generally a sort of mantle thrown loosely over the shoulders, and hanging as low as the ankles; but this covering appeared to be intended chiefly as a protection against the sun and the weather, as it was frequently laid aside - and then the upper part of the body was entirely exposed, and it is not possible to conceive more beautiful forms than they exhibited. They sometimes wreath caps or bonnets for the head, in the most tasty manner, to protect the face from the rays of the sun; and though, as Captain Pipon observes, they have only had the instruction of the Otaheitean mothers, "our dress-makers in London would be delighted with the simplicity, and yet elegant taste, of these untaught females."

Their native modesty, assisted by a proper sense of religion and morality, instilled into their youthful minds by John Adams, has hitherto preserved these interesting people perfectly chaste, and free from all kinds of debauchery. Adams assured the visitors, that since Christian's death there had not been a single instance of any young woman proving unchaste, nor any attempt at seduction on the part of the men. They all labour while young in the cultivation of the ground; and when possessed of a sufficient quantity of cleared land and of stock to maintain a family, they are allowed to marry, but always with the consent of Adams, who unites them by a sort of marriage-ceremony of his own.

The greatest harmony prevails in this little society; their only quarrels, and these rarely happened, being, according to their own expression, "quarrels of the mouth;" they are honest in their dealings, which consist of bartering different articles for mutual accommodation. Their habitations are extremely neat. The little village of Pitcairn forms a pretty square, the houses at the upper end of which are occupied by the patriarch, John Adams, and his family, consisting of his old blind wife, and three daughters, from 15 to 18 years of age, and a boy of 11; a daughter of his wife by a former husband, and a son-in-law. On the opposite side is the dwelling of Thursday-October-Christian; and in the centre is a smooth verdant lawn, on which the poultry are let loose, fenced in so as to prevent the intrusion of the domestic quadrupeds.

All that was done was obviously undertaken on a settled plan, unlike to any thing to be met with on the other islands. In their houses, too, they had a good deal of decent furniture, consisting of beds laid upon bedsteads, with neat covering; they had also tables, and large chests to contain their valuables and clothing, which is made from the bark of a certain tree prepared chiefly by the elder Otaheitean females. Adams's house consisted of two rooms, and the windows had shutters to close at night. The younger part of the females are, as before stated, employed with their brothers, under the direction of their common father, Adams, in the culture of the ground, which produced cocoa-nuts, bananas, bread-fruit tree, yams, sweet potatoes, and turnips. They have also plenty of hogs, and goats. The woods abound with a species of wild hog, and the coasts of the island with several kinds of good fish.

Their agricultural implements are made by themselves, from the iron supplied by the *Bounty*, which, with great labour, they beat out into spades, hatchets, &c. This was not all. The good old man kept a regular journal, in which was entered the nature and quantity of work performed by each family, what each had received, and what was due on account.

There was, it seems, besides private property, a sort of general stock, out of which articles were issued on account of the several members of the community; and for mutual accommodation, exchanges of one kind of provision for another were very frequent, as salt for fresh provisions, vegetables and fruit for poultry, fish &c.; also, when the stores of one family were low, or wholly expended, a fresh supply was raised from another, or out of the general stock, to be repaid when circumstances were more favourable; all of which were carefully noted down in Adams' journal.

But what was most gratifying of all to the visitors, was the simple and unaffected manner in which they returned thanks to the Almighty for the many blessings they enjoyed. They never failed to say grace before and after meals, to pray every morning at sun-rise, and they frequently repeated the Lord's Prayer and the Creed. "It was truly pleasing," says Captain Pipon, "to see these poor people so well disposed to listen so attentively to moral instruction, to believe in the attributes of God, and to place their reliance on Divine goodness." The day on which the two captains landed was Saturday, 17th September; but by John Adams' account it was Sunday the 18th, and they were keeping the Sabbath by making it a day of rest and prayer. - This was occasioned by the *Bounty* having proceeded thither by the eastern route, and our frigates having gone to the westward; and the *Topaz* found them right according to his own reckoning, she having also approached the island from the eastward. Every ship from Europe proceeding to Pitcairn's island round the Cape of Good Hope, will find them a day later - as those who approached them round the Cape Horn, a day in advance; as was the case with Captain Folger, and Captains Sir T. Staines and Pipon.

The visit of the *Topaz* is, of course, a notable circumstance, marked down in Adams' journal. The first ship descried off the island was on 27th December, 1795; but as she did not approach the land, they could not make out to what nation she belonged. A second appeared some time after, but did not attempt to communicate with them. A third came sufficiently near to see the natives and their habitations but did not attempt to send a boat on shore; which is the less surprising, considering the uniform ruggedness of the coast, the total want of shelter, and the almost constant and violent breaking of the sea against the cliffs. The good old man was anxious to know what was going on in the old world, and they had the means of gratifying his curiosity, by supplying him with some magazines and modern publications. His library consisted of the books that belonged to Admiral Bligh, but the visitors had not time to inspect them.

They inquired particularly after Fletcher Christian. This ill-fated young man, it seems, was never happy after the rash and inconsiderate step which he had taken; he became sullen and morose, and practised the very same kind of conduct towards his companions in guilt, which he and they so loudly complained of in their late commander. Disappointed in his expectations at Otaheite, and the Friendly Islands, and most probably

Representation of Malay Proas, on the south side of Compang Bay, in the island of
Timor. Engraved by Bennet, from a drawing by Mr. W. Westall. ^{Plate 264}

dreading a discovery, this deluded youth committed himself and his remaining
confederates to the mere chance of being cast upon some desert island; and chance
threw them on that of Pitcairn. Finding no anchorage near it, he ran the ship upon the
rocks, cleared her of the live stock and other articles which they had been supplied with
at Otaheite, when he set her on fire, that no trace of inhabitants might be visible, and all
hope of escape cut off from himself and his wretched followers. He soon, however,
disgusted both his own countrymen and the Otaheiteans, by his oppressive and tyrannical
conduct; they divided into parties, and disputes, affrays, and murders, were the
consequence. His Otaheitean wife died within a twelvemonth from their landing, after
which he carried off one that belonged to an Otaheitean man, who watched for an
opportunity of taking revenge, and shot him dead while digging in his own field. Thus
terminated the miserable existence of this deluded young man, who was neither deficient
in talent, energy, nor connections, and who might have risen in the service, and become
an ornament to his profession.

John Adams declared, as it was natural enough he should do, his abhorrence of the
crime in which he was implicated, and said that he was sick at the time in his hammock:
- this, we understand, is not true, though he was not particularly active in the mutiny: -
he expressed the utmost willingness to surrender himself, and be taken to England;
indeed, he rather seemed to have an inclination to revisit his native country; but the
young men and women flocked round him, and with tears and entreaties begged that
their father and protector might not be taken from them, for without him they must all
perish. It would have been an act of the greatest inhumanity to remove him from the
island; and it is hardly necessary to add, that Sir Thomas Staines lent a willing ear to
their entreaties, thinking, no doubt, (as we feel strongly disposed to think), that, if he
were even among the most guilty, his care and success in instilling religious and moral

principles into the minds of this young and interesting society, have, in a great degree, redeemed his former crimes.

'This island is about six miles long by three broad, covered with wood, and the soil, of course, very rich, situated under the parallel of 25° S latitude; and in the midst of such a wide expanse of ocean, the climate must be fine, and admirably adapted for the reception of all the vegetable productions of every part of the habitable globe. Small, therefore, as Pitcairn's island may appear, there can be little doubt that it is capable of supporting many inhabitants, and the present stock being of so good a description, we trust they will not be neglected. In the course of time the Patriarch must go hence; and we think it will be exceedingly desirable, that the British nation should provide for such an event, by sending out, not an ignorant and idle missionary, but some zealous and intelligent instructor, together with a few persons capable of teaching the useful trades or professions. On Pitcairn's island there are better materials to work upon than missionaries have yet been so fortunate as to meet with, and the best results may reasonably be expected. - Something we are bound to do for these blameless and interesting people. The articles recommended by Captain Pipon appear to be highly proper - cooking utensils, implements of agriculture, maize, or the Indian corn, the orange tree from Valparaiso, bibles, prayer-books, and the proper selection of other books, with implements for writing.

1815 – Buonaparte's Surrender

FOLLOWING NAPOLEON BUONAPARTE'S DEFEAT at Waterloo, he fled, knowing that he would receive little mercy in Paris. He attempted to escape to the United States, but was captured and taken to Plymouth on board HMS *Bellerophon* where he was held until the Government decided what to do with him. Again, for political reasons, he was spared an execution, but his attempt to claim British hospitality was rebuffed and he was sent a prisoner to St Helena where he ended his days in futile regrets. *The Naval Chronicle* published extensive accounts of Buonaparte's last days as a public figure, which have been reproduced in the Consolidated Edition. The Convention between Great Britain and Austria, signed at Paris on 2 August 1815, granting to Britain responsibility for keeping Buonaparte in custody, was printed in Vol. xxxv, p422.

Emperor Napoleon a Prisoner of the Royal Navy
From 'Nautical Anecdotes.' XXXIV 118-128

The following particulars have been selected as a journalized narrative of the surrender and transmarine transfer of Buonaparte. Having terminated his military career at Waterloo, and finding the Jacobins not inclined to make any further sacrifices, his views seem henceforth to have been solely directed to his personal safety; he accordingly made a pretence of abdication, that he might withdraw himself from public notice, and having prepared for his reception at Rochefort, he passed through Rambouillet on the 1st of July, on his way thither, his suite being composed of Generals Bertrand, Savary, Lallemand, Labedoyere, Moutholon, and Gorgau; Colonels Baillon and Descham, Chiefs of Squadron; Morin, Resigny, and St. Gow; Captain Pierson; Lieutenant Autrie; Messrs. Delacasse, Chamberlain, and his son; St. Catherine, Page; Rattery, Secretary; Regan, Surgeon; Cotin and Appiani, Maitres d'Hotel; Planat St. Jacques and Chiappe, and eight domestics.

Information of his departure from Paris having been received, orders were immediately sent to our cruisers to keep a sharp look-out, in the expectation of his embarking at some one of the southern ports for America. The following particulars of the subsequent proceedings respecting him appear in the subjoined extract of a letter from an officer on board H.M.S. *Cyrus*, dated Basque Roads, July 16:

View of Plymouth Dock, taken from Mount Edgcombe. Engraved by Baily, from a drawing by Owen. Plate 363

"As we have assisted in securing Buonaparte, allow me to give you a journal of the proceedings previous to that event.

July 1. While within Isle Dieu, at anchor, assisting the royalists, a boat came on board from his Majesty's ship *Bellerophon*, with despatches, announcing that Buonaparte had quitted Paris for some port to the southward, intending to go to America; and requiring us to come down and assist her in the blockade of Rochefort. We immediately proceeded to Quiberon Bay to Admiral Hotham with this intelligence.

July 5. Arrived at Quiberon Bay at three P.M. communicated with Admiral Hotham, and sailed again directly to join the *Bellerophon* off this port.

July 6. At six A.M. chased and boarded a Prussian just come out of the Charente, notwithstanding the hostility between the two nations. - Examined her minutely, but found no suspicious characters on board. - Received information that Buonaparte was not at Rochefort, but daily expected, as three successive messengers had arrived in the night of June 29, ordering two frigates lying at the Isle d'Aix, to be got ready with all despatch. In the evening we spoke his Majesty's ship *Slaney*, and received orders to resume our station within Isle Dieu.

July 8 - Resumed our station, after capturing a boat, containing three soldiers, belonging to Isle Noirmoustier, who endeavoured to pass for fishermen - gained no information.

July 9 - Spoke his Majesty's ship *Falmouth*, proceeding to the westward, who told us, from the information of the *Sheldrake* brig of war, off the Loire, that Buonaparte was at Nantes, and that the force off that river was not sufficient to oppose his departure. We immediately weighed, and proceeded off the Loire. Found the *Dwarf* had joined the brig, and that the *Opossum* was also close at hand; so that being strong enough, we bore up to regain the *Bellerophon*, off the light-house of Oleron.

July 12 - At one P.M. passed near to her and the *Slaney*. *Bellerophon* telegraphed us

- "Keep close off Balaine light-house: Buonaparte is here, endeavouring to escape.
Examine every description of vessels closely for him. I have two of his generals, who
have asked for the frigates to pass."

At three P.M. saw a brig coming out of the Breton Passage; chased her for 12
hours, and found her an American without passengers, who told us he had no doubt but
that Buonaparte was at Rochefort, but it was not publicly known at the place he had left
(St. Martin's Isle Rhé.)

July 13. At half-past one P.M. saw the *Bellerophon* and *Slaney* some distance to
leeward, with flags of truce at their mast-heads, and a chasse marée with a similar flag,
so that we had little doubt of Napoleon having surrendered, or being at least negotiating
for that purpose.

July 14. The *Superb*, Admiral Hotham, directed us to anchor within the Breton
Passage, the more effectually to blockade it, and then passed on to Basque Roads to join
the *Bellerophon*.

July 15. The *Slaney* passed us, and telegraphed, "For England, with important
despatches."

July 16. We were recalled to this place, and found the *Disturber of the World*, whom
we had been so anxiously looking for, safe on board the *Bellerophon*. He was just returning
to the latter ship from breakfasting on board the *Superb* with the Admiral, who ordered
the yards to be manned, as a mark of respect.

We passed close to the *Bellerophon* several times; Captain Maitland told us, "*I have
got Buonaparte on Board.*"

Napoleon stood exposed at full length on the gang-way, about twenty yards distant,
to survey us; and we, in return, examined him, as you may be assured, with minute and
eager attention. He was dressed in a green uniform coat, with two epaulets, and a red
collar - a broad red sash over his shoulder, a large star on the left breast, white waistcoat,
pantaloons, boots, and a large cocked hat, with the tri-coloured cockade. I knew the
figure and face instantly; it was impossible for any one, who had ever examined the
lineaments with attention, to mistake them. Bertrand, L'Allemand, Savary, and others,
were with him.

He first sent out to Captain Maitland for permission to proceed to America in the
frigates, which was refused; but an offer made of referring him, if he came out, to the
Admiral. He then asked for a brig, and afterwards for a schooner - requests equally
inadmissible. Afterwards he formed the plan for going in two chasse marées out of the
Breton Passage in the night; and being informed that this ship would intercept him, he
replied, "*He would try, for we would not suspect such small vessels.*" This determination
was altered, probably, by reflecting, that if taken prisoner, he would have no claim on
our generosity; while, by throwing himself into our power, there might at least be some
hope in setting up such a claim. *He then surrendered, after threatening to force his passage.*

On board the *Bellerophon*, he seemed to think himself Emperor, taking possession
of Captain Maitland's cabin, and shortly after inviting him to dinner. When he went on
board the *Superb* this morning, Bertrand first ascended the side, and was introduced to
the Admiral; Napoleon followed. "The Emperor," said Captain Maitland - Napoleon
bowed to the Admiral, without further ceremony walked to his cabin, and sent his
compliments that he would be glad to speak with him!!

Nothing escapes his notice; his eyes are in every place, and on every object, from
the greatest to the most minute. He immediately asked an explanation of the ropes,
blocks, masts, and yards, and all the machinery of the ship. He sent for the boatswain,

to question him; that officer always fitting out the French ships. He requested the marines to pass in review before him, examining the arms, evolutions, dress, &c &c and expressed himself highly pleased. He inquired into the situation of the seamen, their pay, prize-money, clothes, food, tobacco, &c and when told of their being supplied by a purser or commissary, asked if he was not a rogue.

In conversing with the Admiral, he said, "I have given myself up to the English; but I would not have done so to any other of the Allied Powers. In surrendering to any of them, I should be subject to the caprice and will of an individual: – in submitting to the English, I place myself at the mercy of a nation. – Adieu."

In his passage to the British coast, he demanded all the homage due to a sovereign, as he considers himself as still sovereign of Elba.

July 24. Between five and six o'clock in the morning, Captain Sartorius, of the *Slaney* sloop, arrived with despatches from Captain Maitland, and was also the bearer of a letter from Buonaparte to the Prince Regent. Buonaparte had delivered this letter to one of his own suite, who was to present it. This person, however, upon his arrival at Plymouth in the *Slaney*, was not permitted to proceed to town, but the letter was given in charge to Captain Sartorius, who immediately upon his arrival proceeded to the Secretary's, Mr. Barrow's. Lord Melville came to town from Wimbledon, between ten and eleven, and had an audience of the Prince Regent at Carlton House, who had returned to town from Windsor on Sunday night, between ten and eleven o'clock. He remained with his Royal Highness upwards of an hour, when his Lordship proceeded at twelve o'clock to the Foreign Office, at which hour a Cabinet Council was summoned to be held, and which continued sitting till between four and five. At the breaking up of the Council, Mr. Pegler, the King's messenger, was ordered to hold himself in readiness for a journey, and the exertions to get him off were so great, that he had started at about six.

The following is a translation of the letter:

Rochefort, 13th July
Your Royal Highness, Exposed to the factions which divide my country, and to the enmity of the great Powers of Europe, I have terminated my political career; and I come, like Themistocles, to throw myself upon the hospitality (*m'asseoir sur le foyer*) of the British people. I claim from your Royal Highness the protection of the laws, and throw myself upon the most powerful, the most constant, and the most generous of my enemies.

NAPOLEON

In the evening of the same day it was announced by telegraph, that the *Bellerophon* was arrived at Torbay.

July 25. Lieutenant Fletcher, flag-lieutenant to Sir H. Hotham, arrived in town with despatches, giving an account of the *Bellerophon*'s arrival, with Buonaparte and his suite, consisting of 45 persons. He had required accommodations for 50 cavalry! Telegraphic orders were given to prohibit all communication between the ship and shore.

July 26. The *Bellerophon* in consequence of orders left Torbay for Plymouth, about 5 o'clock this morning, and about 5 o'clock in the evening of the same day, came to an anchor just inside the breakwater, and immediately afterwards the *Eurotas* and *Liffey* were directed to place themselves at a short distance on each of her quarters, and keep off boats that had anxiously hastened from the shore to obtain a glance of the imperial magnet. Admirals, captains, and other distinguished persons, were among the number, but all alike were refused admittance, and obliged to content themselves with a distant view. He gratified the spectators with his appearance frequently on the poop and gangway, on which occasions the *British*, as well as French, officers, *stood uncovered*, and apart!! One of his officers intimating to him, that Sir Richard Strachan was in a barge alongside, Buonaparte instantly took off his hat, and bowed to him, with a smile. This was a favourable opportunity for the various observers, as he continued walking in full view nearly an hour. Mrs. Maitland was also complimented with a bow. Yesterday Admiral Lord Viscount Keith had a short interview with Buonaparte, at the request of the latter, when orders were given that he should be treated as a prisoner and foreign general.

The number of spectators was immense. The principal time for beholding his whole figure was generally a little before six o'clock, just previous to his dinner hour, at which time the mass of surrounding boats exceeded both in breadth and length every thing that can be imagined concerning it, 1000 boats, and 10,000 persons, at least, were supposed to be at some time congregated, partly attracted by the ex-imperial phenomenon, and partly by a wish to see the breakwater, only a few hundred yards from the *Bellerophon*, where, to their surprise, they found a supply of porter, biscuits, fruit, and even tea, coffee, and cream; on which, after viewing the chief object, several thousands landed, at low-water, absolutely covering its extent with population.

We regret to say, that a large portion of the spectators not only took off their hats, but cheered him, apparently with the view of soothing his fallen fortunes, and treating him with respect and consideration; him, whose whole life has been a series of exultations in the calamities of others! To what cause shall we ascribe this tergiversation of the British character? Can there be a stronger proof of our growing depravity, than this tendency to commiserate vice, when men allow such a dangerous impulse to overcome their reason, their ideas of justice, and all the sober feelings of their minds? All history proclaims the dignity due to suffering virtue. Is it left for us to venerate unsuccessful villainy? Do great talents alone, unaccompanied by a single other good quality, carry with them a sufficient title to the esteem and admiration of mankind? It is impossible, in our opinion, to speak too harshly of such a mode of conduct, and the excuse assigned for it, still more degrades our natural spirit; this is, a love of war, because it enriches individuals more than the avocations of peace, and as Buonaparte administered to that love, in full perfection, he was necessarily entitled to our regard and affection! - Horrible confession! Disgraceful to our religion, to our morality, to our country! Shall the mean self-interest of individuals be permitted to weigh down the public good, (and surely war cannot be considered very compatible with the latter!)? Heaven forbid! When self is every thing, and country nothing, that country rapidly approaches its downfall! If there be a virtue in Frenchmen it is their nationality, which, under all circumstances, whether prosperous or unprosperous, ever adheres to them, and is the beacon to their thought and actions.

July 28. The fate of Buonaparte was finally determined at a Cabinet Council held at the foreign Office, and the following morning Sir H. Bunbury, the Under Secretary of State for the War Department, set out for Plymouth, accompanied by the son of Earl Bathurst and Mr. Guy, the King's messenger, to communicate to Napoleon the final determination of our Government to consign him as a prisoner to St. Helena; to make all the arrangements consequently necessary; and to witness in part their execution, by the departure of the ship. In all the official documents issued upon this occasion, the Usurper is designated as "General Buonaparte."

August 4. Sir George Cockburn cleared St. Helen's in the *Northumberland*, the ship destined to carry Buonaparte to St. Helena, in company with the *Ceylon* and *Bucephalus*, troop ships, having on board a company of artillery, and the 53d regiment, under Sir George Bingham. Sir George Cockburn's sailing was hurried, by the circumstance of Buonaparte's having expressed the most violent determination not of suffer himself to be taken to St. Helena. When the Commission was read to him by Colonel Bunbury, appointing his place of future residence, he exclaimed – "You may take my body to St. Helena, but you shall never take my spirit." Frequently, afterward, to Captain Maitland, he said – "You shall never take me over the side of this ship alive."

August 4. A writ of *Habeas Corpus* having been obtained by some British Buonapartist, addressed to Lord Keith, to deliver up the body of Buonaparte, whom he had in custody, for the purpose of transporting him against his consent, and contrary to the laws of the kingdom, the Admiralty having been advised of it, telegraphed to Plymouth, to caution Lord Keith to keep out of the way; his Lordship immediately proceeded to Plymouth Sound, where finding the *Prometheus* under weigh, he immediately went on board that ship, hoisted his flag, and made signals for the *Bellerophon*, *Eorotas*, and *Tonnant* to follow him to sea: when he was clear of the Sound, he shifted his flag to the *Tonnant*, and cruised between the Eddystone and the Start, until he fell in with the *Northumberland*.

August 7. Buonaparte was taken from on board his Majesty's ship *Bellerophon*, accompanied by Admirals Lord Keith and Sir G. Cockburn, two French ladies, and two French Generals, and sent on board the *Northumberland*. His Majesty's ship *Tonnant*, with Lord Keith's red flag flying at the main, was stationed in the centre to superintend the trans-shipment, and supported by his Majesty's ships as below. A schooner and a cutter kept sailing about to keep off boats that had come from the shore.

Ceylon		*Morgiana*
**		*
	Tonnant	
	***	
Bucephalus		
**		
	Northumberland	*Bellerophon*
	***	***
Eurotas	*Myrmidon*	Store ship
**	*	*

The despatches which announced the trans-shipment of Buonaparte from the *Bellerophon* to the *Northumberland*, were brought by Lord Viscount Lowther, who had proceeded in the *Northumberland* from Portsmouth, and who, with the Honourable Mr. Lyttleton, M.P. for Worcestershire, remained for two hours in earnest conversation with Buonaparte, after such of his suite as were not to accompany him had left him.

The *Bellerophon* and *Tonnant* put to sea from Plymouth Sound on Friday; (the 4th August) and here we must contradict the statement that they sailed to avoid the service of a writ of *Habeas Corpus*.

The facts of the case are, that the concourse of boats in Plymouth Sound, and the loss of some lives which had already taken place, induced the government to remove the *Bellerophon* to a greater distance; and the writ which is spoken of was no more than a common subpoena from the Court of King's Bench, obtained by some person who has some cause pending in that Court, in which he fancied he wanted the evidence of Napoleon and Jerome Buonaparte, and Admiral Villaumez [Willaumez].

The *Northumberland* sailed from Portsmouth on Friday, August 4; and, on nearing Torbay on Sunday, perceived two line-of-battle ships approaching her, which proved to be the *Bellerophon*, with Buonaparte on board, and the *Tonnant*, with Lord Keith. In a few hours the *Northumberland* hailed them, and asked after Buonaparte, who, she was informed, had not come out of his cabin for some days. The ships came to an anchor off Torbay.

General Bertrand went first on board the *Tonnant*, where he dined with Lord Keith and Sir George Cockburn. He is a man of about 50 years of age, and extremely well behaved. At dinner, Sir George gave him a general explanation of his instructions with respect to Buonaparte: one of which was, that his baggage must be inspected before it was received on board the *Northumberland*. Bertrand expressed his opinion strongly against the measure of sending the Emperor (as he and all the suite constantly style him) to St. Helena, when his wish and expectation were to live quietly in England, under the protection of the English laws. Lord Keith and Sir George Cockburn did not enter into any discussion upon the subject.

After dinner, Lord Keith and Sir George Cockburn, accompanied by Bertrand, went on board the *Bellerophon*. Previously to their arrival, Buonaparte's arms and pistols had been taken away from him - not without considerable altercation and objection on the part of the French officers.

Those who were not to accompany him were sent on board the *Eurotas* frigate. They expressed great reluctance at the separation, particularly the Polish officers. Buonaparte took leave of him individually. A Colonel Pistowski, a Pole, was peculiarly desirous of accompanying him. He had received 17 wounds in the service of Buonaparte, and said he would serve in any capacity, however menial, if he could be allowed to go with him to St. Helena. The orders for sending off the Polish officers were peremptory, and he was removed to the *Eurotas*. Savary and Lalleman, however, were not amongst those sent on board the frigate: they were left in the *Bellerophon*.

When Lord Keith and Sir George Cockburn went on board the *Bellerophon* on Sunday afternoon (August 6th), Buonaparte was upon deck to receive them, dressed in a green coat with red facings, two epaulets, white waistcoat and breeches, silk stockings, the Star of the Legion of Honour, and a *chapeau bras*, with the three-coloured cockade. His face is remarkably plump, and his head rather bald upon the top. After the usual salutation, Lord Keith, addressing himself to Buonaparte, acquainted him with his intended transfer from the *Bellerophon* to the *Northumberland*.

Buonaparte immediately protested with great vehemence against this act of the British Government: - he did not expect it, - he did not conceive that any possible objection could be made of his residing in England quietly for the rest of his life.

No answer was returned by either Lord Keith or Sir George Cockburn. A British officers who stood near him observed to him, that if he had not been sent to St. Helena, he would have been delivered up to the Emperor of Russia.

Buonaparte. - "*Dieu me garde des Russes!*" (God keep me from the Russians!) In making this reply, he looked at General Bertrand, and shrugged up his shoulders.

Sir George Cockburn - "At what hour to-morrow morning shall I come, General, and receive you on board the *Northumberland*?"

Buonaparte, with some surprise at being styled merely General - "At ten o'clock."

Bertrand, Madame Bertrand, Savary, Lallemand, Count and Countess Moutholon, were standing near Buonaparte.

Sir George Cockburn asked him if he wanted any thing more before they put to sea. Bertrand replied, 50 packs of cards, a backgammon and a domino table; and Madam Bertrand desired to have some necessary articles of furniture, which, it was said, should be furnished forthwith.

One of Buonaparte's officers, the nephew of Josephine Beauharnois, his first wife, complained that faith had not been kept with the Emperor, who expected to reside with his suite in Great Britain.

Buonaparte asked Lord Keith's advice. His Lordship merely replied, that he had to obey the orders he had received from his government. Buonaparte then desired another interview with his Lordship: Lord Keith declined it, alleging that it could not but be unsatisfactory - he had no discretion - his fate could not be altered.

An officer who stood near him said "You would have been taken if you had remained at Rochefort another hour, and sent off to Paris." Buonaparte turned his eye upon the speaker, but did not speak a word. He next addressed himself to Sir G. Cockburn, and asked several questions about St. Helena.

"Is there any hunting or shooting there? - Where am I to reside?"

He then abruptly changed the subject, and burst into more invectives against the government, to which no answer was returned.

Whether he had any idea of a writ of *Habeas Corpus* or no, we know not; but he was very solicitous to go ashore.

He then expressed some indignation at being styled General - saying, "You have sent Ambassadors to me as a Sovereign Potentate, you have acknowledged me as First Consul." He took a great deal of snuff whilst speaking.

After reminding him that the *Northumberland*'s barge would come for him at ten on Monday morning, Lord Keith and Sir George Cockburn retired.

Early on Monday morning (August 7th), Sir G. Cockburn went on board the *Bellerophon* to superintend the inspection of Buonaparte's baggage; it consisted of two services of plate, several articles in gold, a superb toilet of plate, books, beds, &c. They were all sent on board the *Northumberland* about eleven o'clock.

Buonaparte had brought with him from France about forty servants, amongst whom were a groom, postilion, and lamplighter. Two-thirds of these were sent on board the *Eurotas*.

At half-past eleven o'clock, Lord Keith, in the barge of the *Tonnant*, went on board the *Bellerophon* to receive Buonaparte, and those who were to accompany him. Buonaparte, before their arrival and afterwards, addressed himself to Captain Maitland and the officers of the *Bellerophon*. After descending the ladder into the barge, he pulled off his hat to them again. Lord Keith received in the barge the following personages:

Buonaparte; General Bertrand and Madame Bertrand, with their children; Count and Countess Moutholon, and child; Count Lascasas; General Gorgaud; nine men and three women servants.

Buonaparté's surgeon refused to accompany him: upon which the surgeon of the *Bellerophon* offered to supply his place.

Buonaparte was this day dressed in a cocked hat, much worn, with a tri-coloured cockade; his coat was buttoned close round him, a plain green one with a red collar; he had three orders, two crosses, and a large silver star, with the inscription *Honneur et Patrie*; white breeches, silk stockings, gold buckles.

Savary and Lallemand were left behind in the *Bellerophon*.

Savary seemed in great dread of being given up to the French government, repeatedly asserting that the honour of England would not allow them to be landed again on the shores of France.

About twelve o'clock the *Tonnant*'s barge reached the *Northumberland*. Bertrand stepped first upon deck, Buonaparte next, mounting the side of the ship with the activity of a seaman. The marines were drawn out and received him, but merely as a general, presenting arms to him. He pulled off his hat. As soon as he was upon deck, he said to Sir George Cockburn - "*Je suis à vos ordres.*" He bowed to Lord Lowther and Mr. Lyttleton, who were near the Admiral, and spoke of them a few words, to which they replied. To an officer, he said, "*Dans quel corps servez vous?*" (In what corps do you serve?) The officer replied, "in the artillery." Buonaparte immediately rejoined - *Je sors* [sic] *de cette service moi-même* - (I was originally in that service myself.) After taking leave of the officers who had accompanied him from the *Bellerophon*, and embracing the nephew of Josephine, who was not going to St. Helena, he went into the after-cabin, where, besides his principal companions, were assembled Lord Keith, Sir G. Cockburn, Lord Lowther, the Honourable Mr. Lyttleton, &c.

Bertrand - "I never gave in my adhesion to Louis the 18th. It is therefore palpably unjust to proscribe me. However, I shall return in a year to two to superintend the education of my children."

Madam Bertrand appeared much distressed: said she was obliged to leave Paris in a hurry, without clothes, or any necessary. She had lived in the house now occupied by the Duke de Berri. She spoke most flatteringly of her husband; said the Emperor was too great a man to be depressed by circumstances, and concluded by expressing a wish for some Paris papers.

Count Moutholon spoke of the improvements made by Buonaparte in Paris; alluded to his bilious complaint, which required much exercise.

The Countess Moutholon is a very interesting woman; she said little.

Bertrand asked what we should have done had we taken Buonaparte at sea?

As we are doing now, was the reply.

Lord Keith took leave in the afternoon of Buonaparte, and returned on board the *Tonnant*.

Lord Lowther and the Honourable Mr. Lyttleton now entered into very earnest conversation with him, which continued for two hours. As he was very communicative, and seemed desirous of a very free conversation with these two accomplished young noblemen, they availed themselves of the opportunity, and entered into a review of much of his conduct. We understand that they asked him how he came to commit the impolicy of attacking Spain - the motives for the Berlin and Milan Decrees - the war against Russia - the refusal of the terms of peace offered him before the first capture of Paris, &c. To all these questions we hear he gave full answers, not avoiding, but rather encouraging, the discussion. We hope to be able to give the particulars which ought of be known. They are materials for history.

At the expiration of two hours, Lord Lowther and Mr. Lyttleton took leave of them and went ashore.

His cabin in the *Northumberland* is fitted up with great elegance. His bed is peculiarly handsome, and the linen upon it very fine. His toilet is of silver. Among other articles upon it is a magnificent snuff box, upon which is embossed in gold, an eagle, with a crown, flying from Elba to the coast of France; the eagle just seeing the coast of France, and the respective distances, are admirably executed.

The valet de chambres are particularly fine men. They and all about him always address him by the title of Emperor.

August 8th. The *Bellerophon*, *Tonnant*, and *Eurotas* returned to Plymouth Sound.

The *Northumberland* was lying-to off Plymouth, though the wind was fair; supposed waiting for the *Weymouth* storeship, which was taking in stores, &c. and was to complete them by the next day."

Buonaparte's Arrival at St. Helena XXXIV 465

The following are extracts of letters received from officers on board H.M.S. *Northumberland*:

H.M.S. Northumberland, October 20, 1815
We arrived here on the 15th, after rather a pleasant, though long, passage, of ten weeks: and General Buonaparte landed on the 16th, in the evening, when it was quite dark: he was muffled up in a large surtout coat. A guard went before him to disperse the mob. You must judge of the state of his mind and spirits by what he did, and what he did not do, during the passage. He never came out of his cabin, but in the evenings, after dinner: he then, almost without exception, went and leant against the breech of the foremost gun, on the weather side of the quarter-deck, whence he never moved. Generals Bertrand and Lascassas always came out with him, and with whom he ever continued in conversation: he appeared to take little notice of his other companions. His dress, upon these occasions, was, invariably, a green coat, white waistcoat, with two plain epaulets, light-colour small clothes, with silk stockings, and pumps, with gold buckles. At the usual ceremony of passing the Line, which we did on the 23d of September, General Buonaparte made a present to *Old Neptune* of one hundred Napoleons; the French generals and children gave him a double Napoleon each. The Countess Bertrand is one of the most pleasant and agreeable women I ever conversed with. She said, she wished we had missed the island; and I do not wonder at it; for if its boundless craggy rocks and lofty mountains strike the senses of a stranger, who can depart at his pleasure, with a cold heart-appalling effect, what must be the feelings of banished *Majesté*! Nature seems to have formed it for security to its inhabitants. Had General Buonaparte ever entertained a hope of escape, when he came in sight of this place, it must have been banished for ever; the whole world besides, I should suppose, does not present such another spot.

Northumberland, October 18, 1815
Buonaparte was very much pleased with the attention shewn to him, whilst on board this ship, however he might have felt upon subjects connected with bringing him here. He publicly thanked Captain Ross, on the quarter-deck, for his kindness, and requested he would do the same for him to the officers. He appeared very solicitous not to give the least trouble whilst on board. Every thing is very scarce and dear here. The *Redpole* returns to England with the Admiral's despatches.

Further Particulars XXXV 27-29

Further particulars of Buonaparté's arrival at St. Helena have reached us in letters from that island, to the 22d of October. On the 16th of that month, his Majesty's ship *Icarus* arrived there with the first tidings of Buonaparté's downfall, of his being a second time so strangely saved from punishment, and of his destination to that island as a place of confinement. The inhabitants were naturally struck with no small degree of surprise. It was of course learnt at the same time, that a very considerable addition would be made to the population of the island by the new garrison, as well as the attendants of

Saint Helena, with an East Indiaman coming to anchor, from an original drawing by Owen. Engraved by Ellis. Plate 54

the celebrated rebel, the commissioners to watch him, their suites, &c. Accordingly all was immediately hurry and bustle. Provisions experienced a sudden and enormous rise in price. Eggs, which were before about 3 shillings a dozen, now advanced to a shilling a piece. Almost every other article of produce rose in the same proportion and even land itself assumed an increased value of 50 per cent, which is not much to be wondered at considering the small extent of the island, and the still smaller portion that is fit for cultivation, to feed the increased number of mouths. Upwards of 900 troops arrived out in the squadron under charge of the *Northumberland*. A great bustle took place on the 11th in making preparations for Buonaparté's reception; 80 of the Company's soldiers were stationed to guard the gates, and orders were immediately issued by the governor, that no fishing boats were to be out of harbour after four o'clock in the afternoon. On the 15th the fleet arrived; when some persons from the town were allowed to go on board the squadron to dine. It was some days before all was ready for conveying Buonaparte to the house allotted for his reception. When he landed, he was dressed in a green coat, white waistcoat, light coloured small clothes, white stockings, and cocked hat. The coat was trimmed with gold, and a plain gold epaulette was placed on each shoulder. He held in his hand an elegant telescope, and cast his eyes around him with great eagerness to survey the new objects; possibly not without hope of noticing some particulars, which might, on a fit occasion, assist him to escape. The Company's troops on the island were immediately to be sent to the Cape to do duty there. . . .

View of the Landing Place, St. Helena. Engraved by Baily, from a Drawing by
Pocock.

On drawing near the land, St. Helena appears to be girded with a chain of
inaccessible precipices; behind which, craggy and barren mountains shoot up to a
great height, on whose summits are telegraphs, for the purpose of announcing the
approach of ships. Barns Point is one of the most stupendous cliffs ever beheld;
being nearly perpendicular, and fifteen or sixteen hundred feet high. Steering
thence (on the return from India) close alongshore for Sugar-Loaf Hill and Point, on
the peak of the former appears a telegraph, and on a jutting crag of the latter, about
80 or 90 feet above the level of the sea, is a small battery of three or four guns, to
compel vessels to heave-to and send their boats on shore. After complying with this
regulation, ships, in making sail for the anchorage, pass close to Rupert's valley, (the
landing place) and several ranges of batteries constructed amongst the precipices.
On rounding Rupert's Hill, James Town and valley present themselves, abreast of
which is the anchorage, about a quarter of a mile from the beach. St. Helena Bay
being formed by two promontories, and situated on the lee side of the island, is, of
course, completely sheltered from the S.E. trade winds by the mountains; and
protected from the long swell of the southern ocean, by the island itself. It thus
affords a safe and commodious anchorage, where ships may lie close to the rocks, in
water as smooth as glass. (*Vide* Johnson's *Oriental Voyager*, p. 365 to 386.) ^{Plate 349}

1815 – The Problems of Peace

ALTHOUGH THE FIRST of the following two papers is directly concerned with an injustice committed during the war, it is consistent with the work of the postwar navy, the most arduous aspect of which was the anti-slaving patrols on the African coast. The second, an advertisement for crew, is eloquent of the new world without impressment, or the incentive of prize money.

Breach of Faith with American Negroes
From 'Nautical Anecdotes.' XXXIV 213

An extraordinary transaction, which is stated to have taken place off the coast of Georgia, in the month of April last, is become the subject of general animadversion. It is said, that about 150 negroes, who had joined our army in consequence of Sir Alexander Cochrane's Proclamation, were restored by an officer of rank to their original owners, contrary to the faith of that Proclamation. Several British officers who were present, strongly remonstrated against the restoration, which they regarded not only as a breach of national honour, but as a result of undue partiality, while the poor Blacks themselves, among whom were several females, deprecated the act with the most piteous lamentations, especially as to the fate that awaited them from the resentment of the owners whom they had been induced to desert, as well from the experience of harsh treatment as from the natural reliance upon the pledge of a British admiral. That resentment these unhappy beings have no doubt severely felt. But the whole of this transaction is of such a nature as to call loudly for inquiry. It certainly appeals with peculiar force to the benevolent advocates for the Abolition of the Slave Trade, by some of whom it will, we trust, be brought under the consideration of Parliament.

The Puff Nautical; or Jack Invited to Glory! XXXV 211

Who would enter for a small craft? whilst the *Leander*! the finest and fastest sailing frigate in the world, with a good spar deck over head, to keep you dry, warm, and comfortable; and a lower deck like a barn, where you may play at leap-frog when the hammocks are hung up; has room for one hundred active smart seamen, and a dozen stout lads for royal-yard men? This whacking double-banked frigate is fitting at Woolwich to be flagship on the fine, healthy, full-bellied Halifax station, where you

Representation of some ice islands, as seen by a squadron of his Majesty's ships on their passage to Newfoundland. Engraved by Wells. ^{Plate 125}

may get a bushel of potatoes for a shilling, a cod-fish for a biscuit, and a glass of boatswain's grog for two pence. The officers' cabins are building on the main deck, on purpose to give every tar a double berth below. Lots of leave on shore! Dancing and fiddling on board! And four pounds of tobacco served out every month!!! A few strapping fellows, who would eat an enemy alive, wanted for the admiral's barge. The officers already appointed are Captain Skipsey, late *Maidstone*; Lieutenant J.P. Baker, late *Royal Sovereign, Rippon*, and *Barham*; H. Walker, late *Courageaux* and *Menelaus*; J.S. Dixon, late *Caledonia* and *San Joseph*; A.P. Le Neve, late *Maidstone*; E.A. Haughton, late *St. Lawrence*, and *Princess Charlotte*, (on the Lakes,) who will give every encouragement to their old ship-mates. Every good man is almost certain of being made a warrant officer, or getting a snug berth in Halifax dock-yard. All brave volunteers whom this may suit must bear a hand, and apply either on board the *Leander*, at Woolwich; at her rendezvous, the Half Moon and Seven Stars, Ratcliffe-highway, nearly opposite Old Gravel-lane; on board the *Enterprise*, off the Tower; or at any other general rendezvous in the kingdom, from whence they will be immediately forwarded to the *Leander*.

God save the King!!

The *Leander*, and a full-bellied station!!!

General Index

The First Edition of *The Naval Chronicle* was often inconsistent in its spelling of names, and sometimes made clumsy anglicisations of foreign names. An attempt has been made in this index to identify officers, using the Navy Record Society's Volume, *The Commissioned Sea Officers of the Royal Navy, 1660–1815* (David Syrett and R L DiNardo editors, Scolar Press, 1994), and the annual *Army Lists*, and to employ the spellings used there, with variations given in parentheses. The rank given for naval officers is the highest reached by the officer during the war, but for the sake of identification, honours and hereditary titles are given even if only acquired after the war. Generally, ranks for seamen and warrant officers, and for officers in the army or in foreign services, are those employed in the first edition. Where possible, foreign officers have been identified from secondary sources, but there is every possibility of incorrect spelling and identification. Where no first name is given, and identification has not been possible, a separate entry has been made. References to last name and rank have been indexed, but there is no guarantee that all the references under a particular entry refer to the same person.

The standard employed by this index is to note all the references to people, but to be selective of references to places, excluding entirely places mentioned only as navigational points, and those listed in organisational charts, and perforce being selective of references to naval dockyards. The index also includes references to such concepts as ship design, with many entries being grouped under 'naval'. A separate index provides reference to all ships' names, divided by nations.

Battle of Trafalgar, III 232
Batz, *IV* 286, 288, 292, 294, 297-98
Baudin, *Fr.* Adm. Charles, *III* 180, *IV* 299-304
Bavaria, *II* 318
Bayley, James, *III* 237
Baynes, Lt. R.M., *I* 196-97
Bayntun (Baynton), R.Adm. Sir Henry William, *I* 86, *II* 126, *III* 105, 200, *IV* 68-69
Bayonna Isles, *IV* 116, 118
Bazeley (Bazely), Capt. Henry, *I* 234
Bazely, Adm. John, *I* 124, *II* 56
Beatty, Dr. Sir William, *III* 196, 205-07
Beatty, R.M., *II* 17
Beauchesne, Baron de, *V* 219
Beauclerk, R.Adm. Lord Amelius, *I* 11, *IV* 273
Beaudouin, *Fr.* Capt. Louis-Alexis, *III* 202, 220
Beaver, Capt. Philip, *IV* 225, 227-29, *V* 54-56, 76-77
Becher, Capt. Alexander, *I* 110
Becker Bey, *Turk.*, *IV* 64
Beckwith, Lt.Gen. Sir George, *IV* 220, 224-28, 316, 323
Beckwith, Gen. Sir Sydney, *V* 182, 247
Bedford, R.Adm. William, *I* 124, *II* 36, *III* 102, *IV* 192, 203
Bedford, Duke of, *I* 34
Bekir Pacha, *IV* 50
Beliamo, *Neap.* Lt. Chev., *III* 328
Belize, *I* 202, 208-09
Bell, Capt. George, *I* 167-68
Bell, Mr. John, *IV* 120
Bell, Lt., R.A., *III* 358, *V* 226
Bellegarge, *Fr.* Gen., *V* 14
Belle Isle, *I* 111, 121, 125, 134, 138, *II* 114
Belle-Rock Lighthouse, *III* 376
Belling, *US* Lt., *V* 32
Bellingham, John, *V* 86
Bencoolen, *III* 38
Benesa, Don Raphael, *I* 205
Benfield, Mr., *III* 127
Bennet (Bennett), Lt. James, *II* 127
Bennet, Capt. Richard Henry Alexander, *I* 52
Bennet, *Artist and Engraver*, *I* 244-45, *II* 2, 41, *IV* 144, 171, 224, 324, 335, *V* 165, 184, 300
Benson, Capt., *I* 11
Bentham, *Engraver*, *II* 73
Bentinck, V.Adm. William, *I* 90, *IV* 281, *V* 224
Bentinck, Lt.Gen. Lord William Cavendish, *Amb. to Sicily, 1811-14*, *IV* 208, *V* 67
Bequiers Road, *I* 280
Berbice, *II* 313
Berenger (Barouger), *Fr.* Capt. Charles, *III* 202, 221, 242
Beresford, R.Adm. Sir John Poo, *II* 126, 191, *III* 323, *IV* 193, *V* 96, 124, 177
Beresford, Maj.Gen. W.C., *III* 285, 286, 293, 297-300, 309, 334, *IV* 51, 73, 129, 175, 209, *V* 24
Bergen, Netherlands, *II* 47
Bergen, Norway, *IV* 39, 147
Bergeret, *Fr.* Capt., *V* 15
Berkeley, Adm. the Hon. George Cranfield, *I* 90, *II* 38, 117, 280-81, 330, *III* 347, *IV* 52-53, 98-99, 218, *V* 24
Berkeley, Capt. *Aide-de-Camp to Gen. Bowyer*, *IV* 136
Berkley, Capt. Velters Cornewall, *I* 70,
Berlin, *II* 9
Berlin Decree, [*See:* Economic Warfare], *IV* 95
Bermett, Capt. R.H.A. [not in NRS], *II* 126

Bermuda, *II* 54
Bernadotte, Jean Baptiste Jules, *Fr.* Marshal, Duke of Sudermanland, *K. of Sweden*, *IV* 315, 338-39, 344, *V* 16-17
Bernstorff, Count, *II* 90, 99, 150
Berry, Capt. Sir Edward, *I* 172, 182, 187-89, 193, 240-42, 243, 250-51, 253, 255, 258-59, 269, 277-78, 280, *II* 9, 75, 77-78, *III* 173, 183, 200, 261, 265
Berry, T., *I* 186
Berry, Lt. William, *IV* 99-100
Berthier, *Fr.* Marshal Louis Alexandre, *III* 29
Bertie, Adm. Sir Albemarle, *I* 7, 91, 133-34, 138, 241, *II* 56, 180, 243, *IV* 319-320, 358-360
Bertie, V.Adm. Sir Thomas, *IV* 352, 388
Bertrand, *Fr.* Gen., *V* 308-311
Bertrant, Mm., *V* 308-311
Best, Serjeant, *III* 115, 119, 121, 124-125
Betson, Mid. Nicholas, *I* 258
Bettesworth, Capt. George Edmund Bryon, *III* 153-55, *IV* 147
Beveland, *IV* 270, 272, 275, 292, 296-97, 307
Bevians, Cmdr William, *IV* 191
Bickerton, Adm. Sir Richard Hussey, *II* 83-84, 123, 198-99, 205, 214-15, 219, *III* 21, 46, 78, 105, 189-190, 375, *V* 88, 166
Bilbao, *III* 79, *V* 79
Bingham, Capt. Arthur Batt, *V* 29-34, 105
Bingham, Capt. Joseph, *I* 191, *II* 37, 128, *III* 105
Bingham, Capt., *V* 20
Birch, Lt.Col. T., *III* 48
Biscay, Bay of, *I* 121, *II* 32, 48
Bissell, Cmdr William, *IV* 239, 246
Bissett, Brig.Gen., *V* 247
Bissett, Capt., *V* 68
Bitchenskoy, *Rus.* Capt., *IV* 178
Black, Capt. James, *V* 185, 188-89
Blackeman, *III* 46, 56-58
Blacks, *I* 237, *V* 63-65, 262-63, 314
Black Sea, *IV* 323
Blackwood, R.Adm. Hon. Sir Henry, *I* 125, *II* 75-76, 78, 81, 141, *III* 194, 200, 210, 215, 218, 222-24, *IV* 19-20, 33, 192, *V* 147
Blad, *I* 136
Blake, *II* 190
Blake, W., *Master*, *III* 67
Blakely, *US* Lt., *V* 125
Blane, Dr. Gilbert, *II* 368-72, *IV* 364
Blankett, R.Adm. John, *II* 128
Blanquet du Chayla (Blanquett), V.Adm. Armand Simon Marie de, *I* 256, 272, 275-76, *II* 7
Bligh, Adm. Sir Richard Rodney, *I* 91, 112-14
Bligh, V.Adm. William, *I* 7, 226, *III* 103, *IV* 205, 281, *V* 2, 8-10, 13, 295
Bligh, Capt., *III* 31, *IV* 237-38, 244, 249
Blight, Lt. William, *IV* 69
Blockade, *See:* Naval Blockade, and Economic Warfare
Block Making, *III* 22
Blood, *Engraver*, *III* 32, *V* 13, 161
Bloye, Capt. Robert: *V* 192
Bloye, *Master's Mate*, *V* 217
Bluckhart, G.M., *Publican*, *V* 38-39
Blundell, Col. Bryen, *I* 78
Blyth, Capt. Samuel ?, *V* 167
Blyth, Lt., *IV* 222

45; Sant'Elmo, *I* 268, *II* 33, 41, 44-45; Nuovo, *I* 268, *II* 33, 41, 44

Castenschield (Castenschiold), *Dan. Gen., IV* 76

Castile, *IV* 151

Castlereagh, Robert Stewart, Lord Visc., *Sec. of War 1805, 07-09; Foreign Sec. 1812-22 I* 287, *III* 6, 119, 288, *IV* 71, 77, 85, 105, 107, 129, 158, 162, 207-08, 231, 278, 325, *V* 67, 87, 92, 95

Catalonia, *V* 35, 79-83

Cathcart, Gen. Lord, *III* 346, *IV* 41, 49, *Copenhagen* 76-77, 80, 84-87, 105

Cathcart, Capt. Robert, *V* 169-170

Catherine the Great, Czarina of Russia, *II* 152, 185, 187, *III* 47

Catholics, *IV* 6, 8, *V* 86, 88

Cator, Capt. Bertie Cornelius, *IV* 359

Cattinelli, Lt.Col., *V* 224

Cattle, Lt. [R.M.?], *V* 81

Caulfield, Capt. Thomas Gordon, *I* 291, 295, *III* 105

Cavan, Maj.Gen. Richard Ford William Lambert, Earl of, *II* 202, 206, 272

Cavita, *I* 236-37

Cawsand Bay, *I* 285

Cayenne, *I* 78, *III* 34, 257, *IV* 190, 220-224

Caz (Case) Navires Bay, *I* 71, 81-82

Celebes, *I* 142

Cette, *IV* 299, 302

Ceuta, *IV* 322, 324

Cevellos, M., *III* 83

Ceylon, *I* xi, 139-143, *141, II* 266

'C.H.', *Pseud., V* 232

Chabert, M. de, *III* 140

Chacra-Braganza, *IV 121*

Chads, Capt. Sir Henry Ducie, *V* 157, 159

Chambers, Richard, *II* 138

Championnet, *Fr.* Gen. Jean Étienne, *II* 42

Champlain, Lake, *V* 244, 246-47, 263

Chancellor, Lord, Great Seal, *See:* 28 Jan. 1793, Alexander Wedderburn, Lord Loughborough; 14 April 1801, John Scott, Lord Eldon; 7 Feb. 1806, Thomas Erskine, Lord Erskine; 1 April 1807, Lord Eldon again.

Chancellor of the Exchequor, *See:* 1783, William Pitt; 20 Mar. 1801,.Henry Addington; 10 May 1804, William Pitt; 5 Feb. 1806, Lord Henry Petty, Marq. of Lansdowne; 26 May. 1807, Spencer Perceval; 9 June 1812, Nicholas Vansittart

Chaplains, *II* 353

Chapman, *Boatswain, I* 258

Charante, *II* 32, *IV* 190, 232, 236-258 *passim*

Charfield, Capt. Allen

Charity, *II* 362, 363

Charles IV, *K. of Sp., I* 155, *III* 68, *IV* 105, 123

Charles V, *Emp., II* 287

Charles XIII, *K. of Sweden, See:* Bernadotte, J.

Charles, *Archd. of Aust., IV* 204, 260, 315

Charles, Maj., *I* 65

Charlestown, *I* 65

Charlotte, *Q. of the Two Sicilies, IV* 18

Charmilly, *I* 64

Charnley, Privateer Capt. John, *III* 94-95

Charnock, John, *Biographer, I* 189

Charruca, *Sp.* Capt. Don Conne, *II* 304

Chatham, *II* 144, *IV* 192

Chatham, Earl of, *See:* Pitt, J.

Chatterton, *I* 104

Chaumant, Treaty of, *V* 287-88

Chauncey, *US* Capt. Isaac, *V* 30, 201, 264

Chesapeake, *IV* 142, *V* 110, 179-181, 207

Chesshyre, Lt. [R.M.?], *V* 216

Cheyne, Lt. George, *V* 216

Chiesa, Joseph, *Artist, I* 291

Chilcott, Cmdr. William, *II* 127

Chile, *IV* 67

Chouans, *I* 134-37

Christian, Lt. Fletcher, *V* 299

Christian, R.Adm. Sir Hugh Cloberry, *I* 202

Christian VII, *K. of Denmark, II* 150, *V* 16

Christian, Lt., *IV* 205

Christian, Thursday October, *V* 296-98

Christiansand, *II* 143

Christianstadt, *II 196,* 197, *IV* 138

Christie, Capt. Andrew, *I* 70

Christophe, Henri, *Pres. of Haiti, II* 311

Chronicle, III 196

Church, Capt. Stephen George, *I* 51

Churruca, *Sp.* Capt. Brig. Don Cosme, *III* 201, 219

Cinque Ports Lord Warden, *IV* 152

Cintra, Convention of, *IV* 118, 124-25, 166-67, 173-182, 207, 274

Circello, Marq. de, *I* 276

Cisneros, *Sp.* R.Adm. Don Baltaszar H., *III* 201, 202, 221

Ciudadela, *I* 292, 294-95

Civitta Vechia, *I* 243, 261, 268

Clancart, Rt. Hon. Richard le Poer, Earl of, *Amb. to Netherlands 1813-14, V* 174

Clancarty, Earl of, *V* 288

Clarence, HRH the Duke of, *Pr. Regent, I* 5, 172, *II* 284-85, *III* 109, 123, 142, 346, *V* 85-87, 97, 104, 107-110, 132-140, 215, 224-25, 266, 305

Clark, *US* Capt., *IV* 11

Clark, *US* Gen., *IV* 11

Clark, Gen. Sir Alured, *III* 40

Clark (Clarke), Rev. James Stanier, *Chaplain, Author and Editor, I* vi, 116, 120, 193, 195-96, 269-270, *II* 81, *III* 142

Clark (Clarke), Capt. William, *I* 140, 240, *II* 128

Clarke, *Chamberlain, II* 119

Clarkson, *Author, V* 64

Claremont, *I* 361-62

Clements, Cmdr. Nicholas Brent, *IV* 247

Clements, Capt. 71st Reg., *IV* 308

Clinch, Mid., *III* 137-38

Clod, Wales, *Master, I* 258

Clonard, Chev., *IV* 347

Clyde, *Purser, II* 147

Coastal Defences, *II* 325, *III* 48, 58, 98

Cobb, Lt., Charles, *V* 40

Cobb, R.Adm. Charles, *II* 56

Cobbett's Political Register, IV 122

Cocault, *Fr.* Capt., *III* 267

Cochin, *II* 277

Cochrane, V.Adm. the Hon. Sir Alexander, *II* 123, 200, 206, 208, 214, 216, *III* 71-72, 77-79, 105, 150, 257, 261, 265-66, 305, 320, *IV* 133, 137-38, 142, 220, 224-28, 279, 323-24, *V* 207-09, 226, 240-43, 255-260, 273-282, 289, 314

Cochrane, Capt. Nathaniel Day, *III* 264

Cochrane, Capt. Rt. Hon. Thomas, Earl of Dundonald, *I*

18, *II* 125, *IV* 41-42, 190, 202-03, 212-16, *Basque Roads* 232-258 *passim*., *242*, 318, *V* 148
Cock, John, *II* 138
Cockburn, R.Adm. the Hon. Sir George, *I* 176, 178, *II* 124, *III* 347, *IV* 225, 273, 338, *V* 177-184, 256-59, 307-08
Codlin, Merchant Capt., *II* 274
Codrington, R.Adm. Sir Edward, *I* 124, *III* 200, *IV* 337, *V* 35-37, 79-80, 83, 275, 287
Coffin, Adm. Sir Isaac, *III* 22
Coffin, Col., *V* 185-86
Coghlan, Capt. Jeremiah, *V* 173
Colby, Capt. David, *II* 124, 215, *III* 105
Colby, Lt., *IV* 28
Cole, Capt. Sir Christopher, *II* 127
Cole, Capt. Francis, *I* 124
Cole, Capt., *V* 7
Cole, Rev. Mr., *I* 212
Collett (Colet), Fr. R.Adm., *III* 333
Collard, Capt. Valentine, *II* 125, 215
Collier, V.Adm. Sir George , *III* 356
Collier, Capt. Sir George Ralph, *IV* 49, *V* 185, 192-193, 212, 234, 288
Collier, Capt., *IV* 86, *V* 203-06
Collier, Lt., *II* 55,
Collier, Lt. (Army), *IV* 49
Collin, Lawrence, *Brazier*, *III* 365-66
Collingwood, V.Adm. Cuthbert Lord, *I* 90, 172, 176, 186, 189, *II* 121, *III* 104, 167, 187-88, 192, 194, *Trafalgar* 195-238 *passim*., 209, 244; 261, 264, 346, *IV* 12-13, 15, 20, 22, 25, 27, 35, 50, 65-66, 96, 104, 146, 150, 154, 158, 167, 183, 189, 197, 199, 212, 216, 282, 299, 303-04, 315, 328-331, 350, *V* 18
Collins, Lt. John, *I* 257
Collins, Capt. [not in NRS], *IV* 214-15
Collins, Lt., *V* 216
Colman, George, the Younger, *Poet*, *II* 321
Colombo, *I* 140, 143
Colona, 68-69
Colphinston, *See*: Fleeming
Colpoys, R.Adm. Edward Griffith, *II* 124, 199, *III* 105, *V* 243
Colpoys, Adm. Sir John, *I* 5, 210-12
Columbia River, *V* 2
The Columbian, *V* 30
Columbine, Capt. Edward Henry, *IV* 278-79
Comino, *II* 266
Committee . . . for the Encouragement . . . *I* 138
Comora Islands, *IV* 354
Compang Bay, *V* 300
Compton, Cmdr. Henry, *I* 258
Comyn, Rev., *I* 253, 258-59
Concannon, Mr., *III* 314
Concarneau, *III* 257
Congress, US, *II* 2, 13, *IV* 260, 282, 333, *V* 127, 241, 258. House of Representatives, *II* 12, 235-236, *III* 93, *IV* 111, 129, *V* 44-46. Senate, *IV* 111, 129
Congreve, Gen. Sir William, *I* 357
Congreve Rockets, *See*: Naval Gunnery and Pyrotechnics
Conn, Capt. John, *II* 248, *III* 201
Connecticut, *V* 228
Conolly, Edward, *II* 138
Conolly, Lt., *I* 77
'Constant Reader', *Pseud*., *II* 372

Constantinople, *II* 14, 16-17, 21, 26, 29, 31, 309, *IV* 14, 17-18, *23*, 30-35, 50, 63, 134, 148-150, 198-200
Contamin, Fr. Gen. Gédéon Baron de, *II* 211-212, 218
Continental System, *See*: Economic Warfare.
Continho, Don Domingos Antonio de Souza, *Port. Amb. in London*, *IV* 201
Continho, Don Rodrigo de Souza, *Port. Min.*, *IV* 201
Convoy, *I* 6
Conyngham, Capt., *I* 86
Cook, Thomas, *Engraver*, *I* 194, *II* 49, 176, *III* 209, 249, 265, *IV* 146
Cooke (Cook), Capt. Edward *I* 18, 36, 40-41, 54, 233, 236-38, *II* 109, 328
Cooke, Francis, *I* 187
Cooke, Capt. John, *III* 106, 187, 196, 201, 215, 225-28, 246
Cooke, Col., *I* 41
Coote, Gen. Eyre, *I* 74, 233-35, *II* 5, 198, 202, 206-08, 215-16, *IV* 261, 270, 272-73, 291, 306
Coote, Capt. [Eyre?], *III* 325
Copenhagen, *II* iv, 4, 89-90, 97, 139-140, 149-190, *164-65*, 325-26, *III* 50, *IV* 2, 37, 47-48, 50, 74-94, *77*, 105-110, 125, 147, 169
Copley, John Singleton, *Painter*, *I* 219
Corbet (Corbett), Capt. Robert, *II* 125, 203, *IV* 69, 320
Corbet, *I* 71
Corbyn, Lt. Joseph, *V* 187, 190-91
Cordova, *IV* 322
Cordova, Adm. Don José de, *I* 171, 200-201
Corfu, *I* 278, 280, 282, *II* 33, 64, 90, 266, *III* 22, 173, *IV* 17, 49, 101, 109, 323
Cork, *I* 1, *165*, 214, *IV* 37, 51, 151, 157, 161
Cornish, V.Adm. Sir Samuel, *IV* 329
Cornwallis, Capt. James [died 1790 according to NRS], *II* 358
Cornwallis, Adm. Sir William, *I* 111-12, 120-24, *II* 317-19, 321, *III* 71, 73, 78, 153-54, 157, 164-65, 172, 231-32, 241, 256, 258-260, 312
Cornwallis, Gen. the Marq. of, *II* 244, 264-65, 260
Coromandel, *I* 142
Coron, *I* 246, 269
Corregidore, *I* 236
Corsairs, *III* 68-69
Corsica, *I* 18-19, 26, 31, 35, 41, 49-50, 54-55, 59, 153, 171, 180, 243, 268, *II* 39, 300, *III* 129, *V* 1
Corsin, Fr. Gen. Baron, *V* 284
Cortes, Fr. Capt., *III* 145
Corte, *I* 18, 35
Corunna, *III* 171, 172, *IV* 125, 151, 189-91, 207-212, 219
Cosby, Adm. Phillips, *I* 26, 114, *II* 342
Cosmao-Kerjulien, Fr. Capt. Julien-Marie, *III* 162, 202, 218, 220
Cosmez, Fr. R.Adm., *V* 39
Cotiella, Adj. Don Pedro, *I* 44
Cotton, Adm. Sir Charles, *I* 91, 121-22, *II* 36, 121, *III* 103, 332, *IV* 75, 95, 110, 112, 117-122, 124, 129, 143-45, 158, 166, 173-181 *passim*., 331, 348-350, *V* 21, 35, 122
Cottrell, Steven, *III* 80, *IV* 7
Countess, R.Adm. George, *I* 163, 287-88
Courcelles, Fr. Gen., *V* 215, 218-19
Courtney, Hon. Mr., *III* 280
Courtown, Earl of, *III* 261
Courts: Common Pleas, *II* 351; High Court of Admiralty,

Kerjulien, *Fr.* Capt., *see*: Cosmao
Kerr, Capt. Hon. Lord Mark Robert, *I* 291, 295-96, *III* 133
Kerr, Capt., *V* 148
Killala Bay, *I* 156, 284
King, *I* 212, 262
King, Capt. Sir Edward Durnford, *II* 126, 191, 193, 196
King, Philip Gidley, *Gov. New South Wales 1800-06, III* 180
King, Adm. Sir Richard, *I* 158, 160, 214, *III* 106, 201, *IV* 192, 337
King, Richard, *Q'master, I* 297
King, Lt. William Elletson, *II* 179-180, 358
King, Capt., *III* 285, 291, 295, 297
King, Lt., *III* 37
King, Mr. *US Consul, III* 91
King's Lynn, Corporation, *I* 3
Kingsmill, Adm. Sir Robert Brice, *I* 2, 8, 156, 161-64, *162*, 166, 213, 284-85
Kingston (Kingstone), Lt.Col. [James Peter?], *IV* 72
Kinnaird, Hon. Charles, *MP, II* 281, *III* 91
Kirby, Edward, *Master, I* 258
Kirchner, J.S., *Master, I* 257
Kisakewitz, M. de, *Rus. Amb., III* 50
Kittoe, Capt. Edward, *IV* 272, *V* 23
Kléber, *Fr.* Gen. Jean Baptiste, *II* 15, 26-27, 30-31, 107, 198, *III* 301
Knight, Adm. Sir John, *I* 34, 44, 226, *II* 37, *III* 105, 190
Knight, Lt., *II* 16, 20
Knight, Mr., *Solicitor, IV* 312
Knights of St. John, *I* 240
Knowles, Adm. Sir Charles Henry, *I* 176
Knowles, *Boatswain, II* 147
Koefoed (Kofod), *Dan.* Capt. [Hans H.], *II* 172
Koehler, Maj. George Frederick, *I* 31
Kolff (Koff, Kolf), *Neth.* Capt. [D.H.], *I* 227, *II* 57
Koroni, *I* 246
Kotzebue, *German author, II* 187
Krafft (Kraffe), *Neth.* Capt. [Jan Willem], *I* 227
Krowwe, *Rus.* Capt., *IV* 64
Kruse, *Rus.* Adm., *II* 309
Krusenstern, M., *Rus.* Capt., *III* 134-35, *V* 289-291
Kuttner, *II* 158

L

Lachavardiere, *Fr.* Consul, *I* 275
Lackey, *Master's Mate, I* 279
La Caille, *Fr.* Capt. [Charles Nicholas], *IV* 239, 256
Laconia, *I* 236
Lacy, Gen., *V* 80-83
Lafond, *Fr.* Gen., *V* 80
Laforey, Adm. Sir John, *I* 61, 63-64, *III* 356-57
Laforey, R.Adm. Sir Francis, *III* 105, 147, 200
Lagrange, *Fr.* Gen. [Joseph, Comte de], *III* 132
La Guayra, *IV* 214
Lallemand, Mr. *II* 28, *V* 308
La Londe, *Fr.* Capt., *II* 232
Lamb and Younger, *Merchants, II* 10
Lambe, Hon. Mr., *III* 334
Lambert, Maj.Gen. Sir John, *V* 277-78, 280
Lambert, Capt. Henry, *V* 150, 156, 276
Lambert, Capt. Robert, *V* 150
Lambert, Capt. Robert Stuart, *I* 140, *II* 226, *IV* 356-57
Lambert, Mr., *V* 144

Lambert, *Fr.* Capt., *V* 39
Lamborn (Lamborne, Lambourn), Capt. John, *II* 223, 226
Lamelle, *Fr. Apothecary, III* 317
Lampedosa, *II* 304-05
Lancaster, *Neth.* Capt., *I* 227
Landseer, Thomas, *Purser, I* 116
Lane, Capt. Richard, *I* 124
Lane, Lt.Col. [Thomas Bateman?], *III* 291
Lanfesty, Mid., *I* 258
Langara, Adm. Don Juan de, *I* 17-29
Langlois, *Fr.* Capitain de Frégate, *III* 333
Languedoc, *IV* 212
Lannes, *Fr.* Gen., *II* 25
Lanusse, Gen., *II* 203
Lapenotière, Capt. John Richards, *III* 201, 234-35
La Pérouse (Péyrouse), F.J. de Galoup, *Fr. Explorer, II* 269, 317, 320, *III* 39, *IV* 345, 347
La Pena, *Sp.* Gen., *V* 14, 21
Larcom, Capt. Joseph, *I* 124, *II* 126
Larcom, Capt. Thomas, *I* 116, 124, *II* 128
Larkan, Capt. John, *I* 110
Larmour, Capt. John, *I* 124, 200
Laroche, Capt. Christopher, *II* 126, *III* 104
Lascasas, Count, *V* 309
Lascy, Gen., *IV* 338
Lassen, *Dan.* Capt. [Lorentz F.], *II* 172
Latellier, *Fr.* Capt. M., *III* 202
La Tonie, *Fr.* Capt., *IV* 239
Lauderdale, Earl of, *See*: Maitland, Anthony.
Launder, Lt. Philip Watson, *I* 257
Laurie, Lt., *V* 249
Laville, *Fr.* Capt., *V* 39
La Villegris, *Fr.* Capt. Guilliem-Jean-Noël, *III* 202
Lawford, R.Adm. Sir John, *II* 56, *III* 104, *IV* 192, 337
Lawless, Lt. Paul, *IV* 188
Lawrence, Capt. James, *V* 30
Lawrence, Capt., *V* 177-80
Lawrence, *US* Capt., *V* 124
Lawrence, Chevalier, *V* 218
Lawrence, Dr., *Advocate, IV* 45
Lawrence, Lt., *II* 312
Lawrence, Mr., *III* 314
Lawrie (Laurie), Capt. Sir Robert, *II* 128, *V* 186
Lawrie, Lt. [William], R.M., *IV* 28
Lawrie, Lt. R.M., *IV* 24
Laws of War, *II* 89, 91-92, 94-96, 234-240, *IV* 45-46, 109, 125, 134-36, 148, 317, *V* 2, 17
Lawson, Brig.Gen. [Robert], *II* 209
Lawson, W., *Master, I* 257
Layman, Cmdr. William, *II* 160-163
Leach, Cmdr James, *IV* 275
League of Armed Neutrality or Northern Confederacy, *II* 89, 100-101, 142, 149, 165, 251, *IV* 48
Leake, Lt. William Thomas Martin, *III* 22
Lear, Mr. Tobias, *US Consul, III* 89, 143
Le Bigot, *Fr.* Capt., *IV* 239
Lechmere, V.Adm. William, *I* 116, *III* 201
Leclerk, *Fr.* Gen., *II* 291
Ledayo, *V* 77
Lee, John Theophilus, *Artist, I* 15, 30, *II* 211-212, 336, 363, *III* 237, 249
Lee, Capt. John, *I* 30, 336,

Ship Index

The following index is divided first by nationality. Alternative spellings of ships' names are given in parenthesis. Anglicised spellings of foreign ship names have been retained. Identification of British ships has been assisted by reference to David Lyon's *The Sailing Navy List* (Conway Maritime Press, 1993).

Austrian

General Otto II 74

British

Abergavenny 54, Guard Ship: *I* 207, *II* 126
Abundance 16, Store Ship: *II* 128
Acasta 40: *II* 126, *III* 189, 264, 266, *IV* 225, 227-29, *V* 125, 148
Achille (Achilles) 74: *II* 122, 180, *III* 7, 106, 188, 200, 216, *IV* 192, 337
Active (several ships) *I* 117, 226, *III* 142, *IV* 15-16, 22, 28, 348-49, *V* 17
Acute 14: *IV* 40
Adamant 50: *I* 222, 226, 229, *II* 127, *III* 103
Admiral Devries 68, Prison ship: *II* 126
Adventure 44: *II* 274
Aeolus 36: *III* 241-42, *IV* 225, *V* 96
Aetna Bomb: *IV* 80, 234-35, 237, 242-44, 263, 273, *V* 260-61
Africa 64: *III* 107, 200, 215, 226, *IV* 188, 194, *V* 112, 125
Africaine (L'Africaine) 38: *III* 29, 200, *IV* 105, 358-360, *V* 12
Agamemnon 64: *I* 33-35, 49, 144-49, 151-52, 187, *II* 104, 107, 139, 145, 151-53, 156, 162-63, 166, 168, 178, *III* 104, 183, 200, 215, 261, 266, *IV* 40, 118, 142
Agincourt 64/74: *I* 226, *II* 128, *III* 106, *IV* 40, 269
Aigle 44: *IV* 152, 235, 237, 242-43
L'Aimable 32: *I* 52, *II* 38, *III* 64
Aimwell Gun Brig: *IV* 343
Ajax 80/74: *I* 349, *II* 123, 200, 214-16, *III* 7, 104, 191-92, 200, 216, 220, *IV* 13, 15-16, 19-20, 22, 33, *V* 186
Alacrity 16/18: *IV* 40, *V* 20
Alarm 8, Lugger: *I* 87, 204, *IV* 342
Albatross 18: *II* 128
Albicore 16: *II* 127

Albion 74: *II* 145, *III* 105
Alceste 48: *IV* 340
Alcmene 32: *I* 267, *II* 6, 124, 153, 162, 168, *IV* 151
Alecto 14, Fireship: *II* 242
Alert 16: *I* 42, *IV* 40
Alexander 74: *I* 91, 111-13, 126, 128, 242-43, 247, 250-52, 255-58, 265-66, 269, 271-72, 290, *II* 37, 70-72, 82, 123, 205, *III* 107, 178, 265, *V* 169-170
Alexander 6, Tender: *II* 127, 192, 194
Alfred 74: *IV* 40, 211
Alfred Indiaman: *I* 91, 103-104, *III* 40-41
Alliance 20, Station Ship: *II* 16, 19, 125
Alligator 28: *II* 124, 215, 312-13, *III* 36
Amazon 28: *I* 156, 161, 166-69, *II* 139, 145, 153, 162, 168, 178, *III* 49
Amboyna 10: *II* 128
Amelia 48: *I* 163, 286-88, *II* 110, *IV* 217, *V* 150, 153
America 64: *I* 281, *II* 50, 55-56, 128, *III* 142
Amethyst 44/40: *I* 51
Amethyst 36: *II* 110, *III* 96, *IV* 170, 269-272
Amphion 32: *I* 156-161, *II* 82, 126, *III* 65, 61, 72-74, *IV* 348-49, *V* 17-18
Amphitrite 32/28: *II* 126, 191-92, 194, *IV* 141, 342
Anaconda 18, Brig Sloop: *V* 279
Andromache 32: *II* 341, *IV* 342
Andromeda 32: *I* 6, 63, *II* 63, 126, 128, 191-94, 34, *IV* 342
Anholt Schooner: *V* 26
Ann Brig: *IV* 130
Anna-Maria Despatch Boat: *V* 260-61
Anson 38 Razé: *I* 133, 137, 163, 286, 288-89, *II* 106, *III* 143, *IV* 4, 125, 127
Antelope 50: *III* 66-67, 103, 181, 240, *V* 211-12
Apollo 36/38: *I* 11, *II* 126, *IV* 36, 284, 303
Aquilon 32: *I* 91, 124, 129, 250, 256, 282
Arab 22: *II* 126
Archer 14: *IV* 40
Ardasein Merchantman: *III* 40
Ardent 64: *I* 226, 230, *II* 56, 96-97, 145, 151, 153, 156, 162, 166, 168, 178-180, *III* 103, *IV* 194

Danish

French

Neapolitan

Netherlands

Portuguese

Spanish

Swedish

United States

ERRATA

The first numeral is the page, the next if preceded by 'p' is the paragraph,
the last numeral, preceded by 'l', refers to the line.

Volume I

vii, p1, l12 - "S and J" should be "Stephen and John"

6, after entry 4 (line 3 from bottom) Add: [See also "List of the French Navy as Presented to the National Convention, March 23, 1793", Vol. XX Appendix 4.]

14, l7 from bot. "Pros*p*erpine" should be "Proserpine"

17, p4, l2 - "S*y*dney" should be "S*i*dney"

114, p4 header - "S*y*dney" should be "S*i*dney"

125, l16 - "Pros*p*erpine" should be "Proserpine"

156, p3, l8 - "Amp*r*ion" should be "Amp*h*ion"

l9 - "Amp*r*ion" should be "Amp*h*ion"

157, p2 header - "Amp*r*ion" should be "Amp*h*ion"

162, l9, insert - "Suffrein *[Suffren]*"

179, p3, header - "Ten*n*erifa" should be "Tenerif*e*"

186, p3 header - "Edward" should be "T."

190, p4 header - "*St.* George's" should be "*Prince George's*"

233, p3, l1 - "Cook" should be "Cook*e*"

240, p2, l9 - "Willyam" should be "Willyam*s*"

291, p2, l9 - "*J.*G. Caulfield" should be "*T.* G. Caulfield"

319, bottom Add: *[See also Volume 4 pp. 139-141.]*

Volume II

1, p3, l1 - "S*y*dney" should be "S*i*dney"

3, after entry 2, Add: [See also: State of the Royal Navy of Great Britain at the Commencement of the Year 1799, 18 pp, Vol. XX Appendices 1 and 2.]

9, p3, header and four times in text, "Pros*p*erpine" should be "Proserpine."

14, p1, l4 - "S*y*dney" should be "S*i*dney"

l7 - "S*y*dney" should be "S*i*dney"

p2, l1 - "S*y*dney" should be "S*i*dney"

14, p4, l3 - "S*y*dney" should be "S*i*dney"

p5, l3 - "S*y*dney" should be "S*i*dney"

l4 - "S*y*dney" should be "S*i*dney"

23, p5, header - dated of*f* Mount

39, l4 from bot. B*e*tave should be B*a*tave

56, p3, l2 - italic for "*Victor*"

l2 from bot. - Jun*o*

64, p2 header - "S*y*dney should be "S*i*dney"

65, p4 header - "S*y*dney should be "S*i*dney"

l2 from bottom - "S*y*dney should be "S*i*dney"

89, p2, l7 - "pus*h*ing" should be "pa*ss*ing"

91, p1, l5 - insert "*Buonaparté*" after "Napoleon"

94, p3, l6 - "Reliant" should be "Reliance"

97, p3, l8 - it. "*Romney*"

105 Caption - "*J.* Medland" should be "*T.* Medland".

124, l6 - "Seven" should be "S*t*even"

l4 from bottom - "Bow*d*en" should be "Bowen"

125, l13 - "D*i*vies" should be "D*a*vies"

l29 - "Lou*i*sa (hd. *[?]* brig) - add "i" and eliminate [?]

26, l23 - "Ner*i*ede" should be "Ner*e*ide"

l28 - u.c. *R.*

127, l19 - "Fishl*e*r" should be "Fishl*ey*"

128, l1 - "Wal*t*er" should be "Wal*l*er"

l10 - "Vice Admiral Sir R. Curtis",

l10*a* "Captain T. Larcom"

129, l21 - "Invinci*p*le" should be "Invinci*b*le"

133, l13 from bottom - "12 *12* 6" should be "12 6"

140, p1, l1 - "Dick*e*nson" should be "Dickson"

p2, l7 - "Marm*o*rice" should be "Marm*a*rice"

145, p2 header - "Gan*th*eaume's" should be "Gan*t*eaume's"

note 2, l2 from bottom - "T*r*igress" should be "Tigress"

149, p2, l7 - "Rev*e*l" should be "Rev*a*l"

150, p3, l4 - "Rev*e*l" should be "Rev*a*l"

152, note 2 - "Hawksbury" should be "Hawk*e*sbury"

198, p3, l1 - "Gan*th*aume's" should be "Gan*t*eaume's"

199, p1, l1 - "Gan*th*aume's" should be "Gan*t*eaume's"

p2, l2 - "Gan*th*aume's" should be "Gan*t*eaume's"

201, p1, l1 - "Savil*i*e" should be "Savil*l*e"

210, p4, l6 - "Hi*c*hinbrooke" should be "Hi*n*chinbrooke"

215, l19 - "Vesta" should be "Vesta *[Vestal?]*"

243, p2, l6 - "Bert*is*" should be "Bert*ie*"

252, p2, l5 - "S*y*dney should be S*i*dney"

276, middle, reference - should be "*VIII 502-511, IX 49-66*"

311, cap. l2 - "Hal*i*" should be "Hal*f*"

317, p4, l2 - "Pé*y*rouse" should be "*La* Pérouse"

325, cap. l3 - w.f for reference

328, middle - "Chancellor of the Exchequer *[Addington]*"

358, bottom - add: "*See also Vol. IX Appendix, List of Officers in the British Navy, January 1803.*"

368, p1, l11 - insert "Dr. *John* Harness"

p1, l12 - "Bla*i*ne" should be "Blane"

372, p4, l1 - "Bla*i*ne" should be "Blane"

Volume III

22, p6, header - "Patt*e*n" should be "Patt*o*n"; "Russel" should be "Russel*l*"
24, l14 from bottom - "Ramilies" should be "Ramil*l*ies"
39, p2, header - "La Peruse" should be "La P*é*r*o*use"
45, p4 - "Suffrein" should be "Suffrein */sic/*"
71, p5 - "*V*allis" should be "*W*allis"
88, p4 address - "Ma*d*dalena" should be "Ma*g*dalena"
91, p6 header - "Halifax" and "Newfoundland" in italics.
99, left col. - "Pelag*o*" should be "Pelago */Pelage?/*"
100, right col. - "[Sem*m*ilante]" should be "[Semilante]
103, middle para. - "Gaul*i*ore" should be "Gauliore */Gaulois?/*"
104, left col. "*80* Ajax" should be "*80 /74/* Ajax"
105, right col. "Griffith*s*" should be "Griffiths */sic/*"
106, "Salvador del Mund*i*" should be "Salvador del Mund*i* */sic/*"
174, caption - "Bail*e*y" should be "Baily"
200, list - "Captain Sir C*/harles/* Laforey" should be "Captain Sir F*/rancis/* Laforey"
202, l14 - "P.A. Magon" should be "P.A. */sic/* Magon"
   l21 - "Bellanger" should be "Berenger"
   l26 - "Baudoin" should be "B*e*audo*u*in"
201, l3 - "R[ichard]" should be "R[ichard*s*]"
   l18 - "G[*eorge*] Rutherford" should be "G[*ordon*] Rutherford"
205, "By Command . . . Bronte" wrong font, justify right, raise 1 line
217, l6 from bottom - "Aliva" should be "Aliva */Alava/*"
220, #16 - "Infornet" should be "Infornet */sic/*"
   #22 - "Bruaro" should be "Bruaro */Brouard/*"
223, p2 - "Royal Charlotte" should be "Royal Charlotte */ie Queen Charlotte/*"
242, l3 - "Troufflet" should be "Troufflet */Touffet/*"
267, header - "Lesse*i*gues" should be "Leissegues"
   p3 - "Lesseigues" should be "Lesseigues */sic/*"

293, middle - "Captain Don*o*lly" should be "Captain Don*e*lly"
301, last para. - "General K*i*eber" should be "General K*l*eber"
305, p2, l14 - "Willeaum*è*z" should be "Willeaumez */sic/*"

Volume IV

40, col. 2 - "Com*o*s" should be "Com*u*s"
68, p3 address - "Ner*i*ede" should be "Ner*e*ide"
116, p3, l8 - "Caleraft" should be "Cal*c*raft"
124, p4, l2 - "S*i*niavin" should be "S*e*niavin"
160, p2, l8 - "H.M. Herbert" should be "H.M. [M.H.?] Herbert"
172, caption - "Bail*e*y" should be "Baily"
179, l2 - "*Dournoff, of 26 guns, and 222 men*" should be "*Bytchenskoy, of 80 guns, and 646 men*"
190, p3, l3 - "Saints" should be "Saint*e*s"
192, l4 - "S*o*utheby" should be "Sotheby"
194, p2 - "Honourable John Hope" should be "Honourable */William/* John*/stone/* Hope"
211, p1, l5 - "the *44*th" should be "the *14*th"
244, p6, l5 - "Thunder*er*'s" should be "Thunder's"
245, p1, l3 - "Pallas" should be in italics
   p4, l2 - "of 84" should be "of 84 */sic/*"
255, p2, note - "A.F.*V.*" should be "A.F.*Y.*"
270, p4, l3 - "Huntley" should be "Huntley */sic/*"
303, note - "*Scout*" should be in roman
315, p2, l7 - "Francis I" should be "Francis I*I*"
325, l4 - "Craufo*/u/*rd" should be "Crauford */sic/*"
334, p4 header - "Louis *Napoleon*" should be "Louis *Buonaparte*"
350, 2nd header - "Cart*h*agena" should be "Cartagena"
352, l4, - "Port South*west*" should be "Port South *East*"
356, note - "Port South*west*" should be "Port South *East*"
358, note - "Port South*west*" should be "Port South *East*"